THE RENDERMAN®
SHADING LANGUAGE GUIDE

"DON" RUDY CORTES AND SATY RAGHAVACHARY

D0768068

THOMSON

™

COURSE TECHNOLOGY

Professional ■ Technical ■ Reference

Publisher and General Manager, Thomson Course Technology PTR:
Stacy L. Hiquet

Associate Director of Marketing:
Sarah Panella

Manager of Editorial Services:
Heather Talbot

Marketing Manager:
Jordan Casey

Executive Editor:
Kevin Harreld

Project Editor:
Marta Justak

Technical Reviewer:
Mike McNeill

PTR Editorial Services Coordinator:
Erin Johnson

Copy Editor:
Gene Redding

Interior Layout:
Jill Flores

Cover Designer:
Mike Tanamachi

Indexer:
Sharon Hilgenberg

Proofreader:
Heather Urschel

ISBN-10: 1-59863-286-8

ISBN-13: 978-1-59863-286-6

Library of Congress Catalog Card Number: 2006904403

Printed in the United States of America

08 09 10 11 12 BU 10 9 8 7 6 5 4 3 2 1

THOMSON

COURSE TECHNOLOGY

Professional ■ Technical ■ Reference

Thomson Course Technology PTR, a division of Thomson Learning Inc.
■ 25 Thomson Place ■ Boston, MA 02210 ■ http://www.courseptr.com

Dedication

Dedicated to RenderMan's developers and its community of students, professional users, and hobbyists.

Acknowledgments

Rudy

I would like to thank my parents for their undying support and guidance. For teaching me at an early age that you must always work hard to achieve your goals, and that there is never a good enough reason not to try your best. Also for being so supportive of all of my career changes and all my "creative business ventures." To Rich Pickler, who first introduced me to RenderMan and convinced me that I would be able to understand it if I stuck with it. To Kevin Harreld for his belief that this book has a market and that we could deliver it. To Marta Justak for her enormous patience and guidance through the many revisions of this book. To Mike McNeill for his attentive eye during tech editing. This book and my current career would not be possible without the continuous support of my wife Alexandra who stuck with me through all the long nights of frustration and doubt. Through all the small geeky discoveries that while she might not have understood what on earth I was talking about, she shared the excitement with me. She even stepped up to the plate to become the main provider while I made the transition from the graphic design world to the animation/vfx industry. For all of the above, thanks a lot princesa! To Ana and Nicole, you are my inspiration and my drive, and I will love you forever.

Saty

The RenderMan team at Pixar (past and present members) deserves a big "thank you!" for coming up with a wonderful rendering platform that amazes and delights so many of us, and for continuing to innovate and change it on a regular basis.

Thanks to the folks at Thomson Course Technology PTR for commissioning this book, and for their patience while it was being completed. Kevin, here's the status of the book now: "DONE!" Marta has been a gentle but firm editor, skillfully guiding how the material evolved. Mike McNeill's invaluable technical comments have helped produce a better result.

My dear wife Sharon offered great support while the book was being written, as did my parents from the other side of the world. Thanks also to our delightful little twins Becky and Josh for allowing me to work during several weekends when I should have been playing with them, and for hanging out with me and providing company while I worked. The book is now done, and I'm all yours, kids!

Thanks to several Gnomon students who previewed a lot of material in this book. Their support and feedback means much to me. Thank you Chris, Jim, Alena, Sani, Raqi, Ju Hee, Wallace, Craig, Paula, and Brian. Thanks too to the founders of Gnomon for my long-standing RenderMan teaching gig that goes back to 2001.

Thanks to my very special friend and colleague Gigi for being there for me all these years. Thanks likewise to Valerie Lettera and Chris Eddington.

I've been fortunate to have even more well-wishers who have offered encouragement and support while I worked on the book. These include Dylan Sisson, Gavin Hogben, Malcolm Kesson, Peter Lu, and Salima Poonawala. Thank you very much.

Finally, I'd like to gratefully acknowledge Ray Davis and Wendy Wirthlin from Pixar for eval. licenses of PRMan.

About the Authors

"Don" Rudy Cortes was born and raised in Ecuador. He has been working in the 3D animation industry for the past seven years. He started his career in Kansas City, Missourah! as a generalist and demo artist for a local 3D software distributor. He then worked as a 3D visualization specialist for one of the country's leading architectural and engineering firms before making a jump to the film industry. He initially wanted to be an animator until a good friend introduced him to a small rendering program named BMRT. From that point on, he dedicated himself to learning RenderMan and all the "nerdy" techniques required to run a production with RenderMan. His film credits include *The Day After Tomorrow, Sky Captain and the World of Tomorrow* as a lighting and vfx TD, *The Ant Bully* as a RenderMan shader writer and TD, and the latest Disney movie *Meet the Robinsons.*

Saty Raghavachary is a Senior Trainer and Curriculum Manager in the training department at DreamWorks Feature Animation, where he also has written graphics production software for 11 years. On a part-time basis, he teaches an introductory CG course at USC, as well as classes on Maya (MEL/Python), RenderMan, and visual math at the Gnomon School of Visual Effects. His movie credits include *Bee Movie, Shrek 3, Flushed Away, Over the Hedge, Madagascar, Shark Tale, Sinbad, Spirit, The Road to El Dorado,* and *The Prince of Egypt.* He was previously Software Manager at MetroLight Studios. Saty was awarded three M.S. degrees and a Ph.D. at The Ohio State University and also did postdoctoral research there. He obtained a B.Tech degree from the Indian Institute of Technology (IIT), Madras. He is a member of ACM, IEEE, and American Mensa. Saty is also the author of *Rendering for Beginners: Image Synthesis Using RenderMan.*

Contents

PART II SHADER DEVELOPMENT

6 Shader Design Methodology   157

PART III BASIC SHADING

7 Displacement and Surface Shaders   183

Introduction

Welcome to RenderMan

Over the past 15 years, movie audiences all over the world have witnessed the emergence of one of the most revolutionary tools ever created to aid in the creation of films, the use of Computer Generated Imagery (CGI). Through the use of CGI, filmmakers have transported us to distant places, put us right in the middle of very dangerous shots, and introduced us to several "synthetic" actors, some of which were so convincing that they made you forget you were staring at a careful creation by a team of fantastic artists and technicians—a team that manipulates data that at its core is nothing but a bunch of ones and zeros.

None of these effects would have been possible without the use of 2D painting, 3D modeling, and animation software in conjunction with a rendering program that transforms 3D data into finalized frames for film. Of all the available rendering programs (which are also referred to as *rendering engines*) available today, there is only one that can trace its roots to the first CGI elements incorporated into a film. Pixar's PhotoRealistic RenderMan (PRMan) was the first, and for a long time the only, commercial implementation of the RenderMan Interface Specification [pixar]. Audiences were dazzled by the genesis effect sequence on *Star Trek II: The Wrath of Khan* (1982), which marked the first use of CGI in a film. They were flabbergasted by the stained glass knight from *Young Sherlock Holmes*, the first CG character ever in a film, and sat completely in awe when that first brontosaurus walked into frame on *Jurassic Park*. Visual effects would never be the same. Photo-Realistic RenderMan, or an earlier version of it, was used to render those CGI elements. In those early days, the only studios that had access to PRMan were ILM and its spin-off company Pixar until it became a commercial product in 1989. Back then, the price tag for a license of PRMan was astronomical. Therefore, only the big studios were capable of using it for generating special effects.

Years have passed and new rendering engines have hit the market along with more accessible 3D software. This has created a fertile market for smaller boutique shops that, even though they are incapable of handling big jobs (400 plus shots), are creating fantastic work within very reasonable timeframes and budgets. Even with the introduction of new rendering engines, PRMan is still the film industry's most popular renderer, and the RISpec is slowly becoming the format of choice, or at least supported by several other renderers. Within the past five years, a vast number of new RenderMan-compliant renderers have become available, and most of them offer a number of the features found in PRMan at a much smaller cost. This means that the rendering technology that was once only available to the big studios is readily available to everyone who has the will to learn it. Learning RenderMan and the RenderMan Shading Language (RSL) is a great career investment. There is usually a shortage of knowledgeable RenderMan TDs and with the decreasing prices of software, things don't look as if they will slow down soon.

The Road Ahead

Learning RenderMan is not easy or quick; however, it is not rocket science either. It just requires the right mind and skill set, plus the right personality to become a successful RenderMan TD. Becoming a RenderMan TD is not for everyone, though. There are plenty of other lucrative and fulfilling career opportunities in the animation and visual effects fields. Among the skills necessary to become a successful RenderMan TD are a decent level of math (or at least the ability not be intimidated by it), an inquisitive nature, good problem-solving and organizational skills, a keen eye for what makes something look real without spending a lot of time in useless details, and the resourcefulness to get jobs done on time.

Most TDs get introduced to RenderMan either out of curiosity, out of need, or by a school program. Of these three groups, those exposed to RenderMan by need (because of work) or by a school program tend to stick longer with RenderMan and go on to become knowledgeable TDs. The reason for this is probably because under such circumstances, users tend to understand the benefits of using a high-end renderer since they are guided either by other co-workers or by a professor. However, those exposed to RenderMan by curiosity usually tend to play around with it for a while and then switch back to a renderer with which they are more comfortable. Only a small number of them stick with it long enough to get past "the point of no return." This point is usually the moment when things come into perspective, the planets realign, and all the mysteries of the universe are solved! Or at least that's how it feels. It is the moment when things finally click, and RenderMan stops being a complicated rendering technology that only super math-programmer geeks can use and becomes a very powerful tool at your fingertips. The point where all that nasty shading code starts making sense, and you know exactly what is going on when you read the source file.

Reaching this point might take longer for some people. It might take a month, two months, or maybe a year. In my case (Rudy's), it took about two years of reading and shelving my RenderMan books until things made enough sense that I could actually attempt to do things with it. So don't get discouraged if you are part of this group; the fact that you are holding this book is a clear indication that you have the initial curiosity. Be persistent at it, talk to other RenderMan TDs, and get involved in rendering forums. You will eventually reach the point of no return, and when you do, a world of possibilities will open to you.

Who This Book Is For

This book is designed as a reference and instructional guide for people interested in learning to use RenderMan, more specifically the RenderMan Shading Language, or RSL. It is assumed that the reader has a solid understanding of basic 3D terms, concepts, and techniques. Basic knowledge of math and algebra would also be helpful since we will go over some very important math concepts for shader writers. Programming experience is not necessary, as this book will introduce the user to the necessary programming techniques needed for shader writing. This might also be a good way to introduce people who are more visually inclined, as most 3D artists are, to the world of programming and scripting. This book is also designed to be used as a textbook at universities, colleges, and technical schools where image synthesis is taught. We will not cover any concepts of 3D production other than rendering, so there will be no modeling, rigging, lighting, or animation covered. Neither will we cover any of the 2D processes of animation and VFX production, such as texture or matte painting, rotoscoping, compositing, or editing. There are plenty of great books available in these areas. It's our firm belief that a solid RenderMan TD needs to know the concepts of all these areas since most of them are touched in one way or another by rendering and for those that aren't, well, the more you know the more you can help your production, right?

PART I

RSL FUNDAMENTALS

1

Introduction to RSL and RenderMan

Background and Industry Insight

The process of creating film quality CGI is very complicated. It requires the mastery of many different aspects of 3D production such as modeling, texturing, rigging, animation, lighting, and rendering. It also requires the use of highly specialized software tools to generate the proper data. A long time ago there were different tools for each of these aspects. This resulted in a broken workflow because sometimes the data that one program would generate would not transfer properly to the other applications. Renderers were also separate programs that would load a scene description program and compute a 2D image. Eventually programs began to consolidate the different aspects of 3D production into a single application, which led to the modern programs used nowadays. These programs integrate all aspects of 3D production and some of them go as far as integrating compositing, which used to be a part of 2D post processing. These new programs are complete production packages in one application. Such 3D programs usually have an integrated renderer, but most of them are limited either by their own design shortcomings, lack of speed, or lack of an easy way to write extensions.

Back then there were tons of different renderers, and everyone had a different scene description language or API. With new renderers springing up all over the place, it was pretty clear that there was a need to standardize things by creating a common scene description language that would allow programs to define what needs to be rendered and not how it will be rendered. The idea behind this was that someday there would be companies that would only write renderers and others that would develop animation and modeling tools and that this new standard would be used to move data from a modeling/animation tool to the renderer. The API had to be simple yet extensible to allow other developers to add their own calls to support their renderer features. The engineers at Pixar designed an API that was supposed to become the 3D standard, kind of a PostScript for 3D or HTML for Web browsers. An HTML file can be read and displayed by any Web browser. Each browser will display the page somewhat differently, depending on how well the browser adheres to the HTML standards and what algorithms it uses to render the page. The Pixar API (RiAPI) was to be pretty much the same. Any renderer that supported the standard could read the description file and render a 2D image. Small differences from one image to another were to be expected but the images would still look the same at a glance. But this standard never really caught on, and for a very long time Pixar's own Photo Realistic RenderMan (PRMan) was the only commercially available implementation of the RenderMan standard.

Over the last couple of years, things have come full circle, and we are slowly going back to the trends of years ago. New programs that are very specialized are being released, but this time around they are designed to work in conjunction with most of the already established "big programs." Same thing goes for renderers. Most of the standalone renderers are designed to work with all major programs. This trend has resulted in the rapid adoption of the RenderMan Spec. Now there are several rendering programs that either adhere to the standard or at least support a way to read RenderMan-compliant files. The result of this is that the RenderMan Spec has become a pseudo-standard, since it is not really used by everyone or everywhere, but many renderers can handle RenderMan-compliant files. Not just that, but the release of other high-end rendering engines has affected the price of the most popular RenderMan implementation (PRMan), resulting in it dropping its price more than half over the last five years.

So what does this mean to you, the established technical director (TD), the student, or the self-taught artist looking to break into the industry? It means that there is a huge deficit of knowledgeable RenderMan shading TDs because more studios use RenderMan now that it is more accessible. Knowing RenderMan is a very precious skill to have, even if you are not looking to become a shader or rendering technical director (TD) or if you are looking to work somewhere that doesn't use RenderMan. Most studios that don't use RenderMan as their renderer still search for people with RenderMan knowledge to fill their shading or rendering TD positions. Why? Because someone who knows RenderMan shading usually has a deep understanding of how rendering works, of how illumination models are constructed, and how vectors are constantly manipulated to achieve certain looks. This knowledge is transferable to any other renderer that you might need to use, so it is very valuable to employers.

RenderMan Overview

The RenderMan Interface Specification (or RiSpec) is a 3D scene description language used to connect modeling and animation applications with a rendering engine. It is made up of two separate but intimately related parts: The RenderMan Scene Description API (RiAPI) and the RenderMan Shading Language (RSL).

The RiAPI is the part of the spec that defines the camera and image attributes, the geometry and lights, with their positions and custom attributes. The RiAPI is used to tell the renderer *what* to render, not *how* to render it. A RenderMan-compliant renderer could use scanline, REYES, raytracing, raymarching, OpenGL, or a combination of any of these techniques. The RiAPI tells the renderer where things are located and some important information about the scene. When a piece of geometry or a light is defined in the 3D scene, it is usually given a shader, which will be responsible for computing its appearance in the case of a surface shader or how it affects the scene in the case of a light or a volume shader. That's where the RSL plays its stellar role. It is the shaders that allow you to take an average harshly lit, gray, plastic-looking scene and turn it into beautiful masterpieces such as the frames from *Toy Story*, *Finding Nemo*, *Meet the Robinsons*, or *Ratatouille*. Shading and lighting are usually where shader technical directors spend the most time. This is because exporting the scene into a renderer is usually handled automatically by a third-party, off-the-shelf plug-in or by an in-house plug-in written by a company's software developers.

While developing renderers on the late 1970s, graphic researchers realized that to describe materials that were capable of fooling the eye into believing that a 3D scene was an actual photo, users needed a more extensible and controllable way to define their materials. Back then, and still today, many renderers provide the users with precoded procedurals, texture mapping, and built-in or hard-coded illumination models. These can get the users very far, but it limits the look that could be created. In order to create a new illumination model or a new procedural pattern, users need to write plug-ins using the program's API, which is somewhat complicated for nonprogrammers. In 1984, Rob Cook introduced the concept of *shade trees,* which allowed TDs to write small pieces of code that returned a certain value that could be plugged into other pieces of code successively until a full material would be described. Eventually Pat Hanrahan and Jim Lawson put together all their knowledge of shading trees and texture synthesis and created the RenderMan Shading Language (RSL), a standardized C-like language that allowed users to program shaders for RenderMan-compliant renderers. RSL was first introduced in the 1990 paper, "A Language for Shading and Lighting Calculations."

Since its inception, the RSL has evolved and grown into a large but simple language that most TDs with a little knowledge of programming can pick up rather quickly. This is what sets RSL apart from shading schemes used by other renderers that might use C or C++ (or any other programming language). C and C++ are very strong languages, but they are a lot more complicated than RSL. They are also very low level, which means the programmer has to take a lot of things into consideration while writing shaders. When you work in production you usually want to spend more time in the creative, artistic tasks such as creating procedural patterns or cool illumination models rather than having to keep track of memory addresses, garbage collection, and memory leaks. C and C++ code will certainly execute faster, but there will be portability problems. Since these low-level languages are compiled into machine code, they are not portable across platforms. RSL code is also compiled, but most RenderMan renderers compile their shaders into a machine independent "virtual machine," which interprets the RSL calls and applies it to the shading engine. This is why you can easily take a shader that was compiled with Pixar's shader compiler and use it in any platform where PRMan is supported. The results will be the same because the code is interpreted by the virtual machine. It becomes a matter of sacrificing some speed for the sake of ease of use and portability.

The REYES Rendering Algorithm

Most RenderMan-compliant renderers available on the market today use the REYES (Render Everything You Ever Saw) algorithm or a modified version of it. The most common modification is the inclusion of raytracing and global illumination algorithms. It was designed by Rob Cook, Loren Carpenter, and Edwin Catmull and presented to the CG community in 1987. (REYES also is named after one of Loren Carpenter's favorite spots on the California coastline, Point Reyes.) It was carefully designed to overcome some of the major deficiencies of other rendering algorithms of that time. It was decided that if a renderer were to generate images that would be good enough to be projected next to live action, then the artifacts found on other renderers were simply unacceptable. The new algorithm had to improve on the following areas:

- **Speed:** The algorithm must be as fast as possible and still maintain the necessary level of quality and extensiveness. Speed was important because the resolution required to hold up on a movie theater screen is usually higher than 1K and sometimes closer to 2K. Also, to match the image to film requires 24 frames per second (fps) of screen time. Add to that the number of test renders that are launched in the process of tweaking the parameters to achieve the right look, and you are talking about a lot of rendering!

  The developers knew that computers would become stronger with time, but they also knew that there is a logical relationship between the speed of computers and the complexity of scenes. The faster the systems, the more detail TDs and filmmakers will request. In fact, the need for detail and complexity most times surpasses the speed of the machines. Average frame rendering times have more than quadrupled since the release of *Toy Story* in 1995. Back then, a frame that took 10 hours or more to render would be allowed only if it were absolutely necessary. Nowadays, that same frame that used to take 10 hours to render will probably render in less than 30 minutes with today's fast computers, but now we let our longest frames go way past 10 hours. These render times reflect those scenes that have incredible amounts of data, such as the cars on the stands for the opening or closing sequence of *Cars*.

■ **Capability to Handle Large Amounts of Data:** The real world has an almost unlimited amount of objects, and most of those objects have a lot of detail—levels of detail that most people are not even aware of until they have to take a closer look. As TDs, we always have to observe objects in nature, and it's intimidating to think of the amount of detail that nature includes so effortlessly into something as simple as a rock. Then you think about how many rocks there are in a dirt field that you need to render and someone might have to call 911 to bring you back to consciousness.

■ **Memory Efficiency:** Computers back then were not as strong as they are today. Having 256MB of memory was a luxury, and it was predicted that even if the cost of memory went down, memory limits would always be an issue, just as with speed. It is for this reason that REYES renderers are extremely aggressive when it comes to culling things out of memory. A very simple explanation is that if an object is not being rendered at a particular moment, it will be out of memory, either by dumping it because it is finished being rendered or because it hasn't been loaded into memory yet but will be rendered soon.

■ **Motion Blur (Shutter Speed Simulation):** Live action film cameras operate by exposing film for a limited amount of time; in the case of regular speed film it is exposed at 1/24th of a second. As fast as this might seem, it is not fast enough to capture a fast-moving object without the object smearing or blurring on the screen. This is a kind of aliasing (a signal reconstruction error) that the developers of the first film cameras probably tried to avoid. Eventually they probably gave up on it because our eyes work in a similar way. If an object moves too fast in front of us, it blurs. As an audience we have grown accustomed to this effect, and if it's absent in a film, things look jerky, and it's clear that they are not real. It is very apparent when you see stop motion animation: As good as it may be, it is still jerky and strobby. A renderer had to be able to replicate this effect so that CG images could be mixed seamlessly with live-action footage.

The REYES algorithm introduced several concepts that were so unique that even now they are considered important and innovative. As a shading TD, you will probably not be in charge of debugging scenes, but you need to have a solid understanding of how the REYES algorithm works.

The first step in rendering the scene is the description of the scene, which can be done through direct RiAPI calls or through a RIB file. Originally, animation packages connected with RenderMan through application programming interface (API) calls. The RenderMan API is referred to as the RiAPI, where Ri stands for RenderMan Interface.

This method for connecting to the renderer is very powerful because you can use a number of programming tricks to pass information to the renderer. However, once the image is generated, the data in the API calls is deleted, and if you want to re-render the frame, you must reanalyze the scene and make the same API calls with the new changes. This might not seem like a big deal because you do it all the time with your 3D application. But things would go a lot faster if while lighting a scene you were able to export the unchanged geometry only once, and then every time you re-render, export only the light information. That is one of the many advantages of using RIB.

RenderMan Interface Bytestream (RIB) is a more compact and easier format for describing 3D scenes for RenderMan. It is true that going through the API might be faster and use less disk space, but most production houses use RIB more than API because it contains direct calls, making it a more readable way to pass commands to the API. For example, a RiAPI program to generate a simple constant color polygon might look like this:

```
#include <ri.h>
RtPoint Square[4]= {{.5,.5,.5},{.5,-.5,.5},{-.5,-.5,.5},{-.5,.5,.5}};
main()
{
RiBegin(RI_NULL);
RiWorldBegin();
RiSurface("constant",RI_NULL);
RiPolygon(4, RI_P,(RtPointer)Square,RI_NULL);
RiWorldEnd();
RiEnd();
}
```

This is what its RIB counterpart would look like:

```
WorldBegin
Surface "constant"
Polygon "P" [.5 .5 .5 .5 -.5 .5 -.5 -.5 .5 -.5 .5 .5]
WorldEnd
```

As you see, RIB is a lot more straightforward and easy to read. The previous chunk of commands omits a lot of the calls that are usually used to set up RIB properly. An image is successfully generated because renderers usually insert the necessary RIB calls with some default value in order to render the image. If a RIB file is provided, then there is a parsing stage to convert the RIB stream to RiAPI calls. Then it moves into what is known as the splitting loop, which is responsible for breaking the primitives into manageable pieces of geometry that can be handled efficiently by the renderer. The first step of the splitting loop is the bounding of all primitives.

Bounding

Every piece of geometry that will be processed by a REYES renderer must first be bound. This means that the renderer needs to know the exact dimensions of the geometry before it can be moved down the rendering pipeline. There are no infinite or unbounded primitives such as ground planes or sky domes. This is necessary because of the next step in the pipeline: onscreen testing. An infinite piece of geometry could never be bound, so we could never test whether it is onscreen. This would probably result in a lot of wasted data that would never be seen onscreen.

Onscreen Test

Once all the geometry has been bound, it is tested against the camera frustrum to decide if it is onscreen or not. If it is not inside the frustrum, then it won't show up onscreen or contribute to the scene, and it can be culled from memory. As you can tell from the first steps of the REYES algorithm, optimization is very aggressive. The fact that there is no raytracing in the REYES algorithm means that if the object is not onscreen, then it can't affect the scene through reflections, refractions, or even shadows, as these would be pre-calculated. At the end of this chapter we will discuss the variation that Pixar has implemented into PRMan to turn it into a hybrid REYES renderer. This might not be the same way other RenderMan-compliant renderers that support raytracing implement their raytracing support, but it should give you an understanding of the differences with the traditional REYES algorithm. If the bound geometry is onscreen, then it is run through the size test.

Size Test

The renderer will now estimate how many micropolygons it will take to represent the declared surface. It will do this by projecting the parametric space of the surfaces into raster (a form of screen) space. If the number of micropolygons is higher than the grid size option passed to the renderer, then it will usually be split into smaller pieces. The method by which each primitive is split is different for every type of primitive. Every primitive type must be capable of being diced or split into a primitive type that can be diced. Each of these pieces will be rebound, tested for screen visibility, and if visible, tested for size. The pieces of geometry will stay in this loop, being split and retested until all of the pieces pass the size test. Once a piece passes the size test, it is flagged as diceable, and it can move into the dicing stage.

Dice

The dicing stage is responsible for turning the split primitives that come out of the splitting loop into micropolygons, which are four-sided bilinear patches. The number of micropolygons is determined by either the shading rate option that is defined by the user or just the default value. A shading rate of 1 indicates that each micropolygon needs to be the size of one pixel. Smaller shading rate values result in more detailed and crisp textures and shading at the expense of longer rendering time. A shading rate of 1 is a good mid-high level of detail. A shading rate of 0.25 to 0.5 is typical for production-quality renders because this will make each micropolygon one quarter to half the size of a pixel. A shading rate smaller than 0.25 will usually result in your render times escalating, and the extra expense might not be worth it. A shading rate of 5.0 is great for fast previews where you are trying to position features in a shader, but be aware that this will make your textures lose a lot of detail and make everything very soft.

Shade

Once all the micropolygons have been generated, it's time for the shading engine to come in and do its magic. The shaders are run on the surface in the following order: displacement, surface, lights, volume (interior and exterior), and imager. REYES renderers perform all shading calculations on the corners of the micropolygons. This is different from renderers that use triangles as the base primitive, which use the surface normal that is defined by triangle plane to perform shading calculations. With triangles, it is very easy to determine the surface normal, which is what other renderers use to perform shading calculations. REYES renderers use the derivatives of each micropolygon to determine the surface normal at the corners. Shaders are executed through a virtual SIMD (Single Instruction Multiple Data) machine one grid at a time, not one micropolygon at a time. Some renderers use a single instruction single data (SISD) machine, which parses and performs all of the instructions on a shading point; then it moves to the next shading, parses and executes all of the instructions. A SIMD machine behaves differently. It will parse the instructions once and execute the same instructions on all the points in a grid. Parsing the instructions is usually somewhat expensive, especially if you need to do it once per every shading point. With a SIMD, you only do it once per grid, this makes the process a lot more efficient, especially when you use uniform variables. The whole polygon is shaded either as a blend of all the corners or with constant values based on what kind of shading interpolation the user specified.

Bust and Bound

Once the micropolygons are shaded, they are busted, or exploded into thousands of individual primitives. The renderer doesn't consider them as part of a whole or a model anymore; each micropolygon is its own model. Since each micropolygon is treated as a primitive, the renderer will try to perform one last onscreen test to search for extra efficiency.

Micropolygon Onscreen Test

This last onscreen test is used mainly to cull away any micropolygons that might be hidden by the model they belonged to (such as back-facing micropolygons) or other geometry in the scene and also to cull any micropolygons that might have become hidden after the displacement operations. This is why all micropolygons must be completely shaded before final hiding. The final hiding will create a list of visible micropolygons, which is then passed to the sampler.

Sample

With all the micropolygons shaded and tested for onscreen presence, it is time for the sampling of all the micropolygons that are in the visible points list, which is a list of all the shaded points that remain visible to the camera after all the hiding is completed. Sampling in REYES renderers is performed on a pixel or a subpixel level, depending on the settings you use, and you have controls for sampling the X and Y directions of a pixel. The smallest and fastest sampling rate in a REYES render is 1 by 1, which will sample each pixel only once, resulting in very aliased images. If values lower than 1 are provided, the renderer will round it up to 1, which means that REYES renderers can't do undersampling, only supersampling. If a value of 2 or more is passed, the renderer will split the pixel that number of times in X and Y. Each of these split areas is referred to as a subpixel. The final number of subpixel samples per pixel is the value of xsamples × ysamples, so if you pass a value of 3 and 3 there will be 9 subpixels to shade. The renderer will sample each subpixel and then store a list of color, opacity, and depth values.

Composite and Filter

The final step in the rendering of the image is the compositing and filtering of the stored values. The renderer will use the depth and opacity to sort out whether the sampled values will have any effect on the final image. If the closest sample is 100% opaque, then it will ignore the other values, but if it is somewhat transparent, it will continue to use the values based on depth until the opacity of the pixel is considered opaque, which is determined by the "limit othreshold" option. The renderer will use the specified reconstruction filter to set a final color and opacity value for each pixel. Each pixel is then stored in a file or displayed in a window. This process is demonstrated in Figure 1.1.

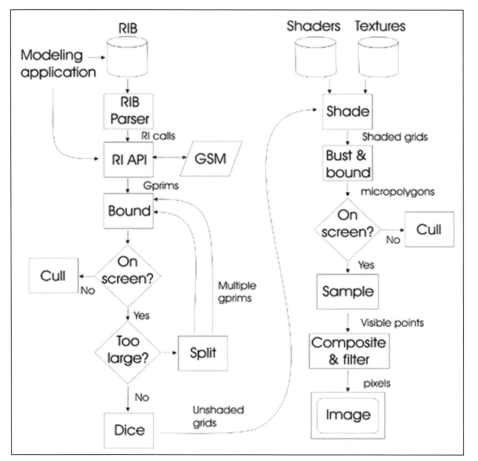

Figure 1.1 A data flow diagram of the steps used by REYES renderers.

Anatomy of a RIB File

RIB files are the most popular way to interface with RenderMan-compliant renderers from modeling packages. They are very simple in their structure, and since RIB is not a programming language but more of a "batch" language, it is very easy to read through them or write scripts that analyze or modify the RIB file. RIB files are structured in blocks, and have their respective commands for opening and closing those blocks.

The outermost block in a RenderMan scene is the `RiBegin`/`RiEnd` block. Everything inside these blocks is passed directly to the renderer as a command part of the Ri state. When using RIB files, you don't need to declare the `RiBegin`/`RiEnd` block because calling the rendering command (such as `renderdl` or `render`) will initialize the Ri state.

Inside the `RiBegin`/`RiEnd` block you will usually find the `FrameBegin`/`FrameEnd` block. These commands tell the renderer that what you are about to render is a single frame that might be part of a sequence of frames. Inside the frame block, you can modify the default values of the rendering options for this frame. When you exit the frame block, all of the rendering options are restored to their default values. The notion of a frame is important because it allows you to declare more than one frame inside each RIB file. This is not a common practice because RIB data for detailed scenes is quite large, and if you try to declare more than one frame per file, that file will get pretty big. It's also an organizational hassle to manage scene files that have multiple frames in a file. It is a lot easier to manage your data if you have a single RIB file for every render that needs to be performed. You don't need to use the `FrameBegin`/`FrameEnd` commands in cases where you are declaring a single frame per file.

Within the frame block and after the initialization of the rendering options comes the world block, which is limited by the `WorldBegin`/`WorldEnd` commands. Within this block you can declare lights and coordinate systems, geometric surfaces, and attributes to control each element. There can be more than one world block per frame, which can be useful if you would like to include any prerender elements such as shadows or environment maps inside a single RIB file.

Options and Attributes

There are two main entities within RIB files that allow the user to control the renderer: options and attributes. They might seem similar, but they are quite different and require a thorough understanding of what each does.

Options are controls that are global to the current frame that is being rendered. An option cannot be changed within a frame because it needs to remain constant for the renderer to do its job. To ensure rendering options remain constant, the renderer will store and freeze all of the rendering options when it finds a call to `WorldBegin`. It will hold those values until the respective `WorldEnd` is found, at which point it will reset all of the rendering options. An example of an option is the output image resolution or the filter used to blend the final sampled values. These values must remain constant, and there can be only one per frame. Other important options are the image name and format, the filtering, and so on. When the renderer is first called, all of the necessary options are initialized to their default values. These values might be different from one renderer to another. As the renderer parses your RIB file, it will replace the default values of any option that has been declared on the RIB file.

Attributes are controls that allow you to modify the current piece of geometry that you are defining. There are certain RIB attributes that allow you to insert shaders at different stages of the RIB file. To assign a shader to a piece of geometry, you need to use the proper command before you define the geometry. You will use and examine these attributes constantly, so it is important to know them well. The keywords for inserting shaders into the RIB stream are listed in the following table, followed by a RIB example demonstrating how to use them.

Table 1.1

Attribute	Action-Declare
Lightsource	A light source with a light shader
Atmosphere	An atmospheric shader to the whole scene
Displacement	The current displacement shader
Surface	The current surface shader
Interior	A shader to handle the interior of a surface
Exterior	A shader to handle the exterior of a surface
Imager	The current imager shader

```
Option "searchpath" "string shader" ["./:@:&:../rsl/rel/"]
Display "sphere.tif" "framebuffer" "rgb"
Format 500 500 1
PixelSamples 3 3
Clipping 0.001 1000
Projection "perspective"
Translate 0 0 1.5
WorldBegin
LightSource "distantlight" 1 "intensity" [1.0]
LightSource "ambientlight" 2 "intensity" [0.1]
Atmosphere "fog"
AttributeBegin
Attribute "displacementbound" "float sphere" [0.15]
Displacement "d_RP_simplenoise" "float noiFreq" [15]
Surface "s_RP_helloworld01"
```

```
Interior "interiorGel" "float fadeValue" [2]
Rotate 55 1 0 0
Rotate -55 0 0 1
Sphere 1 -1 0.5 360
AttributeEnd
WorldEnd
```

Attributes are stored as a stack, where the top of the stack represents the current or active attribute. A stack is a common data structure used in programming; it is very easy to program, and it has very predictable behavior. A stack probably derives its name from a real-world analogy of how it works. Imagine that you will create a stack of dishes. You start the stack by placing a blue plate on a table. This makes the current color value of the dish stack blue. If you put a red plate on top of a blue plate, you have just "pushed" the value of the plate stack, and that top plate becomes the current value of the stack, which is now red. The value of the stack will continue to be red until you push it again by adding another plate on top of it or "pop" the stack value by removing the red plate. You can push and pop a stack value as many times as you want, but you need to remember that the previous value on the stack can only be accessed by popping the current value.

This is how attributes are managed, so when you declare an attribute such as a surface shader, that surface becomes the current value of the surface shader stack. This means that every geometry defined after the surface shader will receive that value until you declare another surface shader, at which point that second surface shader will become the current value.

```
WorldBegin
#Declare the current surface shader
Surface "plastic"
#Define the current color - all objects from now on
#will receive this shader and color
Color [1 0 1]
Transform 1 0 0
Sphere 1 -1 1 360
#Override the current surface shader and color
Surface "matte"
Color [1 1 0]
Transform -2 0 0
Sphere 1 -1 1 360
WorldEnd
```

By just declaring surface shaders in the RIB stream, we are not actually pushing or popping the values in the surface shader stack, we are just replacing the current surface shader. To push and pop attributes from the stack, you need to use the AttributeBegin and AttributeEnd commands. An AttributeBegin call means that

every attribute declared afterward will become active (pushing the stack) until
AttributeEnd is found. At that point every attribute will revert to the previous
attribute value.

```
WorldBegin
#Declare the current surface shader
Surface "plastic"
#Define the current color - all objects from now on
#will receive this shader and color
Color [1 0 1]

#Now we start a new attribute block,
#we can override the previous shader and color
AttributeBegin
#Name the sphere
Attribute "identifier" "name" ["nurbsSphere1"]
#Apply a transform to the sphere's coordinate system
ConcatTransform [2.1367 0 0 0 2.1367 0 0 0 2.1367 0 0 0 1]
#Change the current shader
Surface "rudycplasmaball" "float additive" 0.75
#Change the current color
Color [0.5 0.7 0.8]
#Declare a sphere
Sphere 1 -1 1 360
#The end of the attribute block, we go back to the
#original Surface and Color
AttributeEnd

#This sphere will use plastic and the color [1 0 1]
Sphere 1 -1 1 360
WorldEnd
```

Transformations

This stack data structure is also perfectly suited for handling the type of hierar-
chical transformations we are so accustomed to in our 3D applications. In most
3D applications, when you parent an object to another, transforming the parent
object will result in that transformation affecting the child object. This is because
in 3D graphics every object has a pivot point, which is referred to as a "coordinate
system." These coordinate systems are also handled with a stack, which can be
pushed and popped and which always has a current coordinate system. Coordinate
systems (coordsys) are extremely important for shader development because using

the right coordsys can save you a lot of time and trouble, and using the wrong coordsys will usually create very strange artifacts. We will talk more about coordsys and shading later on when we cover pattern generation.

The transformation stack is initialized when the WorldBegin call is found. Every transformation for every other object has to be placed between the TransformBegin and TransformEnd calls, which are responsible for pushing or popping the transformations on the stack.

End of Line and Comments

As you have seen in previous examples, RIB files don't use a semicolon (;) at the end of a line, which might make you think that RIB uses the end of line character as a delimiter for its commands. A RIB stream doesn't really have an end of line delimiter; it uses its commands as delimiters. So when a command is called, that command will be active, and all subsequent data will be considered parameters to that command. Such a command will remain active until the renderer finds a new command. This means that a command and its parameters can apply to multiple lines and remain active.

```
AttributeBegin
    # This Identifier attribute spans two lines
    Attribute "identifier" "string name"
        ["|nurbsSphere1|nurbsSphereShape1"]
    # As well as this transform command
    Transform [ 1 0 0 0 0 1 0 0 0 0 1 0
        0 0 0 1 ]
    Surface "defaultsurface"
    ObjectInstance 1
AttributeEnd
```

RIB files support one type of commenting through the # symbol. All text between the # symbol and the end of that line is considered a comment and is ignored by the renderer.

Image Control Options

Before the WorldBegin command, you will usually find a set of options that allows the user to control the image that will be generated by the current scene. We will discuss the most popular and useful options available to the user. If you would like to read about all of the options, feel free to read the RiSpec. All of these options have default values that will be used if you don't override them.

Format

The Format command allows you to declare the horizontal, vertical, and pixel aspect ratio of the image. The syntax for calling the format command is Format 640 480 1. These values represent the horizontal and vertical resolution plus the pixel aspect ratio. The first two values must be integers, and the last argument is a float. A pixel aspect ratio allows you to control the horizontal to vertical ratio of the pixels in the image. An aspect ratio of 1 is typical for film output, as well as for computer movies. The NTSC 720 format uses a pixel ratio of 0.9, and images for widescreen anamorphic projections usually use a pixel aspect ratio between 1.2 and 2, depending on how extreme the anamorphic distortion is.

Projection

The Projection command tells the renderer what kind of parameters you want to use to project the 3D scene to a 2D image. The projection can be thought of as the camera description, but this is not entirely correct because a camera description would need extra parameters such as shutter speed and depth of field controls. This control only gives you access to the viewing portion of a camera.

The projection can be of two types: orthographic and perspective. When using an orthographic projection, you don't need any extra parameters, but when declaring a perspective projection, you need to provide a field of view (fov) parameter, which is a float value that represents the angle of view in degrees.

```
#Perspective Projection
Projection "perspective" "fov" [ 37.84929 ]

#Orthographic Projection
Projection "orthographic"
```

Clipping

The viewing volume of a camera is defined by the angle of the field of view and by the near and far clipping planes. These planes let the renderer know at what distance from the camera to start considering the geometry for rendering and at what distance to stop. The near clipping plane is always at a depth value of 0 and the far plane at 1. The distance (or depth) stored on each sampled point is a value that is extracted from a linear interpolation between the near and far clipping planes. Wherever the sampled point lies, that's the value it will receive. The following sets the near plane to 0.01 and the far to 10000.

```
Clipping 0.01 10000
```

It is recommended that you always set your clipping planes properly, meaning the far clipping plane will be a bit further than the farthest object in your scene (the near clipping plane is not quite as important). This will allow the renderer to be more accurate on the depth values computed on the sampled points.

Display

The Display command tells the renderer what to do with the final computed pixel values. You can store them in a file or display them in a window of some sort. The target for the pixels is also referred to as the *display driver*. Each renderer can support different display drivers, but no matter which they support, they need to be able to handle two basic drivers: the *file driver* and the *framebuffer driver*. The framebuffer driver will send the pixels to a window drawn on the screen. Some renderers use advanced windows with tons of features, while others just display the image. The file driver saves the image in whatever image format the renderer specifies as its default. Most renderers use TIFF as the default, but this is not mandatory, so please read your user's manual to make sure.

Renderers should also ship with directions and/or examples on how you can write your own custom display drivers to be able to save images in formats not supported directly or for proprietary formats. A Display command has the following syntax:

```
Display ImageName DisplayDriver ImageMode
```

The following will render an image named myimage.tif in TIFF format with an imagemode of rgba (red, green, blue, and alpha channels):

```
Display "myimage.tif" "tiff" "rgba"
```

PixelSamples and ShadingRate

The PixelSamples option allows you to control the number of samples that will be performed on the X and Y axes of a pixel. The combination of PixelSamples and the ShadingRate command are the two main components that will affect the quality of the image. The more samples and the higher the shading rate, the crisper the image will look (see Figures 1.2 and 1.3), but the longer the rendering will take. In rendering there is always a speed against quality trade-off, and these are the controls that allow you to modify the quality to fit your needs. You can use these controls in combination with the pixel filter to generate images that might be softer looking and still render quite fast. Another thing to consider is that if the scene will be motion blurred, you should be able to reduce the value of the shading rate to speed up the rendering times.

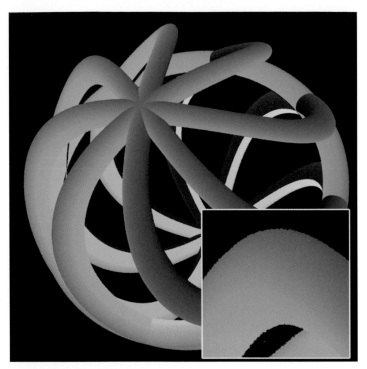

Figure 1.2 Image with a PixelSample value of 1 1.

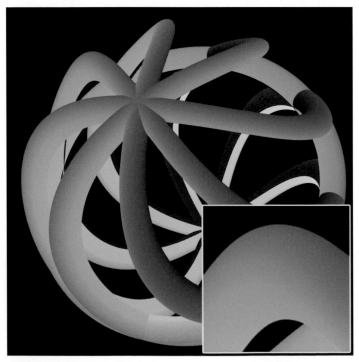

Figure 1.3 Same image but with a PixelSample value of 4 4.

PixelFilter

In the last stage of rendering, when the values are being composited together, the renderer will use whatever filter type you define with PixelFilter. This is the syntax for the PixelFilter command:

```
PixelFilter "FilterType" xwidth ywidth
```

The RiSpec specifies that every compliant renderer must support at least the box, triangle, catmull-rom, sinc, and gaussian filter types. Each filter has its pros and cons. Figures 1.4 to 1.6 show the same scene rendered with different filters with a filter width of 8 8. Notice how the box-filtered image becomes very blurry right away and aliasing starts showing badly on the horizon. The gaussian and box filters provide very similar results while the catmull-rom returns a very sharp image. When using smaller widths, they usually render with similar results, but when you increase the filterwidth value beyond 3, the results become more apparent. The difference is quite obvious when comparing Figures 1.7 and 1.8.

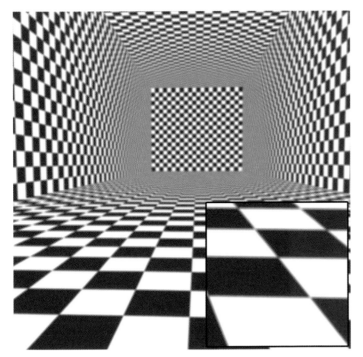

Figure 1.4 PixelFilter box 8 8.

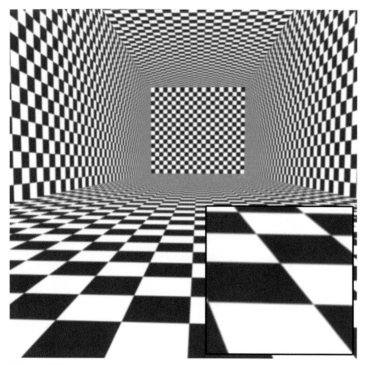

Figure 1.5 PixelFilter gaussian 8 8.

Figure 1.6 PixelFilter catmull-rom 8 8.

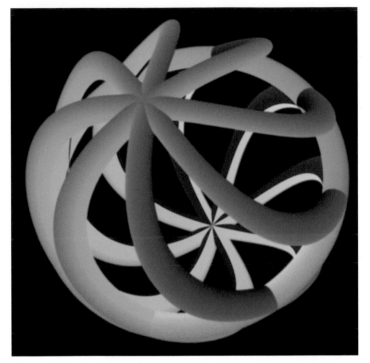

Figure 1.7 PixelFilter gaussian 10 10. Notice how soft the image is.

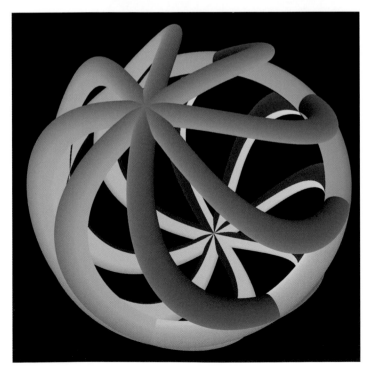

Figure 1.8 PixelFilter catmull-rom 10 10. The exact same value but a different filter. The image remains extremely sharp.

More About RIBs and the RiSpec

We have covered the basics of RIB and RiSpec in this chapter, but we have barely begun to scratch the surface of the options and possibilities of working with the RiSpec. Throughout the book, we will reinforce knowledge in certain areas of the RiSpec that are essential for shader technical directors. If you want to learn more about the spec and using RenderMan in general, you can read any of the following materials to broaden your knowledge:

- *Rendering for Beginners* by Saty Raghavachary
- *Essential RenderMan Fast* by Ian Stephenson
- *The RenderMan Companion* by Steven Upstill
- *Advanced RenderMan* by Larry Gritz and Tony Apodaca
- *The Official RiSpec V 3.2* by Pixar Animation Studios

2

RSL Details

Language Overview

The RenderMan Shading Language (RSL) is a C-like, higher-level programming language designed specifically for surface materials, light, and phenomena description. It was designed to be simple enough to allow non-computer scientists to use it but still have enough power to let savvy TDs create astounding images that rival those captured by a camera. There are several slight differences, restrictions, and caveats in RSL that those familiar with C might find annoying sometimes, but once they understand the design of the language, they will realize that these limitations make the language a lot simpler and that there are several ways to get around them. If you are a complete "C head," you will be happy to know that there is a way to extend RSL by writing DSO shadeops, which are pre-compiled C plug-ins for RSL.

The RSL is made up of about 90 to 100 built-in functions at the time this book is being written. At this moment, the RiSpec v. 3.3 is still an unofficial release, which means that some of the new calls are being tested, modified, added, and discarded to ensure that they are as useful as possible. A note must be made here to those who are using renderers other than PRMan. Most renderers implement their own calls, which are different from those in the RiSpec, and sometimes they don't exist in the spec at all, so please read the user manual of your renderer closely to find out which calls do and don't apply to your renderer.

When working on a shader, you will be dealing with a minimum of two files: the source code file and the compiled file. The source code file contains the RSL code plus all the comments that you add to it and it is human readable. The compiled file can be ASCII or binary, and it contains a set of instructions that only the renderer can understand. You could use the same source code to compile shaders for different renderers, assuming that the renderer adheres to the RiSpec. All shader source code files use a .sl extension. This extension is not necessary, but everyone uses it (just like .txt for text files). The compiled file uses different extensions depending on what renderer you are using. Table 2.1 lists the extensions used for compiled shaders by the most common renderers.

Table 2.1 Compiled Shader Extensions for Common Renderers

Renderer	Extension
PRMan	.slo
3Delight	.sdl
Aqsis	.slx
RenderDotC*	.dll, .so

*RenderDotC generates a system library, not a virtual machine shader.

Shader Types

The RiSpec defines six different shader types that can be used to describe the appearance of a geometric surface. These shaders are executed at very specific times and are responsible for calculating small amounts of information and passing it to the other shaders before the final pixel is drawn and saved to the file. These shaders are discussed in the following sections in order of execution (see Figure 2.1 for one example).

Displacement

Displacement shaders are responsible for modifying the actual surface position of the geometry, which is referred to as displacement, or just modifying the surface normal, which is known as *bump mapping*. Displacement will actually change the geometry of the object, while bump mapping will make it appear as if the geometry has been modified. Figures 2.1 and 2.2 show the effect of a displacement shader on an object. This is the first shader type run on a surface because, when an object is displaced, certain parts of its surface that were visible before shading become hidden (or vice versa). This allows further memory and speed optimization at execution time of the other shaders, resulting in faster render times. Another reason for its position in the execution tree is that displacement shaders modify the shading normals, which need to be computed before the surface shaders.

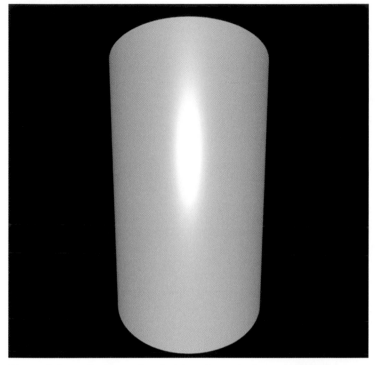

Figure 2.1 A cylinder rendered with a plastic shader and no displacements.

Figure 2.2 The same cylinder file, but with a displacement shader modifying the geometry.

Surface

Surface shaders are the second ones to be evaluated by the shading engine and are responsible for providing the surface color, which is usually pre-multiplied by the opacity calculations. Pre-multiplication is done in the shader source by multiplying the final opacity by the final surface color; it is not mandatory, but it is common practice. Surface shaders are usually made up of a collection of functions that generate procedural patterns, do texture lookups, or a combination of both. They usually also include a section of code referred to as the *illumination loop*.

The illumination loop is responsible for querying all the active lights in the scene and adding their light contribution to the surfaces. The surface shader will then combine the final surface color and the opacity to create a final surface color. This color will be passed to the volume shaders (if they exist) for further modification. Figures 2.2 and 2.3 show the difference between using a single plastic shader (2.2) and using individual custom shaders per object (2.3).

Figure 2.3 A simple scene with the default plastic shader.

Figure 2.4 The same scene with surface shaders added. *Image courtesy of Pixar.*

Lights

Light shaders are essential for image rendering. Without them, you could generate only images that use constant shaders (and those are not too exciting). However, light shaders are not written as commonly as surface or displacement shaders. Most studios actually use a single uber-light or a handful of light shaders that have tons of parameters and are sophisticated enough to allow the user extreme control over how the light behaves, allowing a single shader to behave as several different types of lights.

Light shaders don't run after the surface shaders. They run in parallel with the surface shaders because they query the lights for their intensity. Light shaders are responsible for passing to the surface shader the color and intensity of that light. These values can also be calculated by using procedural patterns, texture lookups, and shadow calculations. Lighting can have a very dramatic effect on a scene, as seen in Figure 2.5. It is the same scene we used in Figures 2.3 and 2.4.

Figure 2.5 The same scene with user-defined lighting.

Volume (Atmosphere, Interior, and Exterior)

Volume shaders were originally designed to simulate the existence of small atmospheric particulate matter that exists almost everywhere in real life. CG images are rendered as if they are inside a vacuum chamber, free of all dust and miscellaneous particles. If CG images are to be used for visual effects on films, then there must be a way to replicate the effect that dust has on photographic images. Originally all volume shaders in PRMan had to be declared as "atmosphere" shaders, but after version 12 of PRMan, the software finally caught up to the RiSpec, and now a volume shader can also be assigned as two other types: interior and exterior volume. Both of these shaders depend on the inclusion of the `gather()raytracing` command inside the surface shader. Exterior volumes are used to simulate dust or haze outside an object. Interior shaders are used to simulate effects such as tinted glasses or even a gelatinous surface inside the object.

After the volume shader evaluation, the surfaces have a final color that can be saved to an image, displayed on the screen, or passed over to the imager shader. Figures 2.6 and 2.7 use a model donated by Serguei Kalentchouk to the 3D community at cgtalk.com for one of its lighting challenges. It is available for free download from 3dRender.com.

Figure 2.6 Underwater scene rendered without an atmospheric volume shader.

Figure 2.7 A simple fog shader enhances the feeling of water's depth dramatically.

Imager

Imager shaders are the last ones to be run by the shading engine. They are designed to behave sort of like a post-process 2D filter. Imager shaders can only modify the final color of a surface. They don't have access to any 3D attributes, only to 2D pixels. PRMan doesn't officially support imager shaders, but it does support a couple of them named "background" and "clamptoalpha." The background shader is used to control the color of the background of the images, which is black by default. The clamptoalpha imager shader is used to restrict values greater than one and lower than zero to make it into the image, as such values can create problems while compositing later. Imager shaders are great for generating non-photorealistic renders (NPRs) such as the following images generated with 3Delight. Figure 2.8 is what the image would render like without the imager shader. Figure 2.9 is what the image looks like once the imager shader is applied.

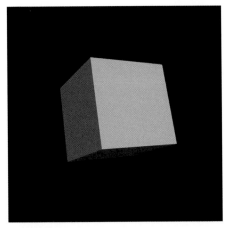

Figure 2.8 The original image without the imager shader applied.

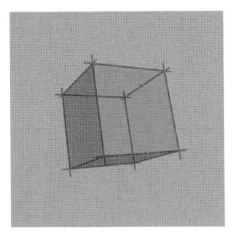

Figure 2.9 A completely different result once the imager shader is applied.

Image courtesy of Katsuaki Hiramitsu

Variables

The most essential and necessary operation in RSL and most other programming languages is the creation or declaration and assignment of variables. Variables are data holders that you are allowed to name. A variable becomes an alias or a nickname for your data, making it easier to identify and track how your data is handled. To declare a variable in RSL, the following syntax should be followed:

```
[class] type variableName;
```

The uniform or varying `class` declaration is optional and is described in the next section. `type` refers to the type of data that will be used, and the variable name can be anything you want it to be as long as you follow these rules:

- You cannot use any of RSL's predefined keywords.

- A variable name cannot include special symbols such as *, - , +, /.

- Variables can't have space between them.

- A variable name can't start with a number.

Once a variable is declared, it can be assigned a value. The variable will keep that value until you assign it a new value or pass it to a function as an output variable. To assign a value to a variable, you use the assignment operator =.

```
variableName =  25;
```

You can also combine the variable declaration and assignment into a single line that initializes the variable:

```
varying float myvar = 25;
```

After a variable is initialized, you can use it at any point in your shader to access its value. For example:

```
uniform float varA = 2;  // Declare and initialize varA
uniform float varB = 5;  // Declare and initialize varB
uniform float varC = varA * varB; // varC value is 10
varB = varC - varA;  // varB value is overwritten to 8(10-2)
```

Data Classes

RSL supports two data classes that are evaluated differently and provide different memory requirements for the renderer. The available classes are *uniform* and *varying*. These two classes allow you to have further control over the efficiency of your shader. As a shader designer you need to know the benefits and the caveats of using them.

To understand the difference between these two classes, we must recap on an important design element of the REYES algorithm. As you might recall, shader evaluation is performed as a Single Instruction Multiple Data (SIMD) machine. This means that a function is parsed only once and executed over all the micropolygons of a shading grid instead of being parsed and executed on every micropolygon. This scheme allows further optimization for certain operations, such as illumination loops, because the resulting values for an evaluated micropolygon will be the same over the whole patch as long as the variables of the illumination loop don't change over the shading grid.

Variables that have the same value over the whole grid are of the uniform class. Most parameters used to control values such as diffusion, specularity, or ambient are declared as uniform variables. Varying class variables are those that change value inside a shading grid. They are commonly used to hold information on texture patterns or on primitive variables stored in the mesh. In case the user doesn't explicitly declare a class, most renderers will assume shader parameters are uniform and variables declared inside a shader as varying. We will go deeper into this topic as needed.

Data Types

The RSL uses a very limited number of data types to store data. Programmers experienced in other languages might realize that there are several common types not used in RSL, and that RSL introduces some types that are not common in other programming languages. This is because RSL is designed specifically for shading, and therefore it excludes some types that are not necessary or useful and includes some very necessary types.

Float

The float data type represents all numerical values in RSL. Other programming languages have more data types to store numbers. It is of particular importance to note that RSL doesn't have an integer data type, which is used to represent a whole number (with no fractions). RSL doesn't have Booleans, either, which are used to represent either a 1 or a 0 and are very common for switches and flow control. This design might be somewhat limiting at times, and it might not make the code as fast as other programming languages, but it does simplify things greatly. If you find yourself needing to use an integer or a Boolean and you want your shader to execute faster, make sure you declare those variables or parameters as uniform.

String

Strings are designed to store text data. The most common use for strings is to read image maps from a hard drive, but they are also used for message passing and to pass custom attributes to the renderer. An important note about strings is that

RSL is not very efficient when working with them, especially for string comparison. This is due to the fact that even though strings are usually of uniform type (which means that variables will be evaluated only once per patch instead of once per shading point), the string must still be compared once per patch, and there could be hundreds or thousands of patches in a single model. Strings are always surrounded by double quotes, but if accessed through a variable, then the quotes are not necessary.

```
// Quotes are necessary to assign it to a string variable
string imageMap = "/home/maps/myimage.tx";
// We use the variable without quotes
color surfaceColor = texture(imageMap,s,t);
// Or without the variable
color surfaceColor = texture("/home/maps/myimage.tx",s,t);
```

Points, Vectors, and Normals

Points, vectors, and normals are very similar in the way they are represented in RSL, but in fact, they are very different. Points are used to represent a position in 3D space based on a given coordinate system. They hold no information about direction at all. Vectors represent directions in 3D space and they have no position. They are used to represent rays and directions. Normals are very similar to vectors, but they are designed to represent the direction in which a surface is pointing. Normals have a position and an orientation. You can easily convert a normal to a vector and to a point, but you must be careful because there are operations, such as multiplication or scaling, that will have a different effect on a vector than on a normal.

All three of these data types are represented by a one-dimensional, three-element array. You can access any of the components of these arrays by using specialized functions, which will be covered later. Use the following examples to help you declare a point, vector, or normal:

```
// A normal that points up the y axis
normal NN =  (0,1,0);
// A point on the origin
uniform point Porig = (0,0,0);
// A vector  that goes from the second value to the first
vector newV = vector ((1,1,0) - (0.5,0.1,0));
```

Color

Color in RSL is represented by a three-value array just like vectors, normals, and points. Colors can be represented in different color spaces, also referred to as *color coordinate systems*. By default, all colors are represented in RGB space. However, some operations are a lot easier if you convert the color to HSV (hue, saturation, and value). To declare a `color` variable, it is advisable to typecast the three-value array explicitly as a color. You can also initialize a color in a different color space as you are declaring a variable by providing the name of the color space right before you type in the three-value array. Note that the color space must be inside quotes because it is a string identifier. If a single float is assigned to the color, then the single float will be copied to all three elements of the color three-value array. Here are some examples of color variable declarations, followed by Table 2.2, which lists all the available color spaces in RSL.

```
// Medium Grey
color color1 = color (0.5,0.5,0.5);
// Pure red defined in hsv
color color2 = color "hsv" (0,1,1);
// white - the single float will be copied to all 3 values
color color3 = 1;
```

Table 2.2 Color Spaces Supported in RSL

Color Space	Description
"rgb"	red, green, blue (default)
"hsv"	hue, saturation, value
"hsl"	hue, saturation, lightness
"xyz","XYZ"	CIE coordinates
"YIQ"	NTSC coordinates

Matrix

RSL includes support for a matrix type that is used to represent transformations inside shaders and their coordinate systems. A matrix is made up of a 16-element float array that corresponds to a 4 3 4 homogeneous transformation coordinate. The math of matrices is not terribly complicated, but it does require more knowledge and practice than the math of integers. Using homogeneous coordinates greatly simplifies the math involved. The most important math operations and concepts will be covered in Chapter 5. Matrices have special rules for initializing variables. Here are some examples of how you can declare a matrix:

```
// A totally useless matrix in the current coordsys
matrix m1 =  (0,1,2,3, 4,5,6,7, 8,9,10,11, 12,13,14,15);
// An identity matrix in shader space
matrix ident = "shader" 1;
// A Zero matrix in world space
matrix zero = "world" 0;
```

The first example creates a valid matrix (although completely useless) in the current coordinate system. The second one creates an identity matrix, which has a 1 diagonally on the components of the matrix like Figure 2.10. The last example creates a matrix with a value of 0 for all of its components.

$$I_3 = \begin{bmatrix} 1 & 0 & 0 \\ 0 & 1 & 0 \\ 0 & 0 & 1 \end{bmatrix}$$

Figure 2.10 An identity matrix has a value of one diagonally.

Arrays

The RenderMan Shading Language supports one-dimensional arrays of all the basic data types. Support of one-dimensional arrays means that you can't have an array of arrays. Arrays are very common for those instances in which you want to perform similar operations on a large amount of data of the same type. This is an important concept because you can't mix and match RSL types within the same array. If you are defining an array of floats, then all the elements in that array must be floats. An array is created using the same notation as in C. Here is the syntax for declaring an array variable, followed by a couple of examples.

```
class type variablename[arraysize] = {element1,element2,..., elementN}
// A 2 element string array with two
string textureMaps[2] = {"./texture1.tx","./texture2.tx"};
// An ERROR! trying to declare a 2 dimensional array
float myArrays[2][2] = {{0,1},{3,4}};
```

Local variable arrays must be fixed and of predeclared length, so you must tell the compiler how many elements an array will have before you compile the shader. To access the value of an array element, you use the same square bracket notation as in C. The value inside the bracket must be a constant float, which will be rounded off to the nearest integer. This value represents the position index of the element inside the array. Be aware that array index positions start at 0, not at 1. Just as in C, arrays are not atomic objects, which means that you cannot assign one array to another or compare two arrays using math unary operations such as =, !=, or >=. You can, however, write RSL functions that can compare, arrange, or copy arrays.

```
float myvalues[3] = {24,45,76};     //Intialize an array
float value1 = myvalues[0];          //value 1 = 24
constant float arrayindex = 2;
float value2 = myvalues[arrayindex]; // value2 = 76
float anotherArray = myvalues;       // ERROR - cannot assign one array
                                     // to another.
```

Syntax Rules

Like every programming language, RSL has a very strict set of syntax rules. For people with no programming experience, these rules will probably be a nuisance and on occasion result in a frustrating search for that one character that is not letting your shader be compiled. Some shader compilers are a little more strict on certain rules, especially when it comes to declaring the class of your variables. The following sections discuss the rules that every RSL shader compiler will always follow.

White Space

White space is usually made up of a single or multiple consecutive spaces, tabs, and end of line or new line characters. There are two important aspects of white space in RSL.

All white space is ignored by RSL compilers. This means that to an RSL compiler the following two statements are exactly the same:

```
float myvar = 25 ;
float          myvar       = 25      ;
```

White space is used as a separator to identify keywords or variables. They are not necessary to identify built-in operators or symbols such as ( ) and { }.

```
float myvar=25;    // Legal
floatmyvar = 25;   // Error - no space between float and myvar
```

The first line is legal because the compiler can clearly tell that you are declaring a float variable and assigning a value of 25 to it. The second example will return an error because the compiler will assume that the word floatmyvar is a variable, and since floatmyvar hasn't been declared, it will cause an error at compile time.

End of Line

As explained before, RSL compilers ignore all white space, including new line characters. This means that to an RSL compiler a line that ends with an enter or a return is not a separate line from the one that follows it. It is for this reason that RSL uses the semicolon character (;) as an end of line character. This allows you to write commands that expand beyond one line, since to the compiler it will all be one line until the semicolon is found.

Comments

Every programming language has comments. Comments are parts of the source code that the compiler will skip entirely. They exist to aid the programmer in documenting the source code. Documenting or commenting is a very important aspect of any programming task. It helps other members of your team understand what your intentions were when you wrote the code and how you implemented certain features. Commenting is still important even if you write shaders that only you will use and edit. It is very easy to forget what you were trying to do in a shader that you wrote three months ago and haven't edited since. Be careful, though, about over-commenting. Inserting unnecessary comments in your code will make it a lot larger and probably hard to read with all the interruptions in the code's flow.

RSL supports two kinds of comments: C style and C++ style. C-style comments are those that start with a double slash (//). Everything between the double slash and the end of the line will be ignored by the compiler. Note that in this particular case the compiler will use the return character as an end of line instead of the semicolon, so you don't need to use the semicolon to indicate that the end of the line has been reached.

```
// This is a valid C style comment
// C comments are only valid until the end of each line
float myvar = 5 ;       // note that we did need the ; to indicate
                        // the end of the previous line of code
```

C++-style comments allow you to comment things out by blocks. They are characterized by commenting out everything, including other comments, between the two delimiters /* and */. Be careful that you don't nest comments. *Nesting* means to include one kind of code inside another of the same kind. If you put a C++ comment inside another C++ comment, the compiler will return an error.

```
/* This is a nice but unnecessary
two line comment */

/* These nested comments will cause the compiler
to fail since it will ignore
/* <- this comment opening but close the
comment with this one ->*/
making this last "open" part of the comment an error */
```

Shader Structure

To create a shader, the compiler needs to recognize it as such, and for this to happen, there needs to exist a structure that tells the compiler "Here is where the shader code starts…and here is where it ends." The structure of a shader is very simple. Most production shaders are somewhat more complicated because they use preprocessor macros, include files, and external functions (we will cover all of these later), but they all still follow the following structure for declaring a shader:

```
shaderType shaderName (shaderParameters)
    {
  executable RSL code;...
    }
```

The shader type can be any of the shader types described in the "Shader Types" section, earlier in this chapter. The most common of these are displacement and surface. The shader type tells the compiler what kind of shader we are working on so that it can initialize certain predefined shading variables that are available to the different types of shader. Lists containing all the available predefined variables will be presented as we go into detail on the shader execution environment of each shader type.

The shader type is also important to the renderer so that it knows what and where it can be used. You can't assign a displacement shader to a light, and you can't assign a light shader to a geometry (although you can declare area lights using information from some geometry).

The shader name can be anything you want as long as you follow the same rules as those that apply to variable names, previously discussed in the "Variables" section of this chapter. It is common practice to use the name of the shader to name the file you are working on. So if you are working on a shader named oldOak, it is preferable that you name the file oldOak.sl. This way you won't have to open the file to find out what shader is contained in it. This is possible because of one important rule of RSL. *Only one shader can be defined per source file.* That's why you can name your file the same as the shader.

After the shader name comes the shader parameters (also known as *shader instance variables* or the *shader argument list*), which are enclosed in parentheses and are controls that the shader writer makes available to the user so that he can have control over certain features of the shader. If you are writing a shader to replicate the look of marble, then you might want to give the user access to the scale of the marbling pattern, the colors of the veins, the fill, the amount of distortion the veins have, and so on. You, the shader designer, must decide which features require a parameter and which would just be overkill, remembering that too much control sometimes gets in the way. Shader parameters are declared like any other variable, with the slight difference that a shader parameter must be initialized on declaration. The initialized value will become the default value of the parameter, so try to set it to something that will give results that showcase the shader's features. It must be noted that all shader parameter variables are assumed to be of uniform class unless specified by the user. Here is a quick example of a shader declaration with its parameters.

```
surface checker ( float checkerSize = 1.0;
                  color colorA = color (1,0,0);
                  color colorB = color (0,1,0);
                )
```

The values of shader parameters are usually a constant for the whole surface being shaded. However, if the user provides a value (through a variable) for each point on the mesh and that variable has the same name and type as a shader parameter in the RIB file, the renderer will use those values instead of the constant provided in the shader or in the shader assignment command. Such variables are known as "primitive variables," and the workflow outlined here is a very powerful way of working because you can use the 3D application to animate those primitive variables based on hand-set keyframes, dynamic collisions, particle events, mesh painting, or whatever you can think of.

The final part of a shader is the shader body or code body. Here is where all the magic happens. The body of the shader is delimited by curly braces ({}) and goes immediately after the shader parameters. All variables declared inside the body of the shader are assumed to be varying unless specified.

Operators

RSL supports several basic operators in such a specialized manner that operations that would usually require several lines of code or the use of external libraries can be performed very easily. The language has built-in knowledge of the different data types and the types of operations that can be performed with each type. Using an operator with the wrong kind of data will usually result in a compile error or a warning. Be very careful when you get a warning because the shader will compile, but your results might not be correct. Table 2.3 lists the operators supported by RSL.

Table 2.3 Mathematical Operators in RSL

Symbol Operator Description

=	Assignment
+	Addition
-	Subtraction
*	Multiplication
/	Division

Vector-Only Operators

.	Dot product
^	Cross product

Matrix-Only Operators

*	Matrix multiplication
/	Inverse multiplication

The assignment operator is used to assign values to variables. The +, -, *, and / are the default mathematical operators. They can be used for all data types except for strings, arrays, and in a limited way matrices. You must be aware that RSL will usually try to warn you if it finds an operation that doesn't seem to be legal, but this is not always the case, so you will need to know what data types you are dealing with and how mathematical operations between those data types will be executed. Here are the rules that all data types adhere to when performing arithmetic operations on the different data types:

- Applying an operation on a point, normal, vector, or color, the operation is performed in parallel for every component of the type. So multiplying two vectors (2,3,4) and (4,3,3) will return a new vector with the values (8,9,12).

- A vector added to a point returns a point.

- A vector added to a vector returns a vector.

- A point subtracted from a point returns a vector.

- A vector multiplied by a float returns a scaled vector.

More detailed information on how math is applied to the different data types can be found in Chapter 5. RSL allows you to join either of the mathematical operators with the assignment operator. This is used to simplify and condense source code.

You can only combine one mathematical operator at a time, and the operator you are assigning a value to must already have been initialized, not just declared. Here is a code example:

```
float A = 1; // The A variable must be initialized
A += 4;      // smaller than using ' A = A + 4 '
A *= 5;      // Value of A is now 25
```

The cross product (^) and the dot product (.) are used only for vectors or normals. Trying to use these operators on colors or points should result in a compiler error. These two operations are essential to shader writers, especially the dot product, and they will be covered to detail in Chapter 5. For performing matrix operations, RSL supports two mathematical operators: * for matrix multiplication and / for inverse multiplication.

These are all the operators supported by RSL. Other programming languages allow you to implement operator overloading, which is the ability to declare new uses for standard symbols based on the data type you are dealing with. For example, you could overload the % symbol to do a very common "screen" operation (such as the screen blending mode in Photoshop) between two colors. RSL doesn't support operator overloading, not even through the DSO C plug-in mechanism, which is the reason why people have written plenty of functions for doing operations such as a screen color blend.

Flow Control

When writing any type of software program, it is usually necessary to embed into your code some intelligence about how to deal with the data or the flow of the program. Some languages have a large number of flow control commands and operators that are very specialized to handle special types of data. RSL provides three commands for flow control: one conditional and two loop commands. All of the control flow commands (also referred to as *control flow statements*) resemble the C programming language in syntax. They also follow the grouping mechanism implemented in C, which dictates that all the statements associated with a control function (or any user-defined function) need to be enclosed between curly braces. Note that the braces are not necessary if the statement that follows a control function is only one line long.

Conditional execution is performed with an if-else command. This command will test the supplied condition and will execute the following statement only if the returned value of the condition is true. The else is an extension, and it is optional. It indicates what commands to execute in case the condition returns a false value. The if-else command has the following syntax (remember that code between [ ] is optional):

```
if ( condition) {
   statement1;
} [else {
   statement2;}]
```

Conditional execution can also be chained together in what is known as an if-else-if statement. When using a chained else-if statement, you should try to always finish the statement with an else. This will become a catch-all statement for when none of the "if's" are met.

```
if (condition1){
   statement1;
}else if (condition2) {
   statement2;
} else {
   statement3; }
```

The condition part of an if statement is usually a Boolean expression. "You said there were no Booleans in RSL." There are no Boolean data types, but there are Boolean operations. Boolean operations are those that return a value of 1 or 0, also known as true or false. They are the heart of flow control statements, as conditions (also known as Boolean expressions) can contain only expressions that contain relational operations. This means that you cannot have a condition that looks like this:

```
if (1 - 0) s = s * 2;
```

This is because you are providing an arbitrary float expression where you can only provide a Boolean expression. You can't use float, color, or point arbitrary expressions where Boolean expressions are expected. This also holds true for a reverse situation; you can't use a Boolean expression to provide a 0 or 1 value to a float, color, point, or any other type.

Table 2.4 lists the available Boolean relational operations.

Table 2.4 Comparison Operators in RSL

Symbol	Name	Returns 1 If
==	equal	left is equal to right
!=	not equal	left is not equal to right
<	less than	left is less than right
<=	less or equal to	left is less than or equal to right
>	greater than	left is greater than right
>=	greater or equal to	left is greater than or equal to right

These binary operations have a small number of caveats that you need to be aware of. You can freely compare values of the same type without any problem. When comparing values of different types, the following rules apply:

- When comparing a float to a three-point type such as colors or vectors, the value of the float will be propagated into the values of all three components.

- It is illegal to compare a color and a point.

- You can compare two matrices using == and =!.

Here is an example of a very common use of the if statement. When performing a texture lookup, it is advisable to first test whether a texture has been provided to the shader. If there is, then perform the lookup; if it's not provided, then assign a proper value to the variable.

```
varying color myColor;
if (myTexture != ""){
   myColor = texture(myTexture,s,t);
}else{
   myColor= color (1,1,1);
}
```

In this case, the else statement could be omitted if the myColor variable were initialized to color (1,1,1) upon its declaration. Sometimes it might be necessary to chain together Boolean operations so that more than one condition must be met. In such cases, you can use the && (and) and the || (or) operators. When chaining together Booleans with &&, conditions are evaluated from left to right as long as the current operation returns true. If any of the operations return false, then the else part of the statement will be evaluated.

```
color baseColor = color (0.5,0.5,0.5);
if ((myTexture != "") && (textureValue > 0)) {
   textureCol =  texture (myTexture,s,t);
   colOut = mix (baseColor,textureCol,textureValue);
} else if ((myTexture == "") && (textureValue > 0)) {
   colOut = mix (baseColor, color(1,0,0), textureValue);
}
```

In this example, we will mix the value of myTexture with the baseColor only if the texture is provided and the textureValue is greater than 0. If the first conditional returns true, then the second conditional will still be evaluated. However, if the first conditional returns false, then the else statement will execute. The chained if will mix a pure red color with the baseColor if myTexture is not provided but the textureValue is more than 0. This will be good visual feedback that the texture wasn't found.

```
if ((Ks <= 0) || (specColor == (0,0,0)) {
  Cspec = color (0,0,0);
} else {
  Cspec = specular(V,Nf,roughness) * Ks * specColor;
}
```

In the previous piece of code, we restrict the specular calculations from taking place if the specular coefficient (usually Ks) or the specular color (specColor) is set to 0 or black. This is done because either one of those values would force the specular call to return black. If the first condition returns true, then the second condition is never evaluated because only one of the conditionals needs to be true.

It may take some time to get used to the logic of the operation and what results you will get. It also takes some time to figure out what is the best condition to use, because it is not the same to use

```
if ( myValue >0 )
```

as it is to use

```
if (myValue >= 0)
```

RSL also provides a more compact form of the if-else statement, known as the C conditional expression. This expression is very useful for those instances in which you need to make decisions just like with if else, but the statements to be executed in each branch are short commands. The syntax for this expression is

```
(binary relation ? statement 1: statement 2)
```

The following is an example of how this expression would be used to determine whether we want to flip the s or t texture coordinates before we do the texture lookup.

```
uniform float flips = 0;
uniform float flipt = 0;

varying float ss = (flips == 0 ? s: 1 - s);
varying float tt = (flipt == 0 ? t: 1 - t);
color textureColor = texture ("mytex.tx",ss,tt);
```

One final warning on the use of Boolean operations within if-else statements should go out to experienced programmers. In other languages, you can use statements such as

```
if (variableName){
}
```

And the compiler will return true if `variableName` has a value (it is not NULL). In RSL the previous statement will return an error, so you will more than likely have to use

```
if (variableName != 0)  or if (variableName != "")
```

depending on whether you are comparing against a float or a string. Another way to control the flow of the code inside your shaders is to use iteration constructs, such as `for` and `while` loops. These commands allow you to repeat a segment of code based on one or more text expressions. They are extremely useful for creating shaders that support large amounts of code that is quite similar. For example, if you write a shader that generates a fractal pattern, you will more than likely use a `for` loop to create several layers of noise at different sizes, which are then combined into a single noise texture. The `for` loop has the following syntax:

```
for (initialization, boolean expression, loop statement){
... statement;
}
```

`initialization` is usually a variable with an assigned value at the beginning of a loop. The text expression is evaluated before the statement is executed. If the expression returns true, then the body is executed. Once the code is executed, the loop statement is evaluated. The loop statement will usually modify the value of the `initialization` variable. After the loop statement is evaluated, the test expression gets evaluated once again, and if it returns true, it will run the statement one more time, followed by the loop statement. This process will be repeated until the test expression returns a false, at which point the loop will exit. Here is an example of the `for` loop used in a fractal texture.

```
float octaves = 4;
float amp = 1;
varying point pp = p;
float lacunarity = 2;
float gain = 0.5;
float i;
varying float sum = 0, fw = filterwidthp(P);

  for (i = 0;  i < octaves;  i += 1) {
sum += amp * filteredsnoise (pp, fw);
amp *= gain;  pp *= lacunarity;  fw *= lacunarity;
  }
```

The other form of looping in RSL is provided by the `while` construct. The `while` construct is very similar to a `for` loop. The main difference is that the `while` construct doesn't really force you to provide a loop statement to test against the Boolean expression, so you could quite easily end up with an infinite loop, which will hang your renderer. The syntax of the `while` construct is presented below, followed by an implementation of the `for` loop we just explained as a `while` loop:

```
while (boolean expression){
    statement;
}


    float octaves = 4;
    float amp = 1;
    varying point pp = p;
    float lacunarity = 2;
    float gain = 0.5;
    float i = 0; // we initialize the variable here
    varying float sum = 0, fw = filterwidthp(P);


    while(i < octaves) {
    sum += amp * filteredsnoise (pp, fw);
    amp *= gain;  pp *= lacunarity;  fw *= lacunarity;
    i += 1;    //we have to provide an increment to the i variable
        //or we would have an infinite loop
    }
```

In this example you can see a couple of important differences with the `for` loop. The first difference is that when we declare the variable `i` we must also initialize it because the `while` loop doesn't have an initialization portion for the loop. The other difference is the increment line we perform at the end of the loop. This line is extremely important; without this line the Boolean expression (`i < octaves`) will always be true, and therefore our renderer will hang up and we will have to kill the process. In both of these constructs, as well as in the `if-else` construct, the statement needs to be inside curly braces (`{}`) only if the statement is longer than one line. For one-line statements you can omit the braces.

Functions

Writing code can be very long, arduous, and many times repetitive work. As a shader writer, you will find that you almost never have as much time as you would like to develop a shader, especially when working in high-paced productions such as are common in the VFX industry. Working smart and efficiently is a basic instinct of successful shader TDs. It is for this reason that it is essential that TDs learn how to write and organize their functions properly.

Functions are neatly organized pieces of code that can be reused at any time by inserting them into the proper place in the source code of the shader. They can be typed directly into the source file of the shader or into a header file, which can be imported into the shader with a #include preprocessor directive. More information about header files can be found in Chapter 3, "Shader Writing Process." Functions can be declared in RSL using the following syntax:

```
type functionName (function parameters){
   rsl code;
   return value;
}
```

type can be any of the supported data types in RSL except for arrays. There is an extra type that can be used, which is the void (or null) type. Next comes the name of the function, followed by the parameters to the function. Function parameters can be declared exactly as the shader parameters, except that in a function they shouldn't be initialized.

After the parameters comes the code to the function. At the end of the function there needs to be a return statement, except for void functions, which don't return any values. The returned value must be of the same type as the one used in the declaration of the function. Here is an example of a function that returns the passed value elevated to the power of two.

```
float sqr ( float val) {
   return val * val;
}
```

You can use this function at any time in the following manner.

```
float x = sqr( 4);
```

There can be only one return statement per function, so if you need to return different values based on some logic inside the function, you can store the values in temporary variables and return that temporary value at the end.

```
color getTexture (string texturename; float u, v, scaleU, scaleV,
      flipU, flipV){

   float uu = u * scaleU;
   if (flipU = 1){
      uu = (1 - u) * scaleU;
   }

   float vv = v * scaleV;
   if (flipV == 1 ) {
      vv = (1 - v) * scaleV;
   }
```

```
color Cout;
if (texturename != "") {
  Cout = texture(texturename, uu, vv);
} else {
  Cout = color (1,0,0);
}
return Cout;
}
```

The C Preprocessor

When compiling a shader, RSL behaves like many other programming languages, which usually run a preprocessor program before they actually call the compiler. A preprocessor, as its name clearly describes it, is a program that is run on your source code. Its purpose is to help expand and/or replace several symbols that are very useful in software development. The expanded text is then piped as a stream into the compiler. It is important to know how to use the preprocessor properly because it can greatly simplify and streamline the creation of shaders. Preprocessors support constants, commands, and macros.

Constants

Constants, also referred to as simple or object type macros, are similar to variables in the sense that you can assign a useful or easily identifiable name to hold a value, but that's as far as the similarities go. One key difference is that variables can be overwritten and reassigned within the shader code. Constants, on the other hand, are read-only and cannot be overwritten, hence their name. The novice coder will probably wonder why he would use a constant that is limited instead of a variable.

This is where the second and probably most important difference comes in. Variables are an entity of your code and as such will be inserted into the compiled shader. Therefore they will use up memory at render time. Granted, the amount of memory used is not that much, but efficiency should always be a goal. Constants, on the other hand, are replaced according to their values by the preprocessor before the shader is compiled, so they have no extra memory requirements than the data they replace. Here are some examples of constants.

```
#define RED (1,1,1)
#define SKYTEX  "/home/textures/sky.tx"
#define HALFPI  1.5707963267848966
```

For every preprocessor command or macro, the pound symbol (#) must be the first character in a line other than white space so that the preprocessor can recognize the line as a command, a constant, or a macro. After the pound symbol comes the name of the command, which can be separated from the pound sign with one or more white spaces.

To create a constant, you need to tell the preprocessor that you are about to define a new constant. This is done by using the define command. After the define command comes the name of the constant you want to declare. It is a common practice to use only capital letters when declaring a constant; this is not a rule—you can name your constants whatever you want, and the preprocessor will still be able to replace the constant. However, using only caps will allow you and other readers of your code to distinguish quickly between a preprocessor constant and a shader variable. Next to the constant name goes the value assigned to the constant. This is the value that will be replaced by the preprocessor before the code is sent out to the shader compiler.

Commands

Preprocessor commands are keywords that tell the processor to behave in a predefined way while expanding the source code. Each preprocessor supports a different number and type of commands. Most RenderMan-compliant renderers use the C preprocessor because it was designed to resemble the C language, which was quite popular when RSL was developed. The C preprocessor supports many commands, and we will go over the most popular ones in the following sections.

include

The include command is perhaps the most-used preprocessor command. It is this command that makes software development a manageable and organized task because without it you would always have to copy and paste your prewritten shared code into the source file. This would result in code that would be virtually impossible to maintain because with every revision of your shared code you would need to update every source file that uses it!

The include command allows you to load into the current shader source file all the contents of any other file with RSL code. These loadable files usually have an *.h extension and are referred to as *header* or *library* files, even though they are not truly libraries. These files may only include preprocessor macros, constants, or RSL functions, so there can be no surface, displacement, light, or any of the shader type calls inside the header files.

The include command comes in two flavors that behave slightly differently. The first flavor or notation has the following syntax:

```
#include <filename>
```

This notation will cause the preprocessor to search for the given filename in the paths provided with the -I flag at compile time. This search is progressive, meaning that it will search until it finds a file with the matching name, at which point it will stop searching. It is important to remember this, otherwise the preprocessor might use the wrong file if you have files with the same names in different directories.

The second flavor of the `include` command uses this syntax:

```
#include "filename"
```

In this case, the preprocessor will look for the file inside the current directory. If it doesn't find it, then it searches the paths provided to the compiler with the -I flag. This is common in software development with C or C++, where you commonly create header files for your source code. In my experience this is not a typical workflow or organization for shader development.

If Defined and If Not Defined

As you develop your shaders and libraries, you will soon realize that there are several files that you will include into other source or header files quite often. What happens when such files are included in several files used to compile a given shader? The preprocessor is not smart enough to know that the file has already been loaded, which means that you might end up loading one or more header files more than once. There is a well-known mechanism to get around this problem, guaranteeing that the file is loaded only once.

To implement this mechanism, we will be using the commands #ifdef (if defined) and #ifndef (if not defined) to provide some logic to the steps that the preprocessor takes. Consider the following code snippet:

```
#ifndef FLOATUTILS_H
#define FLOATUTILS_H 1
float afunction (){
   some code;
   ...;
};
#endif // FLOATUTILS_H
```

The first line asks the preprocessor if the constant FLOATUTILS_H has *not* been defined. If it has not been defined, then all of the following statements are included in the preprocessor. The first step we need to take is to define the constant. Then we can declare as many functions as we want associated with the file floatutils.h. Once we are done with all the float functions in this file, we tell the preprocessor to escape out of the #ifndef condition by using an #endif command. This command marks the end of the code that will be included in other files from the floatutils.h file. This code only tells the preprocessor to define the FLOATUTILS_H constant if it hasn't been defined, but how do we use this code to prevent the preprocessor from loading the file more than once? All you have to do is include the following in any shader or header file:

```
#include <floatutils.h>
```

This code will make the preprocessor include the `floatutils.h` file. The first time the file is included, the code at the top of `floatutils.h` is evaluated, defining the `FLOATUTILS_H` constant. The next time the preprocessor tries to include this file, the `FLOATUTILS_H` constant will already be declared, so the preprocessor won't load all of the float functions again.

if, else, elseif

These commands are just like the flow control commands used in RSL, with the difference that the logic is performed in the code that gets passed to the compiler and not in the shader while running. These commands are very usable when you are trying to multipurpose your shader code. A good example of this is something we used in the development of shaders for *The Ant Bully*.

All of the shaders for *The Ant Bully* included preprocessor logic so that from a single source file we would get a Houdini OTL (which is a custom object type in Houdini) and a RenderMan-compiled shader. Granted, in those instances we used a lot of `ifdef`s, but we had to use several `if` and `else` statements. These statements work like the ones in RSL: If the test returns true, then the code after the `if` is passed to the compiler; if it returns false, then the code after the `if` is excluded or the code associated with the `else` gets passed to the compiler. This is the syntax:

```
#if expression

    controlled text

    #endif /* expression */
```

Where *expression* could contain any of the following:

- The integer 0 or 1
- Macros or constants
- Math operations using addition, subtraction, multiplication, division, bitwise operations, shifts, comparisons, and logical operations (`&&` and `||`)
- The defined operator, which is the same as using `ifdef`

Macros

Preprocessor macros are also referred to as function-like macros because they take arguments. They are a convenient way to insert commonly used code into the shader without having to create a function, which has a little more expense. Another good use for macros is the dynamic expansion of names and variables for repetitive code. The syntax for declaring macros is the following:

```
#define MACRONAME (param1, param2,..)
```

You use the define command just as when declaring a constant, but now you follow the macro name with a set of parentheses, which encompass the macro's parameters. To access the parameters, you just type the parameter name where you want it:

```
#define FGAMMA (x,gamma)  pow(x,1/gamma)
```

You can also concatenate (combine) the parameters to create new names. This is done with the ## operator, and it is very useful to help you minimize the amount of repetition in your code. When writing macros that cover more than one line, you need to add a slash at the end of the line. Make sure there are no spaces or other symbols after the slash. Here is an example as well as a use for a macro.

```
#define MY_TEX_CALL(texname,texnum)        \
uniform string texname##texnum = "";       \
uniform string texname##texnum##Filter = "gaussian";\
uniform float texname##texnum##FilterSize = 1

surface myshader (
        MY_TEX_CALL(colortex,1);
        MY_TEX_CALL(colortex,2);
        MY_TEX_CALL(spectex,1);
        MY_TEX_CALL(spectex,2);
```

There are more commands that are supported by the C preprocessor. If you would like to read more about the commands or about details on how to use the C preprocessor, please go to http://gcc.gnu.org/onlinedocs/cpp/.

3

Shader Writing Process

As we prepare to write our first shader, we must first get acquainted with the methodology or the process involved in basic shader development. For those readers who have never experimented with any type of coding for software development, this section of the book might seem a little bland, especially since there is a lot of preparation involved. However, these are the basics of shader development, and if you have no previous development experience, then you must read this chapter carefully.

Shader development is no different from any other software development. There is a design phase, a research and development (R&D) phase if necessary, the actual coding of the shader (also known as implementation), plenty of testing and optimization (if time permits), an official release, and then updates and maintenance (see Figure 3.1).

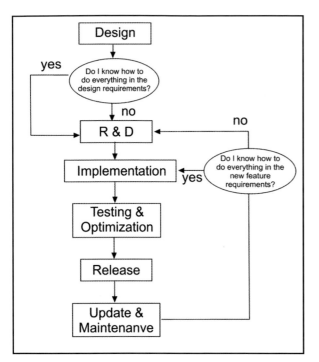

Figure 3.1 Diagram depicting a typical development process.

Design

This is the first step of the development cycle. Before you write a single line of code, you must have some kind of design. It is very useful to write down your initial ideas about the shader, even if it is on a spare piece of paper or a cafeteria napkin. There are several questions that you should ask yourself as you approach a new shader:

- What is the goal of this shader; what is it supposed to accomplish?

- Have I ever written a shader like this one or seen something similar online?

- Are there any special attributes that will be provided by the geometry?

- Will there need to be any arbitrary output variables (AOVs) for multi-pass rendering or special considerations such as message passing or user attributes?

- Do I know how to write such a shader?

Once you know the answers to these and any other question you can come up with, you will need to make a rough outline of how you will write the shader. If you are lucky, you will know how to do everything you need for your shader. If you do, then you will have no need for an R&D phase, and you can jump straight into the implementation.

Research and Development

Also known as R&D, this can be the most exciting or daunting part of shader development. It is in this stage that you need to apply all the knowledge you possess, all the knowledge you can get your hands on, and a good level of ingenuity to think "outside the box." Thinking of different uses for a certain technology that was never intended for such uses can sometimes end up providing some of the most significant advances in CGI. One of the latest such discoveries is the use of *ambient occlusion*. Ambient occlusion (AO) was "invented" by ILM and introduced to the RenderMan community in a course called "RenderMan in Production" at the SIGGRAPH conference in 2002. Curiously enough, it was also presented by Imageworks in the same year and the same RenderMan course. Ambient occlusion uses the very simple concept of testing whether a ray hits another object along its path or not, and I'm quite sure that AO was not the original use for the `rayhittest()` function of Entropy*, which was used to develop the technique.

R&D sometimes involves reading some recently published, SIGGRAPH papers and sometimes some older ones. For older papers, you might want to search the Internet in hopes that someone else has already done an RSL (or similar language) implementation. If there is no previous implementation, then you are probably going to have to dissect the papers and figure out the math yourself. Unless you have a good amount of math under your belt, this can bring your shader development to a screeching halt. If you find yourself in such a situation, you will need to be resourceful and figure out a way to get help. Go to forums, colleagues, community college math labs, or any other place where you might be able to get help.

When coding your R&D tests, you must not obsess over writing clean, fast, or user-friendly code. Your only objective must be to test whether your implementation works, making sure you comment the code so that you understand what is going on. Once you know that your approach works, then you can start thinking about how you are going to merge that code with the rest of the shader. This applies to smaller, localized solutions for your current shader. More complex or global solutions will require a little more design integration on your behalf. Remember, R&D for shaders means getting to a usable solution as quickly as your schedule will allow, using whatever means necessary.

Entropy, developed by Exluna, was a very capable RenderMan-compliant renderer. It is no longer in development.

Implementation

After finishing your design requirements and the R&D (if necessary), you will be ready to start coding. It is advisable to write a pseudo-code description of all the steps and operations that you plan to follow to reach your goal. You can write these steps within comments so that they are inside your file and not on a piece of paper or some other file. Here is a sample of a shader in pseudo-code:

```
/*************************
 * watermelon.sl
 * by Rudy Cortes
 *************************/
surface watermelon()
{
/* Layer 1 - Base color */
/* Layer 2 - Dark green stripes */
/* Layer 3 - Veins / Detail within the stripes */
/* Layer 5 - Markings or spots */ /* Illumination model - Use regular
plastic*/
}
```

While writing your shaders, always look out for areas in which you can streamline your code. If you create a procedure that you think you might use again within the shader or in any other shader in the future, you might want to make a function out of that procedure. If you believe the function to be usable on other shaders, then you should move it to a header file (also known as a library file).

Testing and Optimization

These steps go hand in hand with implementation. They are actually weaved into a loop where you code, test, and optimize over and over until you get the results you are looking for. This stage might take a long time while you find out whether your code actually works and while you constantly ask yourself how to make things faster or simpler. It is very beneficial to have a formal beta testing stage in which you provide the shader to a limited number of users so that they can use it in a production environment. Be sure to let them know that the shader is still in beta stage and not to use it for final objects.

Having input from users will usually reveal bugs, misbehaviors, and sometimes design deficiencies. As the shader writer, you might have done something that makes perfect sense to you because you know the "insides" of the shader quite well, but when a user tries to use a feature you implemented, it behaves in a way that is not expected. At that point you might have to reconsider your implementation. Talk to other users and ask if they also get the results the first user did. If they do, then you will have to do some recoding.

At this stage you will also receive a lot of "it would be really cool if the shader could do…" requests. Take your time looking at these requests because many of them might create problems down the line or send you into a complete recode of your shader. Make a list and prioritize the requests, discuss them with your direct supervisor, and implement only those that are absolutely necessary. This level of selectiveness is not so that we have less work to do, it is simply because the larger the amount of code, the higher the probability for bugs to show up. Once all the changes are made to the code, release the shader to the same limited number of users and let them use it once more as a beta version. Repeat these steps until you are sure that your code is working and optimal for production work, at which point you should get it ready for release.

Release

Before releasing your shader, you must clean up your code. As a gesture of kindness to other shader writers and to yourself, you must comment the shader properly. Also make sure to get rid of any hard-coded variables that you were planning to make shader parameters. As stated before, shader parameters are controls you, as the shader designer, make available to the users of the shader. You must think carefully about what kind of controls you will offer to the users. A shader with too few controls will be very limiting and restrictive to users, while a shader with too many parameters might make the shader hard to use and tweak. How many parameters you provide to the users can be determined through common sense and by understanding the level of technical knowledge of the users. If most of the users are TDs, then you could expose more parameters to provide precise control.

Another thing to consider is the names you provide to your shader parameters. Throughout this book, we use parameters such as Ka, Kd, and Ks to control ambient, diffuse, and specularity, respectively. These Kx parameters are pretty standard for shader writers, but for most users they will make no sense, so you might have to rename those parameters.

End user documentation will be important when you release your shader. It would be great if you could create an HTML page that describes your shader, its parameters, and also provides some parameter settings that could be used as a starting point. In most production environments, you will not have the time to create such a Web page. If time is an issue, you might want to consider writing a Python, Perl, or whatever scripting language you are comfortable with that will analyze your .sl file and create an HTML page when you compile or release the shader.

Update and Maintenance

Just like death and taxes, updates and maintenance are parts of the process that shader developers are stuck with. It would be great if we could release our shaders into the wild and never hear from them again, constantly telling ourselves that the shader is doing fine, living a happy life with a she-shader or he-shader somewhere. This is not the case, not by a long shot. Be ready to roll up your sleeves and dive back into a shader or function you created several months ago. This stage is where you will realize how important commenting and documenting are, and you will be glad you took the extra time to do it right when you were writing your shader.

There are several programs that can aid you in the generation of user-friendly documentation. My favorite is doxygen, which is free and available for download at http://www.stack.nl/~dimitri/doxygen/. If for some reason this link does not work, just search the Internet for doxygen.

Learning to use doxygen is very straightforward. Just follow the documentation on the doxygen Web site, and you should be up and running in a jiffy. The source tree that ships with this book has an HTML directory where you will find a file named index.html. That file is the front page for a Web site that contains documentation for all of the functions and files in the source tree for this book. Figure 3.2 shows a screenshot of what the documentation from doxygen can look like.

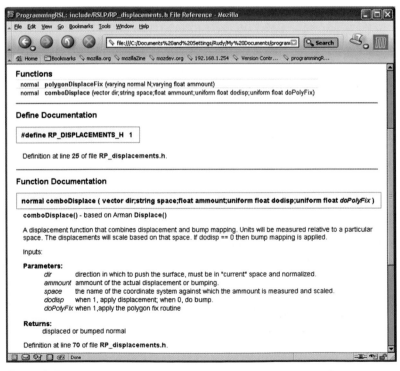

Figure 3.2 Screenshot of a doxygen-generated documentation Web page

Shader Development Files

When developing shaders, there are usually at least two files you will be dealing with: an RSL source file and a compiled file. The source files usually have a `*.sl` extension, and the compiled file might have any extension the developer of the renderer decides. The source file is a plain ASCII text file that usually has the same name as the shader contained in the RSL code. The compiled file can be of many different types, usually decided by the renderer developers, and it has a lot to do with the overall design of the renderer.

Later on, as your shaders increase in complexity, you will have to deal with libraries or header files. These files have a `*.h` extension, and they can be included in any source file with the use of a preprocessor macro. Once you have enough shaders to manage and compile, you will more than likely need a way to compile and release all those shaders. You could write complex scripts with Perl, Python, or any other high-level language, or you could use GNU's Make, which is a program that allows you to declare rules that control what commands are executed for building object files from source code. More information on preprocessor macros, make files, and header files can be found in Chapter 4, "Setting Up a Developing Environment."

The Basic Tools

Using the right tools can make a huge difference in the speed and organization of your shaders. There are many different ways and tools to develop shaders. There are GUI programs designed to make shader development more artist friendly. The problem with these programs is that the artist usually has no idea what is going on under the hood of his shader. At the end he has a shader that looks nice but might be extremely slow, and he ends up blaming the renderer for being too slow when in fact it is a programmer error. We will go over some of the most common tools for shader development, outlining their pros and cons.

Text Editors

The most basic way of developing shaders is using a text editor. Any text editor will do, as long as it supports plain ASCII text files. Never write your shaders using a Rich Text format or any other text document such as MS Office's `.doc` format. Basic text editors are very fast to run, and they usually have some functionality such as search and replace. For writing simple shaders they will do the job, but when you find yourself writing a shader with 500 or more lines, it will be very easy to get lost in the code without tools that help you move around.

IDE Programs

IDE stands for integrated development environment. You can think of it as a text editor on steroids, designed specifically for code development. Some IDEs are designed to support a very specific language or group of languages. There are other IDEs that are very open and customizable. Those used most for shader development are very powerful and customizable text editors that have been tweaked and customized to the point where they can handle any language. Some of these programs are not quite IDEs, but we will refer to them as such to separate them from simple text editors such as Microsoft's Notepad.

The most popular are Vim, Nedit, XEmacs, and Emacs. Some of these programs already have a module that makes them support RSL with easy-to-read syntax highlighting and customized functions for compiling and previewing your shader. My personal favorite is XEmacs, for which there is a support module for RSL that was created by Steve May of Pixar. The module has been updated and extended by several people, including myself. A copy of this module is included on the CD that comes with this book.

The most popular of these programs is Vi or Vim (*Vi improved*). Vi is extremely powerful and lightning fast once you learn how to use it properly. I have seen some programmers who use only Vi, and it is scary to see how fast they move in that program. The problem with Vim is that there is no GUI to it. It runs inside the shell or command prompt. It is strongly advised for every shader writer to learn at least the basics of Vi for the simple reason that any machine you might have to use will have Vi or Vim on it (if it's a Linux machine). Vi is also available on virtually every available platform, and if you end up working at anyplace bigger than a mid-size studio, it is very probable that every machine will have Vi installed.

Most shader developers in the industry use IDEs along with a well-designed library of functions and some kind of automatic building program such as GNU Make to develop their shaders. If you have thought of doing most of your development with a visual development program, you need to erase that idea from your head. As a shader writer, you will write a lot, so pick a good IDE and learn it top to bottom.

Shader Authoring Tools

As mentioned before, there are several shader authoring tools that use a GUI to make the shader development process more accessible to the average artist. They resemble node-based compositing programs such as Shake or Digital Fusion. Every node inserts either a prepacked piece of code or a function.

Some of these tools are very well designed, such as Pixar's Slim, which allows you to create *dynamic functions*, Tcl functions that use all the functionality of Tcl to generate the RSL code. Slim is so strong that it has been used in production for several movies.

There are several drawbacks with these tools that keep them from being used predominately in the industry. The biggest drawback is that the code they tend to produce is either not that efficient or it is very hard to read and debug.

Another major problem is that sometimes an operation that would usually take a single line of code ends up taking three or four nodes. Some of these programs provide a way to comment your shader network, but most of them don't, so it is really hard to maintain your shaders or share the development with other team members.

One final annoyance is the fact that the smallest change to your shader network will trigger a recompile, which could take a couple of seconds and eventually add up. This might be especially annoying to those 3D artists who are used to the material editors that are built into their 3D applications, which are usually near real time.

GUI authoring tools have several positive advantages. If your production is more artist driven and has a limited number of shader TDs, this might be your only solution to generating the number of shaders necessary for a large production. Another advantage is that GUIs can be really fast for prototyping shaders. When you want to try something really quickly, and you don't need the code to be optimal or clean, it is quite fast to turn out a shader to verify that what you are trying to do does indeed work.

Among the most popular shader authoring tools you will find are Shaderman by Alexei Puzicov, Pixar's MtoR, Sitex Graphic's V-shade, and Sidefx's Houdini (with the external renderer support option). Shaderman is extremely popular in the open source community because it is free for personal and commercial use. However, it is not open source, so users must wait for the developers to release patches and updates. Shaderman uses a simple XML file format to declare shading nodes, which are referred to as blocks. This makes extending Shaderman quite easy because all you need is knowledge of RSL, the XML tags, and code conventions established by Shaderman.

One of the nicest features of Shaderman is the code view window that is accessible with a small tab at the bottom of the workspace editor, as shown in Figure 3.3. The code view updates automatically as you connect and disconnect shading blocks. It would be fantastic if you could type in RSL code in the code viewer and then have a "custom" shading block inserted into the workspace network. This would be an ideal scenario to combine the best of both worlds: the speed of using shading nodes and the accessibility of hand-typed RSL code. At this point the main developer of Shaderman is working on a new generation of software. Maybe he can figure out a way to make such a workflow possible.

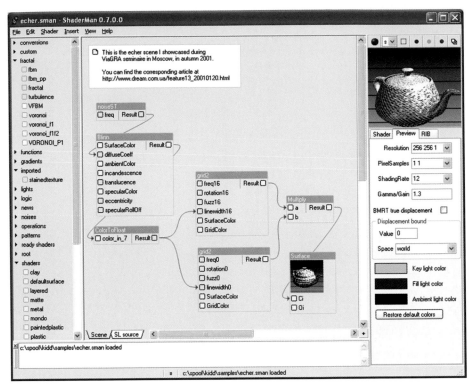

Figure 3.3 Shaderman by Alexei Puzikov.

Pixar's Slim, part of the RenderMan Artist Tools (RAT) package, is perhaps the most popular shader authoring tool in the market today (see Figure 3.4). You can get Slim only if you purchase the RAT, which might be the reason why it is so popular. This also makes the price tag of Slim rather high. It is constantly evolving and improving. It is extremely extensible through the use of Tcl\Tk and the Slim file format, which is a set of precompiled Tcl custom commands.

Another great feature of Slim is that it also runs in batch (command line) mode, which allows you to create scripts to automate tasks. This is an extremely useful feature, especially in large productions where there are hundreds of shaders that constantly need to be rebuilt and recompiled. In such productions, automation is not just helpful but essential.

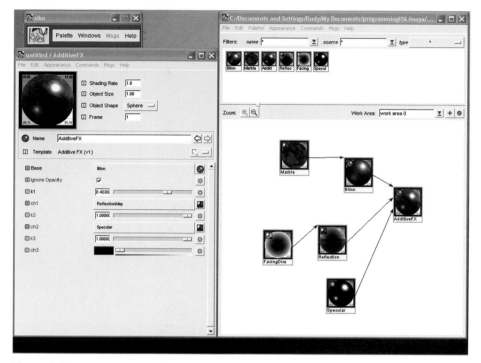

Figure 3.4 Screenshot of Slim in action

The Shader Compiler

The shader compiler is an essential part of your renderer. It is in charge of taking your RSL source code and turning it into usable machine code that the renderer can use to calculate the final color of a pixel. You must learn all the options of your shader compiler because it can give you options ranging from optimization to debugging tools. To access the quick help of your shader compiler, you can usually type one of the following commands:

```
shadcompiler -h
shadcompiler --help
```

The `shadcompiler` part is the name of the compiler program provided by your renderer. It is usually located in the same place as the renderer binary program. The quick help is a very abbreviated version of the documentation of the compiler; for the complete documentation, refer to your renderer's user manual. Here is a list of the compiler programs for the most common renderers.

Renderer	Compiler
Photo Realistic RenderMan	shader
3Delight	shaderdl
Aqsis	aqsl
Pixie	sdrc
Render DotC	shaderdc

Your First Shader: "Hello World Shader"

We will now proceed to write our first shader. Since RenderMan shading is done with RSL, which is a programming language, we will do the typical "hello world" program used to introduce people to a programming language. In our case, a hello world program is represented by what is known as the "constant" shader which gives every point in a surface a fully lit value, completely disregarding all the lights on the scene. This might seem like a useless shader, but they are quite handy for debugging scenes and creating mattes for compositing. To write your first shader, open your favorite text editor and type the following:

```
surface helloWorld()
{
Oi = Os;
Ci = Oi * Cs;
}
```

Save the file as `helloWorld.sl`. Make sure that your text editor doesn't add an extension or change the file type from ASCII to a binary format (such as Rich Text or a Word document). The first line of the shader declares that this shader is a surface type, and it gives it the name `helloWorld`. Next is a set of parentheses, which will usually contain the shader parameters, but since this shader has no parameters, it is left empty.

Next we open the body of the shader with a set of curly braces. All the code between these braces is what will be evaluated by the renderer to determine the initial color and opacity of the surface. We then set the value of `Oi` (opacity output) to be the same as `Os` (opacity input provided by the RIB stream), and then we set the value of `Ci` (color output) to be a multiplication of the output opacity (`Oi`) and `Cs` (color input from the RIB stream).

This last multiplication of the opacity by the color is very common in shaders because it creates a pre-multiplied alpha (opacity) mask for compositing. It is a good idea to be consistent with your opacity handling because having some shaders pre-multiply and others not can create problems down the line. Go ahead and compile this shader by changing to the directory where the `helloWorld.sl` file is and then compile the shader using the shader compiler command.

```
Shadercmd helloWorld.sl
```

If everything was typed correctly, you should get a message confirming that the shader has been compiled, and you should have a file named `helloWorld.xxx`, the xxx being the extension used by your renderer. Now open the file `sphere.rib` and change the surface call to

```
Surface "helloWorld"
```

Save the modified file in the same directory as the compiled `helloWorld` shader and render it using your renderer command by typing

```
rendercmd sphere.rib
```

If everything went well, you should get an image of a white circle in a black background, as shown in Figure 3.5. This circle is actually a sphere, but since there are no lighting calculations being made, all you see is the circular silhouette of the sphere.

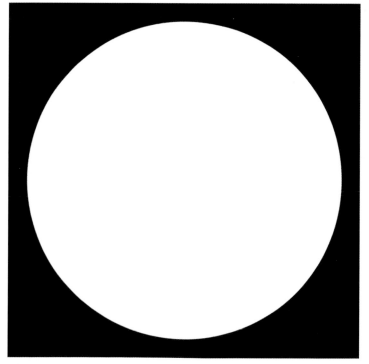

Figure 3.5 The RSL "hello world" equivalent.

Adding Color and Opacity Control

At this point, the surface shader derives its color and opacity information from the input provided by the RIB stream. From experience I can tell you that this is not a common practice. You usually want most of the controls that affect the look of a shader to be part of the shader parameters. Otherwise it can become cumbersome to debug or tweak a look when there are parameters and properties being read from different places.

To add color and opacity control to the shader, we will add a couple of shader parameters to the shader. These will be controls that you as a shader writer make available to the shader user to control aspects of this shader. To add color and opacity control to the shader, make the following modifications to helloWorld.sl:

```
surface helloWorld(
        color surfaceColor = color (1,1,1);
        color surfaceOpac = color (1,1,1);
        )
{
Oi = surfaceOpac;
Ci = Oi * surfaceColor;
}
```

As you can see, all we changed was to add the surfaceColor and surfaceOpacity parameters at the top of the shader and then replace the Os and Cs values in the body of the shader for the new parameters. Go ahead and compile the shader. To modify the values of surfaceColor, change the surface call in the sphere.rib file to

```
Surface "helloWorld" "color surfaceColor" [1 0 0]
```

Save and render the sphere.rib file, and you should now get a red sphere over a black background because you provided the shader with a red value for surfaceColor (see Figure 3.6).

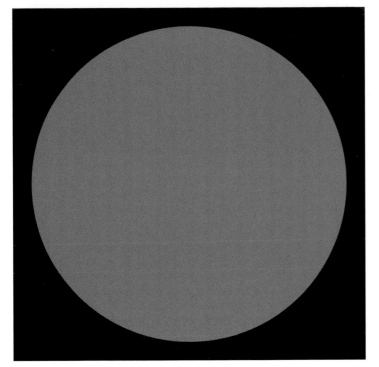

Figure 3.6 The constant surface renders the color provided by `surfaceColor`.

Ambient Illumination

We will now add some controls and features that will make this shader a little more usable as it starts to interact with the lights in the scene. We will do this by using some default shading functions that are part of RSL and that every compatible renderer should support. The first and most basic type of lighting that we will add to the shader is *ambient lighting*. As you might know, ambient lighting is a type that is uniform throughout every point of the surface. It's a very old and cheap way to try to approximate light bouncing around in a scene. Nowadays, ambient lighting is combined with an occlusion pass, also referred to as ambient occlusion, which we discussed earlier in this chapter, and will be covered in detail further along in the book. To add ambient illumination to the shader, make the following changes to `helloWorld.sl`:

```
surface helloWorld(
        uniform float Ka = 0.5;
        color surfaceColor = color (1,1,1);
        color surfaceOpac = color (1,1,1);
        )
{
Oi = surfaceOpac;
Ci = Oi * surfaceColor * Ka * ambient();
}
```

We have added to the shader a parameter named Ka, which stands for coefficient of ambient. We started using K for Koefficient apparently because the first people to use this terminology were German. Compile the shader and re-render sphere.rib. The bright red sphere should now be a dimmed, dark red sphere because the shader is now using the value of the scene's ambient light, which is declared on the line that reads

```
Lightsource "ambient" "float intensity" [1]
```

Since Ka has a value of 0.5, this value is multiplied by the ambient light intensity, the surfaceColor, and the surface opacity, which is why the surface is dimmed to half its intensity, as you can see in Figure 3.7.

Figure 3.7 The red sphere with ambient contribution.

Lambert Illumination

Ambient illumination is very boring and flat looking. To make a surface appear to have dimension, you need some kind of diffuse illumination, which will be bright where lights hit it and dark where they don't. The Lambert illumination model is the most basic form of diffuse illumination, and RSL provides a diffuse function that calculates these values. The Lambert illumination model will be described in detail in chapters to come, but for now we will just use the diffuse call. To add diffuse illumination to the shader, make the following modifications to the helloWorld.sl file.

```
surface helloWorld(
        uniform float Ka = 0.5;
        uniform float Kd = 0.85;
        color surfaceColor = color (1,1,1);
        color surfaceOpac = color (1,1,1);
        )
{
/* Variables */
normal Nn = normalize(N);
Oi = surfaceOpac;
Ci = Oi * surfaceColor * (Ka * ambient() +  Kd * Diffuse(Nn));
}
```

We have added a Kd (diffuse coefficient) parameter to control the amount of light reflected by the surface. We also declare the Nf variable, which holds a normal that has been normalized. The last line has been edited to multiply the surface color and opacity by the sum of the ambient and the diffuse contribution. If you compile this shader and re-render sphere.rib, you will finally get an image of a red sphere. It's true that this is not very impressive, but you can see how little code it took to create a usable Lambert shader with RSL (see Figure 3.8).

Figure 3.8 Lambert shaded sphere.

Specular Reflections

A final step to create a more complete shader is to add a specular term. This will give the shader the appearance of plastic. We will also add a parameter to control the color of the specular highlight. With these controls, we can manipulate the parameters to get many different looks, including very simple and basic metals. To get a more advanced-looking metal, you would need to add a reflective component. Advanced materials that use reflections and raytracing will be covered in Chapter 14.

There are many different models available for calculating specular reflections, of which Phong and Blinn are the most popular. Every renderer is responsible for providing a specular shading function. How the function is calculated is different for each renderer, so the results of each renderer are likely to be different. Here is the modified version of the `helloWorld.sl` shader that includes the specular highlights:

```
surface helloWorld(
        uniform float Ka = 0.5;
        uniform float Kd = 0.85;
        uniform float Ks = 1;
        uniform float roughness = 0.2;
```

```
        color surfaceColor = color (1,1,1);
        color surfaceOpac = color (1,1,1);
        color specularColor = color (1,1,1);
        )
{
/* Variables */
normal Nn = normalize(N);
vector V = -normalize(N);

Oi = surfaceOpac;
Ci = Oi * surfaceColor * (Ka * ambient() +  Kd * Diffuse(Nn)) +
    specularColor * Ks * specular(Nn,V,roughness);
}
```

We could keep adding features to our shader to achieve the look we are after (see Figure 3.9 for a standard shader). However, we need to stop the coding examples to explain some basic CG concepts that every shading TD needs to know. We also need to set up a proper shading development environment and discuss some methodology and approaches to writing production quality shaders.

Figure 3.9 A very standard plastic shader.

PART II

SHADER DEVELOPMENT

4

Setting Up a Developing Environment

A properly set up development environment can be the difference between a fast, enjoyable, and well-managed shading development experience and a clunky, rocky, and at times annoying one. Setting up a proper development environment can take some time, but once you have it up and running, it will make your coding so much easier.

It is also important to learn the most common tools used in the industry so that when you land a job you won't have a hard time working in a development environment that is shared by many TDs. Every studio has a different development environment, but the basics behind them and the tools used usually share similar concepts. This chapter is entirely dedicated to setting up a shader development environment that will allow you to work faster and gain important experience as shader TD. This is not the only way to set up a development environment, but it is a simple environment that can be expanded or customized as you gain more experience.

CYGWIN

Most popular renderers are available for all three major platforms: Windows, Linux, and Mac OS/X. This means you should have access to them no matter what OS you use. Since Windows is the most popular OS on the planet, I assume that most readers use this OS. If you use Linux or OS/X as your OS, you can disregard this section. Without trying to spark a controversy or to seem as if I have something against Windows, I will state my opinion based on personal experience. I will not be able to compare OS/X since I have never used it in a production environment.

Windows is a very good OS, and it has improved a lot over the years probably because it has some serious competitors, but there are a lot of tools and features in Linux that make shader and software development so much easier. There are tons of ways to automate tasks, to create symbolic links between folders and files, and to create an environment that in my opinion allows you to work a lot faster than in Windows. It is for this reason that most high-end 3D software runs better in Linux than in Windows. Most major VFX and animation studios use either Linux or Windows for their work, but Linux is still more used than Windows. It is for this reason that it is highly recommended that you gain Linux experience if you want to work in the film VFX or feature animation field.

But you don't have to install a whole OS just to be able to learn some of the core concepts of Linux. Installing a second OS takes a good amount of time and knowledge. Also, it would be impossible to work on shader development in Linux if most of your other applications are in Windows. Fortunately, there is a group of people that have put together an open source project called CYGWIN, available at www.cygwin.com. CYGWIN is a shell program that allows your Windows computer to emulate a Linux working environment by providing tons of command-line tools that are essential in the Linux OS. We highly recommend that you download and install the default CYGWIN install. This will enable you to learn some of the tools that are used by the big studios while remaining in your native Windows OS.

Most Used Commands

When you launch CYGWIN, a window similar to the Windows DOS command prompt will appear. It is inside this window that a Linux environment is emulated. To be able to do anything at all in this window, you will need to know some basic commands. Most of these commands take extra arguments and options. Let's take the ls command for example. It could be used in these different forms:

```
ls
ls -l
ls /home/username
```

The first form will list the contents of the current directory, and the second will list the contents of the current directory in expanded form (with file owner name, permissions, time saved, and so on). The last form will list all the contents of the user's home directory. Table 4.1 lists the most frequently used commands.

Table 4.1 Most Used Commands

Command	Operation
ls	List contents of given directory
cd	Change directory
pwd	Print path of current directory
mkdir	Make directory
rm	Remove file
rmdir	Remove directory
mv	Move or rename file
cp	Copy files
man	Display the manual of a command
source <file>	Execute the commands in file

Most of these commands will display a simplified help message if you pass a --help option to the command. If you type **pwd --help** you will get:

```
pwd: usage: pwd [-PL]
```

This tells you how to use the pwd command. However, if you type **man pwd**, you will get the full manual of pwd. To exit the manual, hit the Q key. Most built-in commands have a manual installed.

UNIX Folder Structure

The Linux OS uses a very different file structure than Windows. First, there are no drive letters as in Windows. In Linux everything is inside folders that exist inside the root, which is accessed with a back slash (/). Inside this directory you will usually find the following directories: bin, etc, home, lib, tmp, usr, var. You might have more folders, depending on your Linux distribution. The folder where you will be doing all of your work is the /home/username folder. Launching CYG-WIN will place you in your home directory; type **pwd** to verify this.

The real location of this folder in Windows is usually c:\cygwin\home\username. You can create any directories you please in this directory, but more than likely you want to place your development folder somewhere else (I try not to keep any of my working data in C:, as you never know when you might need to re-install Windows). You can create your development folder wherever you please and then create a symbolic link (symlink) inside your home directory. Symlinks are similar to shortcuts used in Windows, but they have a lot more uses. Symlinks are used extensively in Linux, and they behave just like any directory or file. Let's create a symlink so that you can grasp the concept properly.

1. Create the `- c:\rsl` directory.

2. Launch CYGWIN and make sure you are in your home directory (using `pwd`). If you are not there, type **cd ~** to go there.

3. Type the following command: `ln -sf /cygdrive/c/rsl rsl`.

This will create a link named `rsl` in the current directory that points to /cyg-drive/c/rsl. This is the location of `c:\rsl` in CYGWIN. You can now work inside /home/username/rsl as you please within CYGWIN. This will be the directory where we will work from now on.

It's All About Speed

Working in a shell and navigating file structures will be slower at the beginning, but with time and with the use of several simple tricks you can easily speed up your work inside the shell. I have met several TDs who are so fast in a shell that it is scary. Here are some tricks that can help you with speed.

Shortcuts and Environment Variables

There are several places that you will always be accessing. Linux systems provide shortcuts to these places, so you have less to type. The most common shortcuts are ./, ../, and ~, which represent the current directory, one directory above, and the user's home directory, respectively. If there are any directories that you constantly access, it might be beneficial to create an environment variable or an alias for that place. An environment variable is just like a variable in a programming language; it is a symbol that holds a value with which it is replaced when called. To create an environment variable, type the following in CYGWIN:

```
export DEV=/home/username/rsl
```

This will create a variable called DEV that points to your `rsl` directory. Environment variables are usually written in uppercase, but it's not a requirement. To use this variable, you can type

```
cd $DEV
```

The shell will replace $DEV with its stored value and will change the current directory to /home/username/rsl. Of course there is nothing stopping you from setting the DEV variable to

```
export DEV="cd /home/username/rsl"
```

This way, when you type $DEV you will be sent to that directory automatically. The only problem with this is that if you ever need to use the variable for anything other than going to that directory, you won't be able to do so. A better way to accomplish this is to set up an alias for the `cd $DEV` command. If you close the shell and start it again, you will find that the $DEV variable doesn't exist anymore. This is because environment variables are local to the current shell session and are discarded when you close the shell.

How can you declare variables that always exist? When a shell is launched, a file located in your home directory is sourced. This file is used to customize the working environment of that user. When you use the bash shell (the default for CYGWIN), the file named `.bashrc` is sourced from the user's home directory. You can use this file to add any environment variables or customizations that you want to be available whenever the shell is launched. Just add the first described environment variable to your `.bashrc` file.

Aliases

Aliases are similar to environment variables in the sense that they are used to hold a value. They differ in that you don't need to use a $ symbol as the first letter to access the variable's value. Aliases are usually used to abbreviate constantly used commands. To set up an alias, open up the `.bashrc` file and type the following command:

```
alias dev = "cd /home/username/rsl"
```

Save and close the file and then start up a new shell. Typing the word **dev** and hitting Enter should move your current working directory to whatever value you set in the alias call. You can have as many aliases as you want in the `.bashrc` file, so feel free to create as many as you need to get your work done faster. If you are using the bash shell, then you won't be able to pass arguments to an `alias` command, but if you use other shells such as csh you can. Please read the documentation of the `alias` command for your shell by typing **man alias**.

Tab Completion

Most Linux shells and CYGWIN support tab completion, which is the capability to complete what you are typing based on the contents of the current directory, a path in your system, or commands that exist in the system's PATH environment variable. All you need to do is hit the Tab key after you have typed the first letters of the file, command, or path that you are trying to access. If you type

```
/usr/lo -Tab
```

the shell will more than likely expand this to `/usr/local`. To try this with a command, type

```
xe -Tab
```

The shell will fill the command if it finds only one command that starts with xe. If not, it will list all of the commands that start with xe. You can use tab completion as a quick way to look at the contents of a directory or to look up commands that match the letters you type.

Text Editors

As explained earlier in Chapter 3, "Shader Writing Process," a shader writer will spend most of his time in front of a text editor, pounding away on those tiny keys. Type, save, compile, render, type, save, compile, render.... It is for this reason that choosing the right text editor is extremely important for a shader writer. Any text editor will do the job, but this is the one area where you should invest some time deciding which editor you want to use. Once you have decided, you should use it constantly, taking some time to read the documentation for key shortcuts or bindings and how you can customize the editor to suit your needs.

In Chapter 3 we listed Vim, Nedit, Emacs, and XEmacs as the most popular text editors used for shader writing. They are all available in every platform, and they can all be customized for fast shader development by including syntax highlighting, compile command shortcuts, and versioning system integration. You are welcome to use any text editor you like, but in this book we will guide you through the setup and basic use of Emacs or XEmacs.

Emacs and XEmacs

Emacs is a highly customizable text editor that has been available for quite some time. It is an interpreter for the Emacs Lisp language (Elisp), which is a dialect of the Lisp programming language. Using Elisp, you can configure and extend Emacs to perform a large array of tasks. Some people have actually written games such as *Tetris* in Elisp that can be played inside a buffer of the text editor! Emacs runs inside your shell just like Vim does. This means that you don't have access to your mouse pointer for anything other than copy and paste functions; everything else must be done with shortcuts or commands. XEmacs is kind of the next generation of Emacs. I say "kind of" because they are actually two different products and projects. XEmacs was created by a group of programmers who were not content with the direction in which Emacs was heading, so they took it upon themselves to create a newer program that supported all of the original features of Emacs plus the functionality of a GUI. This way, the program is more usable to those who are new but still fast and powerful for the experienced user.

XEmacs should be installed by default when you install CYGWIN. Launch your CYGWIN shell and type **xemacs &**. The & symbol tells the shell to fork the new process so that your shell remains usable after XEmacs starts. If XEmacs is not installed, you should get a message that lets you know that the XEmacs command couldn't be found. If this is the case, run the CYGWIN setup program once again and follow the Installation Wizard until you reach the screen where you get to select your packages. Scroll down to the Editors category and select all of the components for XEmacs. Once XEmacs is properly installed, you should get a window that looks like Figure 4.1.

Figure 4.1 Intro screen for the XEmacs editor.

I'll be the first to admit that XEmacs has a very simple and unimpressive GUI. I was a bit perplexed the first time I ran this program because I had heard so much about how powerful it was. Most of the power of XEmacs comes from the fact that programmers don't concentrate on making pretty, shiny buttons that blink or an animated, annoying paperclip that is always trying to "help" you in your task.

The main window area where the XEmacs logo appears at launch is the buffer editor. If you click on the main area, you will be taken into the scratch buffer. This buffer is like a sandbox where you can type notes, text, or commands that you don't intend to save. Each file that you load into XEmacs will have its own buffer, and you should be able to have as many buffers open as your computer memory and your sanity will allow. To switch from buffer to buffer, you can go to the top Buffer menu and select one of the entries.

You can split the window into several editing areas, so you can have two or more files displayed at the same time. This is done by going to View>Split Window. You can also create new separate windows with the View>New Frame command. At the bottom of the screen there is a mini-buffer that is used for command input. Commands are essential to increasing your working speed. We will list the most used commands, but first we need to go over some XEmacs semantics of command input.

Go to the File menu, and to the right of the Open menu item you will see the symbols C-x C-f. This stands for Ctrl-x Ctrl-f and is the shortcut command for opening a new file. To open a file, you need to hold down the Ctrl key and then hit the X and F keys. You will see an input message displayed in the mini-buffer that reads Find file:/home/username. Type in the full path of the file you are trying to open or the file that you are about to create (you can use tab completion to move faster).

If you give this command a directory, the contents of the directory will be displayed in the buffer editor. Here you can move up and down with the arrow keys as in any text file. Place the cursor on top of a file or a directory and type **enter**. If it's a file, it will be opened into a buffer, and if it's a directory, the contents of that directory will be loaded into another buffer. That's how you enter commands in XEmacs. Table 4.2 lists the most commonly used commands.

Table 4.2 Commonly Used XEmacs Commands

Abbreviation	Meaning
M-	Alt
C-	Ctrl

Shortcut	Command
C-x C-s	Save the current buffer
C-x C-w	Save current buffer as
C-x C-f	Find (open) or create a file
C-x C-k	Kill the current buffer
C-s	Search for all occurrences of text
M-%	Replace text
M-g	Go to line
C-x u	Undo edit
C-x 2	Split window horizontally
C-x 3	Split window vertically
C-x 1	Unsplit, keep this window
C-x 0	Unsplit, keep other windows
C-M-1	Go to previous buffer
C-x C-b	List all buffers

Common Customizations

Using XEmacs right out of the box will not help you work any faster. In fact, without customizations you might as well just use Notepad or any other text editor. With the proper customizations, we will turn XEmacs into an efficient IDE. We will go over only the most important customizations; any other customization is left up to you as an exercise.

Syntax Highlighting

Syntax highlighting might be one of the simplest yet most useful features a text editor will have. Reading code that is highlighted is much easier than reading code that has the same type and color throughout. Once you get used to the patterns and faces that have been assigned to the different elements in the source code, you will be able to skim through them quickly.

For syntax highlighting to work, the text editor needs to know what type of file is being edited. The file extension is a pretty good indicator of the type of code that is being edited, so if the editor loads a file with the *.c extension, it knows it is a C file; if it loads a *.py file, it knows it is Python code that is loaded.

Each language has its own highlighting scheme based on language conventions and on keywords that have been predefined. Once the editor has recognized the file type, it will apply not just highlighting but also formatting rules such as tab spacing and indentations when you are inside certain blocks of code.

To turn on syntax highlighting, go to Options>Syntax Highlighting>In This Buffer. The color of the text should change slightly to let you know that highlighting is active. To save this preference, go to Options>Save Options to ini File. This will save some configuration commands in the file custom.el, which is usually located in /home/username/.xemacs. This is the file that holds all the customizations that need to take effect when you launch XEmacs. You can open this file if you want to read the commands that have been added to it, but please don't modify anything for now as you might break the customizations and will need to start over again.

Face Colors

Syntax highlighting is usually done by reading a programming mode file written in Elisp. In this file the author will specify what type, size, and style of font will be assigned to each component of the source code. For example, the author of the c-mode, which is a file that tells XEmacs to treat the current buffer as a C development platform, will more than likely program that file to use the comment font type for all lines that start with // or for all text between /* and */. However, he will not tell the program what the comment font type will look like because that is something that most users will want to change to their preference. The rsl-mode file that is supplied with this book includes an extensive number of syntax highlighting directives that rely on the font-lock font types. You can edit the look of each font type as you wish by going to Options>Advanced>Face and hitting Enter. This will change your buffer to the Face Customization page. Type **ctrl-s**, and the command area will prompt you for a string to search for. Type **Font**, and the buffer will update to the first occurrence of that string.

Now let's edit the Font_Lock_Builtin_Face type, which should be the first one found by the previous search. To edit the look of the font, click on the little triangle pointing right. This will expand to let you see all the modifiable properties of the font. Click the small square next to each property to activate it. Let's change the foreground color by typing the word **red** in the Foreground Color input field. You will see the sample next to the input field update to the color you typed.

In these color fields you can enter certain color names or hex-indexed colors such as the ones used for HTML. You can google for "hexadecimal colors" and use one of the many interactive applets to find the hex code for the desired color. Go ahead and make any changes you want to the Builtin Face type, then right-click State, which is under Font_Lock_Builtin_Face, and select Save for Future Sessions. This will make the change permanent. After you have loaded rsl-mode (installation of rsl-mode is described later), you might want to come back to this screen and modify the font lock colors to suit your needs. Another important font you might want to change is the Default font. This font will change the appearance of all the letters that are not highlighted, and if you change the background, it will change the background color for the editor, too.

Line and Column Numbers

Making mistakes is part of human nature, and as such you are bound to make mistakes when coding your shaders. With time you will reduce these mistakes, but you will still make some. Thankfully, most RSL compilers are pretty good at finding mistakes and letting you know where they are. A compile error from PRMan's shader might look like this:

```
"s_RP_tile01.sl", line 55: ERROR: syntax error
"s_RP_tile01.sl", line 55: ERROR: Invalid or absent parameter default
"s_RP_tile01.sl", line 213: ERROR: Undeclared variable reference "Nf"
"s_RP_tile01.sl", line 216: ERROR: Undeclared variable reference "Nf"
"s_RP_tile01.sl", line 217: ERROR: Undeclared variable reference "Nf"
```

This lets me know that there is a syntax error in line 55. To be able you find that line quickly you can use the goto line command in XEmacs (Alt-g), or you can just scroll down to the line. However, XEmacs doesn't display the line or column numbers by default. Line numbers are really useful for debugging shaders when you have compile errors and also when you are merging files versioned with CVS or SVN.

It also provides a small sense of accomplishment when you write your first shader that is over 500 lines. The largest shader I have ever been connected with was an uber-surface shader at one of the previous shows I worked on. That beast was over 6,000 lines and spanned across five files, not counting the headers and libraries. Line and column numbers were extremely useful at compile time.

The column number is used less than the line number, but it is really useful for making sure that you type fewer than 75 columns per line. Using fewer than 75 columns is not a rule but is a generally accepted limit for source code files. It is really annoying when you have to work on someone else's code and there are lines that go on forever, slowing down your reading and editing. To display the line and column numbers, go to Options>Display>Line Numbers and Options>Display>Column Numbers. The numbers will be displayed at the bottom separator bar of the current editable area; a capital L will appear next to lines and a C next to columns.

Tab Space

Source code usually becomes a lot more readable if certain blocks of code are indented from the previous lines of code. This is such a common practice that a very popular and powerful language like Python depends entirely on indentations to separate blocks of code. To code faster, most programmers hit the Tab button to indent parts of code that haven't been indented automatically by the editor. The problem with this is that the default size of tabs is different from editor to editor. More than once I have opened a source file written by another shader TD in a different editor than the one I use and run into a file that is almost unreadable. This is usually because the author of the file didn't set his tab size properly. The default size for indentations used by most coding standards is four spaces. To set the tab size to four spaces in Xemacs, go to Options>Advanced (Customize)>Editing> Basics>Tab Width. Type **4** next to the small triangle and then right-click State and choose Save for Future Sessions.

rsl-Mode Installation

Included on the CD that comes with this book is a file named `rsl-mode.el`, which provides RSL support for XEmacs and Emacs. This file provides syntax highlighting, indentation support, and shortcuts for compiling and previewing the shader with the most common renderers. The rsl-mode is nothing but a series of Elisp commands and variables, so feel free to modify it to fit your needs. For information on how to do this, you can read the documentation available at www.gnu.org/software/emacs/elisp-manual/html_mono/elisp.html. Be sure to back up the original file first in case you break it with your modifications. To install the file, copy it into your `home/.xemacs` directory. Then open the `custom.el` file in `.xemacs` and enter the following command at the end of the file:

```
(load-library '"~/.xemacs/rsl-mode")
```

To obtain help on the features that rsl-mode provides, type **M-x describe-function** on the command line. This will print out the following message:

```
(rsl-mode)


Documentation:
Major mode for editing RenderMan shaders.
This is actually just C mode with commands for compiling and
rendering shaders.


C-c C-c    save buffer & compile shader for PhotoRealistic RenderMan
C-c C      save buffer & compile shader for BMRT
C-c 3      save buffer & compile shader for 3Delight
C-C a      save buffer & compile shader for aqsis
```

```
C-c C-r    call render with the current RIB file (PRman Unix)
C-c M-r    call render with the current RIB file (PRman Win32)
C-c R      call rendrib with the current RIB filename (BMRT)
C-c M-3    call render with the current RIB file (3delight)
C-C M-a    call render with the current RIB file (aqsis)
C-c C-s    set the current RIB filename (default is rman.rib)
C-c C-i    set the current include directories as LISP list of strings;
           each string denoting one directory. For example (at the prompt):
           ("/usr/local/shaders" "/usr/shaders").
```

Folder Structure

For the sake of consistency and clarity we will establish a working directory tree structure. This is not the only way to set up a folder structure, but it is a system I have settled on after several years of trying different ones. You are welcome to try another setup if you prefer, but you will have to make the proper modifications to suit your structure. Figure 4.2 illustrates how the folders will be organized.

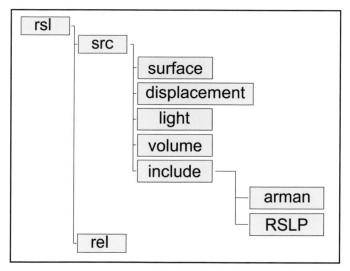

Figure 4.2 Our proposed folder structure

Inside the src (source) directory we will create a folder for each of the shader types that we will be developing. Inside src we will also create an include directory where we will store all of the shader header files that we develop. Within this include directory we will create one folder for each of the libraries we use. Create a folder named arman and extract into it all the *.h files contained in the archive shaderDev.tgz located on the accompanying CD. We will be using the header files developed in Larry Gritz and Tony Apodaca's book *Advanced RenderMan*. Their library of header files is quite good, so it is important that you learn it. As a shader writer, you also need to learn to be resourceful, and there is no reason to reinvent the wheel.

Inside the `include` folder, create a folder named RSLP, which stands for RSL Programming. Here is where we will save all of the libraries that we develop in this book. You might create other folders inside this `include` directory as you start to develop your own libraries. It is a very good idea to keep libraries properly organized.

Inside the `rsl` folder, we will also create a `rel` folder where all the compiled shaders will be copied once they are released. You will need to provide this directory to your renderer when you are looking to use your developed shaders.

Versioning Systems

As you become more accustomed to RSL, you will become more comfortable with the concepts and the language. You will also feel ready to start modifying some of the code from this book, maybe add a feature here or modify a function there. As you modify the code, you will sometimes find that your changes don't work as expected, but you have modified the file so much that you can't return to the original form. You can get around this problem very easily by always working on a copy of the original file.

The down side of this is that you will have lots of files to keep track of, especially if you do incremental saves as you get specific features to work. Another problem is that you will have a hard time remembering what changes you applied to `myshader04.sl` from `myshader03.sl`. You could add a comment at the top of the file with a description of those changes, but you will still have to open the file to read the note.

It is common practice to use a source code versioning system tool to manage your versions and to log the changes from one version to another. The concept behind most versioning is quite simple. There is a central repository from which you check out a working copy of a file, a folder, a module, or the whole repository. When you check out a file, the manager program will create a copy of that file in a local working space. It will also create other folders or files that contain information about the files that were checked out. You can make all the changes you want to those files.

Once you have your changes working, you can check in or commit the file back into the repository. The manager will ask for a comment, and it will stamp the file with time, version, user, and other useful information. The manager will keep the different versions of your files stored, and you can retrieve them at any time. This workflow is ideal for group collaboration, and it's very common in larger studios. You don't need to set up a versioning system to write shaders, but it will help you stay organized, and you will learn useful skills that employers will appreciate. Figure 4.3 demonstrates a typical workflow for versioning systems where there is a central repository and users can check files out of it to a local working directory and then check them back in when done with the changes.

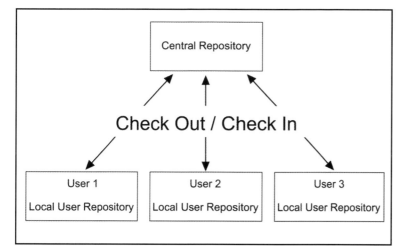

Figure 4.3 Diagram of most common versioning systems

There are many versioning systems available on the Internet, and a number of them are free. Most of them are designed to be used by team members. Others are more geared toward the single developer who is just looking for a way to manage his code better. The following sections discuss Revision Control System (RCS) and Subversion (SVN), two popular versioning systems for individuals and groups, respectively. If you are interested in learning more about these systems, you can go to their Websites, provided in each section.

RCS

Revision Control System (RCS) by the GNU foundation is a command-line program that helps you manage multiple versions of ASCII files. It is extremely easy to set up and very fast for extracting and committing files. It was developed in the early 1980s as an improvement from its predecessor source code control system. RCS works by saving a full copy of the current version of the file and the difference between the current file and the previous files. RCS was designed to help control the chaos that is bound to happen whenever you have more than one developer working on the same source tree. However, it controls this chaos by restricting access to files that might need to be accessed by more than one person at a time, known as a *lock-modify-unlock* workflow. In RCS's design, when a user checks out a file with the intention to edit it, the file is checked out as "locked," which means no one else can check out the file for editing. This makes RCS too restrictive for the speed and level of collaboration that is necessary within a development team. However, it is very well suited for the individual developer looking to keep a well-organized record of all the versions of the files he works with.

Setting up RCS is very simple. First you need to make sure RCS is installed. Type the following command in your CYGWIN shell:

```
> rcs -h
```

If the command is not found, go ahead and install it by running the CYGWIN setup program. Once the program is successfully installed, just create a directory named RCS inside any directory where you want to use version control. These directories are usually your source, includes, and maybe a documentation directory. If RCS finds a directory named RCS within the current directory, it will use that directory to store all the version files. This will help keep your workspace clean. To start using RCS, you will need to check in any file by using the checkin command:

```
> ci filename
```

This will bring up a prompt that asks for a description of the file you are committing. Type whatever you want, and when you are done hit Ctrl-d. The file will be removed from the local directory, and a record of it will be created in the RCS directory. To start editing, you can check out the file by entering the following command:

```
> co -l filename
```

The -l is necessary to check out the file as locked. This will allow you to edit the file. If you don't use the -l option, the file will be checked out as a read-only file. You can save some time by initially committing the file with ci -l filename.

This will check in the file and then check it out as locked in one single step. Every time you check in the file, the program will ask for a log message to be entered. You can provide a log message in one step using the command line with the -m option:

```
> ci -l -m"This is a the log message" filename
```

Make sure there is no white space between the -m and the string of the log message. To retrieve the log messages for a file that is being versioned with RCS, you use the rlog command. This will print out the logs for every version checked in plus additional data such as the date and user of each commit.

```
>rlog filename
```

One final command that will be useful is the rcsdiff command, which prints out the differences between file versions. The most common ways to use this command are

```
> rcsdiff filename
> rcsdiff -r1.1 filename
```

The first command will print the difference between the latest version and the current working file; the second command will compare the working file with whatever version you provide next to the -r option. There are other commands and options associated with RCS. If you are interested in learning more about this versioning system, you can go to the official RCS site at www.gnu.org/software/rcs/rcs.html or do a Web search for "RCS tutorial." For quick reference, Table 4.3 lists the most popular commands. Remember that you can get more information on how to use a command by typing man command.

Table 4.3 Popular RCS Commands

Command	Value
co	Check out
ci	Check in
rcsdiff	Difference between versions
rlog	Print the log history of a file
rcsmerge	Merging versions

Subversion

Subversion (or SVN) is another version control system that is available for free. It was designed to be an accessible replacement for CVS, which is perhaps the most popular open source version control system. It provides most of CVS's features, but it corrects some of CVS's deficiencies. It uses a *copy-modify-merge* workflow that is well suited for large-scale development among many programmers. It is more complicated than RCS to set up, but once it is running, it is quite straightforward to use. Using SVN to version a single-user environment might seem like overkill, but it will prepare you in case you are planning to work for a major VFX or animation studio.

Subversion is available for free at http://subversion.tigris.org/. If you are using CYGWIN, it might have been installed by default. Open the CYGWIN shell and type svn -h. If the command is not found, then you can run the CYGWIN setup program to install Subversion. There are several easy-to-use Subversion clients available at the Website given above. I personally like TortoiseSVN because it is very easy to use. TortoiseSVN is just a set of shell extensions that give you quick access to most of SVN's operations. We will not cover TortoiseSVN because it is a lot more useful to learn how to use the command-line program. This will give you a firm grasp of how SVN is used, making it very easy to adapt to any client you might be inclined to use, if you want to use a client at all.

Setting Up a Repository

The first thing that needs to be done is to create the central repository where all the code will live. Make sure you create this repository in a location you have easy access to. We will use your home directory because you will more than likely be working by yourself. This would not be a good location if you were setting up a repository for several developers, in which case you might want something a little more accessible and protected, such as /usr/local/. For now, just cd into your home directory. Then type the following command:

```
> svnadmin create svn_repo
```

This will create a folder named svn_repo inside the current directory. This is where you can create as many modules as you need to keep your files properly organized.

Importing a Folder and Initial Checkout

Your repository is created and ready for you to start adding modules. We will create a module named shaders inside svn_repo.

```
> mkdir src
> svn import src file:///home/username/svn_repo/shaders/src -m "Initial Commit"
```

You should receive a message confirming that the first revision has been created. It is very important to understand that there is now a versioned copy of the src directory inside of the repository and that the src folder you created is not yet managed by SVN, so it is not suitable for editing. We will delete this directory and check out a fresh copy of the shaders module into our ~/rsl directory. Enter the following commands:

```
> rmdir src
> cd ~/rsl
> svn co file:///home/username/shaders/src
```

A message should let you know if the checkout was successful. Now you are ready to start working inside this directory.

Common Operations

The first thing we will do is create the directories that were outlined in the section "Folder Structures," earlier in this chapter. Navigate to the ~/rsl/src directory and create the include, surface, displacement, and light folders.

```
> cd ~/rsl/src
> mkdir surface include displacement light
```

You now need to add these directories to the repository. This will let SVN know that these directories are to be managed and versioned. To do this, we will use the add command. As mentioned before, SVN is more complicated than RCS. You can't commit a file that is not registered in the system. To add the folders to the repository, type either of the following commands:

```
> svn add surface include displacement light
> svn add *
```

You should see a series of messages that read

```
A        displacement
A        include
A        light
A        surface
```

This means the folders have been added to the repository, but they are still not committed. You need to add your files or folders to the repository only once; from then on you just commit files at different stages of development. To commit the folders, use the following command

```
> svn commit -m "initial commit" displacement include light surface
```

If you are part of a development team, you will need to update your source tree constantly to pick up all the latest changes that have been submitted by the other developers. When doing an update, SVN will replace all the local files that have not being modified, and the files that have been modified locally will be merged with those changes that have been committed. This can sometimes create conflicts with your local copy, which will more than likely break your code. If you get messages that conflicts have been generated, you will need to go into the affected files and correct them manually. To update all the files in the shading repository, go to the src folder and type

```
> svn update
```

To update a specific folder or a file, you can pass the name of it after the command

```
> svn update filename
```

For every processed file, you will get a letter as the first line of the output message. These letters let you know what the update status of each file is. The meaning of these letters is as follows:

- A   Added
- D   Deleted
- U   Updated

- ■ C   Conflict
- ■ G   Merged

The last command that you will use constantly is the `diff` (difference) command, which like RCS will print out the difference between the local working copy and the `HEAD` (latest version) of the repository or with a supplied version with the `-r` option. For example:

```
> svn diff -r 12 filename
```

will print the difference between the current working copy and revision 12, while

```
> svn diff filename
```

will print the difference with the latest committed version. Now that you know the basics of SVN, you can use the command line or any of the clients available at subversion.tigris.org/links.html.

GNU Make

As your development repository grows, you will soon realize that calling the compiler command for every file in your repository is just way too time consuming. It also becomes hard to keep track of file dependencies and inheritance. Imagine a scenario where you realize that an illumination model you so cleverly implemented has a bug in it that is making your renders show up with nasty artifacts. You track down the problem inside the header file where the illumination model is defined, and you figure out what is wrong with it. You go ahead and fix it, so now you need to recompile every shader that uses that illumination model. Which files are using the model? What if there are 30-some files that need to be recompiled? You need a way to have every shader that includes the modified file recompiled automatically. This is one of the workflow nightmares that GNU Make can help you keep under control.

GNU Make is a program that allows you to declare rules for building, installing, releasing, or performing any operation on a file. These rules can be dependent on other rules or on prerequisite files. When a rule is called to be executed, Make will compare the target with the prerequisite files. If any of those files is newer than the target, the rule is executed, which usually rebuilds the target.

Variables

Make files support variables that are extremely useful for keeping your Make files clean. A variable in a Make file is declared when it is assigned a value. There is no need to declare the type of the variable because every variable is a string. Variables are case sensitive and are usually written in uppercase:

```
SLOFILES =  shader01.slo shader02.slo
```

To access variables inside the Make file, you use the following syntax:

```
$(SLOFILES)
```

Make will replace the variable with its value when the file is executed. Use this syntax to access system environment variables.

Writing Rules and Commands

Rules are the heart of a Make file. Writing reliable and smart rules takes a bit of practice, but once you understand the basic concept, they are easy to write. A rule is defined as the first word of a line with no leading white space and follows this syntax:

```
target: prerequisites
   commands
   ....
```

The target is usually the name of the file you are trying to build or another rule. The prerequisites are usually all the source files that are necessary to build the target, passed as a space-separated list of filenames. Commands are declared after the prerequisites and need to have one or more white spaces before the command. When Make finds a line that starts with white space, it will pass that line as a command to the system. So, for example, if you want to write a rule to build a shader named myshader.slo with PRMan's compiler, you would write this rule in the Make file:

```
myshader.slo: myshader.sl
   shader $<
```

When you run make Myshader.slo in the local directory, Make will look for the myshader.slo file. If the file does not exist, Make will run the commands associated with the rule. If the file does exist, then it will compare its timestamp with that of the prerequisite myshader.sl. If myshader.sl is newer, then it will run the commands, but if myshader.slo is newer, then you will get a message that says "There is nothing to be done for myshader.slo." This is a very simple rule that you will more than likely never use. Typing **make myshader.slo** would be too time consuming to do for each file, and for this reason, Make provides a mechanism for evaluating a large number of rules with a single command.

To do large builds you will need to use the all rule. When you type **make** by itself at the command line, Make will look for the all rule, and if it finds it, it will evaluate it. The all rule must have all the objects you want to build as its prerequisites. Here is an example of an all rule and how its dependencies could be written:

```
all: myshader01.slo myshader02.slo myshader03.slo

myshader01.slo: myshader01.sl
    shader $<

myshader02.slo: myshader02.sl
    shader $<

myshader02.slo: myshader02.sl
    shader $<
```

When you type **make** in the local directory, Make will run the all rule, which in turn will run the myshader01.slo, myshader02.slo, and myshader03.slo rules. Those rules will be evaluated as described earlier.

Make files support a large number of features that we will not go over because they are just too much overhead for our needs. What we will do instead is describe the Make files that are part of our shading repository and that are included on the CD-ROM included with this book. We will also cover how to customize the files to support specific scenarios that are very probable. If you would like to learn more about GNU Make, you can go to the project home page at www.gnu.org/software/make/.

Our source repository has two Make files that handle the building and releasing of all the shaders. The main or master Make file is inside the src folder, and it is responsible for calling the Make files in all of the subdirectories.

```
#
# Makefile to build all shaders in the recursive directories
#
# by Rudy Cortes
#
#--- VARIABLES ---
DIRS = displacement surface light imager volume
#--- RULES ---
all: $(DIRS)
$(DIRS): FORCE
    $(MAKE) -C $@
    @echo
release: $(DIRS)
    @echo
    @echo "##############################"
    @echo "##############################"
    @echo "#"
    @echo "# releasing shaders"
```

```
@echo "#"
@echo "##############################"
@echo "##############################"
@echo
@for i in $(DIRS);do\
    $(MAKE) release -C $$i;\
done
FORCE:docs:
  doxygen doxyfile
```

DIRS = displacement surface light imager volume defines the DIRS variable, which is the folders into which Make will go and perform some kind of work. Next we declare the all: target rule, which has the value of DIRS as its prerequisite. Because of variable expansion, the all rule now depends on the directories assigned to DIRS. The next line defines the $(DIRS) target, which uses FORCE as the prerequisite. As you can see, at the end of the file the FORCE target has no prerequisites and no commands. This means that each of the targets in $(DIRS) will always have to be evaluated. Since the $(DIRS) variable is a space-separated list of names, Make will use each of those names as a target. The $(MAKE) -C $@ command will force Make to go into each of the target directories and run make locally. This is an important command, so we will break it down a little further.

The $(MAKE) is a special variable that is used to reference the program that was used to run Make. It is not suggested to use make as a direct call inside a Make file because that will give you strange and unreliable results. The -C flag tells Make that the next argument is a directory and that Make should cd into this directory before it runs the local make command. The $@ is one of Make's automatic variables that allow you to write more generic target rules. This variable is expanded to the name of the target that Make is trying to build. (Table 4.4 lists other useful automatic variables.) So Make will cd into each of the directories listed in $(DIRS) and then execute the same make command that was used to process this file. After the make command, we run an echo command, which will print an empty line that will let us read the output of the program more easily. The @ is necessary before the echo command so that the command gets executed but not printed. By default, Make prints every command it executes to simulate a session in which you are typing the commands. When Make finds @ in front of a command, the command will not be printed, but it will be executed.

Table 4.4 Useful Automatic Variables

Symbol	Value
$@	The filename of the target of the rule.
$<	The name of the first prerequisite.
$?	The names of all the prerequisites that are newer than the target, with spaces between them.
$^	The names of all the prerequisites, with spaces between them.
$+	This is like $^, but prerequisites listed more than once are duplicated in the order they were listed in the Make file.

The next target defined in this file is the release rule, which is used to copy all of the compiled shader files into a release place where they will be found by the renderer. The release target has $(DIRS) as a prerequisite. This is done so that Make will recompile any file that is out of date before it is released. We first print several lines with a nice big notice to let us know at which point the release actually starts in the output of the program. We then write a simple for loop in standard shell commands, which will call $(MAKE) release -C $$i. The i variable holds the name of each of the values of DIRS, and we need to use a double $$ to restrict Make from trying to expand the variable. We need to use this workaround of using a shell for loop because the target to be built is release, which is not a file or a directory, so we can't use it as a parameter to our $(MAKE) command. The final rule in the Make file is used to build the documentation with doxygen. To use it just type **make docs** from the command prompt.

The first two rules in this file won't do anything else on their own. They are heavily dependent on Make files that exist inside of each of the directories in DIRS. This "master" Make file is simply a subcommand executer. The real magic goes on inside the make file inside each of the subdirectories, which look like this:

```
#
# makefile for compiling all shaders in the current directory
#
# by Rudy Cortes - Created 04/24/2006
#

#--- VARIABLES ---
CURDIR = $(shell pwd)
```

```
# hack to eliminate spaces in the "Documents and settings" folder in
# windows
CURDIRN = $(word $(words $(CURDIR)),$(CURDIR))
SHADERTYPE = $(notdir $(CURDIRN))
SLFILES = $(wildcard *.sl)
RELEASEDIR = ../../rel/

ifeq ($(RENDERER), )
COMPILECMD = shader -DPRMAN
COMPILEEXT = slo
else ifeq ($(RENDERER),3delight)
COMPILECMD = shaderdl
COMPILEEXT = sdl
endif


SLOFILES = $(SLFILES:%.sl=%.$(COMPILEEXT))

RELEASEDFILES = $(SLFILES:%.sl=$(RELEASEDIR)%.$(COMPILEEXT))
INCLUDEDIRS= -I../include

#--- Targets ---
all: $(SLOFILES)
    @echo
    @echo --------COMPILE--------
    @echo compile of $(SHADERTYPE) shaders done!!
    @echo ----------------------
    @echo

%.$(COMPILEEXT): %.sl
    @echo
    $(COMPILECMD) $(INCLUDEDIRS) $<
    @echo
    @echo - Moving shader to release dir -
    mv $@ $(RELEASEDIR)

FORCE:

release: $(RELEASEDFILES)
    @echo
    @echo -------RELEASE--------
    @echo release of $(SHADERTYPE) shaders done!!
    @echo ----------------------
    @echo
```

```
$(RELEASEDIR)%.$(COMPILEEXT): %.$(COMPILEEXT)
   @echo
   @echo ................
   install $^ $(RELEASEDIR)
   @echo ................
   @echo
```

The first section defines some very important and useful variables. Let's give them a closer look.

```
CURDIR = $(shell pwd)
# hack to eliminate spaces in the "Documents and settings" folder in
# windows
CURDIRN = $(word $(words $(CURDIR)),$(CURDIR))
SHADERTYPE = $(notdir $(CURDIRN))
SLFILES = $(wildcard *.sl)
RELEASEDIR = ../../rel/

RELEASEDFILES = $(SLOFILES:%.slo=$(RELEASEDIR)%.slo)
INCLUDEDIRS= -I./include
```

The CURDIR variable reads the value returned by the shell command pwd. The $ (*shell command*) is used to read in values from shell commands, so when we type **$(shell pwd)** we are telling make to execute pwd and give us the returned value. We then declare CURDIRN, which is a hack to eliminate the spaces found in a path that uses Documents and settings. The $(word) command has the following syntax:

```
$(word number, string)
```

and returns the word that is in the position number within string. So, for example

```
$(word 2, foo bar tops)
```

will return bar. The $(words) command will return the number of words in the string, so using $(word $(words $(CURDIR)),$(CURDIR)) will return the last segment of c:\Documents and Settings\rcortes\somedirectory, since it will treat the words Documents and and as words because they are separated by white space.

The next variable declared is SHADERTYPE, which uses the $(notdir) command to extract the last part of a file path, so this command:

```
$(notdir /home/rudy/surface)
```

will return the word surface. Since the directories in which our source code is stored are named according to the type of shader they contain, we can use this name to figure out what type of shaders we are compiling.

Next we use the $(wildcard) command to retrieve the value of all the sl files in the current directory. If we don't use the $(wildcard) command and we assign SLFILES = *.sl, then the value of SLFILES will not be the names of all the sl files in the current directory but the string *.sl. This causes problems down the line because we will use the string substitution command $(SLFILES:%.sl=%.slo) later to replace the .sl extension to slo to assign to the SLOFILES variable. The rest of the variables use the same commands that we have already covered, so they should be self-explanatory. Next, we have some interesting control flow statements:

```
ifeq ($(RENDERER), )
COMPILECMD = shader -DPRMAN
COMPILEEXT = slo
else ifeq ($(RENDERER),3delight)
COMPILECMD = shaderdl
COMPILEEXT = sdl
endif
```

This small segment allows our Make file to use either Pixar's shader compiler or 3delights shaderdl compiler. The line ifeq($(RENDERER),) tells the program to use the next segment of code if the environment variable (in your shell environment) $RENDERER is not set. If the $RENDERER variable is set and it is equal to 3delight then we use the next block of variables. This allows us to use the same make file to compile shaders with different compilers based on environment variables. Next, we have a set of useful variables:

```
SLOFILES = $(SLFILES:%.sl=%.$(COMPILEEXT))
RELEASEDFILES = $(SLFILES:%.sl=$(RELEASEDIR)%.$(COMPILEEXT))
INCLUDEDIRS= -I../include
```

The SLOFILES variable is set to all the files that where stored in the SLFILES variable, but we replace the sl by the defined COMPILEEXT variable. This will give us all of the target files that need to be built. The RELEASEDFILES creates a string with the path to where the files are moved after compiled. This allows us to compare the files in the local src folder with the released files to determine if the files need to be rebuilt. The INCLUDEDIRS defines the location of our include directory. We then have a small set of targets:

```
#--- Targets ---
all: $(SLOFILES)
    @echo
    @echo --------COMPILE--------
    @echo compile of $(SHADERTYPE) shaders done!!
    @echo ----------------------
    @echo
%.slo: %.sl
    @echo
```

```
   $(COMPILECMD) $(INCLUDEDIRS) $<
   @echo
FORCE:
release: $(RELEASEDFILES)
   @echo
   @echo -------RELEASE--------
   @echo release of $(SHADERTYPE) shaders done!!
   @echo --------------------
   @echo
$(RELEASEDIR)%.slo: %.slo
   @echo
   @echo ................
   install $^ $(RELEASEDIR)
   @echo ................
   @echo
```

all is the default rule that has every slo file in the current directory as a prerequisite. It will print out a Compile of $(SHADERTYPE) shader done!! message when all the files in SLOFILES are processed.

The next target is interesting because it uses the pattern matching symbol %.slo. This will create a target for each of the files in SLOFILES. The %.sl in the prerequisites will look for a file that has the same name as the target but ends with sl. We then declare this command:

$(COMPILECMD) $(INCLUDEDIRS) $<

This will call proper compile command and provide the paths in $(INCLUDEDIRS) as options and the name of the last prerequisite $< as the source file. Next we have the release target, which depends on the $(RELEASEDFILES) values. This variable holds the names of the files in the release directory. This way the release target will be built only if the timestamp in the local slo file is newer than the one in the release directory.

With the setup of the folder structure, CYGWIN, RCS or SVN, XEmacs, and the Make files, you are ready to start writing shaders in an efficient manner. If you are an experienced programmer, you can use whatever tools or development environment you are most comfortable with. Just remember to compensate accordingly throughout the book.

5

Math for Shader Writers

Math—you might think it's ugly, hard, and boring, but it is also absolutely necessary for anyone trying to become a successful shader TD. You also might think that you just didn't pay enough attention during those math classes in high school or in college and that there is no way you will be able to understand what we are about to cover.

Not to worry. The topics covered don't require you to become a human calculator, and in fact, a handy calculator will help you a lot. The concepts and theory we are about to cover might be somewhat complicated, but since we are not mathematicians, we don't need to trouble ourselves with why the theory works or with mathematical proofs. All we need to do is learn the operations and properties and then apply them when necessary. You will have to practice to get used to some operations, but don't get discouraged. As a shader TD, the amount of math you will use on a daily basis is not extensive, and there are only a small number of operations and properties that you really need to become familiar with. There are a lot of mathematical studies that can greatly improve your value as a shader TD, but those tend to be more complicated, and you will only use the knowledge on very particular cases. In this chapter, we will go over the math that you will deal with on a daily basis.

Useful Operations

We will start our exploration into math-land by first looking at simple numbers like the ones we had to deal with in elementary and high school math. Luckily for us, most of the math used in shader development deals with numbers that are within the 0 to 1 range, although sometimes the range expands to cover from

−1 to +1. This range is important because texturing and parametric coordinates of objects usually span this range and also because most colors and noise fields are within the same range.

It is important to be able to manipulate these values to get the values you need. These are operations that you will use constantly, so make sure you remember them; if necessary, make yourself a cheat-sheet. Do whatever you need to do to make them part of your arsenal. Figure 5.1 shows a graph of y = x, giving us a 0 to 1 linear function.

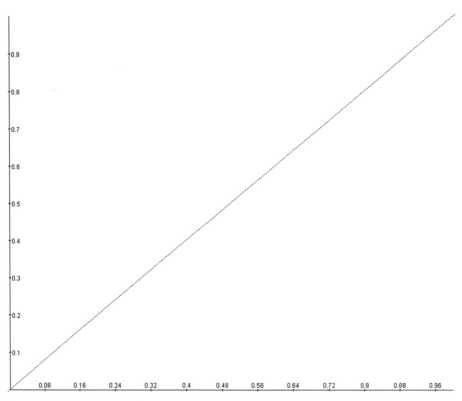

Figure 5.1 A linear map of y = x.

Inverting a Value

If the value you are dealing with (let's refer to this value as x from now on) is within the range 0 to 1, you can invert the value by simply subtracting the value from 1. Note that the operation must be y = 1 - x; because subtraction does not have a commutative property. This means that typing y = x - 1; will give you a completely different result. If x is within the range -1 to 1, then the solution for an inversion is to multiply x by -1, such as y = -1 × x;. Since we are multiplying, the order of the operation does not matter, so you could also type y = x 3 -1;. Another way to do this is by using the negate operator, which is a minus sign (-) placed right before the value, with no space between them, such as -x. This operator is shorthand for multiplying a value by −1. Figures 5.2 and 5.3 demonstrate why these methods of inversion work.

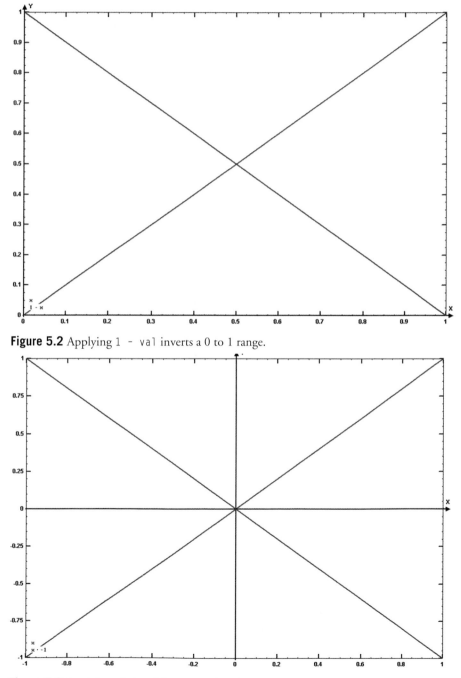

Figure 5.2 Applying 1 - val inverts a 0 to 1 range.

Figure 5.3 Applying -1 * val inverts a −1 to 1 range.

Signing a Value

Sometimes, you have a 0 to 1 range that you need to turn into −1 to 1. This operation is known as *signing*. To sign a 0 to 1 value, you need to multiply the value by 2 and then subtract 1 from it, such as y = (2 × x) -1;. Signing can be very useful when dealing with noise values. noise() returns values that average around 0.5. Sometimes, you need the noise values to average between −0.5 and 0.5. In such cases, all you need to do is sign the noise value. Figure 5.4 demonstrates a graph of signing 0 to 1 value to -1 to 1.

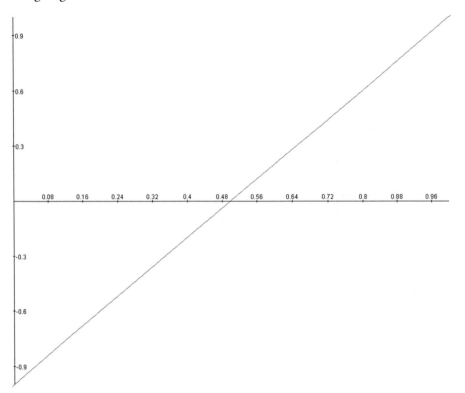

Figure 5.4 Signing a 0 to 1 value turns it into −1 to 1.

Divide Value by 1

As you develop your shaders, you will sometimes need to use a certain value within your shaders, but that value would make no sense at all as a shader parameter. One such example is when you are scaling a texture. Remember that texture spaces (s, t) are usually within the 0 to 1 range. To scale the texture, you could take a shader input txscale and divide by the s or t value.

The problem with this approach is that you will run into a "divide by zero" error when the texture coordinate is 0 (you can't divide a value by 0). The following code will more than likely generate rendering errors:

```
float ss = s/txscale;
float tt = t/txscale;
```

To get around this problem, we will invert our approach and add the logic to avoid division by zero. To do this, we will multiply the s and t values by 1/txscale. What this does is scale down the texture coordinates, resulting in the texture scaling up. To prevent division by zero, we will use the max() shadeop to restrict the value to drop below a very small number. Here is the modified code.

```
float scaler = max(1/txscale,0.000001);
float ss = s * scaler;
float tt = t * scaler;
```

Parametrizing a Value

Another common operation used to massage the shader parameter within a shader is to remap a 0 to 1 value used as an input to a shader parameter into a more useful set of values. This is known as *remapping* or sometimes *parametrizing* the value. I believe that parametrizing is a better description because a true remap would allow you to take a value that ranges from lowA to hiA and remap it to a new lowB to hiB value, which will not necessarily be between 0 and 1.

One example of a use for this is when you are trying to manipulate the specular value that is passed to a phong() illumination call. Let's say you find that good results can be achieved by passing a value that lies somewhere between 20 and 45. How would the user of the shader know this? Chances are that he will play with the shader for a bit, try values between 0 and 10, and then probably give up, cursing the shader writer who can't even code a simple phong() function!

To get around this problem, you parametrize the value by subtracting the low value (20) from the high value (40) and then multiply that value by the user input (x) and add the low value back into the result. This will allow the user to use an input between 0 and 1, but internally it will be handled as a linear interpolation between 20 and 45. Defining a preprocessor macro will greatly simplify the process of normalizing a value. Here is the macro, followed by a quick example of how to use it.

```
#define parametrizeVal(x,lo,hi) lo + x * (hi - lo)
float specval = parametrizeVal(specParam,20,45);
float phongValue = phong(N,I,specval);
```

bias() and gain()

We will now introduce a set of functions that are extremely useful because of their properties. They allow you to manipulate the values within the 0 to 1 range without ever modifying the low or high value. These functions were developed by Ken Perlin and are a must for every shader writer's bag of tricks. These two functions need to default to a value of 0.5, at which point they have no effect on the input value.

The bias() function behaves like a weight modifier: it allows you to control which part of the 0 to 1 range has more weight. Here is the bias() function, followed by Figures 5.5 and 5.6, which illustrate the output of applying the values 0.25 and 0.85 to the bias() function.

```
float bias(varying float val,b){
    return (b > 0) ? pow(val,log(b) / log(0.5)): 0;
}
```

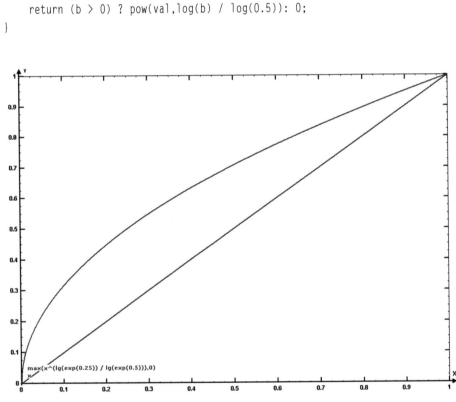

Figure 5.5 bias() function with a value of 0.25.

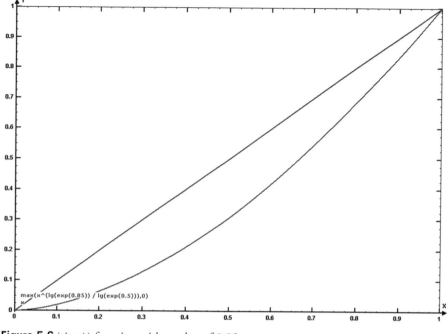

Figure 5.6 bias() function with a value of 0.85.

The gain() function (also known as a *contrast function*) has very different behavior. It leaves the values at 0, 0.5, and 1 unchanged and manipulates the values in the first segment (0 to 0.5) and the second segment (0.5, 1). Internally, it is calculated as two bias() operations applied to the first and second segments. The visual result of the gain() function is the increase or decrease of the value's contrast. Here is the function followed by Figure 5.7 and Figure 5.8, which are graphs of gain() at 0.25 and 0.85.

```
float gain(float val,g){
    return 0.5 * ((val < 0.5) ? bias(2 * val,1 - g) :
           (2 - bias(2 - 2 * val,1 - g)));
}
```

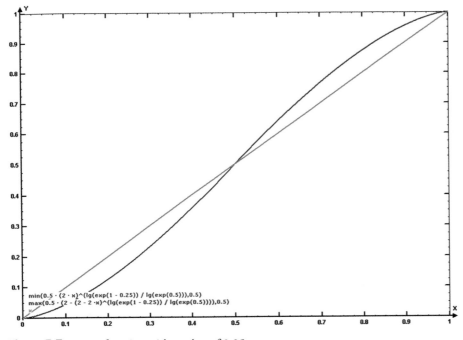

Figure 5.7 gain() function with a value of 0.25.

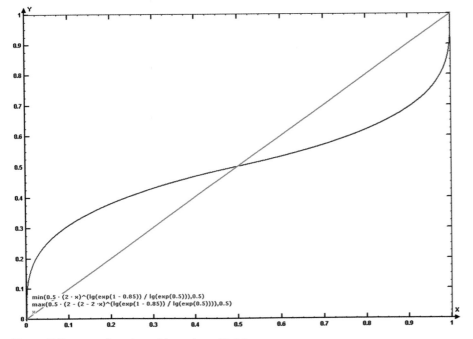

Figure 5.8 gain() function with a value of 0.85.

gamma()

A similar function to bias() is the gamma() function. This function is used in gamma correction, which is the standard way images are manipulated inside the animation and VFX industries. A deeper discussion of gamma correction will be presented later in this chapter when we get to color math and color spaces.

A gamma() function is extremely simple and is defined as y = pow(x,1/gammavalue). Note that this operation returns a float value, so to use it to gamma-correct a color, you will need to apply the gamma() function to all channels of the color.

```
#define gamma(x,value) pow(x,1/value)
color col1 = color (0.5,0.5,0.5);
color gammacol1 = color(gamma(comp(col1,0),gammaval),
                        gamma(comp(col1,1),gammaval),
                        gamma(comp(col1,2),gammaval));
```

You also could use the new color array notation, available since PRMan 13.0:

```
color col1 = color (0.5,0.5,0.5);
color gammacol1 = color(gamma(col1[0],gammaval),
                        gamma(col1[1],gammaval),
                        gamma(col1[2],gammaval));
```

Figures 5.9 and 5.10 show graphs of gamma() at 0.4545 and 2.2.

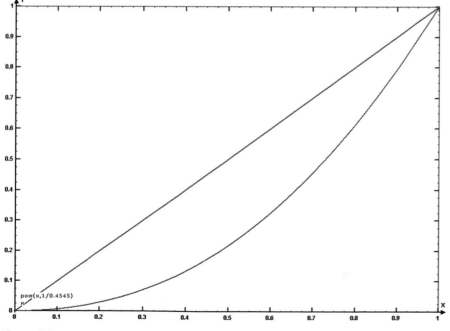

Figure 5.9 gamma() applied with a value of 0.4545.

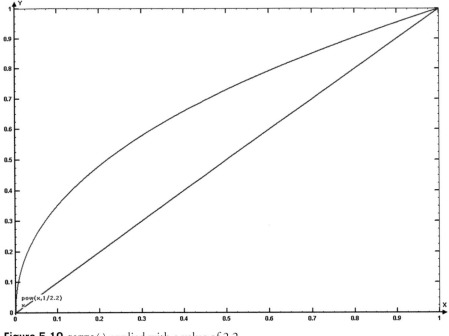

Figure 5.10 gamma() applied with a value of 2.2.

compress() and expand()

Another set of very useful operations is the compress() and expand() functions. These functions allow you to manipulate the dynamic range of the 0 to 1 values. The output of these two operations might seem similar to using gain() to increase or decrease the contrast of the texture. The difference lies in the fact that compress() and expand() actually change the range of the texture, while in gain(), 0 will remain 0, and 1 will remain 1. The compress() function allows you to tighten the dynamic range of the texture. It adheres to the following syntax:

```
compress(value,lo,hi)
```

lo represents the lowest value that will be remapped to and hi the highest. Note that compress() will remap the lo and hi values by pushing them into a lower position in a value graph. Here is a graphic that represents the overall action compress() will take over the mapped values. Setting the compress() values to compress(s,0,2) will remap a value of 1 to 2 and 0.5 to 1 while leaving 0 unchanged. Changing the values to compress(s,0.5,1) will remap the value of 0 to 0.5 and 0.5 to 0.75 while leaving 1 untouched. Figure 5.11 is a graph of compress at (x,0,2) and (x,0.25,0.75) while Figures 5.12 to 5.14 demonstrate the output of using compress().

```
float compress(float x, float lo, float hi) {
    return (hi-lo) * x + lo;
}
```

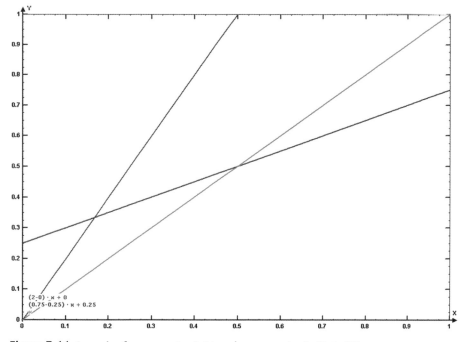

Figure 5.11 A graph of compress(x,0,2) and compress(x,0.25,0.75).

Figure 5.12 S with no compression.

Figure 5.13 s with (0,2) compression; what used to be 1 is now 2.

Figure 5.14 s with (0.5,1) compression; what used to be 0 is now 0.5.

The expand() function does the exact opposite of compress(): It remaps the values
by pushing the values to a higher position in a value graph. Applying an expand()
function with the values expand(s,0.5,1) will leave 0 and 1 untouched, remapping
0.5 to 0. This means that the value of 0 is shifted up to the position of 0.5, therefore remapping 0.5 to 0. Using the values expand(s,0,2) will leave 0 untouched
while remapping 1 to 0.5, because the value of 1 will be shifted up to the position
of 2. Figure 5.15 shows a graph of expand at (0,2) and (0.25,0.75), while Figures
5.16 and 5.17 illustrate the effects of expand() on the s coordinates.

```
float expand(float x, float lo, float hi) {
    float retval = 0;
    if (lo == hi)
   retval =  x < lo ? 0 : 1;
    else
        retval = (x-lo) / (hi-lo);

    return retval;
}
```

Figure 5.15 A graph of expand(0,2) and expand(0.25,0.75).

Figure 5.16 s with (0,2) expanded; what used to be 1 is now 0.5.

Figure 5.17 s with (0.5,1) expanded; what used to be 0.5 is now 0.

remap()

The final float operation we will go over is the remap() function. This operation can also be referred to as a fit operation because it takes the low and high values of x (referred as a1 and b1) and fits them in a linear fashion into a new low and high value (referred to as a2 and b2). If you use the call remap(x,0,1,1,0), the value of x will be inverted. Setting the function to remap(x,0,1,0.25,0.75) will remap the output to 0.25–0.75 as shown in Figure 5.18.

```
float remap(float x,float a1,float b1,float a2,float b2) {
    return (x*(b2-a2) - a1*b2 + b1*a2) / (b1-a1);
}
```

Figure 5.18 s with a remap() of (0,1,1,0) inverts the image, while a remap() of (0,1,0.25,0.75) limits the image range to 0.25-0.75.

Trigonometry

Stepping up one level in the complexity of math concepts, we will take a look at trigonometry. If I had known in high school that I wanted to be a TD, I would have paid a lot of attention. But there is no reason to panic. Although trig can seem hard, there are only a handful of formulas and properties that you need to remember; the rest you can always look up in a trigonometry book or a Website.

Trigonometry is all about triangles, so let's go over some important properties of triangles. Of course, they have three sides. Where the sides touch each other, there is an angle. The sum of the angles of a triangle will always be 180 degrees, or $\pi/2$ in radians. There are many different types of triangles, but for the study of computer graphics the most common is the right triangle. The right triangle has one 90-degree angle; the other two angles add up to 90 degrees. The longest side of a triangle, which is always opposite the 90-degree angle, is known as the *hypotenuse*. The other two sides are known as the *legs* of the triangle. The well-known Pythagorean Theorem provides us with the following formula to calculate the hypotenuse:

$$c^2 = a^2 + b^2$$

This formula can be manipulated to get the length of any of the three sides of a right triangle, as long as you have the length of the other two sides.

Now let's move over to other key aspects of trigonometry. The terms *sine, cosine,* and *tangent* represent the measurement of certain areas of a triangle. Each of these values can be found using the lengths of the sides, as follows:

```
sin=opp/hyp
cos=adj/hyp
tan=opp/adj
```

In these formulas opp represents the side opposite to the angle you are calculating, adj is the adjacent side (a side that touches the angle), and hyp is the hypotenuse, which once again is the longest side of a right triangle. Let's look at a simple example. In the following formula, we will first calculate the hypotenuse, and then we will calculate the sine, cosine, and tangent of angle A. Finally, we will calculate the angle of A. Figure 5.19 illustrates a right triangle.

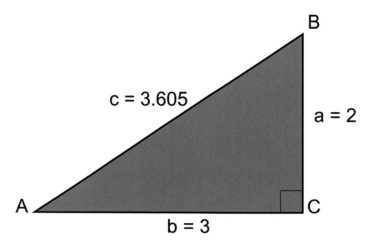

Figure 5.19 A right triangle has one angle at 90 degrees C.

$$hyp^2=2^2+3^2$$
$$hyp=\sqrt{13}$$
$$hyp=3.605$$
$$\sin(A)=\frac{2}{3.605}=0.554$$
$$\cos(A)=\frac{3}{3.605}=0.832$$
$$\tan(A)=\frac{2}{3}=0.666$$
$$A=\arcsin(0.554)=33.641$$

These are the basic trigonometric operations that you will use most often. Now let's take a look at the sine, cosine, and tangent properties. The values of sine and cosine always range from −1 to 1, progressing in a wave-like manner as the angle or radians increase or decrease. They are also an interval apart, so when sin(x) is equal to 1, cos(x) will be equal to 0. A tangent travels from −infinity to infinity while remaining on a tangent to the point where it touches the sin(X) curve, when x = 0. A tangent of a curve is a line that touches the curve on one position but never penetrates or crosses the curve. The repetitive nature of sine and cosine make them quite useful for texture generation. Figure 5.20 shows a graph of sine, cosine, and tangent, while Figures 5.21 and 5.22 show how sine can be used to generate textures.

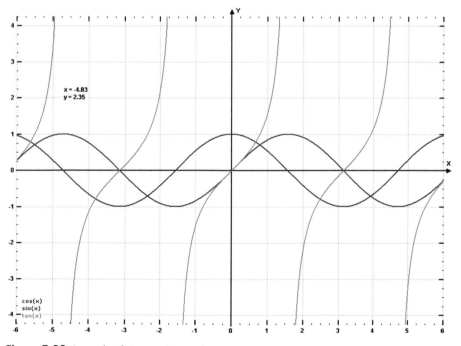

Figure 5.20 A graph of sine, cosine, and tangent.

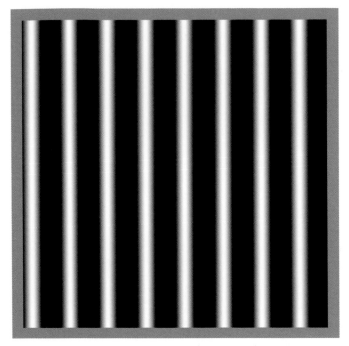

Figure 5.21 Output of using `Cs = sin(s * freq)`.

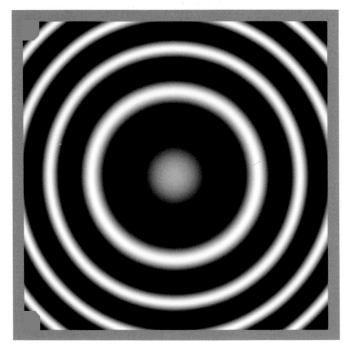

Figure 5.22 Output of using `Cs = sin(distance(point(.5,.5,.5),point(s,t,0))* freq)`.

One common use for these trigonometric functions is to apply rotation to a two-dimensional texture coordinate. The following preprocessor macro allows you to rotate points x and y using ox and oy as the pivot point. It will rotate the a and b points the given rad amount in angles. The output of the rotation is stored in the rx and ry variables.

```
/* rotate2d()
 * from rmannotes.sl
 * 2D rotation of point (x,y) about origin (ox,oy) by an angle rad.
 * The resulting point is (rx, ry).
 *
 */
#define rotate2d(x,y,rad,ox,oy,rx,ry) \
   rx = ((x) - (ox)) * cos(rad) - ((y) - (oy)) * sin(rad) + (ox); \
   ry = ((x) - (ox)) * sin(rad) + ((y) - (oy)) * cos(rad) + (oy)
```

Vector Math

Vectors and matrices are among the most used mathematical entities in computer graphics. Matrices are used to represent transformations such as translations, rotations, and scaling. Vectors are used to represent positions, directions, normals, and sometimes even colors. We will concentrate mostly on vectors because they are a lot more useful to a shader writer. Vector properties and operations are important for any TD in the industry, but they are essential for a shader developer. If there is one section in this chapter that you need to understand completely, it is this section.

Vectors are represented by a three-element, one-dimensional array. The three values of the vector represent the x, y, and z values. As previously stated, RenderMan has three different data types that are represented in a very similar three element array (points, vectors, and normals) but they hold different information. For a point, the three values represent a position in 3D space. For a vector, they represent a direction defined by a line that travels from the origin of the current coordinate system and the value passed to the vector. Normals also represent a direction, but the origin is a surface position, not the origin of the coordinate system. Vectors also contain a length or magnitude that is defined by the distance from the origin to the vector location.

Now let's take a look at the most important properties of vectors and the most useful vector operations.

Vector Addition, Subtraction, and Scaling

Once again we will start by looking at addition and subtraction, as they are the most basic operations that can be performed. Vector addition and subtraction are performed in an element-by-element fashion, where addition of vectors A and B would be performed as:

$$A+B=[A_x+B_x \quad A_y+B_y \quad A_z+B_z]$$

Visually, the result of addition can be seen as placing one vector on the tip of the other vector. For ease of visualization, let's see how addition of two 2-dimensional vectors would take place. Let's add the vectors Q = [2 2] and T = [-3 1].

$$Q+T=[2+(-3) \quad 2+1]$$
$$Q+T=[-1 \quad 3]$$

Figure 5.23 illustrates this addition.

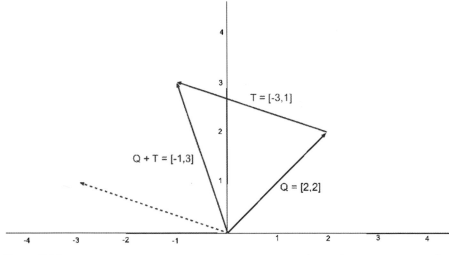

Figure 5.23 Addition is done by moving vector T to the tip of Q and spanning a vector from the origin to T. The dashed line is the original location of T.

The same way, vector subtraction is performed element by element. Visually, vector subtraction connects the tips of both vectors as they emanate from the origin. Figure 5.24 demonstrates a subtraction of the same Q and T vectors.

$$Q-T=[2-(-3) \quad 2-1]$$
$$Q-T=[5 \quad 1]$$

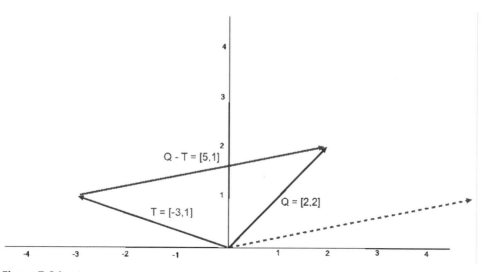

Figure 5.24 Subtraction is done by putting both vectors on the origin and joining their tips. The dashed line is the new Q - T vector located at the origin.

Scaling the length of a vector is achieved by multiplying an integer or a float value by the vector. When multiplying these two entities, the integer value will be multiplied independently by each of the three vector components. Vector scalar multiplication, as well as vector addition, is a commutative operation, so multiplying Q × i is the same as i × Q. Multiplying the integer i =2 by the vector Q=[2 3 1] will result in Figure 5.25.

$$Q×i=[(2×2)\ (3×2)\ (1×2)]$$
$$Q×i=[4\ 6\ 2]$$

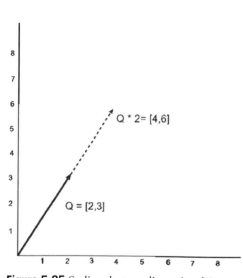

Figure 5.25 Scaling the two-dimensional Q vector by 2 returns a scaled vector with the same direction. The new vector is dashed.

Vector Length and Normalize

Vectors are defined by direction and length (or magnitude). Calculating the length of a vector is a very useful operation that can be applied to a lot of different uses. Among those uses is the normalization of a vector, which will turn the vector's length to 1, thus becoming a unit vector or a normalized vector. We will explain normalization in more depth later on. To calculate the length of a vector, use the following formula:

$$length = \sqrt{x^2 + y^2 + z^2}$$

So the length of a vector Q=[2 4 1] and a vector T=[6 16 3] would be

$$Qlength = \sqrt{4 + 16 + 1}$$
$$Qlenght = \sqrt{21}$$
$$Qlenght = 4.5825$$

$$Tlength = \sqrt{36 + 256 + 9}$$
$$Tlenght = \sqrt{301}$$
$$Tlenght = 17.3494$$

RSL provides a built-in function for calculating the length of a vector. This function adheres to the syntax `ln = length(vector V)`. Internally, it is calculated as

```
ln = sqrt(V.V);
```

The RenderMan developers decided to use a dot product operation using the vector as both components so that the operation would be more compact. Dot products will be reviewed later in this chapter, and you will see why you can replace the vector to the $x^2 + y^2 + z^2$ with a dot product. Normalizing is an operation where you take a vector of any length and turn it into a unit vector. Unit vectors are extremely useful in CG programming and in shader programming. Several mathematical operations are greatly simplified if the vectors used are normalized. RSL takes this into consideration and implements certain built-in functions in a very optimized way (such as the `reflect()` function) that requires the user to provide a normalized vector to the function; otherwise, the result can be erroneous. To normalize a vector, all you need to do is divide the value of each component by the length of the vector. The formula would look like this:

$$Vnorm = [\frac{Vx}{length(V)}, \frac{Vy}{length(V)}, \frac{Vz}{length(V)}]$$

So if you normalize the vector T = [6 16 3] you would get

$$Tnorm = [\frac{6}{lenght(T)} \quad \frac{16}{lenght(T)} \quad \frac{3}{lenght(T)}]$$

$$Tnorm = [\frac{6}{17.3494} \quad \frac{16}{17.3494} \quad \frac{3}{17.3494}]$$

$$Tnorm = [0.345834 \quad 0.922225 \quad 0.172917]$$

This is a vector with the exact same direction as [6 16 3] but with a length that falls within the 0 to 1 range. RSL provides a built-in function that handles normalization quite efficiently. It follows the simple syntax normalize(vector V), which is internally calculated as follows:

$$Vnorm = \frac{V}{length(V)}$$

Dot and Cross Product

We finally arrive at what are perhaps the most used mathematical expressions in computer graphics. These two operations are very useful because they allow you to measure the angle between two vectors (dot product) and to create a vector that is parallel in a third dimension to the two provided vectors. Of these two, the most useful to a shader writer is the dot product (identified in RSL with a period (.) between two vectors). A dot product is calculated as follows:

$$A.B = A_x * B_x + A_y * B_y + A_z * B_z$$

Because of the law of cosines, the dot product between two vectors can also be defined with this statement:

$$A.B = |A||B|\cos(angle)$$

This tells us that the dot product is equal to the multiplication of the length of A by the length of B by the cosine of the angle between the two vectors. Since most of the time we will be dealing with normalized vectors, which by definition have a length of 1, then we can state that A.B = cos(angle). The dot product also gives us the cosine of the angle between two vectors. If the two vectors are parallel and point toward each other, the angle between them is 0, and the dot product returns 1 (cosine of 0 – 1). If the vectors are perpendicular to each other with an angle of 90 degrees between them, then the dot product will be 0 (cosine of 90 = 0). Based on these two cases, we can say that the dot product returns a *facing ratio* value, where if two vectors face each other the value is 1, and as the vectors start pointing away, the value decreases all the way to –1 when the vectors are parallel but point in different directions. It is for this reason that this operation is constantly used in illumination functions such as a Lambertian diffuse model, which uses the dot product of the surface normal N and the light vector L to calculate light contribution. Figure 5.26 illustrates this concept.

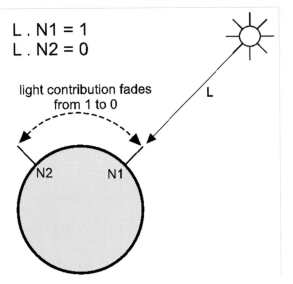

Figure 5.26 The value of the light contribution fades from N1 to N2.

Another important property of the dot product is that when you apply it to a single vector A.A, the result will always be the square of the length of that vector. It is for this reason that RSL replaced the $x^2+y^2+z^2$ from the length equation $length=\sqrt{x^2+y^2+z^2}$ of the length() function with A.A. Here is an example using

```
T = [2 3 2].T.T = 2×2+3×3+2×2
T.T = 17
```

So to calculate the length of a vector all you need to do is solve $\sqrt{A.A}$.

One final manipulation to the dot product rule allows us to calculate the angle between the two vectors. Remember that the position of the vector is not really important. In fact, vectors have no position, only direction, so measuring the angle between two vectors can be done regardless of where the origin of the vector is, as long as both vectors are defined in the same coordinate system. Using simple algebra, we can manipulate the dot product formula to give us the angle between the two vectors:

$$angle=\arccos(\frac{A.B}{|A||B|})$$

As you can see, the dot product operation can be used to gather a lot of information about vectors, which is why it is so important to understand its properties.

A cross product is another important operation that can be performed within two vectors. When performing a cross product operation (identified in RSL with a ^), the result will be a vector that is perpendicular to both supplied vectors with a length (or magnitude) equal to the area of the parallelogram they span. What this means is that by applying the cross product to any two vectors that are not parallel to each other, we will get a vector that is parallel to the plane described by the original two vectors. The most common use for this operation in computer graphics is to find the rendering normal of surfaces and to find the normal to any given plane in space. The vector product is calculated with the following formula:

$$A \times B = [(A_y * B_z) - (A_z * B_y), (A_z * B_x) - (A_x * B_z), (A_x * B_y) - (A_y * B_x)]$$

Let's look at how this operation is applied to get the surface normal. Assume we have a flat polygonal (or NURBS) grid. This grid lies flat on the XY plane. If the grid is only one unit big with one corner touching the origin and the other at (1,1,0), we know it lies in a plane defined by the two vectors $Sx(1,0,0)$ and $Sy(0,1,0)$. Let's apply the cross product to see if indeed we get the surface normal to our grid.

$$Sx \times Sy = [(0*0) - (0*1) \quad (0*0) - (1*0) \quad (1*1) - (0*0)]$$
$$Sx \times Sy = [0 \quad 0 \quad 1]$$

As you can see, the surface normal of a flat grid that lies on the XY plane is always pointing to Z. Figure 5.27 represents a cross product operation.

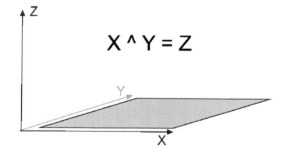

Figure 5.27 Graphic representing a cross product.

Reflections and Refractions

The last of the most popular operations applied to vectors are reflections and refractions. Reflections are the rays that bounce away from a surface based on the point of view. A good example of reflection is a shiny surface, a mirror, and polished metal. The rays that go through a surface and in the process are bent into a direction vector are refractions. Common examples of objects that demonstrate refraction are a glass of water and a piece of solid crystal such as an ashtray.

A reflection is calculated using the following formula:

$$R = I - 2*(I.\hat{N})*\hat{N}$$

Where I is the incidence vector, a vector that travels from the eye to the surface point, and is the normalized surface normal. RSL defines the built-in function reflect(), which has the following syntax:

```
vector reflect( vector I,N)
{
    return I - 2 (I.N)*N;
}
```

You can use the output of reflect() to do an environment texture lookup with environment() or to look up a raytraced reflection with trace(), among other things. Figure 5.28 demonstrates a sphere using the reflect() call.

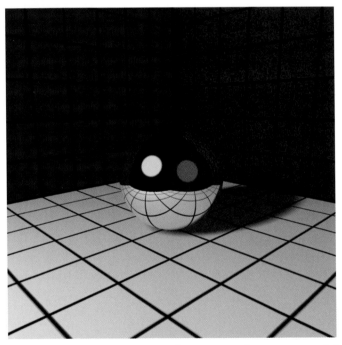

Figure 5.28 Surfaces with pure reflections give the appearance of chrome.

The refraction vector is another very important ray that is essential to simulate effects such as an object made of glass or a glass of water. The refraction vector is also referred to as the *transmission vector*, and in most RenderMan shaders, people use the letter T to identify the variable. The refraction vector is somewhat harder to compute than a reflection, but it is still doable with simple math. The formula for refraction is as follows:

$T = eta * I ? ??1 - eta^2 * ?1 - ?I.N ?? eta * ?I.N ?* N$

This could be simplified by computing each term into a set of variables:

$IdotN = I.N$
$cos1 = ?1 - eta^2 ?1 - ?IdotN??$
$T = eta * I ? ?cos1 - eta * IdotN ?* N$

RSL provides a refract() built-in function that can be used whenever you need to calculate the refracted ray. The refracted ray can be used to do an environment map lookup or in any raytracing function. The refract() function has the following syntax:

```
vector refract( vector I, N; float eta )
{
    float IdotN = I.N; float k = 1 - eta*eta*(1 - IdotN*IdotN);
    return k < 0 ? (0,0,0) : eta*I - (eta*IdotN + sqrt(k))*N;
}
```

I is the incidence vector, and N is the surface normal. eta is a float value that is the ratio of the index of refraction in the volume containing the incident vector to that of the volume being entered, this value determines how much the ray will be bent as it goes through the rendering surface. Figure 5.29 demonstrates the effect of refract().

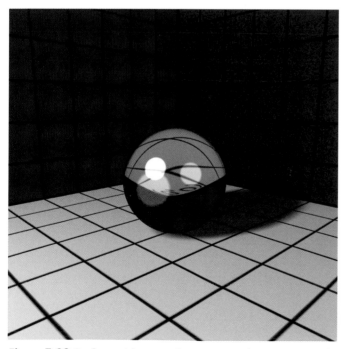

Figure 5.29 Surfaces with pure refractions give the appearance of glass.

The following are the refraction indexes for common materials:

- Vacuum   1.00000 (exactly)
- Air (STP)   1.00029
- Acetone   1.36
- Alcohol   1.329
- Crown Glass   1.52
- Crystal   2.00
- Diamond   2.417
- Emerald   1.57
- Ethyl Alcohol   1.36
- Flourite   1.434
- Fused Quartz   1.46
- Heaviest Flint Glass   1.89
- Heavy Flint Glass   1.65
- Glass   1.5
- Ice   1.309
- Iodine Crystal   3.34
- Light Flint Glass   1.575
- Liquid Carbon Dioxide   1.20
- Polystyrene   1.55
- Quartz 1   1.644
- Quartz 2   1.553
- Ruby   1.77
- Sapphire   1.77
- Sodium Chloride (Salt) 1   1.544
- Sodium Chloride (Salt) 2   1.644
- Sugar Solution(30%)   1.38
- Sugar Solution (80%)   1.49
- Topaz   1.61
- Water (20 C)   1.333

To get the proper eta value just divide 1.00029 (air IOR) by the IOR of the material, so the eta of glass is 0.66686. Another way to calculate the refracted ray is through the use of the fresnel() function (pronounced freh-nel). The fresnel() function is somewhat more complicated because it allows you to calculate several interesting values with one function. It is an essential function to re-create the appearance of certain materials such as shiny plastics. The fresnel() function makes a surface more reflective as the viewing ray hits the surface point at a perpendicular angle in relation to the surface normal. The more perpendicular (or glazing) the angle at which the ray hits the surface, the more reflective the surface becomes. The fresnel() function has the following syntax:

```
void fresnel( vector I, N; float eta, Kr, Kt [; output vector R, T] )
```

I is the incidence vector, N is the surface normal, eta, Kr, and Kt are floats, where eta is the index of refraction that will affect the ray. The variables Kr and Kt will store the values that control how much the reflection (Kr) and the refraction (Kt) will increase as the vector I hits the surface at glazing angles. The optional vector parameters R and T allow fresnel() to return the reflection vector (R) and the refraction or transmission vector (T). Figures 5.30 and 5.31 demonstrate the effect of fresnel().

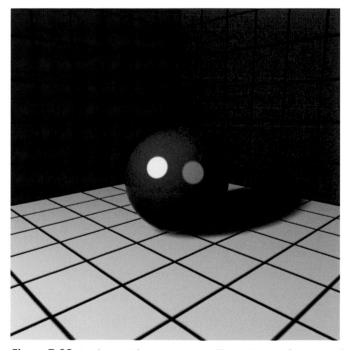

Figure 5.30 A sphere with a fresnel() effect using a refraction index of 1.5. The reflections are a lot stronger where the surface faces away from the camera.

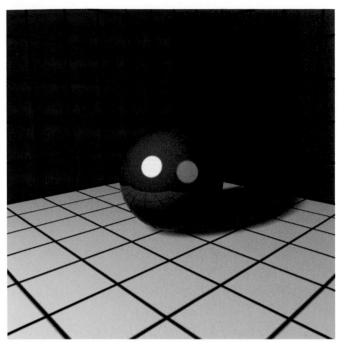

Figure 5.31 The same sphere and shader with a refraction index of 2.5. Note how the reflections are stronger where the sphere faces the camera.

Color Math

Color manipulation is a huge part of shader development. You will constantly run into situations in which representing a color in a different space can make your task a lot easier. You might also need to multiply, add, and subtract colors to achieve the result you are seeking, so you need to be able to manipulate colors and know what the results will be. In this section we will go through the theory of color math and present functions for all key operations that can be applied to two colors.

Color Theory and Spaces

Color. What is it? What is the difference between red and blue? To understand how color works, we first need to take a close look at the physical properties of light. Sometime during 1665 or 1666, Sir Isaac Newton discovered that sunlight passing through a glass prism would be broken down into what he named "a spectrum of colors." The spectrum of colors is made up of all colors, ranging from red to violet. That is what happens when we see a rainbow; it is the sunlight being bent through mist in the air, which acts as a prism. When light shines on an object, that object will usually absorb a certain amount of color from the spectrum. The colors that are not absorbed are reflected into the environment. It is the reflected color that our eyes see, giving the object its perceivable color. An object that seems red absorbs every color but red. A white object reflects all the colors from the spectrum, and a black object absorbs them all. That's why black objects heat up a lot faster and more intensely than white objects when exposed to sunlight.

There are several ways that all colors can be generated from a set of primary colors. In additive colors such as light the primary colors are red, green, and blue (RGB), and in subtractive colors such as printing ink they are cyan, magenta, yellow, and black, which is represented with a k for key (CMYK). Figure 5.32 is a good example of how primary additive and subtractive colors are combined.

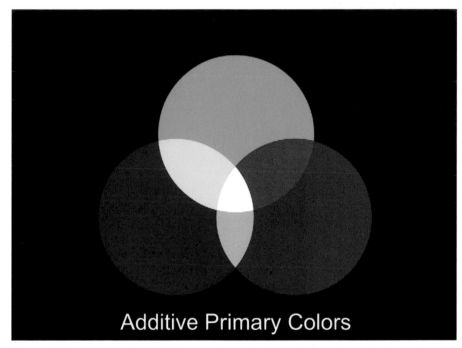

Additive Primary Colors

Figure 5.32 Primary colors and their combinations for additive colors and subtractive colors.

Color in RenderMan is by default stored in an RGB (red, green, and blue) space with a floating-point precision. An RGB image is made up of three channels, each storing a value that when added to the other channels creates a final color. Most images on the Internet or that you take with a typical digital camera are 8-bit images, which can store up to 256 levels for each of the three channels that make up color. In an RGB/8-bit image, a value of (0,0,0) represents black and (255,255,255) represents white. This is enough levels for day-to-day digital images, but for images that will be used in film, VFX, or animation, 256 levels is usually not enough. For this reason, RenderMan calculates color values as floating-point values, which means that each channel can have values with up to six decimal points. This provides more than enough values to represent all the colors you might need.

In float values, black will be represented as (0,0,0) and white as (1,1,1). Note that floating-point precision images are not limited to values between 0 and 1. You can easily compute an image with a value of (10,10,10). This image will still seem white to the naked eye, but if that value is stored in the final image, it could create problems or save a shot when the image moves into compositing.

Add, Subtract, Divide, and Multiply

The most basic mathematical operations that can be performed on two elements are addition, subtraction, division, and multiplication. When these operations are applied to color values (which are represented as a three-element array), the math will be performed just as it is with points, normals, and vectors, meaning that the operation will be performed on each component of color 1 against the same component of color 2. Adding (0.5,0.4,0.1) to (0.3,0.2,0.3) will result in a color with the values of (0.8,0.6,0.4).

Color multiplication behaves the same way. Since addition and multiplication are commutative operations, the order of the elements is not important. Subtraction and division are not commutative; in subtraction the second element will be subtracted from the first, and in division the first element will be divided by the second.

```
(0.7,0.5,0.8) - (0.5,0.4,0.1) = (0.2,0.1,0.7)
(0.9,0.4,0.6) / (0.3,0.2,0.3) = (3,2,2);
```

You must be careful when performing any of these simple operations because you can very easily end up with colors that are beyond the 0 to 1 range. These are not illegal colors, so if you compute them and let your renderer save them into the image, you will have to deal with the image in compositing. Here are the typical results when applying these operations to two colors.

Addition: The color will be brighter and a mix of both colors, and the color will seem washed out. Values can easily go over 1.

Subtraction: The color will be darker and will seem like a dirty, foggy shade. Values can easily end up being negative values.

Multiplication: The color will be darker, as if both colors have been filtered together.

Division: The color will usually be white, with values beyond 1.

Color to Float

The RenderMan standard provides a default built-in method for handling float to color conversions. In such cases, the shader compiler will duplicate the passed value into all three necessary channels to create a color. So something like this

```
color white = 1;
```

will internally be stored as color white = (1,1,1). However, RenderMan does not provide a default way to convert a color to a float. When you try to compare two colors in an if statement, you will run into a shader compiling error. Most colors tend to be varying, and using a varying variable in any type of conditional statement or in a looping statement can generate a lot of problems, not to mention the negative effect it has on performance. For this reason we will create our own "color to float" conversion function.

If you think about how color is represented through three float values, you understand that you can get the average float value of the color by adding its three components together and then dividing that value by 3. This is the simplest way to convert a color value to a float.

We will present two ways of doing the conversion. The first is an RSL function, and the second one is a CPP macro. For these implementations we are using the new array notation to access each individual color channel. If your renderer does not support this new RSL feature, you can use the component (comp()) notation.

```
float  color2float (color col){
   return (col[0]+col[1]+col[2])/3;}
```

```
#define COLOR2FLOAT(x)          (x[0]+x[1]+x[2])/3
```

Advanced Color Mixing Operations

Anyone who has done any kind of image manipulation with Adobe Photoshop is probably familiar with the different layer blending modes that Photoshop offers to the user. Blending modes such as screen and overlay are very commonly used in image manipulation and digital painting. These blending modes are extremely useful, so we will proceed to create RSL functions for the most popular blending modes.

All of the blending mode functions presented in this book will use the following naming conventions:

- colorMode, where Mode is the description of the mode that the function performs.
- BaseMap represents the color value that will be at the bottom of the blend.
- Layer will be the color of the blending layer.
- LayerOpac represents the opacity value used to control the blend.

Throughout the development of these blending mode functions, we will use the image maps in Figures 5.33 and 5.34 as the color values to demonstrate the effects.

Figure 5.33 BaseMap.

Figure 5.34 Layer.

These functions are based on the works of Jens Gruschel (http://pegtop.net). We are grateful to him for allowing us to use his work.

colorOver()

The most basic of the blending modes is Over, a simple linear interpolation between BaseMap and Layer using the value of LayerOpac as a mixing value. The code uses the built-in function mix() to perform the operation. You could use mix() instead of colorOver() any time; we are just defining colorOver() mode for consistency. Figure 5.35 illustrates the output of using an Over operation.

```
/***********
* Over mode
* Over mode is a simple linear interpolation between the base map
* and the blending layer
********/

color colorOver(color BaseMap; color Layer; float LayerOpac){
```

Figure 5.35 colorOver() applied with a LayerOpac value of 0.5.

```
    return( color mix(BaseMap,Layer,LayerOpac));}
```

colorAdd(), colorSubtract(), and colorMultiply()

These three modes are pretty much the same as using the regular add, subtract, and multiply operators except that these operations allow you to use a mixing value that can be any float value, even an alpha or luminance map. The result of colorAdd() and colorSubtract() can be seen in Figures 5.36 and 5.37.

```
/**********
* Add mode
* Color add mode performs a simple color addition
**********/

color colorAdd(color BaseMap; color Layer; float LayerOpac){

    return BaseMap + (Layer * LayerOpac);}


/**********
* subtract mode
* Color subtract mode performs a simple color subtraction
**********/

color colorSubtract(color BaseMap; color Layer; float LayerOpac){

    return BaseMap + ((Layer-1)* LayerOpac);}
```

Figure 5.36 colorAdd().

Figure 5.37 `colorSubtract()`.

Notice that there is a small amount of extra code in the multiply function. This is done so that we can use a blending value to control the multiplication. First multiply the Layer color by the LayerOpac value. The effect of this operation is that Layer will be dimmed by the value of LayerOpac. If we multiply this value directly into BaseMap, the output of the multiplication will be a darkening of the whole texture based on the LayerOpac value (whenever there is a 0 in a series of multiplications, the result will be always be 0). This is not the desired effect. We want the multiplication of the two layers to be driven by LayerOpac, not to be darkened by it. We solve the problem by adding the inverted value of LayerOpac back into the multiplication of Layer and LayerOpac. Figures 5.38, 5.39, and 5.40 demonstrate what would happen if we didn't do the inversion at the end compared to what our colorMultiply function returns.

```
/*********
* Multiply mode
* Multiply mode performs as simple multiplication, taking into account the
* value of LayerOpac
*********/
```

```
color colorMultiply(color BaseMap; color Layer; float LayerOpac){

    return BaseMap * ((Layer * LayerOpac) + ( 1 - LayerOpac));

}
```

Figure 5.38 Direct multiplication with LayerOpac = 0.5.

Figure 5.39 Correct multiplication with LayerOpac = 0.5.

Figure 5.40 colorMultiply() with LayerOpac = 1.

colorDissolve()

Dissolve uses a random noise value to mix between the two supplied colors. Actually, it compares the value returned by the rand() lookup against the supplied LayerOpac value. If the value from rand is less, then the Layer color is used; if it is higher, the BaseMap color is used. The result is a noisy blend of Layer on top of BaseMap. The output of this function can be seen in Figure 5.41.

```
/******
* Dissolve
*
* Use the value of LayerOpac to randomly choose between Layer
* BaseMap
*
******/

color colorDissolve(color BaseMap; color Layer; float LayerOpac){
   color out;

   if (float random() < (LayerOpac))
      out = Layer;
   else
      out = BaseMap;

   return out;
}
```

Figure 5.41 `colorDissolve()` with `LayerOpac= 0.5`.

colorScreen()

`Screen` mode is probably one of the most useful blending modes in Photoshop. It can be thought of as inverted multiplication because both colors will be inverted, multiplied by each other, and then finally inverted once again to make the colors positive again. We need to do a little bit of trickery to get the `LayerOpac` value to have the right effect. Figure 5.42 illustrates `colorScreen()`.

```
/****
* Screen Mode
*
* Screen is almost the opposite of Multiply. Both layers are
* inverted, multiplied by each other and then the result is
* inverted one more time
*
*****/
color colorScreen(color BaseMap;color Layer; float LayerOpac){

    return 1 - ((1-BaseMap) * (1-Layer * LayerOpac));
}
```

Figure 5.42 `colorScreen()`.

colorOverlay()

The `Overlay` mode is a combination of `colorMultiply()` and `colorScreen()`. It uses the value of the blending layer to decide whether to multiply or to screen. If the value of the blending layer is greater than 0.5, then we multiply; if it is less, we screen. For this function we had to modify how we used the `LayerOpac` value so that when the opacity of the layer is set to 0, `BaseMap` remains unchanged as shown in Figure 5.43.

```
/****
* Overlay Mode
*
*   is almost the opposite of Multiply. Both layers are
* inverted, multiplied by each other and then the result is
* inverted one more time
*
*****/

color colorOverlay(color BaseMap; color Layer; float LayerOpac){
    float layerval= colorToFloat(Layer);
```

```
return (layerval > 0.5) ? (2 * BaseMap * Layer * LayerOpac)
        + BaseMap * (1-LayerOpac):
        1 - ((1-BaseMap) *  ( 1 - Layer * LayerOpac))*(2 - (1-
LayerOpac));
}
```

Figure 5.43 `colorOverlay()`.

colorDarken() and colorLighten()

The `Darken` blending mode produces visual results that are somewhat similar to the results of the `Multiply` mode, where a completely white layer won't change the background image, and a black layer will generate a black image output. However, the math used in this mode is very different from that used in `Multiply`. In `Darken` mode, both images are compared to each other pixel by pixel. If the value of the layer is smaller than the base, the base color is used; if not, the `Layer` color is used. Figure 5.44 illustrates the output of `colorDarken()`.

```
/****
* Darken Mode
* Both layers are compared to each other. If the layer is greater than
* the base then the base is used, if not then the layer is used
*****/
```

```
color colorDarken(color BaseMap; color Layer; float LayerOpac){

    float baseval = colorToFloat(BaseMap);
    float layerval= colorToFloat(Layer);

    return (baseval < layerval) ? BaseMap: Layer * LayerOpac +
                                        (BaseMap * (1-LayerOpac));
    }
```

Figure 5.44 colorDarken().

As it would be expected, colorLighten() does exactly the opposite of colorDarken(), as shown in Figure 5.45. All we need to do is switch the comparing term in the return line. The rest of the operation still applies.

```
/****
* Lighten Mode
* Both layers are compared to each other. If the layer is smaller than
* the base then the base is used, if not then the layer is used
*****/

color colorLighten(color BaseMap; color Layer; float LayerOpac){
```

```
float baseval = colorToFloat(BaseMap);
float layerval= colorToFloat(Layer);

return (baseval > layerval) ? BaseMap: Layer * LayerOpac +
                                  (BaseMap * (1-LayerOpac));
}
```

Figure 5.45 `colorLighten()`.

colorDifference()

Using the value from the top layer to invert the colors of the base layer results in a very interesting effect, reminiscent of those psychedelic posters from the 1960s and 1970s. I haven't used this mode that much, but I'm sure it can be handy while painting textures.

Here is how it works. We simply subtract the value of the layer from the basemap. We then apply an `abs()` function to the output; otherwise we would end up with negative values, which are usually not that useful. Since RSL's built-in `abs()` doesn't support colors, just floats, we will create a function that will allow us to return the absolute value of a color.

```
/*********
* colorAbs()
* Returns the absolute value of a color
********/
color colorAbs(color col){
   return color( abs(col[0]), abs(col[1]), abs(col[2])); }
```

Once again we must take into consideration the use of an alpha value to control the opacity of the blend. In this case it is very simple to implement the opacity. All we have to do is multiply the opacity value by the layer color before we subtract it from the base layer. This is what the final colorDifference() function will look like, followed by Figure 5.46, which is its output.

```
/*********
* Difference mode
* Returns the absolute value of the subtraction of layer from basemap
********/

color colorDifference (color BaseMap; color Layer; float LayerOpac){

      return colorAbs(BaseMap - (Layer * LayerOpac));}
```

Figure 5.46 colorDifference().

colorHardlight() and colorSoftlight()

These two blending modes are also very popular, and despite their associative names, internally they are very different from each other. Hardlight mode darkens the base layer where the blending layer is dark and lightens it where the blending layer is bright. It is somewhat of a mix between the Screen and Multiply modes. Softlight provides a similar visual effect but with a lot less intensity. The dark areas of the blending layer darken the base layer, but only a little bit.

As previously mentioned, Hardlight is a mix between colorMultiply() and colorScreen(). It is almost identical to colorOverlay() mode, with the difference that we switch when we multiply and screen. In Overlay we multiplied when the value of the blending layer was greater than 0.5. Hardlight is exactly the opposite, as shown in Figure 5.47.

```
/**************
 * Hardlight mode
 * Hardlight is pretty much the same as overlay but we reverse the condi-
tional
 * statement so that if the value of the blending layers is LESS than 0.5
 * we multiply and if it is larger we screen
 ********/
color colorHardlight(color BaseMap;color Layer; float LayerOpac){

    float layerval= colorToFloat(Layer);

    return (layerval < 0.5) ? (2 *BaseMap*Layer * LayerOpac) +
                         BaseMap * (1-LayerOpac):
                         1 - ((1-BaseMap) * ( 1 - Layer *
LayerOpac))*
                         (2 - (1-LayerOpac));

}
```

Figure 5.47 `colorHardlight()`.

`Softlight` mode produces a similar visual output to `Hardlight`, but the code is entirely different internally. The output is obtained through a series of operations that begins with a multiplication of the two layers. Then we add the base layer, which is multiplied by a screened blend layer. For simplicity we will use the `mix()` function to control the contribution of `LayerOpac` in this blend mode. Figure 5.48 shows the output of `colorSoftlight()`.

```
/**************
* Softlight mode
* Softlight generates an output similar to Hardlight but with a more subtle
* effect.
*********/

color colorSoftlight(color BaseMap; color Layer; float LayerOpac){
    color ctemp = BaseMap * Layer;

    return  mix(BaseMap,ctemp + (BaseMap * (1-((1-BaseMap)*
                        (1-Layer)) -  ctemp)),LayerOpac);
}
```

Figure 5.48 colorSoftlight().

colorDodge() and colorBurn()

The final pair of operations that we will introduce are Dodge (brighten) and Burn (darken). The brightening effect of Dodge is different from that attained by applying colorLighten(). The Dodge operation will increase the color value of the BaseMap based on the intensity of the blending layer. If the blending layer is black, then the Dodge operation has no effect. The final result is that a Dodge operation makes the BaseMap a lot more saturated and intense where the blending layer is bright.

colordodge() is calculated by dividing the color value of the BaseMap by the color value of the blending layer. As simple as it sounds, there are several things that we need to consider to have a finished colorDodge() function that will behave properly.

First we need to always beware of division by zero, which will result in rendering errors. We solve this problem by using a max() function. We then use a mix() function to control how much the layer is blended on top of the BaseMap. The division can easily return values that are beyond the 0 to 1 range, so we apply a clamp() function to make sure the function returns colors within the 0 to 1 range. Figure 5.49 shows the output of colorDodge().

```
/**********
 * Dodge mode
 * The Dodge mode is obtained by dividing the BaseMap by the inverse of the
 * Layer value.
 * NOTE - we must use a max() to prevent a division by zero which
 * would result in rendering errors.
 ***************/

color colorDodge(color BaseMap; color Layer; float LayerOpac){

    color ctemp = mix(BaseMap,BaseMap / max(1-Layer,color(0.00001)),
LayerOpac);

    return clamp(ctemp,color(0),color(1));
}
```

Figure 5.49 colorDodge().

Burn mode is similar in properties to Dodge mode, but instead of brightening the image where the blending layer is bright and having no effect where it is dark, Burn mode will darken the BaseMap where Layer is dark, and it will oversaturate the BaseMap where Layer is bright, as you can see in Figure 5.50. The calculation of Burn is very similar to Dodge except that we divide the inverse of the BaseMap by the blending layer, and the result of that division is inverted again to make a positive image.

```
/**********
* Burn mode
* The burn mode is obtained by dividing the inverse BaseMap by the
* Layer value and then inverting that result.
* NOTE - we must use a max() to prevent a division by zero which
* would result in rendering errors.
***************/
color colorBurn(color BaseMap; color Layer; float LayerOpac){
   color ctemp =  mix(BaseMap,1-((1-
BaseMap)/max(Layer,color(0.00001))),LayerOpac);

   return clamp(ctemp,color(0),color(1));
}
```

Figure 5.50 colorBurn().

There are many other ways to combine color values. There are also other blending modes that we will not cover because they are not used as often as those described here. Using the previously described modes as examples, it is very easy to create new blending modes using Jens Gruschel's Blend Modes page as a reference. The development of blending modes is left as an exercise for the reader.

6

Shader Design Methodology

Why Follow a Methodology?

Shader development is typically not difficult except when you are trying to devise very unique solutions that haven't been implemented before. In those cases, there might be a lot of reading, math, charting, and testing. For the average shader, most of these steps can be skipped, but even the simplest shaders require a certain level of planning and organization.

As stated in Chapter 3, "Shader Writing Process," there is usually a design phase involved in the development of the shader. That phase tells you what your goals are; without it you will be shooting in the dark. A methodology is not "what I need to do," it is "how am I going to do it?" It's good practice to follow a methodology when developing shaders, even if it is a weird, unorthodox methodology that only you understand. In this chapter I will explain certain development strategies that I personally find quite useful and that are used by many professionals I have met. They are based on a couple of documents published by Tony Apodaca at SIGGRAPH 1996 and Steve May's Web tutorial, RManNotes.

I will demonstrate these strategies using a watermelon shader as a subject. We will not write the shader at the moment. I will just point out the steps that might be taken to approach such a task. Here is the outline of your task:

> You receive instructions from your department head that you will be writing a watermelon shader. This shader will be applied to about 100 watermelons in a watermelon fight sequence, so you will need to go procedural because

they want to have each watermelon look a little different. There are mid close-ups in some shots, so the texture needs to be reasonably detailed. You have three days to complete the task.

With this information in hand, we are ready to approach our task. The description is pretty much your design requirements. Remember to be thorough with questions when you are assigned a shader. Will we ever see the inside part of the watermelon? If we do, then we are more than likely dealing with two different shaders because the inside of a watermelon has a completely different appearance and properties than the outer shell. If that is the case, you might want to discuss the issue with your supervisor, because three days to write both shaders might not be enough time. Your show development standards will probably provide you with the rest of the information you need, such as required AOVs, naming conventions, and so on. Once you know what you need to do, you can move over to perhaps the most important part of writing a good-looking shader, which is acquiring some reference.

Reference

Our first step is to gather reference on the subject we are about to try to create. Without reference, we will have to work from memory, and we are more than likely not going to have a good recollection of what we need to shade. It is like shooting in the dark—you have no clue where you are supposed to aim. Ask your department head for some artwork or references from the art or production design department. If they have paintings or clippings of what they are looking for, then you are pretty much done with your reference search, and you can go ahead and start planning how you are going to write your shader.

However, let's assume that for our particular element, the art department didn't generate any artwork, and your department head tells you to make it look just like any regular ol' watermelon. This happens more often than you can imagine and more than we shader writers prefer. The good side is that if there is no production design artwork, you have some artistic input and freedom, but the bad part is that you can end up going down a wrong path and spend valuable production time and effort on something that will ultimately not be approved. And you will have to start over on another path.

Regular ol' watermelons, huh? This could be a good excuse to take a nice long lunch break and head out to the local grocery store or farmer's market. Buy one or two watermelons and take them back to your office. Oh, and don't forget to get a receipt, since you could get reimbursed for those melons—after all, it is a work related expense. Give the watermelon a good inspection, touch it, and feel how lumpy it is. It would be a good idea to take a digital camera and take a number of pictures of the watermelon.

You could also go online and search for pictures of watermelons, but your understanding of what makes a watermelon look like a watermelon will be better if you have the watermelon in your hands. Besides, when you are done, you can cut up the watermelon and eat it with your friends at work, which is great on hot summer days. I went to a local farmer's market and took pictures of watermelons, shown in Figures 6.1 and 6.2. They are pretty high resolution, so for our example they will do just fine.

Figure 6.1 A bunch of watermelons.

Figure 6.2 Watermelon details.

Figure 6.1 gives you a good idea of what several watermelons look like when they are piled together. It also shows you the illumination component of the fruit and the variance in shape, color, and tone from one melon to another. Figure 6.2 provides a lot of detail of the different features and marks that identify a watermelon.

Make Your Efforts Count

After careful analysis of the pictures, you should be able to identify several key components of a watermelon's appearance. At this point, you must prioritize the features that you are about to put into your shaders. What is the most important feature of the watermelon (see Figures 6.3 and 6.4)?

Think of it this way: If you were allowed to use only two colors to represent the watermelon, what would let people know that this is a watermelon? Anyone with a decent eye for detail will tell you that what stands out the most from a watermelon is the big green stripes. If you took everything else out, even illumination, and left only those stripes, you could still tell it was a watermelon.

Figure 6.3 A real watermelon, filled with tons of small details.

Figure 6.4 A simplified sphere with green stripes. Is it still a watermelon?

This should be the first feature you tackle, and it should be where you put most of your effort. Illumination is another important component, so those two will be your main tasks. Illumination will more than likely be a simple plastic-like illumination model. If photorealism is the goal, then you will probably need to add a subsurface scattering component.

Since most of the illumination will be based on work that has been done already, you can quickly code a solution. This means that you will spend most of your time developing the green stripes.

Look at the watermelon a little closer and you will see several other features that are necessary if you want to replicate a photorealistic watermelon. Among those features are small darker green veins inside the dark green stripes, dark green veins within the light green areas, small nicks that are light in the center and dark on the edges, and small scratches. Once you have the stripes and the illumination, you can start adding those details and features that will be the icing on the cake, starting with the most prominent of those features.

Divide and Conquer

When developing shaders, you will usually find yourself writing some small utility shaders or test shaders and then production shaders. Test and utility shaders are usually small enough that you can tackle them in a sequential order based on what your design requirements are. Production shaders, on the other hand, tend to be a lot more complex, with tons of parameters, features, and functions. It is a task that can overwhelm even the most patient and experienced TD.

To face such a shader and keep your sanity (or at least part of it), you can use the tactic of "divide and conquer." This means to break down your shader into smaller tasks until the tasks are small enough that you can create them with relative ease. Creating these small tasks will make the development process a lot easier and a lot more fun as you get a sense of accomplishment as you finish each task. Here is an example of how you might break down the tasks for a shader to create a watermelon.

- Pattern
- Main green stripes
- Small dark veins within green stripes
- Small dark veins inside light green areas
- White spots, "nicks"
- Illumination
- Broad plastic modified by pattern
- sss component, if necessary

Layered Approach

Part of the divide and conquer methodology is the use of layers. Each feature or set of features usually lives as part of an identifiable set of layers. It is advisable to code your shader with a layered approach in which you will create a new layer and composite it on top of your current color. This approach is preferable to other approaches where you just compute different values and put them all together at the end.

The advantage of using a layered approach is that it reduces the number of variables needed for your shader. The more variables you have, the heavier your shader will be memory wise, and it will be more prone to errors and bugs. Another great advantage of using a layered approach is that it makes it very easy to keep track of where features are inserted into the final shader color.

There are times when you will have to break out of the layered approach, such as when you are computing a value that you will need for the color but that you also will need for the specular. You might need to save this value in a variable so that it is available to you further down the line without having to recompute the value.

When using a layered approach to writing shaders, you will need four main variables that will be overwritten and updated, as necessary. These variables will represent the current layer color, current layer opacity, the final surface color, and the final surface opacity. It is advisable to always use the same name for these variables in all your shaders; that way it will be easier to keep track of your layers. The following is a list of variables that I usually use for these values. You are welcome to use any variable names you feel comfortable with, but throughout this book we will use these four variable names.

Variable	Description
lc	Layer Color
lo	Layer Opacity
sc	Surface Color
so	Surface Opacity

All four of these variables are usually declared as varying color type. Over time I have found it a little more convenient to declare the layer opacity as a varying float instead of a color. This greatly simplifies using built-in blending functions such as mix(). Throughout this book, we will write several functions that will allow us to use a float or a color as a mixing value. The lc and lo variables are used to calculate the current layer opacity and color. Once the current layer has been calculated, the value can be composited with the final surface color and opacity. So in pseudocode, this is how you would use those variables.

```
/* Initialize Variables */
varying color lc, lo, sc, so;

/* Layer 1 */
lc = compute layer 1 color;
lo = compute layer 1 opacity;
sc = initialize surface color;

/* Layer 2 */
lc = compute layer 2 color;
lo = compute layer 2 opacity;
sc = composite lc using lo on top of sc;
```

As explained earlier, you need to put most of your effort into the most conspicuous feature of your pattern. This might not be the first layer you work on because layers are created and composited from the inner to the outermost layer. You could calculate your layers in different order if you want, but that requires creating more variables and defeats the purpose of using layers.

Shader Outline

Before you start writing the code for your shader, it is useful to write an outline within your source code. The shader outline is nothing more than a series of comments that explain the steps you are planning to take to create your shader. It is useful to write down details of how you are going to accomplish certain tasks. This will allow you to identify which parts you will code directly into your shader and which could be extracted into a reusable function for your shading library. An outline for our watermelon shader could look similar to this.

```
/************************
 *
 * watermelon.sl
 *
 * by Rudy Cortes
 ************************/
surface watermelon()
{
/** Layer 1 - Base color
 * Use a simple noise pattern to add variation to the base color */

/* Layer 2 - Dark green stripes - the "moneymaker" layer!
 * use an elongated noise pattern which stretches from pole to pole
 * use another noise field to perturb the s and t values*/

/* Layer 3 - Veins / Detail within the stripes
 * use the veins from a marble pattern that I saw out on the net. I
 * think it was Larry Gritz's marble shader from renderman.org*/

/* Layer 5 - Markings or spots
 * use similar algorithm to one found in apple shader by tom porter, sig-
graph 1992?*/


/* Illumination model - Use regular plastic and see how well we do*/

}
```

From this point on, it is just a matter of filling in the blanks. As you can see, I am listing certain features that I will borrow from other people's shaders. Knowing where to look and how to get the patterns you are looking for will become essential as a shader writer. I have three large binders of printed material from SIGGRAPH RenderMan courses, which are SIGGRAPH rendering papers, tips, tricks, and shaders I have found on the Internet that do interesting things. As I became more informed on Web technologies I created a wiki on my personal page, which I keep as an "online notepad." Wiki's are Web pages that can be edited directly on any Web browser. They are usually searchable and are quite convenient. There are tons of different free wiki distributions available on the Internet. To install a wiki, you will need to have your own Web page, though. If you are not that savvy with Web technology, then you can just get a blog on one of the many free blogging platforms out there. Try to get one that allows you to keep your posts private; that way only you can access the material. So whether you go digital or stay old school with printed paper, it is important to gather as much information as possible on shader writing and keep it handy.

Borrowing code is necessary and at times essential to writing shaders. Just remember to credit the author if you are going to use his code. Chances are that if the author made the code public, he or she doesn't mind people using it. What is infuriating is when others use your source code and claim it as their own. Writing shaders is too hard for us to try and reinvent the wheel, so as I have heard other shader writers say, "borrow, cheat, steal, do whatever you need to do to get that shader to work, but remember to credit the right people."

We will now dive into the development of the watermelon shader to demonstrate how to apply our shader design methodology. Note that we will cover several concepts and RSL functions that have not been discussed yet. These concepts will be covered in Chapter 12, "Procedural Patterns," so please don't be discouraged if you find yourself a bit confused with the code.

Layer 1—Base Color

The base color is probably the easiest thing you will have to tackle. First, you will pass a color that you will include in the shader's parameters and assign it to the surface color or `sc` for short. At this point, you start adding parameters to the shader and adding the shader's local variables. You need to figure out the appropriate color to use as a default for the shader's `baseColor` parameter. This can be done by loading the image into a photo editing program such as Photoshop and using the Eye Drop tool. Sampling the light green area gets a value of

143,155,107. RenderMan works on a 0 to 1 color range, while most image manipulation programs work on 0 to 255 (8 bits per channel images). To convert them, simply divide each of the numbers by 255, and you will get 0.56,0.6,0.41.

However, most watermelons don't have a flat color on the base, so let's break up the color a bit by using a noise function and then passing it to a spline call. To do this, you first transform the shading point from current space to shader space, which makes sure that the texture doesn't slide through the model if it is transformed. We will also multiply the shading point by the parameter baseColorFreq so that users can control how big the noise pattern is. Then you can add the parameter label to this transformation so that you can use the same shader to create unique watermelons.

You then calculate a simple noise function and pass it to smallnoise, which is the noise that will be passed to the spline function. Then you must create small variations of your base color. The last color, lightgre, receives a special addition without any blue so that the color becomes a bit yellowish. With your noise calculated and your colors defined, you can now use the spline call and pass it to sc. At this point you can also add the usual outputs for Oi and Ci and pass Oi * sc to Ci. If you compile this image and render a sphere with the surface applied to it, you will get something like the image shown in Figure 6.5.

```
/************************
 *
 * watermelon.sl
 *
 * by Rudy Cortes - Copyright 2004(c)
 ************************/

surface watermelon(
        color baseColor= color (0.56,0.6,0.41);
        float baseColorFreq = 2;
        float label = 0.5;
)
{
 /* Initialize shader variables */
 color sc;
 /************************
  * Layer 1 - Base color
  ************************/
 /* Transform P from "current" to "shader" */
 point Pshad = transform("shader", P) * baseColorFreq + label;
 /*calculate a very simple noise to drive the spline function */
 float smallnoise = noise(2 * Pshad);
```

```
/* create variations of the baseColor to pass it to the spline function*/
color dargre = baseColor - 0.025;
color midargre = baseColor - 0.0125;
color midgre = baseColor;
color midligre = baseColor + 0.0125;
color lightgre = baseColor + color (0.025,0.025,0);
/* use the spline function to color the base of the watermelon  */
sc = spline(smallnoise,dargre
              ,midargre
              ,midgre
              ,midligre
              ,midligre
              ,midgre
              ,midargre
              ,midgre
              ,midligre
              ,lightgre);

/* Illumination model - Use regular plastic*/
Oi = Os;
Ci = Oi * sc;
}
```

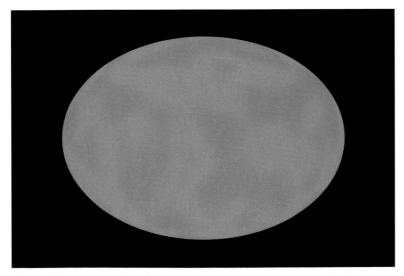

Figure 6.5 A watermelon shape with a simple noise variation applied to it.

Layer 2—Green Stripes

Let's now concentrate on the darker green stripes of the watermelon. This is perhaps the most important feature of the watermelon, so you should plan to spend a good deal of time on it. Looking at the reference pictures, you can see that the green stripes span and get pinched as they get closer to the poles of the fruit. So the built-in s,t coordinates of a sphere will work perfectly. As I think of possible ways to approach the stripe generation, I begin to feel inclined toward using a noise pattern that stretches across the surface from pole to pole. The noise needs to be stretched on the long direction of the watermelon, which on a quadratic sphere is equal to s. You can get the necessary effect by using a noise in the form of noise(25 * s , 0.1 * t) and passing it to the layer opacity variable, lo. Let's replace the number 25 with a stripeFreq parameter. You then use lo to control a smoothpulse() function, and you mix the colors with the mix() function. After making the appropriate changes to the code and rendering a sample image, you get the following (see Figure 6.6):

```
#include "patterns.h"
#include "noises.h"
surface watermelon(
                color baseColor= color (0.56,0.6,0.41);
        float baseColorFreq = 4;
        float label = 0.5;
                color stripeColor = color(0.35,0.45,0.31);
                float stripeFreq = 25;
        float stripeNoiAmp = 0.025;
        float stripeNoiLevels = 12;
        float stripeNoiFreq = 5;
                )
{
  /* Initialize shader variables */
  color sc,lc;
  float lo;
.............


 /*******************************
  *
  * Layer 2 - Dark green stripes
  *
  ******************************/
 /* compute base noise based on texture coords
  * This is a turbulence noise that uses gradual clamping
  * taken from Steve May's RmanNotes */
 float width = filterwidthp(Pshad);
```

```
float cutoff = clamp(0.5 / width, 0, stripeNoiLevels);
float f;
float turb =0;
for (f = 1; f < 0.5 * cutoff; f *= 2)
      turb += abs(snoise(Pshad * stripeNoiFreq * f)) / f;
float fade = clamp(2 * (cutoff - f) / cutoff, 0, 1);
turb += fade * abs(snoise(Pshad * f)) / f;

/* perturb s based on turb, add the label to control randomness*/
float ss = s + snoise(turb + 912) * stripeNoiAmp + label;
lc = stripeColor;
/* use a noise to create broad long noisy stripes */
lo = abs(snoisexy( stripeFreq * ss , 0.6 * t );
lo = smoothpulse(.1 .3,.74,.94,lo);
sc = mix(sc,lc,lo);

/* Illumination model - Use regular plastic*/
  Oi = Os;
  Ci = Oi * sc;
  }
```

Figure 6.6 Stripes applied to the shader, it's starting to look like a watermelon now.

Layer 3—Veins (Detail Within the Stripes)

Back in our shader outline, you identified small veins that are present mostly inside the green stripes. As mentioned before, you need to be resourceful and reuse as much code as you can. So where have I seen a shader with small veins before? I recall that there is a marble shader written by Larry Gritz available at the RenderMan Repository. I open the source code file and after a little digging I find what I need. Now you will calculate a new shading point noise field with a different scale and store it in Pshad (you don't need the old noise field anymore). You also calculate the filter width for Pshad; this is used for anti-aliasing, which we will cover sometime in the future. This is done with the two lines:

```
Pshad = label + detailFreq * transform ("shader", P);
float Pshadw = filterwidthp(Pshad);
```

You then reuse the stripeColor variable and create several variations of it. You build a new turbulence noise field turb and pass it to a spline function to create some small turbulent noise spots. Next, you mix the noise spots with the base color sc using a modified version of the layer opacity lo1 multiplied by a smoothstep() of turb. This will ensure that the detail only shows within the boundaries of lo1, which is a little wider than lo.

```
sc = mix (sc,stripeDetail, lo1 * smoothstep(0.1,.3,turb));
```

Now you will layer the small veins on top of the detail. You first use the previous noise field Pshad and add a vector fBm noise to it. You use a loop to calculate the value of veins, and then you run it through a smoothstep() to make the veins thinner and not as connected. Finally, you composite the surface color sc with a darker version of the stripeColor and use lo1 to restrict the veins to the stripes. You also add a new parameter detailFreq to control the scale of the noise for the small details (see Figure 6.7).

```
#include "patterns.h"
#include "noises.h"
surface watermelon(
                color baseColor= color (0.56,0.6,0.41);
        float baseColorFreq = 4;
        float label = 0.5;
```

```
            color stripeColor = color(0.35,0.45,0.31);
                float stripeFreq = 25;
        float stripeNoiAmp = 0.015;
        float stripeNoiLevels = 12;
        float stripeNoiFreq = 5;
                float detailFreq = 20;
            )
{
  /* Initialize shader variables */
  color sc,lc;
  float lo;

..............
  /* use a noise to create broad long noisy stripes */
  float stripeOp = abs(snoisexy( stripeFreq * ss  , .6 * t ));
  /* create 2 vestions of layer opacity, one a bit thinner than the other
*/
  float lo1 =  smoothpulse(.1, .3,.74,.94,stripeOp);
  lo = smoothpulse(.05,.3,.74,.94,stripeOp);
  Sc = mix(sc,lc,lo);

  /********
   *
   * Layer 3 - Veins  / Detail within the stripes
   *
   ********/
    Pshad = label + detailFreq * transform ("shader", P);
    float Pshadw = filterwidthp(Pshad);
 /*
  * First calculate the underlying color of the substrate
  * Use turbulence - use frequency clamping*/
 /* create variations of the stripeColor to pass it to the spline function*/
    dargre = stripeColor - 0.035;
    midargre = stripeColor - 0.0125;
    midgre = stripeColor;
    midligre = stripeColor + 0.02;
    lightgre = stripeColor + color (0.04,0.035,.01);

    turb = 0.5 * turbulence (Pshad , Pshadw, 5, 2, 0.5);

    color stripeDetail = spline(turb
                ,dargre
                ,midargre
                ,midgre
```

```
                    ,midligre
                    ,lightgre
                    ,midligre
                    ,midgre
                    ,lightgre
                    ,midargre
                    ,midgre
                    ,midligre
                    ,lightgre
                    ,midargre);

  /* mix the stripedetail turbulent spots inside the stripes*/
  sc = mix (sc,stripeDetail, lol * smoothstep(0.1,.3,turb));


   /* Generate the veins */
   /* perturb the point lookup */
   Pshad += vector(35.2,-21.9,6.25) + 0.5 * vfBm (Pshad, Pshadw, 6,2, 0.5);
 /* Now calculate the veining function for the lookup area */
   float veins, freq, i;
   veins = 0; freq = 1;
   Pshad *= .75; // scale down the scale of Pshad
   for (i = 0; i < 4; i += 1) {
         turb = abs (filteredsnoise (Pshad * freq, Pshadw * freq));
         turb = pow (smoothstep (0.55, .98, 1 - turb), 30) / freq;
         veins += (1-veins) * turb;
         freq *= 2;
         }
   veins *= smoothstep (-0.1, 0.05, snoise((Pshad+vector(-4.4,8.34,27.1))));

   /* mix the veins  with the surface color */
   sc = mix (sc, stripeColor * 0.9, veins * lol);


............

/* Illumination model - Use regular plastic*/
   Oi = Os;
   Ci = Oi * sc;
   }
```

Figure 6.7 More detail added within the green stripes.

Illumination

Now let's move to the final part of our shader, the illumination. You will use a simple plastic illumination model that is made up of a diffuse() plus a specular() call. To control the diffuse, you will add a Kd parameter, and to control the specular, you will add Ks and roughness parameters. After making a couple of test renders, I find the values that give the best results, but the watermelon's specular highlight looks way off. Adding some bump mapping will make the specular highlights break up a little bit and give the surface a more uneven appearance. The bump is created by calculating a new normal with the following code:

```
float bumpnoise = noise(Pshad * 0.45);
Nn = normalize(calculatenormal(P + Nn*bumpnoise * Km));
```

Km is a new shader parameter that controls the height of the bump. Here is the final complete shader source code followed by two images that demonstrate the effect that the bump has on the surface (see Figures 6.8 and 6.9).

```
#include "arman/patterns.h"
#include "arman/noises.h"

surface watermelon(
        float Kd = 1;
            float Ks = 0.4;
            float roughness = 0.3;
            float Km = 0.012;
```

```
            color baseColor= color (0.56,0.6,0.41);
            float baseColorFreq = 4;
            float label = 0.5;
            color stripeColor = color(0.35,0.45,0.31);
            float stripeFreq = 25;
            float stripeNoiAmp = 0.015;
            float stripeNoiLevels = 12;
            float stripeNoiFreq = 5;
            float detailFreq = 20;
)


{
 /* Initialize shader variables */
  color sc,lc;
  float lo;


 /***********************
   *
   * Layer 1 - Base color
   *
   ***********************/


 /* Transform P from "current" to "shader" */
 point Pshad = transform("shader", P) * baseColorFreq + label;


 /*calculate a very simple noise to drive the spline function */
 float smallnoise = noise(2 * Pshad);


 /* create variations of the baseColor to pass it to the spline function*/
 color dargre = baseColor - 0.035;
 color midargre = baseColor - 0.0125;
 color midgre = baseColor;
 color midligre = baseColor + 0.02;
 color lightgre = baseColor + color (0.05,0.055,.01);


 /* use the spline function to color the base of the watermelon */
 sc = spline(smallnoise,dargre
        ,midargre
        ,midgre
        ,midligre
```

```
            ,midligre
            ,midgre
            ,midargre
            ,midgre
            ,midligre
            ,lightgre);


/*******************************
 *
 * Layer 2 - Dark green stripes
 *
 *******************************/

 /* compute base noise based on texture coords
  * This is a turbulence noise that uses gradual clamping
  * taken from Steve May's RmanNotes */

float width = filterwidthp(Pshad);
float cutoff = clamp(0.5 / width, 0, stripeNoiLevels); //4 = maxfreq
float f;

float turb =0;
for (f = 1; f < 0.5 * cutoff; f *= 2)
  turb += abs(snoise(Pshad * stripeNoiFreq * f)) / f;

float fade = clamp(2 * (cutoff - f) / cutoff, 0, 1);
turb += fade * abs(snoise(Pshad * f)) / f;

 /* perturb s based on turb, add the label to control randomness */
float ss = s + snoise(turb + 912) * stripeNoiAmp + label;

 lc = stripeColor;
 /* use a noise to create broad long noisy stripes */
 float stripeOp = abs(snoisexy( stripeFreq * ss  , .6 * t ));
 float lo1 =  smoothpulse(.1, .3,.74,.94,stripeOp);
 lo = smoothpulse(.05,.3,.74,.94,stripeOp);


sc = mix(sc,lc,lo);


/********
 *
```

```
 * Layer 3 - Veins  / Detail within the stripes
 *
 *********/


 Pshad = label +  detailFreq * transform ("shader", P);
 float Pshadw = filterwidthp(Pshad);

/*
 * First calculate the underlying color of the substrate
 * Use turbulence - use frequency clamping*/

 /* create variations of the stripeColor to pass it to the spline func-
tion*/
 dargre = stripeColor - 0.035;
 midargre = stripeColor - 0.0125;
 midgre = stripeColor;
 midligre = stripeColor + 0.02;
 lightgre = stripeColor + color (0.04,0.035,.01);

 turb = 0.5 * turbulence (Pshad , Pshadw, 5, 2, 0.5);


 color stripeDetail = spline(turb,dargre
             ,midargre
             ,midgre
             ,midligre
             ,lightgre
             ,midligre
             ,midgre
             ,lightgre
             ,midargre
             ,midgre
             ,midligre
             ,lightgre
             ,midargre);

   sc = mix (sc,stripeDetail, lo1 *  smoothstep(0.1,.3,turb));


  /* perturb the point lookup */
   Pshad += vector(35.2,-21.9,6.25) + 0.5 * vfBm (Pshad, Pshadw, 6, 2, 0.5);
```

```
/* Now calculate the veining function for the lookup area */
float turbsum, freq, i;
turbsum = 0;   freq = 1;
Pshad *= .75; // scale down the scale of Pshad
for (i = 0;   i < 4;   i += 1) {
   turb = abs (filteredsnoise (Pshad * freq, Pshadw * freq));
   turb = pow (smoothstep (0.55, .98, 1 - turb), 30) / freq;
   turbsum += (1-turbsum) * turb;
   freq *= 2;
  }
turbsum *= smoothstep (-0.1, 0.05, snoise((Pshad+vector(-
4.4,8.34,27.1))));

   sc = mix (sc, stripeColor * 0.9, turbsum * lo1);


 /* Layer 5 - Markings or spots */

 /* Illumination model - Use regular plastic*/
   normal Nn = normalize(N);
   vector V = -normalize(I);
   float bumpnoise = noise(Pshad * 0.45);

   Nn = normalize(calculatenormal(P + Nn*bumpnoise * Km));

 Oi = Os;
 Ci = Oi * sc * (diffuse(Nn) * Kd) + specular(Nn,V,roughness)*Ks ;
}
```

Figure 6.8 The watermelon with diffuse and specular but no bumpy noise—very bland looking.

Figure 6.9 The watermelon with a little bit of bump added to it—it looks much better now.

There are several other changes and enhancements you can do to this shader to make it look better, but you must first look at the individual parts of shader development, such as illumination loops and pattern generation. If this shader was a bit over your head, feel free to come back to it once you have read the rest of the book and everything should make sense then.

Additional Reading

The following SIGGRAPH papers are extremely useful, and you should try to read all of them. Some of the material might be old and a bit outdated, but even if the outlined techniques are no longer relevant, they can open your eyes to the history of high-end production rendering, not to mention that sometimes old techniques can become quite useful when combined with new techniques. Most of these files are available at either the ACM SIGGRAPH Website or at renderman.org, the oldest free RenderMan resource Website created and maintained by Tal Lancaster.

"Writing RenderMan Shaders"—SIGGRAPH 1992 Course 21. Tony Apodaca and Darwin Peachey

"Using RenderMan in Animation Production"—SIGGRAPH 1995 Course 4. Tony Apodaca, Larry Gritz, Tom Porter, Oren Jacob, MJ Turner, Joe Letteri, Ellen Poon, Habib Zargarpour

"Advanced RenderMan: Beyond the Companion"—SIGGRAPH 1998 Course 11. Tony Apodaca, Larry Gritz, Ronen Barzel, Antoine Durr, Clint Hanson, Scott Johnson

"Advanced RenderMan 2: To RI_INFINITY and Beyond"—SIGGRAPH 2000 Course 40. Tony Apodaca, Larry Gritz, Tal Lancaster, Mitch Prater, Rob Bredow

"Advanced RenderMan 3: Render Harder"—SIGGRAPH 2001 Course 48. Tony Apodaca, Larry Gritz, Matt Pharr, Christophe Hery, Kevin Bjorke, Lawrence Treweek

"RenderMan in Production"—SIGGRAPH 2002 Course 16. Tony Apodaca, Larry Gritz, Matt Pharr, Dan Goldman, Hayden Landis, Guido Quaroni, Rob Bredow

"RenderMan, Theory and Practice"—SIGGRAPH 2003 Course 9. Dana Batali, Byron Bashford, Chris Bernardi, Per Christensen, David Laur, Christophe Hery, Guido Quaroni, Erin Thomson, Thomas Jordan, Wayne Wooten

"RenderMan for Everyone"—SIGGRAPH 2006 Course 25 . Rudy Cortes, Hal Bertram, Tal Lancaster, Dan Maas, Moritz Moeller, Heather Pritchett, Saty Raghavachary

Another fantastic resource is the Pixar graphics library available at http://graphics.pixar.com/. This is a Website where the folks at Pixar publish all of their papers and presentations. The information on that Website is gold to a RenderMan TD, and there are papers there that date back to 1982 when the Cook-Torrance reflectance was introduced, as well as the original paper where the REYES rendering architecture was presented. Thanks a lot to Pixar for sharing the knowledge.

PART III

BASIC SHADING

7

Displacement and Surface Shaders

Defining a three-dimensional object usually involves two stages. The first is the surface or geometric modeling, which involves generating and manipulating points from a polygon, subdivision, or NURB surface. At the end of this stage you have a complete 3D model that will more than likely look like gray plastic. No matter how impressive or detailed your model is, it will not jump off the screen and cause anyone other than modelers to be impressed.

The second part of the process is appearance modeling, also referred to as shading, texturing, or look development. For some reason, some artists think that texturing can be accomplished with a couple of texture maps downloaded from the Internet and slapped onto the diffuse, specular, and bump channels. Then they are surprised when their gorgeous model looks bad, and no amount of lighting makes their object look as good as those CG elements in VFX shots in films or those frames in CG animation.

The truth is that most studios know that it usually is necessary to spend as much time texturing an object as is spent modeling. If someone spends two weeks modeling a fantastic cargo ship, why would he spend only a day or two texturing the ship and take the sparkle off a beautiful model? The amount of time spent on a model is usually related to the amount of screen time it will have, and as such you need to devote about the same amount of time on texturing the object.

When modeling the appearance of an object, you will usually be dealing with displacement and surface shaders. Once in a while, you will need to use an internal volumetric shader to help with some complex visual appearances. There are certain renderers that allow surface shaders to perform displacements, and others will take any displacement operation inside a surface shader and compute it as a bump. It is advisable to always use a displacement shader for either displacement or bump. The reason for this is that in production there are usually tons of pre-rendering maps, such as shadow maps, that need to be generated before a final image is rendered. For some of these shadow passes, replacing a complex surface shader with a constant white shader can greatly reduce the rendering time. Sometimes, it could be beneficial to replace the displacement in a scene, such as when rendering an object that has blurry reflections. You might think that spending all that time optimizing a scene is a waste of time, but it makes a huge difference when you are rendering a frame in film resolution that is taking over five hours to render.

One final argument for separating the displacement from the surface shaders is debugging of scenes. If an object is rendering with artifacts in a scene, and you suspect that the reason is that your normals are out of whack, it is quite easy to deactivate the displacement shader, either by telling the 3D app not to output it into the scene or by writing a simple Python or Perl script to comment out all displacements. If displacements were part of the surface shader, you would need to know the name of the parameter that controls the displacement amount for every shader used in the scene.

Displacements

Displacement shaders have the capability to modify the position of the shading points or the shading normal in the evaluated surface. It is extremely useful for adding fine detail that would be too time consuming to model and too resource intensive to manage. Most RenderMan-compliant renderers perform displacement on a micropolygon level, also referred to as *subpixel displacement* because micropolygons are smaller than a pixel in production quality images.

Contrary to other renderers that use triangles as their primary primitive and where using displacements has a great impact on performance and resources, rendering displacements on a micropolygon renderer has a significantly smaller impact on performance. In most triangle renderers, it is the user's job to pre-tessellate the geometry that will be displaced, or it is handled automatically by the renderer. Either way, the expense of rendering quickly climbs as you provide a lot more data to the renderer so your displacements will look good.

This is not the case in micropolygon renderers because the amount of data passed to the renderer is still the same. It's the renderer that performs the micropolygon dicing on that data. This operation happens whether or not you are displacing, so the added expense of displacement is only to move the point and to recompute the normal. The expense of rendering displacements is directly proportional to how large the displacements are. Larger displacements take a lot longer to render, as explained later in this chapter, so TDs should be careful not to overuse displacements as a modeling tool. If a feature can be modeled with relative ease, then it should be modeled and not displaced. Figures 7.1 and 7.2 show the difference between a model without and with displacements.

Figure 7.1 Model with no displacements.

Figure 7.2 Model with displacements; note all the extra detail.

Displacement or Bump

To novice 3D artists, the difference between a displacement and a bump is rather ambiguous. Most of them figure out rather quickly that displacements are a lot more expensive to render than bumps, so they rarely use displacements. Displacements are a key feature of REYES renderers and are embraced with open arms by shading TDs.

However, it should always be a TD's priority to get the desired look with the least amount of resources and CPU time, so using a bump is also very popular in look development. As explained earlier, the added cost to render displacements in a REYES renderer is usually not significant, but it is there, and a bump will always run faster than a displacement, especially if the displacements are large. Let's look at the difference between these two techniques and see where the added cost comes from.

Figures 7.3 and 7.4 represent the difference between displacement and bump. Figure 7.3 is a typical bump, and Figure 7.4 is a displacement. A bump is the result of changing the direction of the normals that will be used for shading calculation. The renderer uses these normals to perform illumination and reflection lookups, so the result is that the surface appears to have changed when in fact it hasn't. A displacement actually moves the micropolygon surface in a new direction, resulting in a need to recalculate the normals.

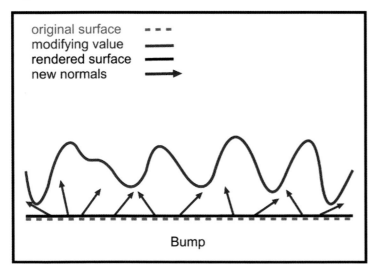

Figure 7.3 On a bump, the surface never changes, just the normals.

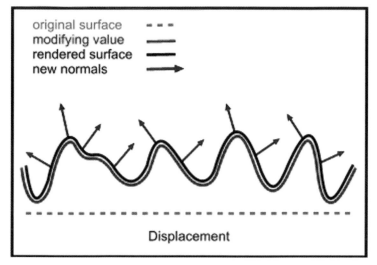

original surface   - - -
modifying value   ⎯⎯⎯
rendered surface   ⎯⎯⎯
new normals   ⎯⎯➤

Displacement

Figure 7.4 A displacement actually changes the surface.

Moving points adds extra expense to the rendering. The rendering time is also influenced by an extra hiding step performed after the displacement to ensure optimum memory efficiency. Rendering large numbers of displacements will also influence your rendering time, as you will force the renderer to evaluate the surface for longer periods of time.

The most obvious difference between bumped and displaced surfaces in a renderer is visible in the object's silhouette. While the bumped surface will remain true to the silhouette of the object being rendered (Figure 7.5), a displaced surface will change the contour of the object (Figure 7.6). If you push the bump of a surface to values that are too high, you might end up getting some artifacts or images that look strange. It is for this reason that we use a bump for small modifications of the surface and a displacement for larger ones. It is also advisable to use a bump on an object that will not be too close to the screen but still needs that extra detail. Let's write our first displacement shader so that we can get familiar with the necessary steps.

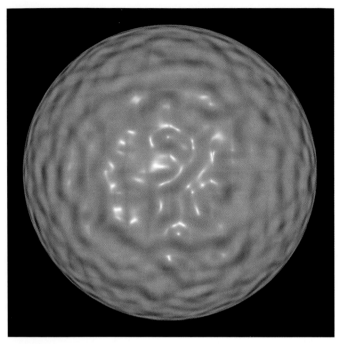

Figure 7.5 A sphere with only bump will appear as if it is lumpy, but the silhouette will remain a sphere.

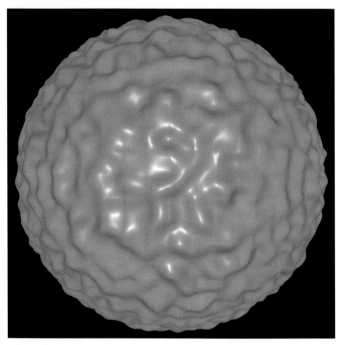

Figure 7.6 The same sphere with displacements. The geometry is modified and so is the silhouette.

A Simple Displacement Shader

We will start by writing a very simple displacement shader that applies 3D noise to any surface. We will enlarge this shader slowly until we have a fully usable shader. Let's start by creating the skeleton of our shader.

```
displacement d_RP_simplenoise()
{
    N = Ng;
}
```

Name the shader d_RP_simplenoise and the filename d_RP_simplenoise.sl. The compiled shader file will have the same name as the source file but with the extension used by the compiler. The d_RP_ identifies this file as a displacement shader, d, and the RP prefix identifies this shader as part of the shaders developed in this book. We use these conventions because eventually you will have tons of shaders, some of your own and some from other sources, and it will be important to be able to identify a shader without opening its source file or using sloinfo. sloinfo is a program that ships with PRM that outputs important information about a shader, such as the parameters and their default values. Every RenderMan renderer ships with a similar program. Please read the manual of your renderer to find out how to use such program.

We will start coding our little shader by adding a couple of parameters to control the strength of the displacement and the frequency of the noise.

```
displacement d_RP_simplenoise(
                        uniform float Km = 0.03;
                        uniform float noiFreq = 15;)
```

We will now add the lines of code that compute a 3D noise field aligned to the coordinate system of the shader.

```
    /* Local variables */
    float noi;

    /* Compute a noise field on the shader coordinate sys */
    noi = noise(transform("shader",P * noiFreq));
```

Now we will use the noi variable value to modify the position of P. Adding the normal N to the surface position P changes the location of P, effectively displacing the surface.

```
    /* Modify the position of P and recalculate the normal */
    P += normalize(N) * noi;
    N = calculateNormal(P);
```

We then add these shader parameters at the proper place, which gives us our final shader.

```
displacement d_RP_simplenoise_disp(
                                float Km = 0.03;
                                float noiFreq= 10;)
{
    /* Local variables */
    float noi;

    /* Compute a noise field on the shader coordinate sys */
    noi = noise(transform("shader",P * noiFreq));

    /* Modify the position of P and recalculate the normal */
    P += normalize(N) * noi * Km;
    N = calculatenormal(P);
}
```

Bump Shader

We will now convert the previous displacement shader into a bump shader. As mentioned earlier, bump shaders don't actually move the position of P, so we will be removing the P+= call and just do this operation when we call calculatenormal(). The final shader would be

```
displacement d_RP_simplenoise_bump(
                                float Km = 0.03;
                                float noiFreq= 10;)
{
    /* Local variables */
    float noi;

    /* Compute a noise field on the shader coordinate sys */
    noi = noise(transform("shader",P * noiFreq));

    /* Modify the position of P and recalculate the normal */
    N = calculatenormal(P + normalize(N) * noi * Km );
}
```

Since there is no assignment operator overriding the value of P, it is never moved, but the normals are calculated as though it were. That is the only difference between coding a displacement shader from a bump shader. The resulting effect of these shaders is demonstrated in Figure 7.5 for bump and Figure 7.6 for displacement.

Built-in Variables for Displacement Shaders

Table 7.1 lists the default built-in variables available to displacement shaders. As you can tell, there are fewer available than for a surface shader. That is because displacement shaders can alter only the surface position and normal, so variables such as surface color and opacity are not useful at all.

Table 7.1 Global Variables Available to Displacement

Name	Type	Storage Class	Description
P*	point	varying	Surface position
dPdu	vector	varying	Derivative of surface position along u
dPdv	vector	varying	Derivative of surface position along v
N*	normal	varying	Surface shading normal
Ng	normal	varying	Surface geometric normal
I	vector	varying	Incident ray direction
E	point	uniform	Position of the eye
u,v	float	varying	Surface parameters
du,dv	float	varying	Change in surface parameters
s,t	float	varying	Surface texture coordinates
ncomps	float	uniform	Number of color components
time	float	uniform	Current shutter time
dtime	float	uniform	The amount of time covered by this shading sample

*P and N are the only variables in this table that are both readable and writeable.

Keep in mind that the latest versions of the RiSpec and PRMan support very sophisticated methods of message passing between different shader types.

Large Displacements and Patch Cracks

When rendering displacements that are larger than the bounding box of the rendering buckets, it is very common to run into a rather nasty artifact called a *patch crack*. These cause your surface to display a lot of small slits cutting through it, breaking all continuity in the shading calculations. If the surface is displaced beyond the size of the displacement bound, then there is a good chance that the bucket will miss rendering the displaced surface since shaders begin to be evaluated once the render bucket is inside the bounding box of an object, resulting in areas where there is no geometry at all. The effects of large displacements are clearly visible in Figure 7.7.

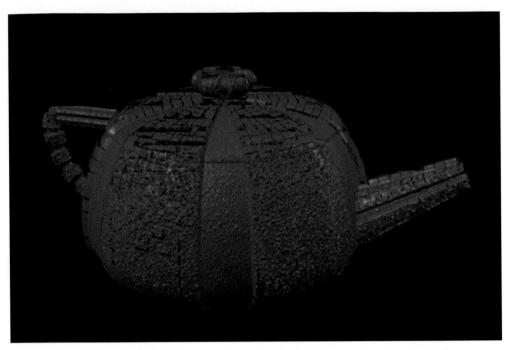

Figure 7.7 A teapot with bad displacement bounds ends up having small cracks all over the geometry.

This is not a rendering bug or shortcoming, but is, in fact, a user error. The renderer has no way of knowing how big the displacement will be before the rendering bucket enters the object's bounding box for the first time. It is only then that the renderer will load and run the shader and know how much to displace the surface.

The problem is that at such time it might be too late to run the shader. What if the displacement is big enough that the surface should have been picked up three buckets ahead of time? That's where the problem arises, and we get those nasty patch cracks, as demonstrated by Figure 7.8.

RenderMan provides a way to alert the renderer that it needs to start running the shader on a surface ahead of time. This is done with a call to the displacement-bound attribute, which allows you to define a new bounding area that will be considered by the shading engine. Large displacement bounds will result in slower rendering times because you are telling the renderer that your surfaces are bigger, therefore using more screen space and forcing the renderer to evaluate the shaders over a larger number of pixels. Figure 7.9 uses the same RIB file as 7.7 but with the displacementbound attribute properly set.

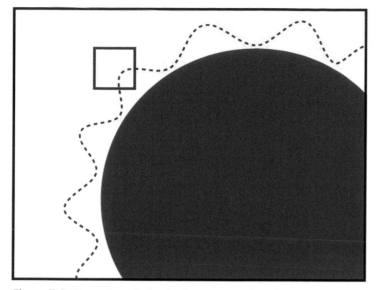

Figure 7.8 Illustration of why displacement cracks can occur.

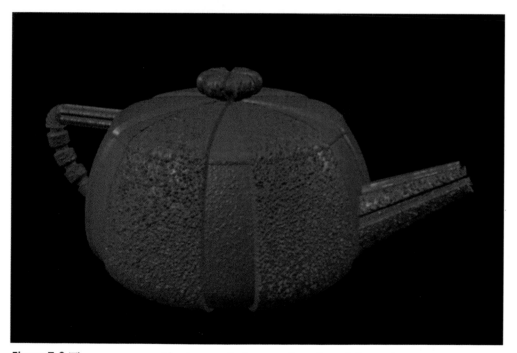

Figure 7.9 The same teapot with a correct displacement bounds, and the cracks are gone.

The `displacementbound` attribute is not officially part of the RiSpec, so renderer developers can choose to ignore it if they want or need to. Not being a standard attribute means that the syntax for declaring this attribute might be different from one renderer to another. The following is an example of how you would call this attribute in PRMan.

```
Attribute "displacementbound" "sphere [2] "coordinatesystem" ["world"]
```

Displacing Polygons

It is common knowledge that REYES renderers are not efficient when trying to render smooth surfaces using polygons. This is due to the large amount of data that must be included in the RIB file to represent a smooth surface. However, once in a while, you will need to use polygons, and you will probably attach a clever, work-of-art displacement shader to the surface just to see it become tessellated like a video game model at render time. This is not an artifact: It is the software doing what it's supposed to do and catching us off guard when we forget or overlook how shading is performed in REYES renderers.

Let's recap some information explained in Chapter 1. When a REYES renderer performs its shading calculations, it usually uses the shading normal N that is supplied by the modeling program to the RIB file. To get smooth shaded polygons, these normals are averaged on every point of the geometry (these normals are also referred to as vertex normals), and the spaces between the points are filled in with normals that are linearly interpolated between those vertex normals. Those averaged normals are used in all the lighting calculations, and the resulting effect is that the surface appears smooth or continuous, as demonstrated by Figures 7.10 and 7.11.

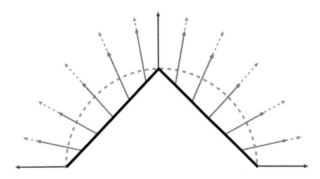

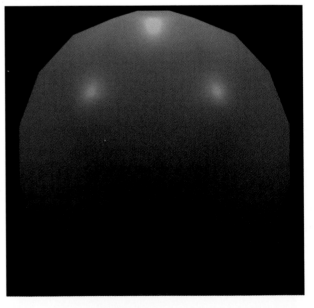

Figure 7.10 and Figure 7.11 Averaged normals and their interpolated values shade as if the surface were smooth.

If the modeling program doesn't provide the averaged vertex normals, then the renderer will automatically initialize N with the value of the geometric normal Ng. This value is the true geometric normal of the surface, which, if polygonal, will display a lot of breaks in continuity. The resulting effect is that the surface looks faceted, as demonstrated in Figures 7.12 and 7.13.

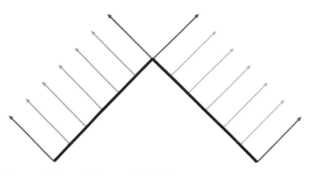

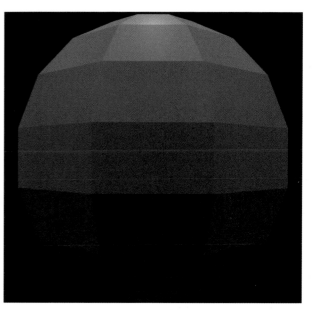

Figure 7.12 and Figure 7.13 When normals are not averaged out, the renderer computes the actual geometric normals, which for polygons will have breaks in continuity.

Why does your surface that was nice and smooth go all faceted after you add the displacement? If you remember, displacements are performed on the surface point, usually in the direction of the normal. If you provided averaged normals, the displacement will be in the direction of those interpolated normals, so why does it break?

The problem is not the direction in which the points are displaced, but the recalculation of the normals executed by calculateNormal(). Let's elaborate on this using Figure 7.14 as a reference. Remember that your polygon surface is made of flat polygons, and this is the position that the renderer uses to add or subtract displacement. The points will be displaced in the direction of the normal N, but since all the points of a face are part of a flat surface, the result is that the new surface positions might be perturbed, but they will be perturbed from a flat plane as the original surface was. The calculateNormal() call will use the tangents (or derivatives) at P to recalculate the normal, and because the tangents are part of a flat plane, the surface becomes faceted.

In the end, it is the calculateNormal() call that creates the problem. Even if you set the displacement to 0, it will still facet the polygons because you are overriding the smooth normals provided by the modeling application by the recalculated normals based on the current position of P.

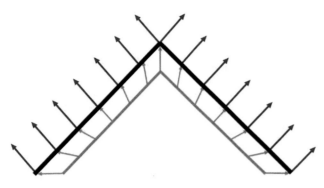

Figure 7.14 The original surface and normals (in orange), the displaced surface in black, and the recalculated normals in blue.

To get around this problem, we use a bit of simple math trickery. What we need to do is subtract the shading normal from the geometric normal. As stated in Chapter 5 when we reviewed vector math, subtracting two vectors will result in a third vector that closes a triangle shape. This vector contains the direction and distance that differentiates the two original vectors. We can store this vector in a variable Ndiff to later add it to the new recalculated normal. This will force the new normal to bend in the direction of the original shading normal by the amount stored in the Ndiff variable.

The result is that the faceting disappears from our polygonal object. Figures 7.15 through 7.17 demonstrate what happens when you apply this hack. In Figure 7.15, there is a square in the middle that is a zoom of the normals in the corner. The normal in magenta represents the geometric surface normal Ng, the orange normal represents the user-provided averaged normal, and the red normal represents the difference between those two normals.

On the surface, we see the recomputed normals in dashed gray and the final normals that are the result of adding Ndiff to the recomputed normals in blue. As you can see, those normals approximate a smooth surface again.

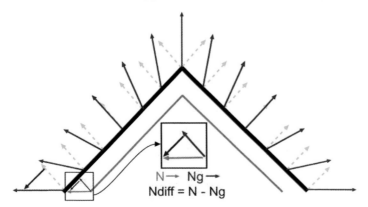

Figure 7.15 A graph of how our normals hack makes the surface seem smooth again.

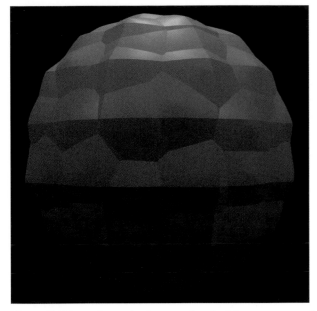

Figure 7.16 A polygonal sphere rendered without our normals adjustment trick.

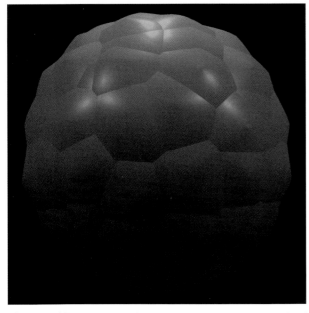

Figure 7.17 The same polygonal sphere with our normals adjustment trick.

Figure 7.17 shows the corrected. smooth-shaded, and displaced surface. Be aware that this hack will still show the facets on close examination and whether the displacement or bump is pushed to be larger. If you really need a smooth surface, the best solution is to switch to a smooth primitive, such as subdivision surfaces or NURBs. Here is a function implementation of the displaced polygon fix.

```
normal PolygonDisplaceFix(varying normal N; varying float amount) {
    extern point P;
    extern normal Ng;
    varying normal Ndiff;

    Ndiff = normalize(N) - normalize(Ng);
    P += ammount * normalize(N);
    return normalize(calculatenormal(P)) + Ndiff;
}
```

Layering and Manipulating Displacements

Creating interesting procedural displacement patterns will more than likely require you to work in layers and to combine such layers in clever ways to achieve the desired pattern. However, we must be careful of how layers are combined, because with displacement patterns you are not really handling color values but float values. Each layer will usually contain a set of values in the 0 to 1 range, and this greatly simplifies the math when combining layers. It is not necessary to stay within the 0 to 1 range, but it is advisable to do so because it is easier to calculate the maximum displacement for the displacement bounds, which should be the value of the displacement multiplier Km.

Add, Subtract, Multiply

These are the three most basic operations for combining texture values, and each will yield different results. Creative use of these operations will allow you to create complex patterns out of simpler ones. We will use two different simple patterns: One will be a set of vertical stripes, and the other will be horizontal stripes. Here is the code of the horizontal stripes, followed by Figures 7.18 and 7.19, which show vertical and horizontal stripes. The code for the vertical stripes is the same as the one for the horizontal stripes except for this line float ss = mod(s * texFreq,1).

```
displacement d_RP_hstripes(
                              uniform float texFreq = 4;
                              uniform float Km = 0.01;
                              )
{
    /* Create tiled texture space */
    float tt = mod(t * texFreq,1);
    /* simple step texture */
    varying float stripes = smoothstep(0.2,0.25,tt) -
smoothstep(0.75,0.8,tt);

    P += normalize(N) * Km * stripes;
    N = calculatenormal(P);
}
```

Figure 7.18 Stripes texture aligned to s.

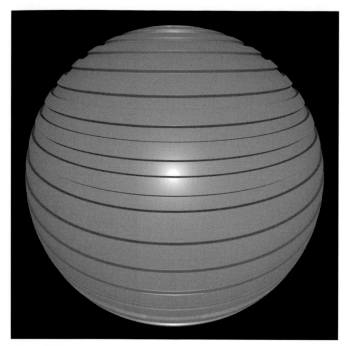

Figure 7.19 Stripes texture aligned to t.

If you look carefully at the code, you will see that these patterns are themselves products of a simple subtract operation to create the stripe, created by subtracting two smoothstep functions. The first smoothstep generates a set of values mapped in the graph in Figure 7.20, and the second one generates the graph in Figure 7.21. Subtracting the first step from the second results in a pulse or stripe texture as shown in Figure 7.22. Note that these graphs are approximations, and I have removed the "smooth" portion for ease of drawing.

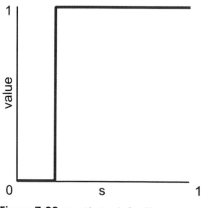

Figure 7.20 smoothstep(.2,.25,s).

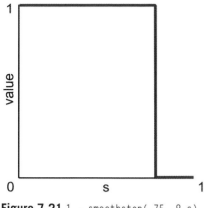

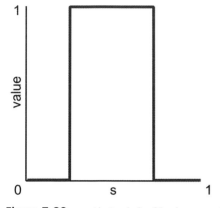

Figure 7.21 1 - smoothstep(.75,.8,s).

Figure 7.22 smoothstep(.2,.25,s) - smoothstep(.75,.8,s).

If you add these two textures together, you will get a result similar to Figure 7.23,while multiplying both textures will result in a square instead of a set of stripes, as seen on Figure 7.24. You can get creative with the ways you combine the images as shown in Figures 7.25 and 7.26.

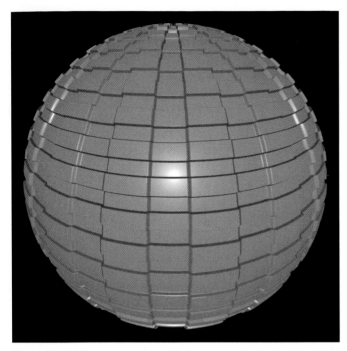

Figure 7.23 The two textures added.

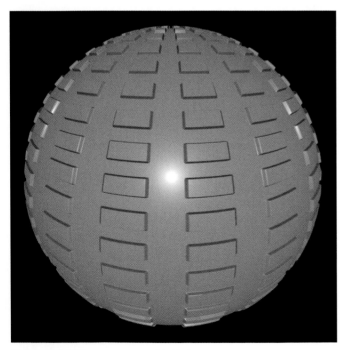

Figure 7.24 Two textures multiplied.

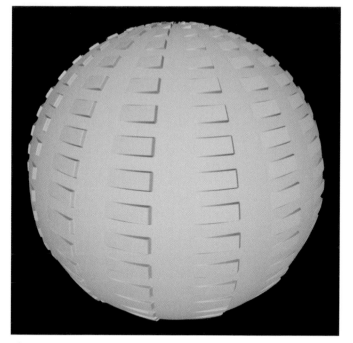

Figure 7.25 Two textures multiplied by themselves and by the tiled s space.

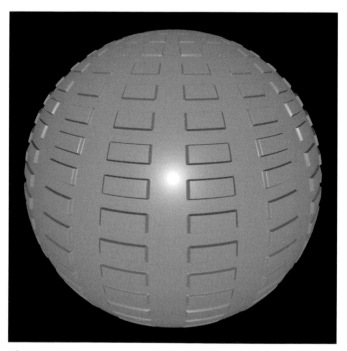

Figure 7.26 Two textures multiplied by themselves and by the t space.

Max and Clamp

The max() and clamp() functions are other helpful operations you can perform on your texture generation. If you want to take the vertical and horizontal patterns and turn them into a grid texture, you can't simply add or multiply them as previously demonstrated. In such cases, the solution is to tell the renderer to read only the maximum value of the texture by using the max() function. If we change the compositing operation to max(), we would get a texture similar to Figure 7.27.

```
displacement d_RP_stripes_max(
                                    uniform float texFreq = 4;
                                    uniform float Km = 0.01;
                                    )
{
    /* Create tiled texture space */
    float tt = mod(t * texFreq,1);
    float ss = mod(s * texFreq,1);

    /* simple step texture */
    varying float vstripes = smoothstep(0.2,0.25,tt) -
smoothstep(0.75,0.8,tt);
    varying float hstripes = smoothstep(0.2,0.25,ss) -
smoothstep(0.75,0.8,ss);

    P += normalize(N) * Km * max(vstripes,hstripes);
    N = calculatenormal(P);
}
```

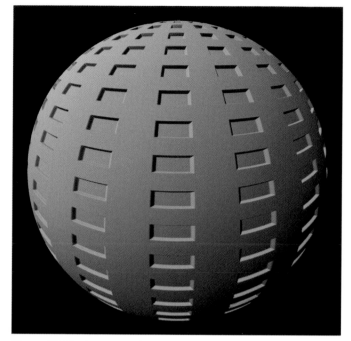

Figure 7.27 The result of using max() to combine layers.

Another useful operation is the clamp() function. Sometimes the pattern you are after can be obtained by chopping off certain values of the generated pattern. An example of this is the stucco pattern applied to houses. If you examine a stucco wall, you will see that it is created by randomly splattering some type of concrete material and then flattening it with a putty knife or other flat surface. Such flattening ends up chopping off the top parts of the concrete, leaving it flat. Here is a shader that generates a pattern that looks like stucco (see Figure 7.28).

```
/* castucco.sl
 *
 * Original by Larry Gritz
 *
 */


#include "arman/noises.h"

Displacement castucco (
                    float freq = 1;
                    float Km = 0.2;
                    float octaves = 3;
                    float trough = 0, peak = 0.25
                    )
```

```
{
    point Pshad;        /* Point to be shaded, in shader space */
    normal NN;          /* Unit length surface normal */
    float fwidth;       /* Estimated change in P between image samples */
    float disp;         /* Amount to displace */

    /* Do texture calcs in "shader" space */
    Pshad = freq * transform ("shader", P);

    /* Estimate how much Pshad changes between adjacent image samples */
    fwidth = sqrt (area(Pshad));

    /* Compute some fractional Brownian motion */
    disp = fBm (Pshad, fwidth, 3, 2, 0.6);

    /* Threshold the fBm and scale it */
    disp = Km * clamp(disp,trough,peak);

    /* displace in shader space units */
    NN = normalize(N);
    P += NN * (disp / length (ntransform ("shader", NN)));
    N = normalize (calculatenormal(P));
}
```

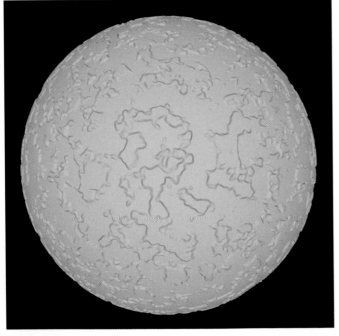

Figure 7.28 A displacement that resembles a typical stucco wall

Offset

As you saw before in our little noise shader, most displacement shaders use a Km multiplier parameter to scale the strength of the pattern. Because we are multiplying and not adding or subtracting, at any point where the pattern returns a value of 0, the pattern will have no effect on the surface. If you want, you can provide a negative value as your multiplier, which will result in a pattern that is inverted. If your original pattern created an appearance of bubbles (Figure 7.29), the inverted pattern will have an appearance of dimples (Figure 7.30). Inverting a pattern is part of your arsenal as a shader writer, so if you need to you can invert the value inside the shader before you multiply it by the Km scalar.

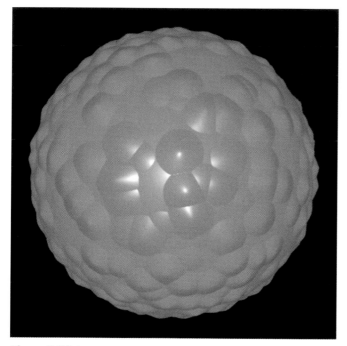

Figure 7.29 A pattern using a positive value for the displacement.

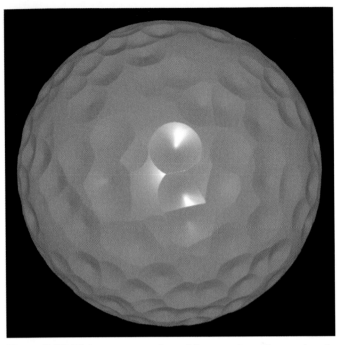

Figure 7.30 The same pattern but with a negative value used as the displacement.

Our shader is capable of pushing the surface out or in with no effect wherever the pattern returns a 0. But what if we need a pattern where the surface must be pulled and pushed at the same time? For such occasions, it is necessary to perform a remapping operation that allows the values of a map with 0 to 1 values to be interpreted as values lower than 0.

There are two ways to perform this offset. The first way will remap all the values between 0 and 1 to fit between −1 and 1. This means that a value of 0.5, which is a gray color, will end up with a value of 0 after the remapping. To perform this remap, the math operation to use is $(x \times 2) -1$, where x is the value in the 0 to 1 range. Translated into an easy-to-use CPP macro named mkSignedValue() (because ranges that include negative values are referred to as signed values), the code will be as follows:

```
#define mkSignedValue(x) ((x * 2) - 1)
```

The second way to handle remapping is even simpler and more useful than signing the value. It is implemented by subtracting a simple offset value from the value read from the texture. With an offset value of 0.5, an original value of 0 will become −0.5, and a value of 1 will become 0.5. Another way to think of this offset value is that the offset represents the value where the texture will have no effect on the displaced surface. So an offset of 1 will make the value of 1 become 0, and a value of 0 become −1, which results in the surface pushing in instead of pulling out. This operation doesn't leave all values between 0 and 1, but the value from the lowest value to the highest will still be 1. A simple implementation of this operation would be this:

```
displacement simpleOffset(
                              float Km = 0.1;
                              float Offset = 0.5;
                              )
{
    float tex = float texture("mytexture.tex");
    P += normalize(N) * Km * (tex - Offset);
    N = calculatenormal(P);
}
```

Tips on Displacement Shading

There are several issues when dealing with displacement shading. These are little "gotchas" that can jump out of nowhere and create problems if you are not aware of them. Most of these issues are not documented, but they are very important.

When using texture maps to drive your displacements, using 8-bit textures will usually work fine and give you good results. However, it is important to be aware that sometimes they can introduce nasty discontinuities or stepping along your displacement. An 8-bit image has only 256 tones between full black and white, so if you have a texture with big transition zones, small steps will show up in your render. It is for this reason that it is usually advisable to use either 16-bit or floating point images for displacements maps with big gradients or transition zones. Chapter 13, "Texture Mapping," covers all of the options available to control the generation of textures with your renderer's texture making program.

Another major issue is the aliasing that can become apparent when using displacements. The reason for such anti-aliasing, as explained by Pixar's Tony Apodaca, is that because a texture lookup in displacements will actually modify the normals of a surface, small changes on the texture lookup will usually have a big effect on the displaced surface.

The worst problem comes from improper filtering of a texture. A small texture filter will cause the displacement to alias horribly, while a filter that is too large will make your displacements look very flat. One way to get around this problem is to use a texture that is sized appropriately to the object's size on the screen.

Routines such as shadingnormal(), which ships with PRMan, allow you to do smarter shading on the front side and the back side of a model. This routine is very useful for proper raytracing in most cases. However, never use these routines inside a displacement shader. It will cause the back of the object not to be displaced or to be displaced in the wrong direction.

While developing shaders for an animated film, I received a request to give our surface shaders the capability to use or ignore the bumped normals when computing specular calls. This is important when you are authoring shaders that have more than one layer of specular or reflection. With such controls, you could add a bump and have a first specular layer that uses a Blinn model and is affected by the bump, then you can have a reflection layer on top that ignores the bump completely. The surface will look as if it were painted in layers—first a layer of paint and then a layer of glossy lacquer. Implementing such a feature is very easy and useful. In Chapter 15, where illumination loops are explained, you will learn that illumination lookups depend heavily on normals. These normals are modified by the bump calls in the displacement shader. The steps to get this to work are as follows:

1. Store the unbumped normal in a variable inside the displacement shader.

2. Read that stored unbumped normal into the surface shader.

3. Add a switch to control whether the bumped normal will be used.

4. Use the proper normal based on the switch.

My first impulse is to store the unbumped normal N in an output variable in the displacement shader and then use message passing to read this normal from the surface shader. Analyzing the steps further, I realize I could just use the true geometric normal Ng from within the surface shader and save myself all the trouble and extra computing time of message passing plus the storage of an extra variable.

I could also try to implement a floating value slider instead of a switch. This will give the artists the ability to dial how much the specular call will respect the bump. This feature could require a bit of vector math to manipulate the normals. Since math is evil (not really but I try to avoid figuring out stuff that others already have as much as I can), I look into the RiSpec and realize that RSL ships with a very useful function for blending normals.

```
mix (normal x, y; float alpha)
```

This function will make the implementation of the feature quite easy. Here is the code for a simple shader that allows you to control how much bump the specular model uses followed by Figure 7.31, which has the bump affect the specular, and Figure 7.32, where the bump does not affect the specular calculation.

```
surface bumpedSpec(
                uniform float specBump = 1;
                uniform float Ks = 1;
                uniform float roughness = 0.2;
                )
{
```

```
/* Initialize variables */
normal Norig = faceforward(normalize(Ng),I);
normal Nbump = faceforward(normalize(N),I);
vector V = -normalize(I);
normal Nspec = normalize(mix(Norig,Nbump,
                             clamp(specBump,0,1)));
/* output */
Oi = Os;
Ci = Oi * diffuse(Nbump) + (Ks * specular(Nspec,V,roughness));
}
```

Figure 7.31 Teapot with a bump noise shader and the specBump parameter set to 1. The specular lookup is affected by the noise.

Figure 7.32 Same scene as before but with specBump set to 0. The specular behaves as though the object is smooth.

Surface Shaders

When you are finished with the displacement, you will more than likely move on to writing the surface shader. The surface shader is the bread and butter of the shader writing profession. You will probably write more surface shaders than any other type. It is true that most objects will have a displacement and a surface shader, but since the surface shader usually provides patterns and features that simulate the look of an object, it is common to first write the surface shader and then move the necessary code over to the displacement shader, either by copying and pasting or by creating a function.

Surface shaders can be very simple or as complicated as some shaders used by production companies. These shaders can have thousands of lines, very complicated preprocessor macros, and tons upon tons of controls.

The code inside a surface shader can usually be subdivided into two segments. The first segment is usually the calculation and generation of patterns, and the second consists of the illumination routines that tell the surface how to interact with the lights in the scene. It is very common to use calculated patterns to affect the illumination loops by masking or modulating the intensity of a given component.

Just as with displacement shaders, there is a list of predefined global variables available to a surface shader. It is important to get acquainted with this list of variables to save yourself from having to constantly look up the reference manual. There are certain variables, such as P, N, s, and t, that you will use constantly, and they will become embedded in your head just like the letters of the alphabet. There are also several variables such as ptime and dPdu that you will use a lot less frequently. It not necessary to memorize these, but it is important to be aware of their existence. Table 7.2 lists the global variables available in surface shaders, as defined by the RiSpec.

Table 7.2 Global Variables Available in Surface Shader

Name	Type	Storage Class	Description
Cs	color	varying/uniform	Surface color
Os	color	varying/uniform	Surface opacity
P	point	varying	Surface position
dPdu	vector	varying	Derivative of P along u
dPdv	vector	varying	Derivative of P along v
N	normal	varying	Surface shading normal
Ng	normal	varying	Surface geometric normal
u, v	float	varying	Surface parameters
du, dv	float	varying/uniform	Change in surface parameters
s, t	float	varying	Surface texture coordinates
L	vector	varying/uniform	Incoming light ray vector*
Cl	color	varying/uniform	Incoming light color*
Ol	color	varying/uniform	Incoming light opacity*
E	point	uniform	Position of the eye
I	vector	varying	Incident ray direction
ncomps	float	uniform	Number of color components
time	float	uniform	Current shutter time
dtime	float	uniform	The amount of time covered by this shading sample
dPdtime	vector	varying	How the surface position P is changing per unit of time, as described by motion blur on the scene
Outputs			
Ci	color	varying	Incident ray color
Oi	color	varying	Incident ray opacity

* Available only inside illuminance statements.

It is important to understand what each of these variables means and how to use them. Since surface shaders are responsible for calculating the initial color and opacity values of a surface, we can use them to visualize the most commonly used variables. We will first create a shader that enables us to visualize the texture coordinates that are embedded in the geometry, either automatically as in NURBS surfaces or quadratic surfaces, or user-generated as in polygons or subdivision surfaces.

```
surface s_RP_showst(
                     string showSorT = "s";
                     )
{
    /* Variables */
    // Assign pure RED to sc, if the value provided by the user is not
    // recognized the use red.
    varying color sc = (1,0,0);

    if (showSorT == "s")
        sc = color(s,0,0);
    else if (showSorT == "t")
        sc = color(0,t,0);
    else if (showSorT == "st")
        sc = color(s,t,0);

    Ci = sc;
}
```

The images in Figures 7.33, 7.34, and 7.35 were generated using this shader. They illustrate the result of using the parameter values of s, t, and st, respectively, for showSorT.

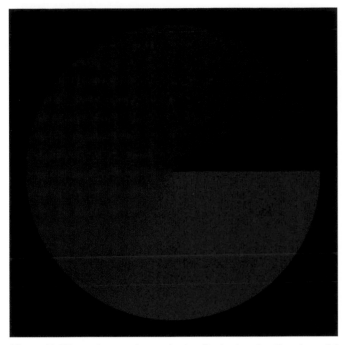

Figure 7.33 A sphere with our shader displaying the direction of the s variable.

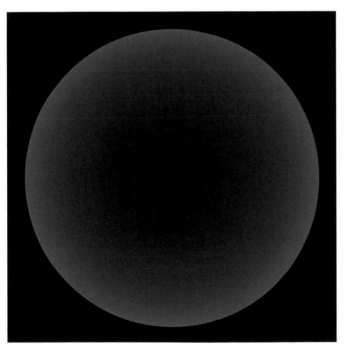

Figure 7.34 The same sphere with our shader displaying the direction of the t variable.

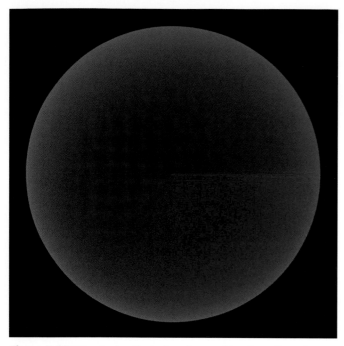

Figure 7.35 The shader displaying the combination of s and t.

Another useful feature that the previous inspection shader could use would be the capability to render the value of the surface position (P) and normal (N). Here is the source code of the file s_RP_showVars.sl, which is an expanded version of s_RP_showst.sl.

```
surface s_RP_showVars(
                      string showVar = "s";
                      )
{
    /* Variables */
    // Assign pure RED to sc, if the value provided by the user is not
    // recognized the use red.
    varying color sc = (1,0,0);

    if (showVar == "s")
        sc = color(s,0,0);
    else if (showVar == "t")
        sc = color(0,t,0);
    else if (showVar == "st")
        sc = color(s,t,0);
    else if (showVar == "P")
        sc = color(P);
```

```
else if (showVar == "N")
    sc = color(normalize(N));

    Ci = sc;
}
```

You can use this shader any time you need to visualize the value of any of those variables. You can expand this shader to support the rest of the surface global variables; just pay attention to how we handled float variables to create colors and how we typecast the vectors and normals into a color. It is very important to be able to visualize a variable as you are manipulating it to generate surfaces.

The following code is a shader that visualizes what happens to the texture coordinates when a modulus operation is applied to s. This operation is used quite commonly when generating texture patterns that are tileable. A more detailed explanation of this operation and other essential ones can be found in Chapter 12, "Procedural Patterns." Figure 7.36 demonstrates the use of this shader to visualize the s and t parameters.

```
surface s_RP_showMod(
                    uniform float tileFreq = 8;
                    string useSorT = "s";
                    )
{
    /* Variables */
    // Assign pure RED to sc, if the value provided by the user is not
    // recognized the use red.
    varying color sc = (1,0,0);
    varying float ss, tt;

    if (useSorT == "s")
        sc = color(mod(s * tileFreq,1),0,0);
    else if (useSorT == "t")
        sc = color(0,mod(t * tileFreq,1),0);
    else if (useSorT == "st")
        sc = color(mod(s * tileFreq,1),mod(t * tileFreq,1),0);

    Ci = sc;
}
```

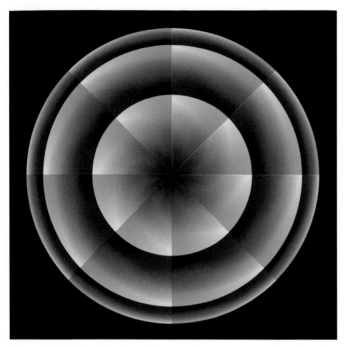

Figure 7.36 Visualization of the s and t parameters when they have been tiled.

As you might recall, surface shaders are evaluated after the displacements. This means that if the displacement shader altered the position of P and the direction of N, then those values will be used by the surface shader. In the case of the surface normals, you can still access the original unmodified normal through the Ng or geometric normal variable.

Another thing to consider is that most often the features in a displacement shader will need to line up with features in the surface shader. Some of those features might have a lot of noise, fractals, power, and vector functions, which are usually very expensive to compute. To get the features to line up, you need to use the exact code along with the same parameters. This can be a nuisance in your workflow because a parameter could very easily slip through with the wrong value, and you will have to edit two parameters every time you want to make a simple change.

In most software packages, you can use a math expression to ensure that the parameters in your displacement and surface shaders have the same values. This solves the workflow problem, but you are still left with the overhead of calculating a very expensive pattern more than once. You can get around this by calculating the pattern once in the displacement shader and then using message passing to query the calculated values into the surface shader.

We already created a simple shader in Chapter 3 that had the appearance of plastic. That shader describes how to use the most popular shading functions. From this point on, writing surface shaders involves illumination and pattern generation. In Chapter 11, "Illumination Loops—BRDFs," we will go over creating custom illumination models to achieve any look you want. In Chapters 12 and 13, we will cover procedural pattern generation and texture access.

wall to be at least three to five f/stops (f/stops control how much the aperture of a camera is open) less than the character? And here is the catch: You can't use back lighting because the scene must look as if all the light comes from a single light source in front of the character. This is a setup that is a bit hard to achieve for people without the right amount of experience. An experienced cinematographer will know how to get the shot, but it will take a lot of careful setup to get it just right.

Now let's picture the same requirements in the world of CG animation. All you have to do is create two lights and link one to the character and the other to the wall. Give the wall light about one-half of the intensity from the character light, and you are done. Easy, huh? Well, there is a catch: In CG lighting you don't get any of the subtle details that real-life lights offer. Whereas in live action you might need five or six lights to get your shot set up, you might need 10, 20, or even more lights to create all the subtle light-bouncing effects that make our world real. With the addition of global illumination techniques to the rendering arsenal, the ease of setting up scenes might go down, but the rendering times will surely go up. Global illumination techniques are more valuable to the VFX artist than the CG animation artist because they need to match the live plates provided by the studio, which are filled with light bounces.

In the end, the name of the game in CG lighting is control. The more control you have over how lights behave, the easier your life will be. This is why I have a hard time believing that those fancy "unbiased" or "physical based" renderers will take over the rendering realm for VFX and animation. Those renderers pride themselves on delivering physically accurate reconstruction of light propagation between objects. Don't get me wrong—accuracy is a fantastic accomplishment and no easy task to implement, and they might take over in architectural visualizations, but for feature work, most directors will pick control over accuracy.

Most renderers out there use a local illumination approach to calculating lights and offer global illumination as an added feature that can get turned on at any moment. Even so, their foundation is still the local illumination model. Local illumination means that only scene lights and the illumination model of the current object can contribute to the lighting portion of such object. The illumination model traces rays from the current point on a surface to each of the active lights and gets each of the lights' intensities and color values. Once the colors and intensities are retrieved, the renderer considers the contribution of each light finished. Then those values are manipulated by the surface shader to create the desired effect. In a global illumination renderer, the light calculations don't end once a light's intensity and color are retrieved. The shader will then use more rays to trace the contribution it has on other objects and that other objects have on it. These extra rays usually result in much longer rendering times. Most renderers have come up with very clever ways of accelerating the calculation of extra rays, either by caching, baking, or using photon maps.

In this chapter, we will cover the standard light shaders, which include ambient lights and regular point lights. Point lights emanate all of their light rays from a single point, contrary to area lights, which emanate light rays from many different points within a given area. Some renderers, RenderMan renderers included, usually refer to an omnidirectional light as a point light. This might create some confusion in terminology, so I'll try to be careful when referring to omni lights. Just like all other shader types, light shaders have a predefined set of global variables that are available to the light at different stages of execution. Table 8.1 lists the light shader global variables.

Table 8.1 Light Shader Global Variables

Name	Type	Storage Class	Description
P	point	varying	Surface position
dPdu	vector	varying	Derivative of surface position along u
dPdv	vector	varying	Derivative of surface position along v
N	normal	varying	Surface shading normal
Ng	normal	varying/uniform	Surface geometric normal
u, v	float	varying	Surface parameters
du, dv	float	varying/uniform	Change in surface parameters
s,t	float	varying	Surface texture coordinates
L	vector	varying/uniform	Incoming light ray direction *
Ps	point	varying	Position being illuminated
E	point	uniform	Position of the light's eye
ncomps	float	uniform	Number of color components
time	float	uniform	Current shutter time
dtime	float	uniform	The amount of time covered by this shading sample

Outputs

Name	Type	Storage Class	Description
Ci	color	varying/uniform	Outgoing light ray color
Oi	color	varying/uniform	Outgoing light ray opacity

*Available only inside solar or illuminate statements.

Light source shaders have their own execution state, which differs from the surface and displacement shaders. In Figure 8.1 we can see how the previously mentioned variables behave inside a light shader state. It is important to note that variables such as P and N have completely different meanings inside a light shader. They refer to the light's origin point and the light surface normal, respectively.

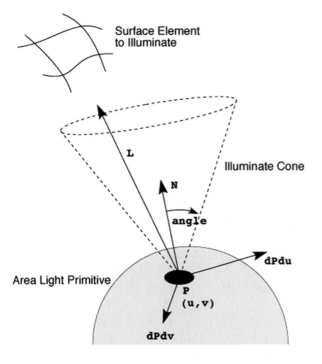

Light Source Shader

Figure 8.1 Variables as represented inside a light shader graphic state.

Ambient Lights

The first light we will explore is the ambient light. Ambient lights have been around since the beginning of 3D graphics. It was the first "quick hack" attempt at simulating the effects of light bouncing around from object to object. The main problem with basic ambient light is that it tends to wash out objects and make them look flat. As time progressed, new techniques were created to replicate ambient lighting with relative low cost and without flattening the object. We will discuss those enhancements later, but for now let's look at the most basic ambient light. The code of a basic ambient light shader will usually look like this:

```
light l_RP_ambientlight(
                            uniform float intensity = 1;
                            uniform color lightcolor = 1;
                            )
{
    /* No solar or iluminate statement turns this light into an
    ambient light. This light will only connect to an ambient() call
    in the surface shaders*/
    Cl = lightcolor * intensity;
}
```

As you can see, the code is extremely simple. It has only two parameters and one line of code, which is assigned to Cl, the final light color that is read by surface shaders. This light doesn't have either a solar() or an illuminate() statement. Lights that lack both of these statements are automatically treated by the renderer as ambient lights, which means that the only way to retrieve their Cl value is through the use of the ambient() RSL call within a surface shader. If we put our ambient light shader into a scene with a simple primitive, such as a teapot, and give the teapot the standard "plastic" surface shader (which uses ambient()), you will see that our shader immediately connects with it as visible in Figure 8.2

```
Option "searchpath" "string shader" ["./:../rsl/rel:@:&"]
Display "l_RP_ambientlight.tif" "framebuffer" "rgb"
Format 500 500 1
PixelSamples 3 3
Clipping 0.001 1000
Projection "perspective" "fov" 30
Translate -1 0 30
Rotate -22 1 0 0
Rotate 19 0 1 0
Translate 0 -3 0
WorldBegin
LightSource "distantlight" 1 "intensity" [1.0]
#Define a red ambient light
LightSource "l_RP_ambientlight" 2 "float intensity" [1] "color lightcolor"
[1 0 0]

## Begin teapot object
AttributeBegin
Attribute "displacementbound" "float sphere" [0.15]
Displacement "d_RP_simplenoise" "float noiFreq" [15]
Surface "plastic"
ReadArchive "teapotArch.rib"
AttributeEnd
WorldEnd
```

Figure 8.2 A teapot with a red ambient light.

Enhanced Ambient Light

The basic ambient light works, but in a production environment it won't get you far. There are tons of improvements that can be made to get more mileage out of an ambient light.

The first thing we are going to do is add an environment texture lookup to our shader. This environment lookup will behave pretty much like an environment reflection map, but instead of using a reflection vector to do the environment map lookup, we will use the normal vector. This way the lookup is not camera dependent, and we won't see the ambient contribution slide through our object as the camera moves. We will also add the proper parameters to control the map lookup and a light category that will allow the user to write an illumination model that restricts the ambient lookup to only this light. Light categories are a very important part of setting up a lighting pipeline and workflow. From the light shader writing stance, implementing a light category is quite simple because most of the work is done in the surface's shader illuminance loop. Illumination loops will be covered in detail in Chapter 11, "Illumination Loops—BRDFs."

To be able to add a normal that will be used to do the environment map lookup, we need to add an `illuminate()` statement that will calculate the light contribution. Once you add an `illuminance()` or `solar()` statement to a light shader, you can no longer use the built-in RSL `ambient()` function to perform ambient lookups. You will have to use a personalized, more advanced illumination loop to do the ambient lookup. That illumination loop will also be described further along. Our enhanced light shader will have the following parameters.

```
light 1_RP_enhambientlight(
                        uniform float intensity = 1;
                        uniform color lightcolor = 1;
                        string ambientMap = "";
                        string envSpace = "shader";
                        uniform float ambientMapBlur = 0.1;
                        uniform float ambientMapFilterWidth = 1;
                        string ambientMapFilter = "gaussian";
                        string __category = "ambient";
                        )
```

The first two are from the previous `ambientlight` shader. Next, we have a group of parameters used to control the environment map lookup. The `ambientMap` is a string that defines the name of the environment texture to be used. The `envSpace` allows you to read a predeclared coordinate system from the RIB file.

This coordsys can be used to control the orientation of the environment map. We will set the default value of such coordsys to `shader`. This means that the environment can be manipulated by simply adding a transformation before the light `shader` is called. The moment the light `shader` is called, the current transformation will become the shader coordsys, and the environment map will be transformed by the declared transformation. The `MapBlur`, `MapFilterWidth`, and `MapFilter` parameters control the blur amount, the filter size, and the type of filter to be used on the texture lookup, respectively.

Finally, we have the light `category` parameter, which is nothing more than a string parameter with the reserved keyword `__category` (with two underscores). The `category` parameter is a comma-separated list of names that defines which category this light belongs to. This category can be used by a surface shader's illuminance statement to restrict the evaluation of the shader to only certain shader categories. Here is the complete code for the enhanced ambient light.

```
light 1_RP_enhambientlight(
                        uniform float intensity = 1;
                        uniform color lightcolor = 1;
                        string ambientMap = "";
                        string envSpace = "shader";
```

```
                                uniform float ambientMapBlur = 0.1;
                                uniform float ambientMapFilterWidth = 1;
                                string ambientMapFilter = "gaussian";
                                string __category = "ambient";
                                )
{
    /* Variables */
    normal Ns = normalize(N);
    vector Nv;
    color ambientMapColor = lightcolor;

    illuminate (Ps + Ns){
        Nv = vector(ntransform(envSpace,Ns));

        if (ambientMap != "")
            ambientMapColor = environment (ambientMap,Nv,
                                          "blur",ambientMapBlur,
                                          "filter",ambientMapFilter,
                                          "width",ambientMapFilter-
Width);

        Cl = lightcolor * intensity * ambientMapColor;
    }
}
```

This shader introduces the use of the illuminate() statement, which is one of two
light contribution statements that can be used within a light shader: illuminate()
and solar(). The illuminate() statement is used to define a light that emits light
through a three-dimensional solid cone. The general two ways that illuminate()
can be used are:

```
illuminate( point position ){..code..}
illuminate( point position, vector axis, float angle ) {..code..}
```

The first form specifies that light is cast in all directions, similar to a light bulb.
The second form specifies that light is cast only inside the given cone, similar to
a spotlight. The length of L vector inside an illuminate statement is equal to the
distance between the light source and the surface currently being shaded.

The solar() statement is used to define a light that shines as a distant light source.
The arguments to the solar() statement also specify a three-dimensional cone.
Light is cast from distant directions inside this cone. The difference from the illu-
minate() statement is that the light rays from a solar() statement are parallel and
shine from infinity, which is why a point position is not needed on either of the
two forms.

```
solar( ) stmt
solar( vector axis, float angle ) stmt
```

The first form specifies that light is being cast from all points at infinity, such as an illumination map. The second form specifies that light is being cast from only directions inside a cone.

In our ambient shader, we are using an illuminate() statement with a point as an argument, but instead of providing a single position, which is what is usually used for omni and spot lights, we are using a new point, which is located at the tip of every normal of the shaded surface. This is done with simple vector math where we add the value of the normalized surface shading normal Ns to the current shading point Ps to create a new point Ps + Ns. Figure 8.3 is a diagram of this operation.

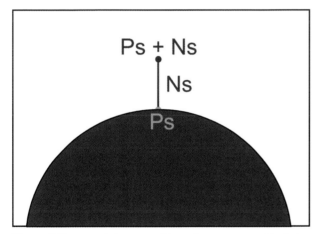

Figure 8.3 A visual diagram of how the position of the light (Ps + Ns) is calculated.

If you use this light in a scene like 1_RP_enhambientlight.rib, you will see the effect of the environment map on the teapot. Instead of it being one flat color all over the object, the ambient lookup will have interesting color variations obtained from the map. It is very easy to re-create the environment lighting for a VFX shot if you can manage to capture several images on the set. If you didn't get a chance to take such pictures (you usually don't), you could still create a decent ambient map from several frames of the final footage. If the shot has noticeable changes in the environment lighting, you could always create an image sequence that matches those changes, convert the images to environment maps, and then use those maps to light the scene. Environment maps were originally designed to fake reflections, but by using one to do an ambient lookup, you can save a lot of setup time. One problem with the way the light is behaving right now is that this ambient light is being read by every illumination loop, so it affects not just ambient but also the diffuse and specular components, as are visible in Figure 8.4.

Figure 8.4 Our ambient light is also contributing to spec and diffuse.

There are two ways we can get this light to behave properly. The first way we could control the spec contribution is to add an output float parameter named nonspecular and give it a value of 1. This is a special name that RSL's built-in specular() call should respect. It allows you to control how much you want the specular component not to affect the current surface. Insert this parameter right under the category parameter. Recompile the light shader and re-render 1_RP_enhambientlight_Nspec.rib, which is the same scene as 1_RP_enhambient-light.rib but with the nonspecular parameter left at its default value. The output of this RIB file can be viewed in Figure 8.5.

The resulting image has no specular contribution, and it appears correct, but the light is still being considered by the diffuse() call, and this is surely not what we want. To get things to behave the right way, we must move over to the second (and better) solution. The other way to control this light and force it to behave properly is to create a customized illumination loop function that will connect to the enhanced ambient light shader. Illumination loops are the part of a surface shader responsible for collecting light information. They are covered in detail in Chapter 11, but we need to get into them right now to get our ambient light shader to behave properly.

Figure 8.5 The same teapot but without specular contribution from the light.

Note that from this point on, we will more than likely have to create our own illumination models for all the functions in our shaders because the RSL built-in functions don't allow us to declare a category to restrict the lighting calculation, and they are rather basic in their implementation. Here is a customized function that will calculate the contribution of our ambient light, followed by the image rendered from using scene 1_RP_enhambientlight2.rib. Whenever you use rpAmbient() in any of your shaders, this function will calculate only the contribution from lights that have the category parameter set to "ambient." Creating customized illumination loop functions will also ensure that you don't get a double or triple contribution from the ambient light shader, if it creeps into the diffuse() or specular() calculations, which will affect the look of the object. Figure 8.6 shows the output of using our custom illumination function.

```
color rpAmbient(varying normal NN; varying point PP)
{
    /* Variables */
    varying color Cout = 0;

    illuminance("ambient", P){
        Cout += Cl;
    }
    return Cout;
}
```

Figure 8.6 Teapot rendered with our `rpAmbient()` illumination model.
It looks just like the image rendered with the `nonspecular` parameter set to 1.

Super Ambient Light

We will now take the enhanced ambient light and expand it to a production ready
ambient light. The next step is to add the capability of computing ambient occlusion. As you might know, ambient occlusion (AO) is a technique that allows you
to provide a very rich amount of detail from self-intersecting objects. Occlusion
and the math behind it will be explained in detail in Chapter 14 when global illumination techniques are covered. So even though the concepts and techniques are
more advanced than anything we have seen so far, we will add this capability so
that we have a finished shader that we can use in production.

In this shader, we will be using the RSL built-in `occlusion()` function, which was
designed specifically for what we need to do: fake ambient occlusion. This function also allows us to pass an environment map to it so that if the occlusion rays
don't intersect with anything, they will get the color of the environment map. This
means we have to get rid of the environment call. The super ambient light shader
source code is as follows:

```
light 1_RP_superambientlight(
                        uniform float intensity = 1;
                        uniform color lightcolor = 1;
                        string ambientMap = "";
```

```
                             string envSpace = "shader";
                             uniform float samples = 64;
                             uniform float maxvariation = 0.02;
                             uniform float maxdist = 1;
                             uniform float coneAngle = PI/2;
                             string traceSet = "";
                             string __category = "ambient";
                             output uniform float __nonspecular = 1;
                             output varying float Cocc = 1;
                             )
{
    /* Variables */
    normal NN = normalize(N);
    color ambientColor = lightcolor;
    illuminate (Ps + NN){
        /* Compute average color of ray misses (ignore occlusion) */
        Cocc *= occlusion(Ps, NN, samples, "maxvariation", maxvariation,
                          "environmentmap", ambientMap,
                          "environmentspace", envSpace,
                          "environmentcolor", ambientColor,
                          "maxdist",maxdist,
                          "coneangle",coneAngle,
                          "subset",traceSet);

        /* Set Cl */
        Cl = intensity * lightcolor * ambientColor;
        }
}
```

The occlusion() call takes three required parameters: the point where the calculations will be performed, the normal direction in which to perform them, and the number of samples to use while calculating the occlusion. The rest of the parameters passed to the occlusion() call are a set of token-value pairs that allow you to have extra control over the occlusion lookup. In this shader, we have not included all of the parameters that the occlusion call will accept. We added only the most essential ones to make our ambient light shader production ready. When you have read Chapter 14 and have better understanding of the options accepted by the occlusion() call, you are welcome to revise this shader and update it to suit your needs. Figure 8.7 demonstrates how much detail an occlusion() call can give to an image.

Figure 8.7 The same teapot rendered with an ambient occlusion component. See how rich the teapot looks now?

Point Lights

The next level of light source shaders, and perhaps the ones used the most, are point light shaders. Point light shaders encompass every light shader that projects its light rays from a single point in space. Omni, directional (also known as *distant*), and spot lights are all point lights. Area and geometry lights fall into a different category because they project light rays from different places at a time.

The simplest point light shader is the omnidirectional light, also known as an omni light or a point light. The word omni is derived from the Latin word omnis, which means all, so omni-directional means "in all directions." (There is your Latin lesson of the day.) An omni light is similar to a light bulb, which shines in all directions. The omni light shader in this section is based on the default light shader that ships with most RenderMan-compliant renderers. We will extend this shader to turn it into a production-ready shader. The only change we have made to the shader so far is to add the category parameter and initialize it to all. All of our general-purpose point light shaders will be of the same category, so all of our custom illumination models should use this name as the category argument for the illuminance call.

The omni light shader uses a new point parameter named from. This parameter represents the position of the light that will be applied to the currently active coordinate system when the light shader is called. It is a quick way to control the position of the light.

Another way to control the position of the light is to apply a transformation before the light is declared and then just leave the from parameter set to (0,0,0). The from point value will be fed to the illuminate() function. Providing a single point parameter to illuminate() results in light being sent in all directions from that single point. The last line of the shader Cl = intensity * lightcolor / L.L presents a very nifty feature of this light shader. The division by the dot product between the unnormalized light vector, L.L, will produce an inverse square light falloff, simulating the physical behavior of light in the real world.

```
light pointlight(
                float intensity = 1;
                color lightcolor = 1;
                point from = point "shader" (0,0,0);/* light position */
                string __category = "all";
                )
{
    illuminate( from )
        Cl = intensity * lightcolor / L.L;
}
```

The scene in Figures 8.8 and 8.9 was lit with a single omni light. Notice how all the domino shapes are brighter on the faces toward the center. Notice also that the attenuation of the light is clearly visible in the scene, in that the plane gets darker on surfaces farther away from the light source.

There are several problems with this light shader. First, we have no control over how the light attenuates, which is something that you absolutely want control over. Another deficiency is that it doesn't support shadow casting, a very important feature. To add support for different falloff rates, we will add a single parameter to the shader and then perform a single operation to calculate the falloff.

To calculate the attenuation, we first need to get the distance between the light position and the surface point being shaded. We can then use this value and perform an exponent operation on it with the pow() function. This way, the farther away the point is, the higher the returned value. Then we multiply the result of the multiplication of the light color and intensity by the return value by the 1/pow() function.

With this scheme, you have control over how the light attenuates. To turn the light into an infinity light that never falls off, just use a falloff value of 1. A falloff value of 2 will result in an inverse square falloff, which replicates the physically correct way that lights fall off inside a dust-free environment. If you want the light to fall off faster, just keep raising the value of the `falloff` parameter. Figures 8.8 and 8.9 show the difference between using our omni light with an intensity of 6. See how dramatic the difference is with a small change to the `falloff` value?

```
light l_RP_omnilight (
                        ...
                        uniform float falloff = 1;
                        ...)
{
...
    /* Get the distance between the light and the shading point */
    float dist = length(L);
    /* Multiply the light color and intensity by the falloff curve */
    Cl = lightcolor * intensity * 1/pow(dist,falloff);
...
}
```

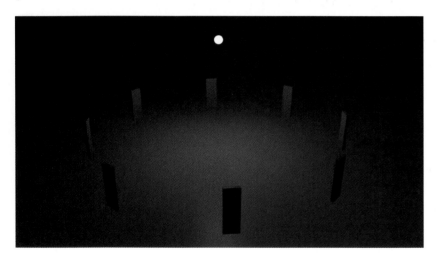

Figure 8.8 Scene with light falloff set to 1.

Figure 8.9 `falloff` set to 1.5. The intensity falls off much faster.

The next upgrade to this light shader will be to add support for shadows. Shadows are important in creating compelling images, and our shader at the moment cannot generate shadows. Before we continue to improve this light shader, we need to discuss the options available to RenderMan users for shadow generation. We will come back to our point light shader later.

Shadow Maps

When the REYES rendering algorithm was designed, it was decided that raytracing routines were too time-consuming and memory intensive to process. They would increase the rendering times and not always give you pleasant results. Raytraced shadows tended to be very sharp and sometimes jagged. To achieve soft raytraced shadows, you need a lot of extra rays to calculate intersections over a larger area and then average the result. This is extremely expensive, so raytracing was discarded as an option and another solution was sought.

Bill Reeves introduced to the computer graphics world the concept of shadow maps. Z-depth shadow maps are quite simple. First, a depth image is rendered from the light's point of view (Figure 8.10). That depth image allows the light to know if an object is in front of or behind another. As the light shoots a ray into the scene, it knows the distance of each visible shading point. If the point is not visible to the light, that means that another object is in front of it from the light's POV, which means that the object is in shadow, as seen in Figure 8.11.

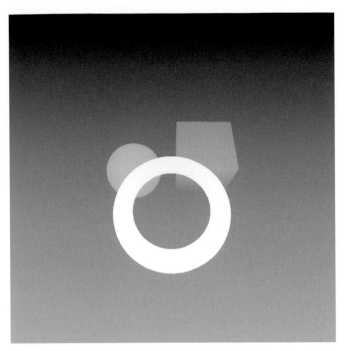

Figure 8.10 A depth image rendered from the light's point of view.

Figure 8.11 The resulting image with the shadow applied.

The upside of shadow maps is that they render extremely quickly, and they are reusable as long as you don't move the geometry or the position of the shadow emitting light. The downside is that shadow maps can't render colored or semi-opaque shadows, they can't cast motion-blurred shadows, and they are terrible at shadowing very small objects such as hair. They also need to be prerendered, which requires the animation program to output the whole scene from the light's perspective, so rendering complex scenes might take a while, especially if there are several shadow-casting lights.

Even though shadow maps have a lot of limitations, they were the only option for generating shadows in PRMan until raytracing and deep shadow maps were introduced in 2003. How did shadow maps, with all those limitations, stand alone for so long? That's where creative and knowledgeable TDs come in. Every movie rendered with PRMan before 2003 used only map-based shadows. Still, good movies such as *Toy Story 2*, *Final Fantasy*, and *Lord of the Rings* were made with the technique.

Deep shadow maps are similar to regular shadow maps in that both need to be prerendered and can be reused if the light and the scene have not changed. Deep shadows overcome most of the limitations of regular shadow maps. They allow you to render colored, semitransparent, and motion-blurred shadows. They also are fantastic at capturing fine detail. Deep shadow maps are largely responsible for hairy creatures such as Sully from *Monsters, Inc.* looking as good as they did. The difference between z-depth maps and deep shadow maps is that z-depth maps store a single depth value on each pixel of the map. Deep shadow maps store fractional values of visibility at all possible depths. This means that deep shadows can store partial transparency generated by a semitransparent object or by an object that is partly visible due to motion blur. Another huge difference is that deep shadow maps are prefiltered, which means you can capture the same amount (or more) of detail with a smaller map than z-depth maps. The good thing from a shader developer's point of view is that both regular map and deep map shadows are accessible using the shadow() call.

Raytraced Shadows

The other shadow types that are supported by RenderMan are raytraced shadows. The benefit of raytraced shadows is that they have the capability to replicate very intricate shadow effects with a small amount of setup. The downside is that some of those fancy shadow effects can take a lot longer to render. Here is where studios and artists need to put the two available options into balance. You can spend your money on a TD's time to set those fancy shadow effects so that the scene renders faster, or you can have the TD spend less time setting up the scene and spend your money on more rendering machines to support longer render times. One hour of rendering time is usually a lot cheaper than one hour of salary for a TD.

In addition, you can always buy more rendering machines to speed up rendering times, but hiring extra TDs can get very expensive. On the other hand, if you are working on a solo project, rendering times will be an issue, so you might want to spend the extra time setting some shadow effects to use maps.

To calculate raytraced shadows in RenderMan, you can use two different techniques. You can use a regular shadow() call and instead of passing the name of a map file as the first argument, you could pass the keyword raytrace. This will calculate the shadows, but they will be single hit shadows that are hard edged. This technique also will not allow you to calculate colored or soft shadows.

The other way to render shadows is to use the transmission() call to trace rays into the scene and gather information from the bounced rays. The transmission() call is designed specifically to gather information for shadows, so it is a lot faster than the more general gather() function. It allows you to declare several parameters, such as the size of a cone inside which to gather samples and the number of samples inside the cone. Using a sample cone will create soft shadows, as seen in Figure 8.12.

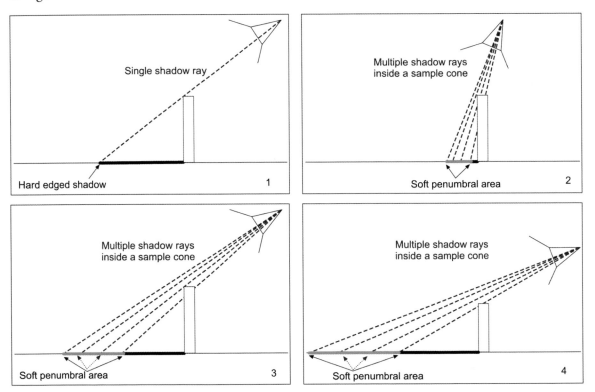

Figure 8.12 Image 1 shows the hard-edged shadow from a single shadow ray. Images 2, 3, and 4 demonstrate how the size of the penumbra increases as the light reaches more parallel angles.

To cast colored shadows, you need to set up the proper RenderMan attributes for your objects. In PRMan, those attributes are

```
Attribute "visibility" "int transmission" [1]
Attribute "shade" "string transmissionhitmode" "primitive"
```

The first line tells the renderer that the following object will be visible to transmission rays. The second line specifies how a transmission ray should evaluate the surface when it hits a point. The accepted values are `primitive` and `shader`. Using `primitive` will make the rays look only for the primitive's `Color` and `Opacity` attribute to determine the value of the hit point. Using `shader` will evaluate the shader for that surface point. As you might assume, using `shader` is a lot more expensive than using `primitive`, but you will need the `shader` option to generate colored shadows for effects such as tinted windows.

Adding Shadow Maps

Now that we have a better understanding of how shadows are generated inside RenderMan, we can move on to implementing shadow support for our omni light. Adding shadow map support for a point light is a different task than adding support to a spotlight. The main reason for this is that spotlights shine in a single direction, while omni lights shine in every direction. For this reason, our shadows need to be cast in all directions. This cannot be accomplished with a single shadow map. You need six shadow maps, one for each side (front, back, left, right, top, bottom). To calculate these shadows you will need to render six maps from the position of the light, one facing each direction. It is usually advisable to set the camera to a field of view of 90.25. More information on generating these maps can be found in the *RenderMan Companion*, in the chapter that describes how to generate environment cube maps.

To read those maps we need to create one map parameter for each of the six maps. We also need to create parameters to control the maps lookup. There is no need to have individual map controls since we want all the maps to behave the same. We will also add a shadow color parameter so that we have more control over the shadows that are cast.

```
light 1_RP_omnilight (

                ...
                uniform color shadowColor = 0;
                string shadowpx    = "";
                string shadownx    = "";
                string shadowpy    = "";
                string shadowny    = "";
                string shadowpz    = "";
                string shadownz    = "";
```

```
        uniform float shadowBlur = 0.01;
        uniform float shadowSamples = 32;
        uniform float shadowBias = 0.01;
        uniform float shadowWidth = 1;
        uniform string shadowFilter = "gaussian";
        ...)
```

We will now implement the map lookup inside the shader body. This will be done using a simple technique. We start by transforming the light vector L from shader space to world space. We do this because the orientation of the shader space could have shifted in the process of positioning the light. For generating the shadow maps, we need the L vector to be aligned with the world coordinates. We then extract the x, y, and z components of the light vector and store them in Lx, Ly, and Lz. The values in these variables have negative and positive values, and we need all values to be positive, as we will use the total distances to identify whether the light ray is facing x, y, or z.

We continue to set up three if-else statements that will make the shader use different shadow() calls based on which direction the L vector is facing. Inside each of those cases, we will test whether the value of L is positive or negative. We use this test to determine if we need to use the map aligned with the positive or negative value of the world. Once we have calculated the attenuation variable, we will use it as the alpha value inside a mix() function to blend lightcolor and shadowcolor. This shader will also support basic raytraced shadows if you provide the keyword raytrace as the map name. Figures 8.13 and 8.14 show the difference between shadow maps and raytraced shadows.

```
{
/* Variables */
    float dist ;
    float Lx, Ly, Lz, AbsLx, AbsLy, AbsLz;
    vector Lrel;
    float attenuation = 0.0;

    illuminate( from ){
        dist = length(L);
        /* Transform L into world coords */
        Lrel = vtransform("world", L);
        Lx = xcomp(Lrel);              // Get the x component of L
        AbsLx = abs(Lx);               // Get the absolute value of Lx
        Ly = ycomp(Lrel);
        AbsLy = abs(Ly);
        Lz = zcomp(Lrel);
        AbsLz = abs(Lz);
```

```
/* test if the value of L is facing more in the x axis than y and z */
if((AbsLx > AbsLy) && (AbsLx > AbsLz)) {
    /* If L points in positive x use the px map, if not use the nx */
    if((Lx > 0.0)&&(shadowpx != ""))
        attenuation = shadow( shadowpx, Ps, "samples", shadowSamples,
                              "width",  shadowWidth,
                              "blur",shadowBlur,
                              "bias",shadowBias,
                              "filter",shadowFilter);
    else if (shadownx != "")
        attenuation = shadow( shadownx, Ps, "samples", shadowSamples,
                              "width",  shadowWidth,
                              "blur",shadowBlur,
                              "bias",shadowBias,
                              "filter",shadowFilter );
} else if((AbsLy > AbsLx) && (AbsLy > AbsLz)) {
    if((Ly > 0.0)&&(shadowpy != ""))
        attenuation = shadow( shadowpy, Ps, "samples", shadowSamples,
                              "width",  shadowWidth,
                              "blur",shadowBlur,
                              "bias",shadowBias,
                              "filter",shadowFilter);
    else if (shadowny != "")
        attenuation = shadow( shadowny, Ps, "samples", shadowSamples,
                              "width",  shadowWidth,
                              "blur",shadowBlur,
                              "bias",shadowBias,
                              "filter",shadowFilter);
} else if((AbsLz > AbsLy) && (AbsLz > AbsLx)) {
    if((Lz > 0.0)&&(shadowpz != ""))
        attenuation = shadow( shadowpz, Ps, "samples", shadowSamples,
                              "width", shadowWidth,
                              "blur",shadowBlur,
                              "bias",shadowBias,
                              "filter",shadowFilter);
    else if (shadownz != "")
        attenuation = shadow( shadownz, Ps, "samples", shadowSamples,
                              "width", shadowWidth,
                              "blur",shadowBlur,
                              "bias",shadowBias,
                              "filter",shadowFilter);
}
```

```
color lc = mix(lightcolor,shadowColor,attenuation);
Cl = intensity * lc  * 1/pow(dist,falloff);
    }
}
```

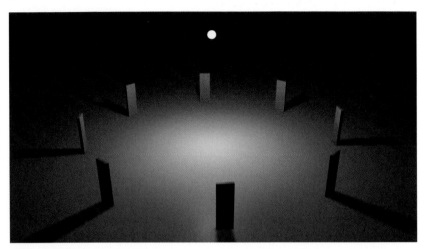

Figure 8.13 The omni light scene rendered with shadow maps.

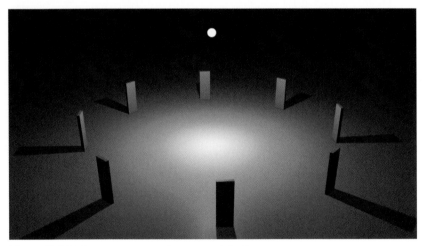

Figure 8.14 The same scene with raytraced shadows.

The last improvement we will make to our omni light shader is to include support for the transmission() function. The transmission() function takes a minimum of two parameters: a destination point and an origin point. The function will calculate the shadow value as a ray is sent from Psource to Pdestiny. Note that the transmission() function is the only shadow calculating method that will respect the opacity color of an object to tint the shadow ray and therefore change the shadow color.

```
transmission(Psource,Pdestiny,...);
```

With this feature implemented, our omni light shader will have access to all the available shadow types, as well as control over how the intensity falls off with distance. To implement the transmission feature, we need to add a parameter to let the light shader know whether we want to use shadow maps or the transmission call, as using both would be overkill. We will use a uniform float parameter named doTransmission, which we will set to 0 as default. Changing this value to 1 will enable the shader to perform transmission calculations. We will also add a set of parameters to control the transmission lookup. Here is the code for our finalized shader. Note that we stripped out the shadow map lookup decisions that were redundant and put them into a function called getMapShadows(). I also added a little more intelligence so that if you want to use raytrace as your shadow map, you don't need to type raytrace on all the map fields, just on the first one. Figures 8.15 and 8.16 demonstrate quite clearly the difference between using raytrace and transmission to calculate shadows for semitransparent objects.

```
float getMapShadows(float LL;string mapP,mapN;uniform float blur, samples,
                    bias,width; string filter)
{
    float res = 0;
    if((LL > 0.0)&&(mapP != ""))
        res= shadow( mapP, Ps, "samples",samples,
                    "width",width,
                    "blur",blur,
                    "bias",bias,
                    "filter",filter);
    else if (mapN != "")
        res = shadow( mapN, Ps, "samples",samples,
                    "width",width,
                    "blur",blur,
                    "bias",bias,
                    "filter",filter );
    return res;
}


light l_RP_omnilightTrans(
                            float intensity = 1;
                            color lightcolor = 1;
                            uniform float falloff = 1;
                            point from = point "shader" (0,0,0);
                            /* Shadow controls */
                            uniform color shadowColor = 0;
                            string shadowpx    = "";
```

```
                        string shadownx    = "";
                        string shadowpy    = "";
                        string shadowny    = "";
                        string shadowpz    = "";
                        string shadownz    = "";
                        uniform float shadowBlur = 0.01;
                        uniform float shadowSamples = 32;
                        uniform float shadowBias = 0.01;
                        uniform float shadowWidth = 1;
                        uniform string shadowFilter = "gaussian";
                        /* Transmission Controls */
                        uniform float doTransmission = 0;
                        uniform float transSamples = 16;
                        uniform float transMinSamples = 4;
                        uniform float transBlur = 0.01;
                        uniform float transBias = 0.01;
                        string __category = "all";
                        )
{
    /* Variables */
    float dist ;
    float Lx, Ly, Lz, AbsLx, AbsLy, AbsLz;
    vector Lrel;
    float attenuation = 0.0;
    color lc = 1;

    illuminate( from ){
        Lrel = vtransform("world", L);
        dist = length(L);

        Lx = xcomp(Lrel);
        AbsLx = abs(Lx);
        Ly = ycomp(Lrel);
        AbsLy = abs(Ly);
        Lz = zcomp(Lrel);
        AbsLz = abs(Lz);

        if (doTransmission == 0){
            if(shadowpx == "raytrace"){
                attenuation = shadow("raytrace",Ps,"samples",shadowSamples,
                                    "blur",shadowBlur,
                                    "bias",shadowBias);
        } else {
            if((AbsLx > AbsLy) && (AbsLx > AbsLz))
```

```
            attenuation = getMapShadows(Lx,shadowpx,shadownx,shadowSamples,
                                shadowWidth,shadowBlur,
                                shadowBias,shadowFilter);
        else if((AbsLy > AbsLx) && (AbsLy > AbsLz))
            attenuation = getMapShadows(Ly,shadowpy,shadowny,shadowSamples,
                                shadowWidth,shadowBlur,
                                shadowBias,shadowFilter);
        else if((AbsLz > AbsLy) && (AbsLz > AbsLx))
            attenuation = getMapShadows(Lz,shadowpz,shadownz,shadowSamples,
                                shadowWidth,shadowBlur,
                                shadowBias,shadowFilter);
    }
    lc = mix(lightcolor,shadowColor,attenuation);
    } else {
        lc = transmission(Ps, from,
                            "samples", transSamples,
                            "minsamples", transMinSamples,
                            "samplecone", transBlur,
                            "bias", transBias);
    }
    Cl = intensity * lc  * 1/pow(dist,falloff);
    }
}
```

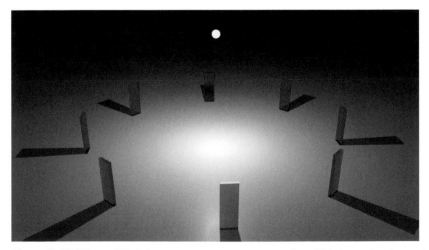

Figure 8.15 We modified the scene to use transparent cubes. This image has transmission turned off and raytrace as the shadow map.

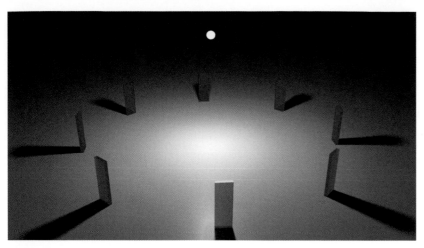

Figure 8.16 This image uses transmission to render colored shadows.

Distant Directional Lights

We have so far created an ambient light that has no position or direction. Then we created an omni light that has a position but no direction. Now we will create a light that is the opposite of the omni light—it has direction but no position. This kind of light is known as a *directional* or *distant light*.

The name *directional light* is more accurate because this light casts all of its rays in a parallel manner aligned to the specified direction vector. Some people refer to it as a sun light because it tends to replicate the effect of a light that is very far away. To implement this shader, we will use a solar() statement instead of illuminate(). Since this light needs a direction, we will need to provide a to point parameter in addition to the from parameter that was specified for the omni light. The to point will be initialized with a value of (0,0,1). Since from is initialized to (0,0,0), this means that our directional light will point by default into the positive Z direction. You can manipulate the position of this light by changing the values of from and to or by transforming the current coordinate system before you define the light and leave from and to at their default values.

We will implement the directional light shader with built-in shadow support. We will start with the finished omni light shader and modify it to turn it into a directional light. To do this, we need to get rid of five out of the six image maps used to cast shadows in the omni light and implement a single shadow call inside the shader. We will also include transmission() support inside this shader, and we will need a bit of trickery to get things to work.

The reason for this is that the transmission() shadeop takes two points as its parameters. If you pass the surface shading point Ps and the from point, you will get shadows that behave as an omni light because every shadow is calculated against the same point, which means that each shadow ray has a different direction vector. Distant lights use a direction vector, not a point, so we need to figure out a way to force transmission() to use that vector.

We need to use the direction vector to somehow create a new point that will be passed to the transmission() shadeop. In Chapter 5, we covered the properties of math operations between points and vectors, and we said that adding a vector to a point creates a new point, so the solution is quite simple. Just add the light direction vector A to the surface shading point Ps. That will create a new point tilted at the same angle for all surface points, creating a distant light.

There is one more thing to consider: If the object is too big, it might not shadow properly because the direction vector (A) is usually just a unit long (to(0,0,1) - from(0,0,0)). What we will do to get around this is to scale the vector by multiplying it by a new float parameter called shadowDist. The last thing to consider is that the light vector (A) travels from the light to the surface point (Ps), and what we need is a vector that travels from the surface point to the light. This is done by simply inverting the vector with a minus sign before the vector. So the new light "from" point PL is calculated like this:

```
point PL = Ps + (shadowDist*normalize(-A));
```

The output of using transmission shadows from a distant light can be seen in Figure 8.17. Here is the final source for our distant light.

```
light l_RP_distantlight(
                    float intensity = 1;
                    color lightcolor = 1;
                    uniform float falloff = 1;
                    point from = point "shader" (0,0,0);
                    point to = point "shader" (0,0,1);
                    /* Shadow controls */
                    uniform color shadowColor = 0;
                    string shadowMap    = "";
                    uniform float shadowBlur = 0.01;
                    uniform float shadowSamples = 32;
                    uniform float shadowBias = 0.01;
                    uniform float shadowWidth = 1;
                    uniform string shadowFilter = "gaussian";
                    /* Transmission Controls */
```

```
                        uniform float shadowDist = 1000;
                        uniform float doTransmission = 0;
                        uniform float transSamples = 16;
                        uniform float transMinSamples = 4;
                        uniform float transBlur = 0.01;
                        uniform float transBias = 0.01;
                        string __category = "all";
                        )
{
    /* Variables */
    float dist ;
    float attenuation = 0.0;
    color lc = 1;
    vector A = to - from;

    solar( A , 0.0){
        dist = length(L);
        point PL = Ps + (shadowDist*normalize(-A));

        if (doTransmission == 0){
            attenuation = shadow(shadowMap,Ps,"samples",shadowSamples,
                                "blur",shadowBlur,
                                "bias",shadowBias);
            lc = mix(lightcolor,shadowColor,attenuation);
        } else {
            lc = transmission(Ps,PL,
                            "samples", transSamples,
                            "minsamples", transMinSamples,
                            "samplecone", transBlur,
                            "bias", transBias);
        }
        Cl = intensity * lc  * 1/pow(dist,falloff);
    }
}
```

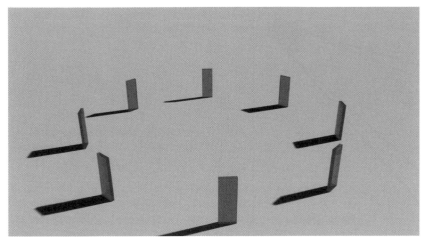

Figure 8.17 Transmission shadows cast from a distant light.

Spotlights

Controlling the direction and position from which a light shines is essential in cinematographic lighting. It offers you a higher level of control over the light rays than a directional or omni light. To implement a spotlight, we will go back to using the `illuminate()` function, except this time we will use a different version of the function, one that uses three parameters instead of a single `from` parameter. The three parameters used on this version are `from`, `direction vector`, and `angle`. `from` is the same as before, the position from which the light shines. `direction vector` represents the direction in which the cone angle will be aligned, and `angle` represents how wide in radians the lighting cone will be. Light rays will only be cast inside this illumination cone, effectively creating a spotlight. Our spotlight will have the same features as the previous light shaders, except for several new parameters necessary to control it effectively.

We will add a `coneAngle`, a `coneDeltaAngle`, and a `beamDistribution` parameter to the shader. `coneAngle` defines the cone where the light rays will be emitted, and `coneDeltaAngle` represents the softness of the spotlight. Note that these two values are in radians, not in degrees, so make sure you pass the values in radians.

The last of the new parameters will be a `beamDistribution` parameter that controls how the light falls off from the core of the cone to the edges. The effect of it is hard to see unless you add an atmospheric shader to help make the light beam visible. Figure 8.18 demonstrates what these new parameters do, followed by the source code of our shader. The comments in the shader explain key sections.

Uberlight

The previous lights will give you a good amount of control, and you should be able to get very decent lighting schemes from them. However, in a production environment, there is usually the need for an even higher level of control and features. In Chapter 14 of Larry Gritz and Tony Apodaca's book, *Advanced RenderMan*, Ronen Barzel describes a light model that he presented at SIGGRAPH 1997. This light model is known in many circles as the *uberlight*. It is a light that has a lot of features, the most important of which are listed here:

- Controls for where the volume of the light starts and ends, including controls to fade the light in and out.

- The capability to function as a spotlight or an omni light.

- Roundness controls for the shape of the light cone. With this control, you can turn the light from a round spotlight to a square "barn doors" type light.

- The cone also has a skew transformation through which you can bend the light cone into a different direction from where the light is actually pointing.

- Slide projection of a texture file that can also be used as a cucoloris or "cookie" to mask the light.

- Blockers, which are 2D super-ellipse shapes that can be used to block light rays. They are great for casting shadows or darkening areas without having to add more geometry to your scene.

You can read all the details on the design and implementation for the shader in the *Advanced RenderMan* (ARman for short) book. This will give you a clear insight of how it is put together and why it behaves the way it does.

As complete as that light model was in 1997, nowadays there are several features that need to be inserted into the light. Some changes are needed to support the latest changes and features that have been added to RenderMan. There are also other controls that can be improved, and the code needs to be updated because it uses some techniques that were relevant to the sadly defunct BMRT rendering engine. We will proceed to make the following improvements to ARman's uberlight:

- Add unlimited support for slides and blockers through the use of arrays. We will also add more controls for the slide projection to enable control of the position, scale, and blur of the slide.

- Add support for `transmission()` generated shadows.

- Clean up and update the code.

We will start by adding unlimited support for slides and blockers. Variable length arrays were introduced in version 13 of PRMan. This new feature allows you to create shaders that can expand and contract to meet your needs. We will add the parameters described below to the shader to support any number of slides and blockers. The arrays for the slide parameters are initialized with the new variable array syntax. For such variables, you don't need to pass a length for the array; you can just use the name of the variable followed by a set of square brackets. You also don't need to pass a value to the array; an empty set of curly braces will do. The blocker parameters are declared in the same manner arrays had to be declared before. You need to give your array a length and initialize the value for each element of your address.

```
{
    ...
    string slideName[] = {};
    uniform float slideScaleX[] = {},slideScaleY[] = {};
    uniform float slideOffsetX[]={}, slideOffsetY[]= {};
    uniform float slideBlur[] = {};
    /* Fake blocker shadow */
    string blockerCoords[4] = {"","","",""};
    uniform float blockerOpac[4]={1,1,1,1};
    float blockerwidth[4]={1,1,1,1}, blockerheight[4]={1,1,1,1};
    float blockerwedge[4]={.1,.1,.1,.1},
    blockerhedge[4]={.1,.1,.1,.1}, blockerround[4]={1,1,1,1};
    ...
}
```

Inside the shader body, we will make some modifications to the uberlight shader. We will use a for() loop to iterate over all the elements inside the array. For this we use the arraylength() shadeop, which returns an integer value of the length of the array. We will use the typical i variable to index each element of the array. It is recommended that you declare the i variable as a uniform float.

```
/* Project a slide or use a cookie */
uniform float i;
for (i = 0; i < arraylength(slideName); i += 1){
    if (slideName[i] != "") {
        point Pslide = PL / point (width+wedge, height+hedge, 1);
        float zslide = zcomp(Pslide);
        float xslide = slideOffsetX[i]+(0.5+0.5*xcomp(Pslide)/zslide);
        float yslide = slideOffsetY[i]+(0.5-0.5*ycomp(Pslide)/zslide);
        lcol *= color texture (slideName[i], xslide * 1/slideScaleX[i],
                               yslide *
1/slideScaleY[i],"blur",slideBlur[i]);
    }
}
```

A similar routine is used to iterate over all the blockers passed to the shader. We will now steal the code for generating transmission() generated shadows. With that code in place, our final shader is as follows:

```
/* Superellipse soft clipping
 * Input:
 *    - point Q on the x-y plane
 *    - the equations of two superellipses (with major/minor axes given by
 *          a,b and A,B for the inner and outer ellipses, respectively)
 * Return value:
 *    - 0 if Q was inside the inner ellipse
 *    - 1 if Q was outside the outer ellipse
 *    - smoothly varying from 0 to 1 in between
 */
Float clipSuperellipse (
                    point Q;           /* Test point on the x-y plane */
                    float a, b;        /* Inner superellipse */
                    float A, B;        /* Outer superellipse */
                    float roundness;   /* Same roundness for both ellipses */
                    )
{
    float result = 0;
    float x = abs(xcomp(Q)), y = abs(ycomp(Q));
    if (x != 0 || y != 0) {   /* avoid degenerate case */
        if (roundness < 1.0e-6) {
            /* Simpler case of a square */
            result = 1 - (1-smoothstep(a,A,x)) * (1-smoothstep(b,B,y));
        } else if (roundness > 0.9999) {
            /* Simple case of a circle */
            float sqr (float x) { return x*x; }
            float q = a * b / sqrt (sqr(b*x) + sqr(a*y));
            float r = A * B / sqrt (sqr(B*x) + sqr(A*y));
            result = smoothstep (q, r, 1);
        } else {
            /* Harder, rounded corner case */
            float re = 2/roundness;   /* roundness exponent */
            float q = a * b * pow (pow(b*x, re) + pow(a*y, re), -1/re);
            float r = A * B * pow (pow(B*x, re) + pow(A*y, re), -1/re);
            result = smoothstep (q, r, 1);
        }
    }
        return result;
}
```

```
/* Volumetric light shaping
 * Inputs:
 *    - the point being shaded, in the local light space
 *    - all information about the light shaping, including z smooth depth
 *      clipping, superellipse x-y shaping, and distance falloff.
 * Return value:
 *    - attenuation factor based on the falloff and shaping
 */
Float ShapeLightVolume (
                        point PL;                   /* Point in light space */
                        string lighttype;           /* what kind of light
*/
                        vector axis;                /* light axis */
                        float znear, zfar;          /* z clipping */
                        float nearedge, faredge;
                        float falloff, falloffdist;  /* distance falloff */
                        float maxintensity;
                        float shearx, sheary;        /* shear the direction
*/
                        float width, height;         /* xy superellipse */
                        float hedge, wedge, roundness;
                        float beamdistribution;      /* angle falloff */
                        )
{
    /* Examine the z depth of PL to apply the (possibly smooth) cuton and
       cutoff. */
    float atten = 1;
    float PLlen = length(PL);
    float Pz;
    if (lighttype == "spot") {
        Pz = zcomp(PL);
    } else {
        /* For omni or area lights, use distance from the light */
        Pz = PLlen;
    }
    atten *= smoothstep (znear-nearedge, znear, Pz);
    atten *= 1 - smoothstep (zfar, zfar+faredge, Pz);

    /* Distance falloff */
    if (falloff != 0) {
        if (PLlen > falloffdist) {
            atten *= pow (falloffdist/PLlen, falloff);
        } else {
            float s = log (1/maxintensity);
```

```
                float beta = -falloff/s;
                atten *= (maxintensity * exp (s * pow(PLlen/falloffdist,
beta)));
            }
    }

    /* Clip to superellipse */
    if (lighttype != "omni" && beamdistribution > 0)
        atten *= pow (zcomp(normalize(vector PL)), beamdistribution);
    if (lighttype == "spot") {
        atten *= 1 - clipSuperellipse (PL/Pz-point(shearx,sheary,0),
                                       width, height,
                                       width+wedge, height+hedge, roundness);
    }
    return atten;
}
/* Evaluate the occlusion between two points, P1 and P2, due to a fake
 * blocker.  Return 0 if the light is totally blocked, 1 if it totally
 * gets through.
 */
Float BlockerContribution ( point P1, P2;
                            string blockercoords;
                            float blockerwidth, blockerheight;
                            float blockerwedge, blockerhedge;
                            float blockerround;
                            )
{
    float unoccluded = 1;
    /* Get the surface and light positions in blocker coords */
    point Pb1 = transform (blockercoords, P1);
    point Pb2 = transform (blockercoords, P2);
    /* Blocker works only if it's straddled by ray endpoints. */
    if (zcomp(Pb2)*zcomp(Pb1) < 0) {
        vector Vlight = (Pb1 - Pb2);
        point Pplane = Pb1 - Vlight*(zcomp(Pb1)/zcomp(Vlight));
        unoccluded *= clipSuperellipse (Pplane, blockerwidth, blockerheight,
                                        blockerwidth+blockerwedge,
                                        blockerheight+blockerhedge,
                                        blockerround);
    }
    return unoccluded;
}

light l_RP_uberlight(
```

```
                 /* Basic intensity and color of the light */
                 string lighttype = "spot";
                 float intensity = 1;
                 color lightcolor = color (1,1,1);
                 /* Z shaping and distance falloff */
                 float cuton = 0.01, cutoff = 1.0e6, nearedge = 0, faredge = 0;
                 float falloff = 0, falloffdist = 1, maxintensity = 1;
                 float parallelrays = 0;
                 /* xy shaping of the cross section and angle falloff */
                 float shearx = 0, sheary = 0;
                 float width = 1, height = 1, wedge = .1, hedge = .1;
                 float roundness = 1;
                 float beamdistribution = 0;
                 /* Cookie or slide to control light cross-sectional color */
                 string slideName[] = {};
                 uniform float slideScaleX[] = {},slideScaleY[] = {};
                 uniform float slideOffsetX[]={}, slideOffsetY[]= {};
                 uniform float slideBlur[] = {};
                 /* Noisy light */
                 float noiseamp = 0, noisefreq = 4;
                 vector noiseoffset = 0;
                 /* Shadow mapped shadows */
                 string shadowmap = "";
                 float shadowblur = 0.01, shadowbias = .01, shadownsamps = 16;
                 color shadowcolor = 0;
                 /* Transmission Controls */
                 uniform float doTransmission = 0, filtWshadCol =
                     0,transSamples = 16;
                 uniform float transMinSamples = 4, transBlur = 0.01;
                 uniform float transBias = 0.01;
                 /* Fake blocker shadow */
                 string blockerCoords[4] = {"","","",""};
                 uniform float blockerOpac[4]={1,1,1,1};
                 float blockerwidth[4]={1,1,1,1}, blockerheight[4]={1,1,1,1};
                 float blockerwedge[4]={.1,.1,.1,.1},
                 blockerhedge[4]={.1,.1,.1,.1}, blockerround[4]={1,1,1,1};
                 /* Miscellaneous controls */
                 output varying float __nonspecular = 0;
                 output float __nondiffuse = 0;
                 output float __foglight = 1;
                 )
{
    /* For simplicity, assume that the light is at the origin of shader
     * space and aimed in the +z direction.  So to move or orient the
```

```
 * light, you transform the coordinate system in the RIB stream, prior
 * to instancing the light shader.  But that sure simplifies the
 * internals of the light shader!  Anyway, let PL be the position of
 * the surface point we're shading, expressed in the local light
 * shader coordinates.
 */
point PL = transform ("shader", Ps);

/* For PRMan, we've gotta do it the hard way */
point from = point "shader" (0,0,0);
vector axis = normalize(vector "shader" (0,0,1));

uniform float angle;
if (lighttype == "spot") {                    /* Spotlight */
    uniform float maxradius = 1.4142136 * max(height+hedge+abs(sheary),
width+wedge+abs(shearx));
    angle = atan(maxradius);
} else {                                      /* Omnidirectional light */
    angle = PI;
}

illuminate (from, axis, angle) {
    /* Accumulate attenuation of the light as it is affected by various
     * blockers and whatnot.  Start with no attenuation (i.e., a
     * multiplicative attenuation of 1.
     */
    float atten = 1.0;
    color lcol = lightcolor;
    uniform float i;
    color lc = 1;

    /* Basic light shaping - the volumetric shaping is all encapsulated
     * in the ShapeLightVolume function.
     */
    atten *= ShapeLightVolume (PL, lighttype, axis, cuton, cutoff,
                               nearedge, faredge, falloff, falloffdist,
                               maxintensity/intensity, shearx, sheary,
                               width, height, hedge, wedge, roundness,
                               beamdistribution);

    /* Project a slide or use a cookie */
    for (i = 0; i < arraylength(slideName); i += 1){
        (slideName[i] != "") {
```

```
            point Pslide = PL / point (width+wedge, height+hedge, 1);
            float zslide = zcomp(Pslide);
            float xslide = slideOffsetX[i]+(0.5+0.5*xcomp(Pslide)/zslide);
            float yslide = slideOffsetY[i]+(0.5-0.5*ycomp(Pslide)/zslide);
            lcol *= color texture (slideName[i], xslide * 1/slideScaleX[i],
                                   yslide *
1/slideScaleY[i],"blur",slideBlur[i]);
            }
        }
        /* If the volume says we aren't being lit, skip the remaining tests */
        if (atten > 0) {
            /* Apply noise */
            if (noiseamp > 0) {
#pragma nolint
            float n = noise (noisefreq * (PL+noiseoffset) * point(1,1,0));
            n = smoothstep (0, 1, 0.5 + noiseamp * (n-0.5));
            atten *= n;
            }
            /* Apply shadow mapped shadows */
            float unoccluded = 1;
            if (shadowmap != "")
                unoccluded *= 1 - shadow (shadowmap, Ps, "blur", shadowblur,
                                          "samples", shadownsamps,
                                          "bias", shadowbias);

            /* Apply transmission shadows */
            if (doTransmission == 1){
                lc = transmission(Ps, from,
                                  "samples", transSamples,
                                  "minsamples", transMinSamples,
                                  "samplecone", transBlur,
                                  "bias", transBias);

                unoccluded *= (lc[0]+lc[1]+lc[2]) / 3;
            }
            point shadoworigin;
            if (parallelrays == 0)
                shadoworigin = from;
            else
                shadoworigin = point "shader" (xcomp(PL), ycomp(PL), cuton);

            /* Apply blocker fake shadows */
            for (i = 0; i < arraylength(blockerCoords); i +=1){
                if (blockerCoords[i] != "") {
```

```
                float block = BlockerContribution (Ps, shadoworigin,
                                    blockerCoords[i],blockerwidth[i],
                                    blockerheight[i],blockerwedge[i],
                                    blockerhedge[i],blockerround[i]);
                unoccluded *= clamp(1,0,block + (1 - blockerOpac[i]));
            }
        }
        if (filtWshadCol == 0 && doTransmission == 1)
            lcol *= lc;
        else if (filtWshadCol == 1 && doTransmission == 1)
            lcol = mix (shadowcolor * lc, lcol   , unoccluded);
        else
            lcol = mix(shadowcolor, lcol,unoccluded);

        __nonspecular = 1 - unoccluded * (1 - __nonspecular);
    }
    Cl = (atten*intensity) * lcol;
    if (parallelrays != 0)
        L = axis * length(Ps-from);
    }
}
```

Figures 8.19 to 8.21 demonstrate the different features of the improved uberlight.

Figure 8.19 An image being projected as a slide from the light.

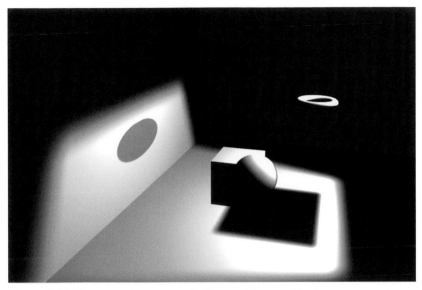

Figure 8.20 This image has no cast shadows and has two blockers: one round, one square.

Figure 8.21 The same scene with `transmission()` shadows, `roundness` = 1, and a `cuton` value of 8. Note how the light doesn't start shining until it's eight units away from the source point.

From Here and Beyond

There are many other things that light shaders can do beyond lighting. In a movie I worked on lately, I created a very simple light shader that didn't actually illuminate an object, but it color corrected the final color returned by the surface shader. This is quite simple to implement; here are the steps you can take to make this work.

Create a new illumination loop function that reads a varying color. This color will be the final unmultiplied color that you calculate from your surface shader.

Inside the function you will translate the color into hsv() space so that you can easily manipulate the values to change the hue, saturation, and value (intensity). When you are finished with the color manipulation, convert the color back to RGB and return it from the function. The trick is that every shader in your production needs to have such illumination function as the last part of the shader, right before it gets multiplied by the opacity.

This and many other tricks are achievable with lights. Just keep in mind that a light does not necessarily have to just illuminate. A great example of how to use lights for other purposes can be found on Moritz Moeller's "Going Mad With Magic Lights" presentation for SIGGRAPH's 2006 "RenderMan for Everyone" course.

Before we wrap up, remember that a light shader can also use procedural routines to modify the intensity and color of a light. To create three-dimensional textures such as noise fields, you need to use the P variable, and to create two-dimensional textures, you can use the s and t parameters or the same routine used to create the texture coordinates for the slide projections. Feel free to experiment with lights and textures once you read the pattern generation chapter.

9

Volume Shaders

We now arrive at what is perhaps the most mysterious and enigmatic of the shader types supported by RenderMan. Volume shaders are a bit hard to understand because they are not really "attached" to a surface or a light. In RenderMan lingo, you attach or assign a volume shader to a surface, but the shader is not evaluated in the surface micropolygons like the displacement or surface shaders. The volume shader lives somewhere between here (the camera) and there (anywhere in the scene besides a surface), and its job is to attenuate or modify the ray value as it travels through space.

A volume shader can exist between the camera and the rendering surface, which is done using an Atmosphere shader call. It can also exist inside a surface, as a ray enters a rendering mesh shell and before it exits the shell; that effect is achieved with the Interior shader call. The final place a volume shader can exist is in a ray that has bounced from a rendering surface, such as a reflection ray. To apply a volume shader to this bounced ray, we use the Exterior shader call. Figure 9.1 demonstrates where each of the three volume calls is executed.

As explained in Chapter 2, "RSL Details," volume shaders were originally designed to replicate environmental phenomena that exist virtually everywhere, but not in the sterile realm of CG graphics. The default values for attributes and options in most RenderMan renderers generate an image that resembles one taken with a pinhole camera (with infinite depth of field) in a vacuum (no dust particles in the environment) and of an object that is not moving at all (no motion blur). Each of these features has to be enabled by the user when needed so that the renderer by default is as fast as it can be.

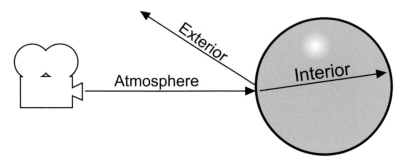

Figure 9.1 Diagram depicting where each of the three volume shaders is executed.

Environmental phenomena are essential for adding realism to shots, especially for long establishing shots, underwater scenes, or anywhere you need to see the beams of light that shine through the environment. A movie such as *Finding Nemo,* which was mostly underwater, could have never looked as good as it did without the use of volume shaders. Fog, mist, and smoke are examples of scattering, one of light's interesting optical properties.

The "Discovering Light" page at ThinkQuest.com describes the scattering property of light this way:

> "Excited electrons emit light waves, and...the opposite is true: Light waves can excite electrons. When electrons are excited by light waves, they jump to a higher energy level. When they fall back to their original energy level, the electrons reemit the light. This process is called scattering. However, when the light is reemitted by scattering, not all of the energy is given back to the light wave, but instead, some is lost to the particle. This will result in a light wave of lower frequency and wavelength...."

Let's start our exploration into volumetric shaders by first analyzing the predefined variables that are available to volume shaders. Since volume shaders are not evaluated on the surface of an object, they have no access to surface variables such as N, s,t, or u,v. The volume shader variables are outlined in Table 9.1.

Table 9.1 Volume Shader Variables

Name	Type	Storage Class	Description
P	point	varying	Light ray origin
E	point	uniform	Position of the eye
I	vector	varying	Incident ray direction
Ci	color	varying	Ray color
Oi	color	varying	Ray opacity
ncomp	float	uniform	Number of color components
time	float	uniform	Current shader shutter time
dtime	float	uniform	The amount of time covered by this shading sample
Output			
Ci	color	varying	Attenuated ray color at origin
Oi	color	varying	Attenuated ray opacity at origin

Atmosphere, Interior, and Exterior Volume Shaders

Atmosphere shaders were the original use for volume shaders in PRMan until version 11, when raytracing was introduced into the renderer. The other types of volume shaders were already defined in the RiSpec before they were implemented by PRMan, which means that other renderers that already supported raytracing could support interior and exterior shaders.

There is an obvious need for an interior volume shader call, such as when you need to shade an object that is all gooey and gelatinous inside, for which you might need to perform extensive calculations that should only happen inside the object. But why are exterior and an environment volume shader implementations needed? After all, isn't everything outside the object considered part of the environment?

If you remember the design requirements of the RiSpec, speed optimization and control were always part of it, so the designers decided to separate the outside of an object into two different types. The first space is covered by the ray between the camera and the rendering surface, and the second space is the rays between all other objects. You can see that the second case (the space between all objects) has the possibility to be much more complex than the first one, between the camera and the surface.

The atmosphere shader is a lot more efficient because once the ray hits a surface, the shader is done executing. If the surface is a reflective material, then a reflection ray will be emitted. It is on these reflected rays that exterior shaders are executed, attenuating the ray value as it bounces around through the scene. Imagine if you had a scene that was a hall of mirrors. That reflection ray would continue to bounce around until it hit the maxspeculardepth ray bounce limit. You can see how much more complex the object-to-object space can be than the camera-to-object space. If we had only the exterior shader call for areas outside the objects, we would always incur the expense of calculating the rays that are bouncing through the scene, which would lead to huge rendering times.

To attach an atmosphere shader to the whole scene, you need to use an Atmosphere call followed by the shader and its parameters (similarly to how Surface and Displacement are used) inside the RIB file. This call is usually placed at the beginning of the world declaration, before all the geometry is defined. It is very important to know that for PRMan, atmosphere shaders can be executed only when there is geometry that the camera sees. If you create a scene with a light and a sphere, you need to add a flat piece of geometry in the background. Otherwise you will not be able to see the smoke or haze in the environment because it will be calculated only where the sphere is. The Interior and Exterior calls are usually right before the object or collection of objects that should use the shader in the same way as the surface and displacement shaders are. Be sure to place the calls within AttributeBegin and AttributeEnd calls to restrict the execution of the shaders to the object you want.

Simple Fog

A simple but essential environment volume shader is a fog or haze shader. The implementation of this shader can be very simple or somewhat complicated, depending on what features your shader will support. The main visual feature of fog is that the visibility of objects is reduced with distance, and an object will fade into a clear whitish tone. If we are dealing with haze or—even worse—smog, objects will fade to some kind of coloration. There are several ways to implement the attenuation. The simplest way is to use an exponential absorption model by fading into a supplied fog color. This shader is very simple, but it offers little control.

```
volume v_RP_simplefog (
                        color fogColor =  color(0.5,0.5,0.5);
                        float distance   =  1;
{
    float dist = 1 - exp(-length(I)/distance);
    Ci = mix(Ci,fogColor,dist);
    Oi = mix(Oi,color(1,1,1),dist);
}
```

Another way would be to provide a parameter that controls the point at which the fog completely covers all objects, reducing visibility to zero. To do this we need to measure the distance of the current shading point and run it through a smoothstep() operation to control where the fading starts and ends. Then we will feed that value to a pow() function to control how fast it fades. We will also create a set of parameters that allow us to define a limit and a fade rate for the fog on the Y (up) axis. This is done by dividing the Y value of P in world space over a height fade limit.

With this operation we will get a value of 1 once the value of P in Y is equal to groundpos plus heightFadeLimit. We then clamp() this value to make sure that once the Y value of P is greater than our heightFadeLimit, we don't go past 1. After that we will use another pow() function to control how fast the fade takes place. This can be used to replicate layered fog a little bit, where the fog does not quite continue all the way to the floor. Here is the shader code, followed by Figure 9.2, which is a sample output of the shader.

```
volume v_RP_fog (
                color  fogColor = color(1,1,1);
                float  fogDensity = 1;
                float  near = 0;
                float  far   = 100;
                float  fogExponent = 1;
                float  groundPos = 0;
                float  heightFadeLimit = 40;
                float  heightFadeVal = 0;
                )
{
    /* Get the depth of the current shaded point and use a pow() and a
smoothstep()
    * to control how the fog fades with distance*/
    float Pdepth = length(I);
    float atten  = pow(smoothstep(near,far,Pdepth),fogExponent);
    /* Create a height fade field. Start by transforming P into world
        coordinates.
    * Then use a clamp function to create a 0 to 1 height field, which will
        be used
    * to control the fade. Finally, use a pow() function to control the
        rate of the fade*/
    point Pw = transform("world",P);
    float Hdepth = clamp(ycomp(Pw)/(heightFadeLimit+ groundPos),0,1);
    float YY = pow(Hdepth,fogExponent);
    atten = atten * ((YY * heightFadeVal) + ( 1 - heightFadeVal));
    if (fogDensity != 0){
        Ci = mix(Ci * (1 - (atten * fogDensity)),fogColor ,atten *
```

```
            fogDensity );
        Oi = mix(Oi * (1 - (atten * fogDensity)),color(1,1,1),atten *
            fogDensity);
    }
}
```

Figure 9.2 The previous fog shader applied to a scene with evenly separated cubes.

Raymarching

The previous shader uses a simple distance field to calculate the contribution or attenuation of the ray color as it travels through space. The attenuation has no variation at all as it travels, and the only real control is the pow() function that we applied to control the rate at which the fog fades in or out. Things in nature are rarely so simple. Particles of dust tend to move and hover in the air based on air currents. This creates areas where there might be more particles present, affecting the density and variation of the fog or smoke. To achieve this effect, we use a shading technique named *raymarching*.

Raymarching gets its name from the way in which volume contribution is calculated. As a ray is cast within a scene from an Atmosphere, Interior, or Exterior call, the ray will be split into intervals that can be even or uneven (if some kind of weighting or randomness is used) and at which the atmosphere will be sampled, as shown in Figure 9.3. This way, if the ray travels through a three-dimensional noise field, the intensity of the environment will vary.

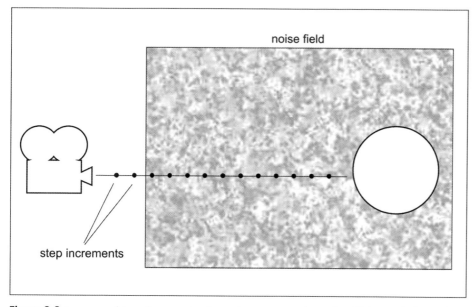

Figure 9.3 In raymarching, the ray going from the camera to the surface (I) is sampled at each step, and the values are accumulated.

There are several key concepts that we need to be aware of when we do raymarching. Ignoring these concepts will result in inefficient implementation of the shader.

■ Don't evaluate the volume shader once the value of the environment has reached a value of 1. At that point the environment is completely opaque and should cover the pixel completely, not allowing any of the surfaces to be visible. This optimization is more useful in large scenes.

■ Smaller step sizes will result in more accurate and detailed images, but with much longer rendering times.

■ Longer integration areas will result in longer rendering times.

■ Self shadowing and illumination effects will produce images that are a lot richer but a lot more expensive to render.

Let's start our exploration of raymarching by going over the steps to create a standard smoke shader that reacts to light rays. This smoke shader will make no contribution to the scene unless there are lights in the scene that are told to consider the smoke shader.

To perform raymarching, an algorithm similar to the following should be used:

```
/*Use the requested step size (increment) for marching along the ray*/
        total_len = length(I)
    inc = increment
```

```
current_pos = P - I
while inc < total_len do:
        current_pos += increment * normalize(I)
        sample the 3D pattern density and light at current_pos
        adjust Ci/Oi to add new light and extinguish due to smoke
opacity
        inc += increment
endwhile
```

If you read other papers and books about raymarching you will probably find algorithms that are somewhat different than this one, but at their core they perform the same tasks. Some might start sampling at the origin of the ray, as ours does, and increment the position from there, while others might start at the surface position and then decrease the position until they reach the camera. The algorithm outlined above can be used to generate phenomena that go through any 3D pattern. A smoky type of noise (a fractal noise, to be more precise) is the one most used because it emulates the randomness of particles in the air, but any 3D pattern can be used. To move to our implementation of our smoke shader, we will start by defining our shader parameters.

```
volume v_RP_smoke (
                color smokecolor=color(1,1,1);
                float density=.1;
                float scattermult=10;
                color scatter=color(1,1,1);
                float stepsize=0.50;
                float mindist = 0.01;
                float maxdist = 100;
                float accelerator = 0.01;
                float freq = 4;
                float octaves = 4;
                float smokevary = 1;
                float use_lighting = 1;
                float use_noise = 1;
                )
```

smokecolor is the color of the smoke. This color will be multiplied by the color of each light that contributes to the smoke calculation. If you want the smoke to be neutral and be affected only by the color of the lights, then leave it at white or (1,1,1). The density parameter represents how dense the smoke is; as you increase this value, the smoke will become more opaque, and objects behind the smoke will be less visible. scattermult is the multiplier of the scattering coefficient and is similar to a diffuse multiplier in that it will make the smoke more or less illuminated by the lights. scatter represents another color that will be filtered by the light contribution.

stepsize is perhaps one of the most important parameters of the shader. It is one of the main controls to establish how fast/slow your shader will run and how accurate your volume lookup will be. The next three parameters are purely optimization parameters. They allow you to control where the raymarching will begin and end, so to raymarch through the whole scene you would set mindist to 0 and maxdist to the value in the far clipping plane of the camera. This will result in the shader raymarching all the way until it hits a surface.

The accelerator is a previewing parameter and not intended to be used in production. It allows you to render the volume quickly by sacrificing accuracy. This parameter combined with stepsize will allow you to control the detail and render times of your image. freq and octaves are the typical fractal noise parameters, and smokevary determines the contrast or depth of the smoke. A smokevary value of 1 will make the dark area of the smoke 0 and the brightest 1, so the smoke will have a lot of variation. The last two parameters control whether the smoke will be affected by lights and if it will be constant or have noise in it.

Next we will create a group of local variables, of which the following are the most important:

```
point Worigin = P - I;
point origin = transform ("shader", Worigin);
vector Ishad = vtransform ("shader", I);
```

Worigin is the starting point of the ray we will march through in the "current" coordinate system. The origin variable is the exact same point but represented in the shader coord sys, and Ishad is the incident (I) vector transformed into shader space. Having the origin and incident rays in current and shader space becomes important later on. Next we have another round of initialization that will take place only if the stepsize is greater that 0.

```
if (Increment > 0) {
    float end = min(Ilen,maxdist)-0.0001;
    li = color(0);
    dtau = 0;
    d = mindist + (stepsize * random());
    ss = min(stepsize,end-d);
    d +=ss;
```

We begin by setting the value of end, which will be used to control how deeply our shader should traverse the scene. For this value, we will use the smallest value of the length of the I vector or the user-provided maxdist parameter. Next we initialize the value of li, which is the current light contribution, and the value of dtau, which is the current density of the volume. We initialize d to the value of mindist plus the stepsize value multiplied by the random() function. The d variable will be used to make the starting point of the volume equal to mindist plus a small variation for every ray, resulting in the starting point being a little different every time it runs and providing some three-dimensional jittering for our shader. ss is the incremental value that we use to march through the ray. It is set to the smallest value of stepsize and the distance between end and d.

We now move on to what is the core of our raymarching algorithm. The following code has been commented to simplify the reading.

```
/* If the value of l is less that the length of I then do some work */
while (d < end) {
    /* Initialize some necessary variables */
    IN = normalize (Ishad);
    WIN = vtransform ("shader", "current", IN);
    PP = origin + d * IN;
    PW = Worigin + d * WIN;
    last_dtau = dtau;
    last_li = li;

    /* If scatterMult is 0 then our smoke will not do any scattering
    so initialize li to white */
    if (ScatterMult == 0) li = color(1);
        /* if we are doing scattering then give li the output value of
            the light */
    else { illuminance (PP) { li += Cl; } }
    /* Calculate the density based on a 3D pattern. You can use a
            function, RSL
    or a cpp macro to insert the pattern here. The pattern must modify the
    value of li and the density of dtau. We use a routine taken from
        Larry Gritz's
    noisysmoke.sl */
    /* If use lighting is > 0 then we read the light value at the
            current point,
     if not then set li to 1 */
    if (use_lighting > 0) {
        li = 0;
        illuminance (PW) { li += Cl; }
    } else { li = 1; }
    /* if use_noise != 0 then do a fractal lookup, else set dtau to the
     provided parameter value */
    if (use_noise != 0) {
        /* scale the PP by frequency to control the size of the noise
        lookup and initialize smoke to a snoise value */
        Psmoke = PP*freq;
        smoke = snoise (Psmoke);
```

```
    /* Optimize: if the value of li is < 0.01 then don't perform
     this fractal generating loop */
    if (comp(li,0)+comp(li,1)+comp(li,2) > 0.01) {
        f=1;
        for (i=1;  i<octaves;  i+=1) {
            f *= 0.5;  Psmoke *= 2;
            smoke += f*snoise(Psmoke);
            }
        }
/* Multiply the smoke value by the density parameter and use a
    smoothstep
to control the variation of values inside the smoke */
dtau = density * smoothstep(-1,1,smokevary*smoke);
} else
    dtau = density;
/* Give tau the value of half the increment times the sum of the
    previous
density value and the current density */
tau = stepsize/2 * (dtau + last_dtau);
/* Do the same for the light density but the sum is of the li*dtau
    and the
last light value and the last density */
lighttau = stepsize/2 * (li*dtau + last_li*last_dtau);
/* Assign to scat the negated tau value multiplied by the Scatter and
smokeColor parameter. This will result in the internal value of the
    smoke
density by itself*/
scat = -tau * scatter * smokecolor;
/* Assign to the density opacity d0 the value the inverse exponent
    value
of scat */
d0 = 1 - color(
exp(comp(scat,0)),exp(comp(scat,1)),exp(comp(scat,2)));
/* and to the density color dC the light contribution times the
density opacity */
dC = lighttau * d0;
/* Finally, assign the value of d0 and dC to the final color value Cv
and the opacity value Ov */
Cv += (1-Ov)*dC;
Ov += (1-Ov)*d0;
/* calculate a new ss value to be added to d */
ss = max(min(ss,end-d),0.005);
/* Use the accelerator to control the spacing in each iteration.
If accelerator is 0 then all samples will be equally spaced.
```

```
    If accelerator is > 0, then the distance from sample to sample will
    increase in each iteration*/
    ss = pow(ss,1 - accelerator);
    d += ss;
}
```

The final step is to composite the calculated values into the shader output variables.

```
if (ScatterMult > 0) {
    Ci = ScatterMult*Cv + (1-Ov)*Ci;
} else {
    Ci = Cv + (1-Ov) * Ci;
}
Oi = Ov + (1-Ov)*Oi;
```

This shader will generate a nice smoke atmosphere as the ray travels through the scene. One important thing to note is that brute force raymarching (which is what this shader does) gets really expensive quite quickly. The render times are manageable when the increment or stepsize is large. The problem with using large stepsize values is that the smoke will have no detail, it will look like a series of blobs in the environment. If you want nice wispy smoke, the increment will have to be reduced, and as you reduce it the render times will go higher.

The accelerator parameter allows you to control how the samples are spaced. The idea behind it is that as we want the samples closer to the camera to be spaced closer together and as the samples travel further away from the camera, then we increase the spacing between them. This is a hack, and it will modify the look of the image. What I recommend you do is use accelerator while you are setting up your parameters such as frequency, smoke, and light colors. As you get closer to what you want, you can start reducing accelerator to get more accurate lookup. Once you think you have the image you want, set accelerator to 0 and render one image. Then start incrementing accelerator by very small amounts (0.01 at a time). Keep doing this until you find the point where the quality of the image is no longer acceptable and use that. The following images show the difference between setting accelerator to 0 (Figure 9.4) and to 0.005 (Figure 9.5).

To get the shadow streaks as shown in these images, your light should cast shadows. One thing to note is that this shader doesn't perform any type of self-shadowing, so it is not useful for re-creating dense smoke plumes. To implement self shadows, you need to add another raymarching step that traverses from each sample point back into the light. This will make your shader take a lot longer to execute, but if you have enough rendering resources, then it is a viable production technique.

If you are interested in how a self-shadowing smoke shader (using raymarching) can be written, read Chapter 15 in Larry Gritz's and Anthony Apodaca's *Advanced RenderMan: Creating CGI for Motion Pictures*. A very detailed explanation of the

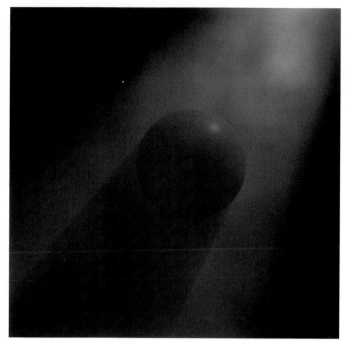

Figure 9.4

The original scene with accelerator set to 0. Render time = 3:05 mins.

Figure 9.5 The same image rendered with accelerator set to 0.005. Render time = 2:18 mins.

algorithm for self-shadowing smoke can be found there. The release of deep shadow maps has made the need for raymarch-based self-shadowing a thing of the past for most shots, though there are still some instances where you will need a true volumetric shader. You can create smoke with 2D sprites that always face the camera and use deep shadows to get the sprites to self-shadow. Make sure that the sprites face the shadow-generating camera when you create the deep shadow map. Figures 9.6 and 9.7 show a rocket trail made completely of sprites. On these images you can compare a smoke shader with no shadows (Figure 9.6) and deepmap shadows (Figure 9.7).

Figure 9.6 Rocket trail with no shadows and lighting.

Figure 9.7 The same rocket trail with deep shadows and lighting.

10

Imager Shaders

The last shaders to be executed before the image is stored to a file or displayed to a window on the screen are the imager shaders. Imager shaders read the value that has been computed after the atmosphere shaders (if there is any) and modify the value of the color. Imager shaders are one of those ideas that seemed great on paper, but they never really caught on, especially once strong compositing packages became available to the public.

The concept behind imager shaders is to perform one last color modification on the rendered image. The problem with this approach is that your final image data is forever distorted. If you need to change your imager shader, which can only modify the color of an image, you will incur all the cost of rendering a 3D scene, which is a *lot* more expensive than modifying those values in a compositing package. Maybe if more thought were put into imager shaders as technology evolved and matured, they would be more useful today, but as they stand, most of the things that you can do with an imager shader you can do with a decent compositing system.

Imager shaders are so rarely needed and used that some RenderMan-compliant renderers don't even support them. Not even Pixar's PRMan supports the loading of imager shaders except for a couple of built-in ones such as a background shader. It is for this reason that documentation and samples of imager shaders are very hard to find. In this chapter, we will demonstrate the basics of using imager shaders and some uses for them. Among the renderers that support imager shaders are these:

- 3Delight

- SiTex Graphics AIR

- Aqsis

Imager Global Variables

The number of variables available to imager shaders is less than any of the other shader types. Only two values are writable; the rest are only readable. Table 10.1 lists the global variables as defined by the RiSpec. Note that since Pixar's PRMan doesn't support imager shaders, other renderers can use other variable names or even add more variables to the table, so please read your renderer's documentation to see what imager shader variables, if any, it supports.

Table 10.1 Imager Shader Variables

Name	Type	Storage	Description
P	point	varying	Pixel raster position
Ci	color	varying	Pixel color
Oi	color	varying	Pixel opacity
alpha	float	uniform	Fractional pixel coverage
ncomps	float	uniform	Number of color components
time	float	uniform	Shutter open time
dtime	float	uniform	The amount of time the shutter was open
Output			
Ci	color	varying	Output color
Oi	color	varying	Output opacity

Working Examples

We will proceed to write some example imager shaders so that we can understand their concept a little better. Remember that most of these effects can be replicated in a 2D package, so if you feel that it is a little overkill to create a shader just to add a background to an image, remember that we are just illustrating the use of imager shaders.

Background Shader

The first and simplest example we will work on is a background color shader. We will set this shader so that you can assign a flat color to the background and use an image as a texture. You could also use any of the techniques explained in later chapters to add more features to this shader. Imager shaders are identified with the keyword `imager`. Our background shader will use gray as the default background. If a texture is provided, it will use a texture with a blurred value of `bgBlur`. This shader could be used when developing the look of an element; you could set a concept painting as the background to see the element in context with the environment in which it will be used. Figure 10.1 demonstrates the use of this shader to place a background image.

```
imager i_RP_background (

                        color bgColor = color (0.5,0.5,0.5);
                        string bgTexture = "";
                        uniform float bgBlur = 0;
                        )
{
    if (bgTexture != "")
        Ci = mix(Ci,texture(bgTexture,u,v,"blur",bgBlur),1-alpha);
    else
        Ci = mix(Ci,bgColor,1 - alpha);
}
```

Figure 10.1 Background imager shader applied to a multitorus image.

As you can see, the shader is extremely simple. First, we test to see if a texture has been provided; if it was, then we mix between the current color of the pixel Ci and the background image using the inverted alpha value. If the texture map is not provided, then we simply mix Ci with the background color using the inverted alpha. Let's take a look at a more complex example.

Old Picture Filter Shader

We will write a shader that will make the rendered output look as if it were an old image, similar to those sepia-toned images that we find in antique shops or historical records. I went to the local library and checked out some books with old pictures from the turn of the century. I am fortunate to live very close to the local library, which is another great place to find reference material. After close examination of those images, I was able to pick out several important features that are present in some of the images. The most important feature, I think, is how faded the values of some of the images are. Some of them are so washed out that the darkest values on them are nowhere near black. To replicate this, we can use the always useful gain() function.

Another feature is that the "filtered color" of the image is not always the same: It is usually close to a light brown, but sometimes the color is reddish, and sometimes it's more orange or even green. We will replicate this by creating a filterColor parameter. The next important feature is the existence of film grain on this image. We can try to replicate this film grain using a cellnoise() function. There are other ways to replicate film grain that are a lot more accurate and controllable, but for our example, cellnoise() will do just fine. The final important feature that I'm able to find is the presence of age marks, water damage, and overall wear and tear of the pictures. With all this information, I fire up my trusty text editor and write the following pseudocode:

```
imager i_RP_oldpicfilter()
{
    /*** Layer 1 ***/
    /* Turn the image to a float and use a gain function to modify the
     * contrast of the float image */
    /* Calculate a grain value */
    /* write the values out to Ci */

    /*** Layer 2 - Age scratches ***/
    /*** Layer 3 - Water spots ***/
    /*** Layer 4 - Edge damage ***/
}
```

We will build up the shader step by step. The first thing we will do is to generate the base layer. We will turn the image into a float using the colorToFloat() function developed in Chapter 5 and then pass it to a gain() function to control the contrast. By reducing the contrast, we can simulate how old pictures fade or wash out with time. We will then composite those values on top of a background color, which will be the same filter color multiplied by half to make it darker. Figure 10.2 shows the original image next to the output when using the old picture filter imager shader.

```
imager i_RP_oldpicfilter(
                          color filterColor = color (0.68,0.507,0.088);
                          float contrast = 0.5;
                          float grainStrength = 1;
                          float grainSize = 1;
                          )
{
    /*** Layer 1 ***/
    /* Turn the image to a float and use a gain function to modify the
    * contrast of the float image */
    float imgval = gain(colorToFloat(Ci), contrast);

    /* Calculate a grain value */
    float rand = compress(cellnoise(P * grainSize),0.75,1);

    /* write the values out to Ci */
    Ci = colorOverlay(imgval * filterColor,color(rand),grainStrength);
    Ci = mix(Ci,colorOverlay((filterColor * 0.5),color(rand),grain-
Strength),1 - alpha);
}
```

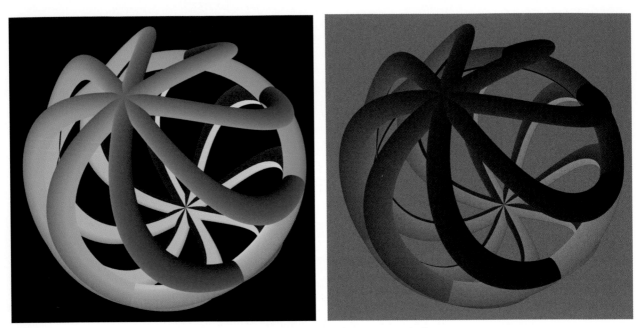

Figure 10.2 The original output image and the output once we add our imager shader.

We will now add the age scratches. This is done by first making a copy of P, which is the position of the current pixel in raster space (within the image). The Z component of P in an imager shader is always 0. We then add a small amount of noise to PP. This distorts its value based on the noise. We then do another noise lookup, but in this case we stretch the noise to be long stripes. We then use smoothstep to change the values of the noise lookup, and finally we use the colorDodge() function to layer the scratches on top of the previous color as visible in Figure 10.3.

```
imager i_RP_oldpicfilter_02 (
                              /* .... */
                              float grainStrength = 1;
                              float grainSize = 1;
                              float scratchFreq = 1;
                              float scratchNoiseScale = 20;
                              float scratchRatio = 0.3;
                              )
{
    /*......... */

    /***************************
    **** Add age scratches ****
    ***************************/
```

```
    point PP = P;
    PP += noise(PP * scratchFreq * 0.01) * scratchNoiseScale ;

    float scratch = noise(xcomp(PP * 0.2),ycomp(PP * 0.005));
    scratch = smoothstep(1 - scratchRatio,1,scratch);

    Ci = colorDodge(Ci,scratch,0.75);
}
```

Figure 10.3 Scratches added to the image.

Image fading, done. Film grain, done. Age scratches, done. Our shader is progressing quite nicely, and now it's time to add the water spots. A water spot is a small splotch that tends to change values within itself. A water spot is not solid because water actually lifts the pigments from the picture. To simulate this feature, we will create a noise field, which we will pass into a smoothstep() to restrict the features only to the highest peaks of the noise field. We will then use a pow() function to make the noise values a little tighter so that the transition between darks and brights is not as soft, creating the appearance of a distorted spot. We then take that value and feed it to a spline() function. This is done so that the water spots are not made up of a single value. The spline() function is a very interesting function, and it can be very handy when you need to manipulate values. It allows you to take a value within a linear 0 to 1 range and insert "knots" at evenly spaced intervals. When you see a call such as spline(value,0,0,0.5,0.1,1,1), the value will be split into four different areas (the first 0 and 1 need to be there, but they don't really affect the mapping):

Original Val	Knot	Output Val
0	0	0
0.25	0.5	0.5
0.75	0.1	0.1
1	1	1

Once we have computed the water spots, we composite them on top of the image using a colorDodge() function. Here is the shader with the new code inserted, followed by an image that features the water spots (see Figure 10.4). If you look carefully at the water spots, you will see the effect of the spline() function.

```
imager i_RP_oldpicfilter_03 (
                               /* .... */
                               float spotSize = 1;
                               float spotEdgeFreq = 10;
                               float spotEdgeScale = 1;
                               )
{
    /* ......... */


    /**************************
    *** Add the water spots ***
    **************************/
    PP  = P * 1/max(spotSize * 10,0.0000001) ;
    PP += noise(PP * spotEdgeFreq)* (spotEdgeScale);
    float fl = noise(xcomp(PP),ycomp(PP));
    float spot = pow(smoothstep(0.8,1,fl),0.5);

    /* use a spline to make some spots be darker in the center */
    spot = float spline(spot,0,0,0.5,0.25,1,1,1);

    Ci = colorDodge(Ci,spot,1);
}
```

Figure 10.4 Water spots added to the old picture filter.

We now arrive to the final feature that we will put into our shader. Some of those old pictures have a peculiar characteristic where the image doesn't cover all the photographic paper. This is due to the fact that years ago there were no machines that perfectly aligned the image to the paper. Image processing was done by hand, and many times there was a small border left around the image. With all the handling of the images throughout the years, some of the borders have completely faded away.

To replicate this feature, we will use another noise field, but instead of using P to drive the noise, we will use the values of u and v, which are the 2D coordinates of the image in raster space. We create several noise fields and then add those values to u and v, which are stored in the new variables uu and vv. We then use smooth-step() once again to create a ramp based on the uu and vv coordinates of the image. We need to apply smoothstep() twice, once for uu and once for vv. We multiply these two values to create a mask that represents the faded edge feature. We finish the shader by adding the value into the image using the colorAdd() function. Figure 10.5 shows the result of the final images shader.

```
imager i_RP_oldpicfilter (
                              /* .... */
                              float edgeWidthX = 0.005;
                              float edgeFuzzX = 0.025;
                              float edgeWidthY = 0.005;
                              float edgeFuzzY = 0.025;
                              float edgeNoiseSize = 2;
                              float edgeNoiseScale = 1;
                              float edgeNoiseStrength = 1;
                              )
{
    /* ..... */

    /***************************
    *** Add the edge damage ***
    ***************************/
    float edgefreq = edgeNoiseSize * 10;
    float noi  = (2 * noise(u * edgefreq, v * edgefreq)) - 1;
    float uu = u + (noi   * edgeNoiseScale * 0.1) ;
    float vv = v + (noi   * edgeNoiseScale * 0.1) ;

    float edgemask =smoothstep(edgeWidthX,edgeWidthX + edgeFuzzX,uu) -
                  smoothstep(1 - edgeWidthX - edgeFuzzX,1-edgeWidthX,uu)
;

    edgemask *= smoothstep(edgeWidthY,edgeWidthY + edgeFuzzY,vv) -
              smoothstep(1 - edgeWidthY - edgeFuzzY,1-edgeWidthY,vv) ;

    edgemask = spline(edgemask,0,0,0.5,0.2,1,1,1);
    edgemask = compress(edgemask,1 - edgeNoiseStrength,1);

    Ci = colorAdd(Ci,1 -edgemask,edgeNoiseStrength);
}
```

Figure 10.5 The final imager shader.

Paper Texture Shader

The last imager shader that we will write applies a texture to our image much like
the canvas effect in Photoshop. To achieve this effect, we will create a fake light
within our imager shader. This light will provide the shading effect necessary to re-
create the texture on our image. For the texture, we will use a texture map to simplify the shader and concentrate on how the embossing is performed. Once you
feel comfortable generating procedural patterns, you will be more than capable of
replacing the simple texture call for any procedural pattern that returns a float value.
The implementation should be quite simple. First, we will initialize some variables
for our shader, next we will create a Pshad variable which will be a copy of P, and
finally we will initialize the NN variable to a normal with a value of (0,0,1) since the
image plane normal should always be pointing toward the camera.

The trick in this shader is to modify Pshad the same way we would modify a surface normal to perform a bump operation by adding to Pshad the value of the texture multiplied by the NN normal. We then need to calculate the normal for the
new position of Pshad. A normal is calculated by applying the cross product operation to the derivatives of the current point. The derivatives are calculated with
Deriv(Pshad,u) and Deriv(Pshad,v), and then we simply apply a cross product to
those two values. We now need to calculate our fake light vector by subtracting

lightTo from lightFrom and assigning the result to the EE variable. We first transform the two vectors to camera space to be consistent with the NN normal. This way it's easier to control and to predict what our fake lights will do. To get the shading of the paper texture, we then apply a dot product to NN and EE. The rest of the shader should be self-explanatory. Figure 10.6 shows the result of using the texurize shader, while Figure 10.7 is the same image scaled and manipulated to show the discontinuities at the bucket edges.

```
#include "RSLP/RP_f_func.h"

imager i_RP_papertexture(
                            string textureFile = "";
                            float textureRepeatX = 1.0;
                            float textureRepeatY = 1.0;
                            float bumpValue    = 1;
                            point lightFrom    = (-1,1,2);
                            point lightTo      = (0,0,0);
                            color backgroundColor = color(0.8,0.8,0.8);
                            float doDuotone    = 0;
                            color duotoneColor = color (1,1,0.5);
                            )
{
    float textval = 0;
    point Pshad = P;
    normal NN = normal "world" (0,0,1);
    point lF,lT;
    /* make a copy of u and v and multiply by the textureRepeat */
    float uu = u * textureRepeatX;
    float vv = v * textureRepeatY;

    /* Perform calculations only if texture is provided */
    if (textureFile != ""){
        textval = float texture(textureFile,uu,vv);

    Pshad += (NN * textval * bumpValue);
    NN = normalize(vector Deriv(Pshad,uu) ^ vector Deriv(Pshad,vv));

    lF = transform("world",lightFrom);
    lT = transform("world",lightTo);
    vector EE = normalize(lF - lT);

    float xx = NN.EE;
```

```
if (doDuotone == 1)
    Ci = colorToFloat(Ci) * duotoneColor;

Ci = mix(Ci,backgroundColor,1 - alpha);
Ci *= xx;
}
}
```

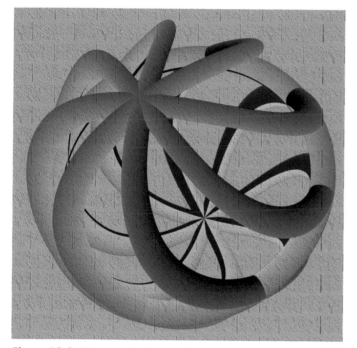

Figure 10.6 Texturize shader applied to texturize the image.

Figure 10.7 The same image as 10.6 but manipulated and zoomed to make the breaks in continuity on the bucket boundaries more apparent. The breaks are circled in yellow.

The problem with this technique, as is apparent in the rendered image, is that most renderers treat each individual bucket as a separate piece of geometry. This results in broken continuity from bucket to bucket. This artifact is caused by letting the renderer compute the derivative of Pshad (which is a copy of P) on u and v. To compute a derivative properly for the current shading point, certain information about its surrounding points is needed. If each bucket is treated as an individual grid, then the renderer will have no way to compute derivatives at the edges, as seen in Figure 10.8. This graph is a visualization of a single scan line in an image. You can see how the discontinuity is not visible when P is constant (flat), but when it is moved, the renderer can compute a derivative at the edges of the bucket

We can get around this by calculating our own derivatives of P and then doing the cross product on those derivatives. Reading the PRMan documentation, we can see that a derivative for u (or v) can be calculated with the following expression (using u as an example, for v just replace the u for v)

```
function(u+du) - function(u) = Du(function(u)) * du;
```

where du is the delta value in u. Solving this equation for Du(), we get

```
Du(function(u)) = function(u+du)-function(u)/du
```

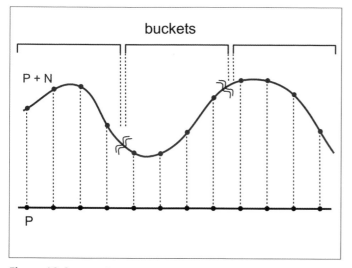

Figure 10.8 A graph visualizing discontinuities at the edges of a bucket.

Based on the above operation, the first thing we need to know is the difference there is in value between each texture lookup (also referred to as the delta). We do this by calculating the distance between each shading point in u and v. This value can easily be determined by dividing the side's textureRepeat value by the side's rendering resolution. The rendering resolution can be queried from within our shader with the following call:

```
float formatV[3];
option("Format",formatV);
```

The x resolution will be stored in formatV[0], the y resolution in formatV[1], and the pixel aspect ratio in formatV[2]. More information on the use of the format RSL command can be found in the RiSpec. We then store those values in the deltaU and deltaV variables. We calculate the difference in the value of the textures by doing a texture lookup of the current point plus the delta value (which gives us the texture value of the next shading sample) and subtract it by the current sample. The result is divided by the proper delta value to finish our derivative calculation.

```
float deltaU = textureRepeatX/x_res;
float deltaV = textureRepeatY/y_res;
textvalDu = (texture(textureFile,uu+deltaU,vv) -
    texture(textureFile,uu,vv))/deltaU;
textvalDv = (texture(textureFile,uu,vv+deltaV) -
    texture(textureFile,uu,vv))/deltaV;
```

We calculate a new set of derivatives along u and v by adding to the current point (P) the value of the normal NN multiplied by bumpValue and the calculated textvalDu (or textvalDv). This will give us a new set of derivatives that are continuous from bucket to bucket. From there, we perform a simple cross product to get the new normal.

```
Uderiv = vector(Deriv(P,uu) + textvalDu * NN * bumpValue);
Vderiv = vector(Deriv(P,vv) + textvalDv * NN * bumpValue);
NN = normalize(Uderiv ^ Vderiv);
```

Here is the final shader that we used to generate the corrected paper texture image (Figure 10.9).

```
#include "RSLP/RP_f_func.h"
imager i_RP_papertexture(
                        string textureFile   = "";
                        float textureRepeatX = 1.0;
                        float textureRepeatY = 1.0;
                        float bumpValue      = 1;
                        point lightFrom      = (-1,1,2);
                        point lightTo        = (0,0,0);
                        color backgroundColor= color(0.8,0.8,0.8);
                        float doDuotone      = 0;
                        color duotoneColor   = color (1,1,0.5);
                        )
{
    float textval = 0;
    normal NN = normal "camera" (0,0,1);
    point lF,lT;
    float formatV[3];

    /* Get the Format option used on the renderer and store them in
     x_res and y_res */
    option("Format",formatV);
    float x_res = formatV[0];
    float y_res = formatV[1];

    float uu = u * textureRepeatX;
    float vv = v * textureRepeatY;

    if (textureFile != ""){
        textval = float texture(textureFile,uu,vv);
        point textvalDu,textvalDv;
        float deltaU = textureRepeatX/x_res;
        float deltaV = textureRepeatY/y_res;
```

```
textvalDu =(texture(textureFile,uu+deltaU,vv) -
            texture(textureFile,uu,vv))/deltaU;
textvalDv = (texture(textureFile,uu,vv+deltaV) -
            texture(textureFile,uu,vv))/deltaV;

Uderiv = vector(Deriv(P,uu)+ textvalDu * NN * bumpValue);
Vderiv = vector(Deriv(P,vv)+ textvalDv * NN * bumpValue);

NN = normalize(Uderiv ^ Vderiv);

lF = transform("camera",lightFrom);
lT = transform("camera",lightTo);
vector EE = normalize(lF - lT);
float xx = NN.EE;

if (doDuotone == 1)
    Ci = colorToFloat(Ci) * duotoneColor;

Ci = mix(Ci,backgroundColor,1 - alpha);
Ci *= xx;
    }
}
```

Figure 10.9 Corrected texturize shader, no bucket continuity breaks.

As stated before, imager shaders might seem useful, but so far, every effect that is attainable through an imager shader can easily be replicated with a strong compositing package, some good technical knowledge, and the proper set of AOV images. Special thanks go to Ramon Montoya of Walt Disney Animation Studios for his help with solving the bucket continuity problem.

PART IV

INTERMEDIATE SHADING

## 11

Illumination Loops—BRDFs

The purpose of this chapter is to examine illumination models using RSL. You can think of an illumination model as a custom procedure to describe the interaction between light and a surface. Knowing how to code illumination models is key to being able to express the look of a variety of real-world materials.

BRDFs

The formal way to describe how light interacts with a surface is via the use of a BRDF, or *bidirectional reflectance distribution function*. The idea is to measure the ratio of outgoing light (radiance) along every possible viewing direction to incoming light striking the surface (irradiance) at every possible direction. For example, 100 light directions and 100 viewing directions would result in 10,000 measurements.

Figure 11.1 shows a single incoming/outgoing direction pair. Given that real-world materials such as skin and household paint are made up of heterogeneous chemicals or internal structures, their BRDF ratios will likely not be identical for all input/output direction pairs. In other words, BRDF measurements validate what we see in real life, namely that many surfaces take on different appearances when viewed from different angles or when their illumination direction changes.

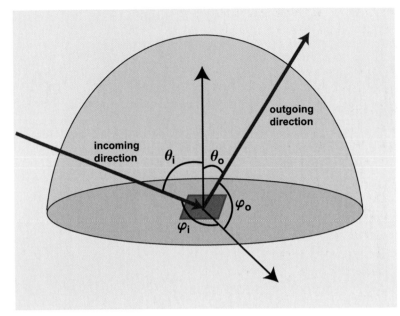

Figure 11.1 BRDF measurement—incoming, outgoing directions.

The reflectance could be also a function of light color (wavelength) in addition to illumination and viewing directions, so these measurements usually need to be done for a series of wavelengths. Given this, BRDF can be denoted as

```
BRDF = f(theta_i,phi_i,theta_o,phi_o,lambda)
```

where `theta_i` and `phi_i` denote incoming light direction in spherical coordinates, `theta_o`and `phi_o` are corresponding values for the outgoing view direction, and `lambda` denotes the wavelength of the light.

For most materials, reversing input and output directions yields the same reflectance value due to a property called *reciprocity*, which cuts down the number of measurements to make (this is what makes the reflectance bidirectional). Also, there is circular symmetry (along the longitudes), which further reduces measurements.

The dependence of BRDFs only on incoming/outgoing angles and wavelength is a simplification. Heterogeneous materials (for instance, a mosaic tile with small embedded chips) have a BRDF dependence on the exact measurement location on the surface, so the actual sample geometry becomes part of the BRDF specification. Also, polarization of the light affects the BRDF as well. In practice, such material and optical dependencies are usually ignored.

BRDFs are acquired using instruments such as gonioreflectometers, sensor arrays, digital cameras, and so on. You can find BRDF data for a variety of real-world materials online. Usually a hemispherical sample of the material is used for the measurements or, in some cases, a full sphere. Ideally, just a small point sample of the material should do, but real-world limitations of the measurement setup necessitate the use of a hemispherical sample volume.

Given a viewing direction V (which is usually `normalize(-I)`) and a light direction L, a true BRDF RenderMan shader would simply look up the reflectance from a BRDF file or table, interpolating between existing data samples. Such data-driven BRDFs are less common in practice compared to the use of alternative illumination models, which include procedural descriptions (arbitrary and possibly nonphysical), phenomenological models (based on empirical observation, qualitatively similar to reality), analytical as well as simulated approximations of real-world surface characteristics, models fitted to measured BRDF data, and so on. For the rest of this chapter, we will concentrate on these simplified versions. Also, note that our shaders will not be computing full-blown BRDFs because that involves sampling irradiance and radiance along multiple directions and integrating the results. Instead, our shaders will take specific light and camera information from a scene and compute shading just for that configuration.

Illumination Models Using RSL

RSL provides three constructs—`illuminate()`, `solar()`, and `illuminance()`—to help create custom illumination models. You encountered the `illuminate()` and `solar()` statements in the chapter on light shaders. `illuminate()` is used to specify local light sources (which have a position and optionally a direction), and `solar()` is used to specify distant light sources (either along a given direction or along all directions). For example, the `pointlight` and `distantlight` shaders are expressed this way:

```
light pointlight(float intensity = 1;
                 color lightcolor = 1;
                 point from = point "shader" (0,0,0);)
{
  illuminate(from)
  {
    Cl = intensity*lightcolor/L.L;
  }
}


light distantlight(float intensity = 1;
                   color lightcolor = 1;
                   point from = point "shader" (0,0,0);
                   point to   = point "shader" (0,0,1);)
{
```

```
solar(to-from,0.0)
  {
    Cl=intensity*lightcolor;
  }
}
```

The complementary function for use in surface shaders is `illuminance()`, which helps integrate the contribution of light sources that are relevant to the shaders. It is a block statement (similar to a `for(){}` loop, for example) with the following syntax:

```
illuminance([string category,]point position)
{
  statements
}
```
or
```
illuminance([string category,]point position, vector axis, float angle)
{
  statements
}
```

Given all lights in a scene, the statements in the body of an `illuminance()` block are executed just for those lights that meet the criteria specified at the top, within the parentheses. You can think of `illuminance()` as a "smart iterator" that knows to loop through relevant lights. Note that the statements within an illuminance block are executed one light at a time, and such per-light calculations are typically accumulated across the loop executions.

As shown above, `illuminance()` comes in two forms. In the first form, a specified position (usually P) is used as a center for a sphere with respect to which lights are queried and used. In the second form, also specified are an axis and a cone semi-angle, resulting in an "inverted umbrella" that is centered at the given position. The axis specified is usually N, and the angle, which is specified in radians, is usually PI/2 (90 degrees)—this leads to a hemisphere centered at the current shading location. Given the illuminance cone, only lights that fall within the cone (orientation-wise) are considered for calculations inside the illuminance block.

The optional `category` specifier can be used with either form of `illuminance()` to further limit the selection of lights to just those that represent the given category. An example of its use is presented at the end of this chapter.

Unlike in the physical world, CG lights in a RIB scene do not continuously illuminate surfaces after they are specified. Rather, when a surface is shaded, its corresponding surface shader "turns on" just the lights it needs (if any, based on the conditions specified in `illuminance()`). The selected light shaders compute light color and direction, which are then returned to the surface shader. The surface shader uses these values to eventually compute an outgoing Ci. Such a surface/light interaction scheme makes for very efficient computations and is in fact the only reasonable way to use programmable lights and shaders together.

Examples of Using illuminance()

We will now illustrate a variety of uses for illuminance(), including the specification of simplified BRDFs. The list of shader variables we will use consists of the usual suspects: P, N, I, L, and such. Think of these examples as elements that you can mix and match to come up with your own customized illumination models. In the following subsections, we'll use the terms "lighting model," "illumination model," and "shading model" interchangeably in an informal manner.

diffuse()

As a first example, the diffuse() function can be expressed using illuminance() as follows (see Figure 11.2):

```
normal Nf = faceforward(normalize(N),I);
color Cdiff=0;
illuminance(P,Nf,PI/2)
{
 vector Ln = normalize(L);
 Cdiff += Cl*Ln.Nf;
}
```

Figure 11.2 Diffuse shading.

Since the cone angle is PI/2, the illumination cone's influence is twice PI/2, or PI, which is 180 degrees. The color contribution from a single light is proportional to Ln.Nf, the dot product between that light's direction and the surface normal. If the surface normal is parallel to the light, the corresponding point receives full illumination from the light. Conversely, if the normal is perpendicular, the point underneath it receives zero illumination. In between these extreme cases, the 0.0 to 1.0 dot product creates the classic Lambertian ("diffuse") lighting. This represents a perfectly diffuse material, where there is no dependence of Cdiff on the viewing angle. In other words, the Lambertian model amounts to constant BRDF.

From this you can see that the illumination from a straight-on orientation to a sphere will be limited to the front hemisphere, since the back hemisphere is beyond the reach of a front light due to the PI/2 cone angle. But what if we want the light to wrap around and extend beyond the hemisphere? We would be able to simulate the look of an area light this way. In some cases doing so will better integrate a CG element with a live-action background.

Wrap diffuse()

We can modify the Lambertian illumination loop by including a user-specified wrap parameter, which will define how much the light is allowed to reach beyond the hemisphere (see Figure 11.3).

```
surface wdiffuse(float Ka=0.1, Kd=0.5, wrap=1., gam=1)
{
  normal Nf = normalize(faceforward(N,I));
  color Cwd=0;
  float wrp=1-0.5*wrap;
  float wa = acos(wrp*2-1); // wrap angle

  illuminance(P, Nf, wa)
    {
      vector Ln = normalize(L);
      float diffuze;
      float dotp = 0.5*(1+Ln.Nf);
      if(dotp<=wrp)
        {
          diffuze=pow((wrp-dotp)/(wrp),gam);
        }
      else
          diffuze = pow((dotp-wrp)/(1-wrp),gam);
      Cwd += Cl * diffuze;
    }
  Ci = Cs*Os*(Ka*ambient() + Kd*Cwd);
  Oi = Os;
}
```

Figure 11.3 Wrapped diffuse shading.

To understand how the `wrap` parameter works, we can directly express the wrap angle `wa` in terms of `wrap` by eliminating the `wrp` parameter:

```
wa = acos(1-wrap); // acos((1-0.5*wrap)*2-1)
```

When `wrap` is 1.0 (the default value), we get the usual behavior because the wrap angle `wa` evaluates to 90 degrees (`acos(0)`). Larger values of `wrap`, such as 1.5, increase `wa` to beyond 90 degrees, past the usual hemispherical boundary. At the extreme case of `wrap` being 2.0, the wrap angle becomes 180 degrees (`acos(-1)`), which means that the frontal illumination can reach all the way around to the back of the object. Likewise, `wrap` can also be less than 1.0 to allow us to restrict the illumination to just a portion of the front hemisphere. Non-unity values of the `gam` parameter can be used to alter the wrapping distribution via the `pow()` function by biasing the wrapping of the illumination. This produces the effect of expanding the darker range of illumination values while compressing the brighter range, or vice versa.

Biased diffuse()

We can also make another simple but useful modification to the original Lambert model. As we saw above, in this model `Ln.Nn` provides the diffuse component. The dot product is equivalent to the cosine of the angle between `Ln` and `Nn` (this is always true when the two vectors that form the dot product are normalized). Going from 0 to 90 degrees—that is, head-on to sideways illumination—the profile of the diffuse illumination is the classic cosine curve. An easy modification to make is to subject the dot product to a bias() function to nonlinearly alter the illumination profile. The code looks like this:

```
float biasFunc(float t;float a;)
{
    return pow(t,-(log(a)/log(2)));
}
color bdiff (float bias;)
{
  color C = 0;
  extern point P;
  extern normal N;
  illuminance (P, N, PI/2)
    {
        extern vector L;
        vector Ln = normalize(L);
        normal Nn = normalize(N);
        float cos_theta_i = Ln.Nn;
        C += biasFunc(cos_theta_i,bias);
    }
  return C;
}
```

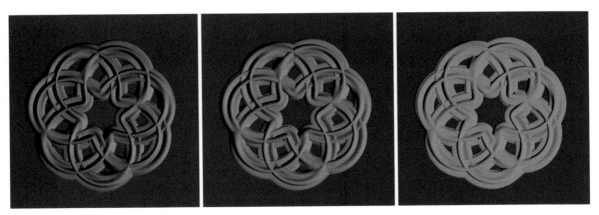

Figure 11.4 Biased diffuse shading.

The results of applying bias values of 0.3, 0.5, and 0.8 are shown in Figure 11.4. As you can see, the bias() function can be used to exaggerate diffuse illumination or to downplay it.

In the rest of the chapter, we present color/float functions instead of complete surface shaders, in the interest of space. These functions encompass illuminance loops, which in turn illustrate a variety of illumination models that we are about to discuss. These functions are meant to be used in creating surface shaders, analogous to the use of built-in RSL calls such as diffuse(), specular(), and so on.

Translucent Surfaces

To render translucent surfaces (see Figure 11.5), we need to be able to light surfaces on the "other side" when the object is situated between the viewer and light source (imagine looking at the sun through a canopy of young green leaves; the leaves are lit from behind, creating a brilliant translucent look). The classic Lambert model restricts shading to the front half of a surface. We need to enable shading the back part, which we can do via a custom illuminance loop:

```
color doublesided(float Kdf,Kdb;string txf, txb;)
{
  color C = 0;
  extern point P;
  extern normal N;
  extern vector I;
  color Ctf, Ctb;
  if (txf!= "")
    {
      Ctf = color texture(txf);
    }
  else
    {
      Ctf = 1.0;
    }
  if (txb!= "")
    {
      Ctb = color texture(txb);
    }
  else
    {
      Ctb = 1.0;
    }
  normal Nn = normalize(N);
  normal Nf = faceforward(Nn, I );
  // front
  illuminance (P, Nf, PI/2)
    {
      extern vector L;
      vector Ln = normalize(L);
```

```
      C += Cl*Ctf*Kdf*(Nf.Ln);
    }
  // back
  illuminance (P, -Nf, PI/2)
    {
      extern vector L;
      vector Ln = normalize(L);
      C += Cl*Ctb*Kdb*(-Nf.Ln);
    }
  return C;
}
```

Figure 11.5 Translucent surface.

Seeliger

Seeliger's Law is a very early (1888!) model of diffuse reflection derived from physical principles. It is an example of a non-Lambertian diffuse calculation. Expressed in terms of N, L, and V, it specifies diffuse reflection as a ratio of (N.L) and ((N.L)+(N.V)). The result is more flat (even) shading across a surface compared to the classical Lambert calculation, which uses just N.L (see Figure 11.6). The Seeliger model is particularly applicable to materials such as skin that call for an even tone. It is best used as a layer to mix with other shading models, since its sole application to a surface leads to a rather "pasty" look.

```
color SeeligerFunc()
{
  color C = 0;
  extern point P;
  extern normal N;
  extern vector I;
  normal Nn = normalize(N);
  vector V = -normalize(I);
  illuminance (P, N, PI/2)
    {
      extern vector L;
      vector Ln = normalize(L);
      C += max(0,(Nn.Ln)/((Nn.Ln)+(Nn.V)));
    }
  return C;
}
```

Figure 11.6 Diffuse versus Seeliger shading.

Oren-Nayar

The Oren-Nayar BRDF, a generalization of the Lambert diffuse model, calculates reflectance from rough surfaces by modeling distributions of microfacets across them. The microfacet distribution is specified by the user via a roughness parameter that is interpreted to be the standard deviation of angles of the facets relative to a light source and view direction. If roughness is 0, the model is equivalent to a pure Lambert one (verify this for yourself from the equations in the code).

The shader code is adapted from PRMan's "Clay" Slim template. (Slim templates are shader blocks that ship with RAT, a collection of tools for use with Maya.) The code also appears in Gritz's and Apodaca's *Advanced RenderMan* book. The roughness values, L, V, and N, are used to derive intermediate quantities such as A, B, and cos_theta_i, which finally come together to create a value for the output color variable C.

Figure 11.7 illustrates the Oren-Nayar BRDF. On the left, the surface is rendered with a roughness value of 0, yielding a classic Lambert look. The image on the right is created with a roughness of 2.0. Due to the flatter look compared to Lambert, the Oren-Nayar model is applicable to dull surfaces such as unglazed earthenware.

```
// OrenNayar() is from PRMan's Clay Slim template
color OrenNayar (normal N; vector V; float roughness;)
{
  /* Surface roughness coefficients for Oren/Nayar's formula */
  float sigma2 = roughness * roughness;
  float A = 1 - 0.5 * sigma2 / (sigma2 + 0.33);
  float B = 0.45 * sigma2 / (sigma2 + 0.09);
  /* Useful precomputed quantities */
  float theta_r = acos (V . N); /* Angle between V and N */
  vector V_perp_N = normalize(V-N*(V.N)); /* Part of V perp to N */

  /* Accumulate incoming radiance from lights in C */
  color C = 0;
  extern point P;
  illuminance (P, N, PI/2)
  {
    /* Must declare extern L & Cl because we're in a function */
    extern vector L; extern color Cl;
    float nondiff = 0;
    lightsource ("__nondiffuse", nondiff);
    if (nondiff < 1)
    {
      vector LN = normalize(L);
      float cos_theta_i = LN . N;
      float cos_phi_diff = V_perp_N .
      normalize(LN - N*cos_theta_i);
      float theta_i = acos (cos_theta_i);
      float alpha = max (theta_i, theta_r);
      float beta = min (theta_i, theta_r);
      C += (1-nondiff) * Cl * cos_theta_i *
      (A + B * max(0,cos_phi_diff) * sin(alpha) * tan(beta));
    }
```

```
    }
    return C;
}
```

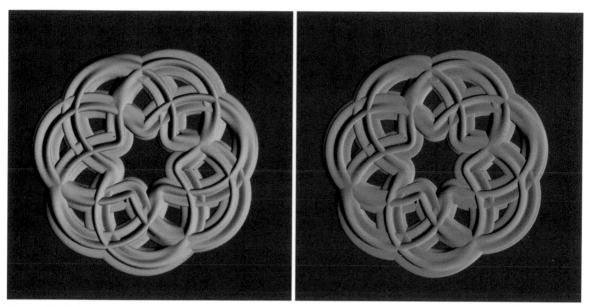

Figure 11.7 Oren-Nayar shading model.

Next, we look at three variations of the Fresnel function—a simple version, Schlick's approximation, and the built-in RSL function, which is the one commonly used in production. The two alternatives to the built-in call are presented just for comparison and study.

Fresnel—Simple Approximation

The dependence on the viewing angle of a material's reflectance/transmittance proportion at an air/solid boundary is called the *Fresnel effect* or *Fresnel phenomenon*. While it is not a full-blown lighting model, it is worth including here along with BRDFs and shading models because it offers one more way to vary shading across a surface.

In accordance with the Fresnel effect, materials such as skin and water are more reflective when viewed edge-on (view direction and surface normal are almost perpendicular) instead of head-on (the directions are nearly parallel). This can be very simply approximated via the term $0.5\times(1+Nn.Vn)$. The resulting shading looks brighter at the edges compared to the interior. To control the extent of this effect, the value is raised to a user-supplied exponent (often this is 2). The Fresnel effect is also wavelength dependent, but we ignore this dependency for our purposes.

Such differential edge enhancement can be used to create rim lighting, transparent edges, electron microscope-like images, two-tone paint (by using the value to blend between two colors), and so on. Figure 11.8 shows the Fresnel effect using our simple approximation.

```
color frnl(float INDEX;)
{
  color C = 0;
  extern point P;
  extern normal N;
  extern vector I;

  vector Vn = -normalize(I);
  normal Nn = normalize(N);

  float Kr = 0.5*(1+Nn.Vn);
  Kr = pow(Kr,INDEX);

  C = color(Kr,Kr,Kr);
  return C;
}
```

Figure 11.8 Simple approximation of the Fresnel effect.

Fresnel—Schlick's Approximation

While the simple approximation to the Fresnel term provided in the previous subsection is adequate, a better approximation that matches well with real-world reflectance measurements was provided by Chris Schlick. Schlick uses a "rational" function approximation where a complex nonlinear curve is expressed using a ratio of polynomial functions that are relatively cheaper to evaluate.

Schlick's Fresnel approximation is that the Fresnel term for arbitrary values of N and V (both normalized) can be approximated by Kr = eta + (1-eta)*pow(1-dotnv,5), where dotnv is N.V and eta is the value of Kr at normal incidence, that is, when N and V are parallel. By way of verification, you can see that when N and V are parallel, dotnv becomes 1, so pow(1-dotnv,5) is 0, therefore Kr=eta.

The resulting value Kr is further modified via biasFunc(), where inputs between 0.0 and 1.0 produce outputs that are also in the range 0.0 to 1.0. biasFunc() provides a nonlinear modification of its input and is used here to control the spread of the edge effect toward the interior. You can also use biasFunc() in other shaders to non-linearly modulate color triplets or other parameters whose values lie in the range 0..1. Figure 11.9 shows an image rendered using Schlick's Fresnel approximation.

Note that the parameter we call eta needs to be between 0 and 1 to get meaningful results. Given a material's refractive index n, eta can be calculated as sqr((n-1)/(n+1)).

```
float biasFunc(float t;float a;)
{
    return pow(t,-(log(a)/log(2)));
}
color FresnelSchlickFunc(float bias;float eta;float Kfr)
{
  color C = 0;
  extern point P;
  extern normal N;
  extern vector I;

  normal Nn = normalize(N);
  vector Vn = -normalize(I);
  float dotnv = abs(Nn.Vn);
  float Kr = eta + (1-eta)*pow(1-dotnv,5);
  Kr = Kfr*biasFunc(Kr,bias);

  C = color(Kr,Kr,Kr);
  return C;
}
```

Figure 11.9 Fresnel effect—Schlick's approximation.

Fresnel—RSL Function

Instead of using either of the above approximations to the Fresnel term, you can use RSL's own `fresnel()` function if you want physically more accurate results. This call takes as input an incident direction, surface normal (`normalize(I)` and `Nf` in our code, respectively), and a refractive index. It uses these inputs in the classic Fresnel formula (whose presentation and discussion are outside the scope of this book) and returns two values: amount of reflection at the material/air boundary and amount of transmission/refraction through the material. Figure 11.10 shows the Utah Teapot rendered using the `FresnelFunc()` function shown below.

Optionally, the call can also return the actual reflection and transmission/refraction vectors via a function signature that looks like this:

```
fresnel( vector I, N; float eta; output float Kr, Kt; [output vector R, T])
```

```
color FresnelFunc(float bias;float eta;float Kfr)
{
  color C = 0;
  extern point P;
  extern normal N;
  extern vector I;

  normal Nn = normalize(N);
  vector Nf = faceforward(Nn,I);
```

```
float Kr, Kt;
fresnel(normalize(I),Nf,eta,Kr,Kt); //*******//

Kr = Kfr*biasFunc(Kr,bias);

C = color(Kr,Kr,Kr);

return C;
}
```

Figure 11.10 Fresnel effect using the RSL `fresnel()` call.

Gooch Warm/Cool Shading

The Gooch model enhances the look of a surface by overlaying complementary warm and cool colors on top of conventional shading. The use of warm/cool tones is a classic technique employed by artists (such as to make surfaces appear as if they recede or advance).

The following code uses a modified version of the standard Gooch model. Here we simply get two colors, blue and yellow, from the user, scale them with user-supplied factors, add the scaled results to `Cs`, and then use the normalized diffuse distribution (1+ldotn) to blend between the two. The result is a pleasing look that shows a gradation between the warm yellow and the cool blue colors (see Figure 11.11). Using the scale factors `alpha` and `beta`, the user can alter the balance between the warm and cool overlay distributions.

This kind of a look is especially suited for medical and technical illustrations where the use of the warm/cool color pair serves to visually enhance local detail.

```
surface Gooch(
float Ka = 0.1, Kd=0.3, Ks=0.6, roughness=.1;
color blue=color(0,0,1), yellow=color(1,1,0);
float alpha=0.2, beta=0.6, bias=0.5;
)
{
  extern normal N;
  extern vector I;
  extern point P;
  extern color Cs;
  normal Nn = normalize(N);
  normal Nf = faceforward (Nn, I, Nn);
  color CGooch = color(0,0,0);
  float ldotn, blendval;
  illuminance(P,Nf,PI)
    {
       extern vector L;
       ldotn = (normalize(L)).Nf;
       blendval = 0.5*(1+ldotn);
       blendval = biasFunc(blendval,bias);

       color kd = Cs*ldotn;
       kd = Cs;
       color kcool = blue + alpha*kd;
       color kwarm = yellow + beta*kd;

       // better if alpha,beta scaled warm/cool cols!!
       kcool = kd + alpha*blue;
       kwarm = kd + beta*yellow;

       CGooch += Cl*ldotn*(mix(kcool,kwarm,blendval));
    }
  Oi = Os;
  Ci = Oi * (Ka*ambient() + Kd*CGooch) + Ks*specular(Nf,-normalize(I),rough-
ness);
}
```

Figure 11.11 Gooch (warm/cool) shading.

Specular: Phong

The Phong illumination model uses the light direction, surface normal, and view vector to create a highlight. The idea is to reflect the light vector about the surface normal as if the surface were a mirror at the point being shaded. The `reflect(-Ln,Nf)` call does this in the following code. If resulting reflection vector R is aligned perfectly with the view direction V, it will enter the eye/camera to create a perfect pinpoint reflection (highlight) on the surface. R.V measures the disparity from such an ideal mirror direction, and the `1/roughness` exponentiation alters the highlight size. Figure 11.12 shows a classic Phong specular highlight. Note that an alternate way to obtain the same result would be to reflect the view vector about the normal and dot the result with the light vector. Also, it is common to raise R.V to a Phong exponent value n instead of using `1/roughness`.

Because of the implied circular symmetry in the dot product (if R sweeps out a cone around V while maintaining the relative angle with it, the dot product would be identical for all the Rs that lie on the cone), the highlight has a perfectly round shape. Real-world highlights are often not perfectly round unless they are reflections of small point light sources on smooth surfaces. As we will see in subsequent sections, there are various ways to distort the highlights to make them appear more natural.

```
color PhongFn(float roughness)
{
  color C = 0;
  extern point P;
  extern normal N;
  extern vector I;
  vector V = -normalize(I);
  normal Nf = faceforward(normalize(N),I);

  illuminance (P, Nf, PI/2)
    {
      extern vector L;
      vector Ln = normalize(L);
      vector R = reflect(-Ln,Nf);
      float rdotv = R.V;
      C += Cl*pow(max(rdotv,0),1/roughness);
    }
  return C;
}
```

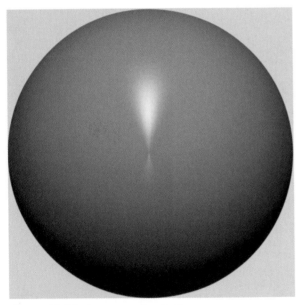

Figure 11.12 Phong specular shading.

The PhongFn call presented above is slightly different from the code for the equivalent phong() function found in the RI Specification:

```
color
phong(normal N; vector V; float size)
{
  color C = 0;
  vector R = reflect(-normalize(V),normalize(N));
  illuminance(P,N,PI/2){
    vector Ln = normalize(L);
    C += Cl*pow(max(0.0,R.Ln),size);
  }
  return C;

}
```

Modifying Specular Reflection Vector

Given a vector Ln and a surface normal Nf, the reflection of Ln about Nf (which is what is returned by the reflect() function call) is 2*Nf*(Nf.Ln)-Ln. You can derive this from simple vector math (try it). This can be generalized to n*Nf*(Nf.Ln)-Ln and the result normalized to produce a pseudo-reflection vector. Values of n other than 2 will produce a nonstandard (not geometrically accurate) reflection vector.

If such a nonstandard vector is used in the Phong specular calculation, it will cause the highlight to be shifted from its expected position (see Figure 11.13). This might provide a useful way to slightly relocate a highlight for artistic purposes without having to reposition the light source.

```
color modReflFn(float n, roughness)
{
  color C = 0;
  extern point P;
  extern normal N;
  extern vector I;
  vector V = -normalize(I);
  normal Nf = faceforward(normalize(N),I);

  illuminance (P, Nf, PI/2)
    {
      extern vector L;
      vector Ln = normalize(L);
      // vector R = reflect(-Ln,Nf);
      vector R = normalize(n*Nf*(Nf.Ln) - Ln);
      float rdotv = R.V;
      C += Cl*pow(max(rdotv,0),1/roughness);
    }
  return C;
}
```

Figure 11.13 Phong shading, altered highlight.

Specular: Blinn

The Blinn specular shading model is an alternative to the Phong one. Here we create a highlight by comparing the "halfway vector" H, which is the vector that lies halfway between L and V [expressed as normalize(Ln+V)] and the surface normal N. The roughness parameter is used to alter the highlight size just like in the Phong model.

Note that for the same L, N, and V values, the Blinn model produces a slightly different highlight compared to the Phong model (see Figure 11.14, and compare it with Figure 11.13). Using a Blinn roughness value that is one-fourth the Phong one produces approximately the same size highlight as the Phong model.

```
color BlinnFn(float roughness)
{
  color C = 0;
  extern point P;
  extern normal N;
  extern vector I;
  vector V = -normalize(I);
  normal Nf = faceforward(normalize(N),I);

  illuminance (P, Nf, PI/2)
    {
      extern vector L;
      vector Ln = normalize(L);
```

```
      // vector R = reflect(-Ln,Nf);
      vector H = normalize(Ln+V);
      // float rdotv = R.V;
      float hdotn = H.Nf;
      C += Cl*pow(max(hdotn,0),1/roughness);
    }
  return C;
}
```

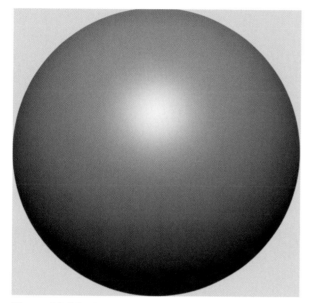

Figure 11.14 Blinn specular highlight.

The Blinn model presented above is equivalent to the following pair of functions from the RI Specification:

```
color
specular(normal N; vector V; float roughness )
{
  color C = 0;
  illuminance(P,N,PI/2)
    C += Cl*specularbrdf(normalize(L),N,V,roughness);
  return C;
}

color specularbrdf(vector L,N,V; float roughness)
{
  vector H = normalize(L+V);
  return pow(max(0,N.H), 1/roughness);
}
```

In production work, the built-in specular() is most widely used. The alternatives (including the one above and the ones below) are presented for comparison and for pointing out ways to extend the built-in functionality (for example, to create streaked/shaped highlights).

Blinn: Anisotropic Shading

As noted earlier, real-world highlights are most often anisotropic and do not look like ideal circles. One easy, ad hoc way to obtain an anisotropic highlight is to use a pair of tangent vectors instead of the surface normal in the Blinn highlight calculation. More appropriately, in addition to a tangent t, we use a binormal b obtained by crossing Nf and t (since by definition Nf, t, and b are orthogonal, in other words, mutually perpendicular vectors). RSL's dPdu is an obvious choice for a tangent vector.

Anisotropy is introduced by scaling the unit vectors t and b via user-supplied factors ax and ay. Further, their dot products with H are raised to user-supplied exponents axp and ayp. Finally, we use another exponent expo as a generalization of the sqrt() call. Since Nf, t, and b are mutually perpendicular, by the Pythagorean theorem we have this:

```
Nf.H = sqrt(1-(t.H)*(t.H)-(b.H)*(b.h));
```

We are simply generalizing the above via this:

```
t = t/ax;  b = b/ay;
float hdotn = pow((1.0 - pow((H.t),axp) - pow((H.b),ayp)),expo);
```

Figure 11.15 shows an anisotropic Blinn highlight rendered using the AnisoBlinnFn() shown below. In subsequent sections, we will look at many other ways to generate anisotropic highlights.

```
color AnisoBlinnFn(float roughness, ax, ay, axp, ayp, expo)
{
  color C = 0;
  extern point P;
  extern normal N;
  extern vector I;
  vector V = -normalize(I);
  normal Nf = faceforward(normalize(N),I);
  illuminance (P, Nf, PI/2)
    {
      extern vector L, dPdu;
      vector Ln = normalize(L);
      vector H = normalize(Ln+V);
      // float rdotv = R.V;
      // float hdotn = H.Nf;
```

```
        // C += Cl*pow(max(hdotn,0),1/roughness);
        // instead of Nf above, use t and b:
        // t can be dPdu, b is cross(Nf,t)
        vector t = normalize(dPdu);
        vector b = Nf^t;
        t = t/ax;
        b = b/ay;
        // float hdotn = sqrt(1.0 - pow((H.t),axp) - pow((H.b),ayp));
        float hdotn = pow((1.0 - pow((H.t),axp) - pow((H.b),ayp)),expo);
        C += Cl*pow(max(hdotn,0),1/roughness);
    }
    return C;
}
```

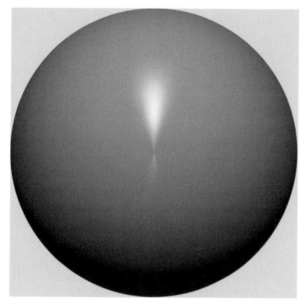

Figure 11.15 Anisotropic Blinn highlight.

Specular: Schlick's Approximation

Earlier, we encountered Schlick's simplification of the Fresnel formula. Here is another one of Schlick's approximations. The exponentiation operation that occurs in the Phong/Blinn model is relatively expensive to compute, so it makes sense to use a simpler approximation for it. Schlick proposed the following substitute for pow(x,n):

```
pow(x,n) ~ x/(n*(1-x)+x)
```

Employing such a simplification for pow(x,n) is acceptable because the Phong/Blinn model is itself empirical (lacks a physical basis). From Figure 11.16, it can be seen that the approximation, which is much faster to compute compared to a pow(), works pretty well since the highlight it creates looks just like one obtained using the power function.

```
color SchlickSpecularFn(float roughness)
{
  color C = 0;
  extern point P;
  extern normal N;
  extern vector I;
  vector V = -normalize(I);
  normal Nf = faceforward(normalize(N),I);


  illuminance (P, Nf, PI/2)
    {
      extern vector L, dPdu;
      vector Ln = normalize(L);
      vector H = normalize(Ln+V);

      float hdotn = max(0,H.Nf);
      float SchlickApprox = hdotn/(roughness*(1-hdotn)+hdotn);
      C += Cl*SchlickApprox;

    }
  return C;
}
```

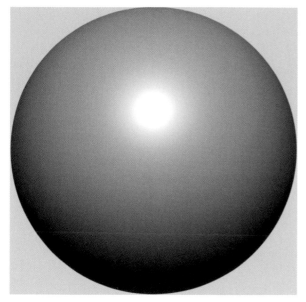

Figure 11.16 Highlight using Schlick's approximation.

Scattered Highlights

Highlights on rough surfaces, such as wind-driven water waves and hammered metal, appear broken up (scattered) due to discontinuities in the surface orientation. A quick, ad hoc way to achieve this look is to perturb H, the halfway vector used in the Blinn specular calculation. Doing so causes a single contiguous circular highlight to fragment into smaller, unevenly shaped regions. In the code below, we simply evaluate noise() using H as an input along with frequency and amplitude. We then add the result to H, thereby perturbing it.

Note that perturbing H affects only specular highlights, not diffuse shading. This is in contrast to bump mapping, where the surface normal perturbation ends up altering both diffuse and specular calculations.

In Figure 11.17, the top-left image is created with an amplitude of 0.0 to show the base case of no scatter. The other three images are made with an amplitude of 0.4 and increasing frequency values of 20, 40, and 80. As expected, the higher spatial variation created by increasing the noise frequency leads to more breakup of the highlights.

```
vector bumped(vector n; float freq, ampl;)
{
    vector bm = (ampl*2*(-1+noise(n*freq)));
    return n+bm;
}
```

```
color hscatter
(
    normal N;
    vector V;
    float roughness, ampl, freq;
)
{
    color C = 0;
    extern point P;

    illuminance (P, N, PI/2)
    {
      extern vector L;  extern color Cl;
      vector H = normalize(normalize(L)+V);

      vector HH = normalize(bumped(H,freq,ampl));


      C += Cl * pow(max(0,N.HH), 1/roughness);
    }
    return C;
}// hscatter
```

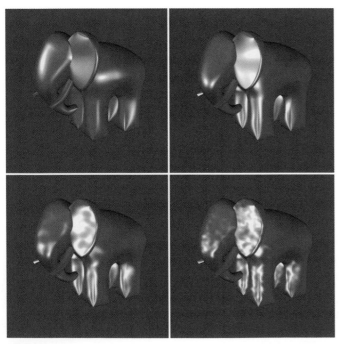

Figure 11.17 Scattering of highlights using noise().

Sparkle

We can use anisotropy to create cross-shaped highlights to simulate a starburst lens filter. The technique here is adapted from the "Jewel" Slim appearance that ships with Pixar's RAT toolset.

We use the RSL functions Du() and Dv(), which measure derivatives of their inputs in u and v, respectively. Du(P) and Dv(P) give us a pair of mutually perpendicular vectors that we can cross with N.(Note that Du(P) and Dv(P) are equivalent to values of built-in variables dPdu and dPdv, respectively.) Further processing is used to create anisotropy, as you can see from the following three lines in the GlossyStar() function:

```
float h = pow(1-abs(H.normalize(N^Du(P))),starhlen);
float v = pow(1-abs(H.normalize(N^Dv(P))),starvlen);
float thinness = (h+v);
```

The resulting thinness value is used as a multiplier in the Blinn highlight calculation. The anisotropy obtained from h and v above flare out the normally circular highlight along u and v directions (see Figure 11.18).

```
color GlossyStar
(
    normal N;
    vector V;
    float roughness, starhlen, starvlen;
)
{
    color C = 0;
    extern point P;
    illuminance (P, N, PI/2)
    {
      extern vector L;  extern color Cl;
      vector H = normalize(normalize(L)+V);

      float h = pow(1-abs(H.normalize(N^Du(P))),starhlen);
      float v = pow(1-abs(H.normalize(N^Dv(P))),starvlen);

      float thinness = (h+v);

      C += Cl * thinness* pow(max(0,N.H), 1.0/roughness);
    }
    return C;
}// GlossyStar
```

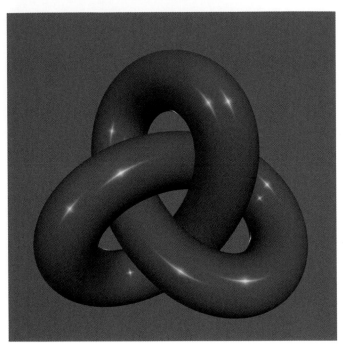

Figure 11.18 Sparkle-shaped highlights.

Hair

The thin cross sections of hair and fur give rise to highly anisotropic shading. There is very little change in shading crosswise (around their cylindrical profile). Most of the shading variation occurs along their length as a function of their orientation with respect to the viewer and light source.

Such anisotropic shading can be modeled by using a vector T that runs along the length of such a thin cylindrical object, such as dPdu or dPdv. Instead of the usual (L,N,V) triplet we use (L,T,V) in the highlight calculation. The relative orientation of T with L with V can be used to derive an anisotropy term via

```
cosang = cos(abs(acos(T.normalize(L)) - acos(-T.V))); // cos of angle
difference
```

Note that for calculating a Blinn highlight, we compare the halfway vector H (which is L+V, normalized) with N. Here, instead of using N, we use T. Also, instead of doing (T.H) for the comparison, we compute the cosine of the angle difference as mentioned above. While the two methods give the same value of 1.0 when T lies exactly midway between L and V, the angle difference result falls off sharply when T diverges from the true mirror (midway) direction. The result is that the highlight is more localized compared to the Blinn case, which is desirable since it mimics the look of natural hair.

The code shown in the hair shader here is a slightly modified version of the one found in Pixar's Application Note #19, "Using the RiCurves Primitive." In the Pixar version, T is always `normalize(dPdv)` where u is the hair's cross direction and the length follows v. For extra visual control, we can generalize this to vary T between Tu (dPdu) and Tv (dPdv) as a function of a user-supplied parameter theta (which takes values between 0 and 90 degrees):

```
vector T = 0.5*(Tv+Tu+(Tv-Tu)*cos(2*PI/180*theta));
```

Plugging theta=0 into the above makes T=Tv, theta=90 yields T=Tu, and in-between values for theta produce an interpolated vector. You can use this expression in other shaders where you need to interpolate smoothly between two vectors.

Figure 11.19 shows four images of identical "hairball" geometry, which is a single NURBS curve oriented along the parametric v direction. From top-left to bottom-right, the theta values are 0, 30, 60, and 90 degrees. As expected, the theta=0 case looks most like hair because T reduces to dPdv for this case. The bottom-right image, where the anisotropy is calculated using dPdu (theta being 90 degrees), looks more like thin copper wire instead of hair. The two intermediate images exhibit visual blends between these two extremes.

```
// From Pixar's Application Note #19, slightly modified
surface hair (float Ka = 1, Kd = .6, Ks = .35, roughness = .15;
              color rootcolor = color (.109, .037, .007);
              color tipcolor = color (.519, .325, .125);
              color specularcolor = (color(1) + tipcolor) / 2;
              float theta=0;
              )
{

    vector Tu = normalize(dPdu);
    vector Tv = normalize(dPdv);
    vector T = 0.5*(Tv+Tu+(Tv-Tu)*cos(2*PI/180*theta));
    vector V = -normalize(I);    /* V is the view vector */
    color Cspec = 0, Cdiff = 0;  /* collect specular & diffuse light */
    float cosang;

    /* Loop over lights, catch highlights as if this was a thin cylinder */
    illuminance (P)
    {
     cosang = cos (abs (acos (T.normalize(L)) - acos (-T.V)));
     // Assuming 'v' is 0 at the root of each hair and 1 at the tip, you
     // can try using it as a scale factor, ie
     // Cl*v*pow(cosang, 1/roughness) for Cspec and Cl*v for Cdiff
     Cspec += Cl*pow(cosang, 1/roughness);
```

```
    Cdiff += Cl;
    }

    Oi = Os;
    Ci = Oi * (mix(rootcolor, tipcolor, v) * (Ka*ambient() + Kd*Cdiff) +
        (Ks * Cspec * specularcolor));
}
```

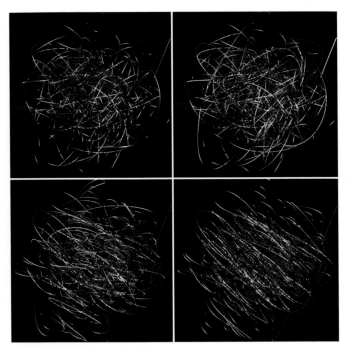

Figure 11.19 Anisotropic shading of a hairball.

Glossy Illumination

The classical Blinn/Phong highlight has a brightness profile across its circular cross section where maximum brightness occurs at the center, tapering off toward the circumference. This is to be expected given that we use a dot product such as R.V or N.H and control its spread via a pow() function. What if we want the highlight to be "flat," relatively uniform across the spot profile? Ceramic coatings, certain types of glass, liquids, and so on exhibit such a featureless highlight profile. Flat highlights are also employed in cartoon rendering (computer-generated or hand-drawn) and poster art.

A glossy look can most easily be achieved using smoothstep(), which returns values between 0 and 1 based on three inputs: two values that specify a range and a third selector value. By making the smoothstep() function's transition from 0 to 1 sharp (narrow) by specifying a narrow range and the usual Blinn specular value as the selector, we can create a flat profile across our highlight (we are essentially thresholding the highlight). Such an illumination model is presented by Gritz and Apodaca in their *Advanced RenderMan* book. The code in our Glossy() function is derived from their LocIllumGlossy() function, including the use of magic constants 0.72 and 0.18, which they arrived at empirically. Figure 11.20 shows a Spirograph surface shaded using the Glossy() function.

```
color Glossy ( normal N;  vector V; float roughness, sharpness; )
{
    color C = 0;
    float w = .18 * (1-sharpness);
    extern point P;
    illuminance (P, N, PI/2)
      {
        extern vector L;
        extern color Cl;
        vector H = normalize(normalize(L)+V);
        // create a 'flatter' highlight by thresholding the usual specular value
        C += Cl * smoothstep (.72-w, .72+w, pow(max(0,N.H), 1/roughness));
      }
    return C;
}
```

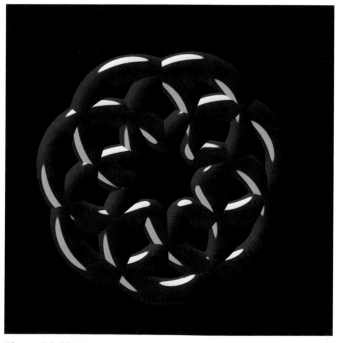

Figure 11.20 Glossy highlights using Ward's technique.

Westin: Brushed Metal

The SHW_brushedmetal shader shown here is originally by Steve Westin and slightly modified by Tal Lancaster. The surface is conceived to be covered with thin, parallel cylinders that lie along the parametric u direction, and these cylinders are shaded anisotropically using dot products of normalize(dPdu) with V and Ln. Note that the hair shader discussed earlier uses a similar approach with (L,T,V). As an exercise, try adding a theta control to SHW_brushedmetal as we did in the hair shader to be able to smoothly vary the anisotropy direction from dPdu to dPdv.

As the name implies, SHW_brushedmetal is useful for creating the look of metallic surfaces such as brushed aluminum or stainless steel, where the brush (machining) marks stretch and diffuse highlights anisotropically along the groove directions (Figure 11.21).

```
surface SHW_brushedmetal (   float Ka = 0.03,
                    Kd = 0.03,
                    Ks = 1.0;
                    float roughness = .04;
                    color specularcolor = 1;
                    )
{

  normal Nf;
  vector tangent;                /* Unit vector in "u" direction */
  color env;
  float Kt;
  vector V;                      /* Normalized eye vector */
  vector H;                      /* Bisector vector for Phong/Blinn */
  float spec;                    /* Total "specular" intensity */
  float aniso;                   /* Anisotropic scale factor */
  float shad;                    /* Phong-like shadow/masking function */
  float sin_light, sin_eye;      /* Sines of angles from tangent vector */
  float cos_light, cos_eye;      /* Cosines of angles from tangent vector */
  vector Ln;                     /* Normalized vector to light */

  /* Get unit vector in "u" parameter direction */
  tangent = normalize ( dPdu );

  Nf = faceforward (normalize(N), I);
  V = -normalize (I);

  /* "Specular" highlight in the Phong sense: directional-diffuse */
  cos_eye = -tangent.V;
```

```
sin_eye = sqrt ( 1.0 - cos_eye * cos_eye );
spec = 0;
illuminance ( P, Nf, 1.57079632679489661923 /* Hemisphere */ ) {
  Ln = normalize ( L );
  H = 0.5 * ( V + Ln );
  cos_light = tangent.Ln;
  sin_light = sqrt ( 1.0 - cos_light * cos_light );
  aniso = max ( cos_light*cos_eye + sin_light*sin_eye, 0.0 );
  shad = max ( Nf.V, 0.0 ) * max ( Nf.Ln, 0.0 );
  spec += Ks * pow ( aniso, 1.0/roughness ) * shad;
}

env = Ks * spec * specularcolor;

Ci = Os * (Ka*ambient() + Kd*diffuse(Nf)) * Cs + env;
}
```

Figure 11.21 Westin's anisotropic shading.

Spirotropic Illumination

This section presents a "spirotropic" illumination model, which is a totally arbitrary, nonphysical model obtained using a Spirograph curve. A Spirograph curve in general crosses itself several times. If such a curve were to be redrawn ("unwrapped") to remove the crossings, the result looks like a polar plot with circularly symmetric lobes. These lobes can be used to compute diffuse, specular, retroreflection (using L.V), and backscatter (via N.V) components. The result is a very shiny surface (top and bottom right images in Figure 11.22) obtained using our spirotropic material and a single directional light. As can be seen from the top and bottom left control images in Figure 11.22, such an effect cannot be obtained just by using standard specular shading with a large roughness parameter to broaden the highlight.

In the unspiro shader, so-called since it uses an unwrapped Spirograph curve, the getrho() function computes the radius of the curve, given an angle between 0 and 360 degrees. This function is used with acos(Ln.Nn), acos(Hn.Nn), acos(Ln.Vn), and acos(Nn.Vn) to calculate diffuse, specular, retroreflection, and backscatter contributions, respectively. The other inputs R, rv, and b to the getrho() function are used for Spirograph curve generation, and the last parameter f introduces non-linearity via pow(rho,f), where rho is the calculated radius value at the given angle.

```
float LCM(float R,rv)
{
   float i=0,cm=1.0;

   if (mod(R,rv)==0)
      {
         // return (1);
         cm = 1;
      }
   else
      {
         i=1;
         while(mod(R*i,rv)!=0)
      {
      i=i+1;
      }
         cm = i;
      }

   return cm;
}


float getrho(float ang,  R, rv, b, f)
{
   float rho;
   float nrev = LCM(R,rv);
   float theta = ang*nrev;
   rho = (sqrt((R-rv)*(R-rv)+ b*b + 2*(R-rv)*b*cos((1+R/rv)*theta)));
```

```
    rho = rho/R;
    rho = pow(rho,f);
    return rho;


}// getrho()



surface
unspiro(float Ksc=1.0, Knorm=1, Ka = 0.05,
                Kd = 0.1,
                Ks = 0.1,
                Kr = .1, Kb=0.1, KS=0.1;
                float roughness = .1;
                float R=400,rv=250,b=175,f=.5;
                float Kspiro=1.0;
    )
{
    normal Nf;                      /* Normalized normal vector */
    vector V;                       /* Normalized eye vector */
    vector H;                       /* Bisector vector for Phong/Blinn */
    vector Ln;                      /* Normalized vector to light */
    float cosine, sine;             /* Components for horizon scatter */
    float NLang, NHang, LVang, NVang, rho;

    Nf = faceforward (normalize(N), I);
    V = -normalize (I);
    color sp = 0, rr=0, bs=0, dif=0;
    normal Nn = normalize(N);
    vector Vn = -normalize(I);
    color C1=0, C2=0;
    illuminance(P,Nn,3.1415) // MUST have 3.1415 due to our ang being 0..360
      {
        vector Ln = normalize(L);
        vector Hn = normalize(Ln+Vn);

        rho = getrho(acos(Ln.Nn),R,rv,b,f);
        dif += C1*rho;

        rho = getrho(acos(Hn.Nn),R,rv,b,f);
        sp += C1*pow(rho,1.0/roughness);

        rho = getrho(acos(Ln.Vn),R,rv,b,f);
        rr += C1*rho;
```

```
    rho = getrho(acos(Nn.Vn),R,rv,b,f);
    bs += Cl*rho;

    C1 += Ksc*Cs*Os*(Ka*ambient() + Kd*dif + Ks*sp + Kr*rr + Kb*bs);

    C2 += Knorm*Cs*Os*(Ka*ambient()+Kd*diffuse(Nf))
          +Ks*specular(Nf,Vn,roughness);



  }

  Ci = mix(C2,C1,Kspiro);
}// unspiro
```

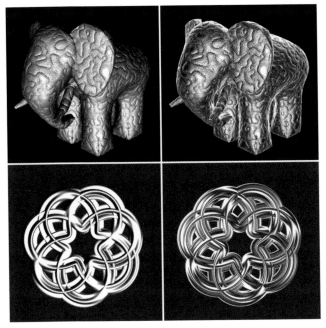

Figure 11.22 Spirotropic illumination model.

Ward: Anisotropic Reflection

The anisotropic Ward illumination model by Greg Ward contains a Lambertian diffuse term and an anisotropic specular one. Here we focus on just the specular part. This model is useful for creating a very metallic look with stretched highlights. In Figure 11.23 this is apparent on the teapot's body, spout, and the knob on the lid.

The `LocIllumWardAnisotropic()` call shown here is from Apodaca and Gritz's *Advanced RenderMan* book. The code is also used in the `LGbrushedmetal` shader found at the RenderMan Repository on the Web.

The overall idea is to use not just one but two `roughness` values in the specular highlight calculation. These `roughness` values model the standard deviation of surface microfacets in two perpendicular directions that lie on the surface. `dPdu` is used as one of those directions, and `N^dPdu` is taken to be the second one. When the `roughness` values are small, we get sharper (shinier) highlights. Also, the ratio of the `roughness` values controls the anisotropy.

The isotropic Ward model is a special case of the anisotropic version where a single `roughness` value is used and the two surface directions are dispensed with. This in turn is a simplification of the Cook-Torrance model, which we will encounter in an upcoming section.

```
/*
 * Greg Ward Larson's anisotropic specular local illumination model.
 * The derivation and formulae can be found in:  Ward, Gregory J.
 * "Measuring and Modeling Anisotropic Reflection," ACM Computer
 * Graphics 26(2) (Proceedings of Siggraph '92), pp. 265-272, July, 1992.
 * Inputs:
 *    N - unit surface normal
 *    V - unit viewing direction (from P toward the camera)
 *    xdir - a unit tangent of the surface which defines the reference
 *           direction for the anisotropy.
 *    xroughness - the apparent roughness of the surface in xdir.
 *    yroughness - the roughness for the direction of the surface
 *           tangent which is perpendicular to xdir.
 */
color
LocIllumWardAnisotropic (normal N;  vector V;
                         vector xdir;  float xroughness, yroughness;)
{
    float sqr (float x) { return x*x; }

    float cos_theta_r = clamp (N.V, 0.0001, 1);
    vector X = xdir / xroughness;
    vector Y = (N ^ xdir) / yroughness;

    color C = 0;
    extern point P;
    illuminance (P, N, PI/2) {
    /* Must declare because extern L & Cl because we're in a function */
```

```
    extern vector L;  extern color Cl;
    float nonspec = 0;
    lightsource ("__nonspecular", nonspec);
    if (nonspec < 1) {
        vector LN = normalize (L);
        float cos_theta_i = LN . N;
        if (cos_theta_i > 0.0) {
            vector H = normalize (V + LN);
            float rho = exp (-2 * (sqr(X.H) + sqr(Y.H)) / (1 + H.N))/
                        sqrt (cos_theta_i * cos_theta_r);
            C += Cl * ((1-nonspec) * cos_theta_i * rho);
        }
    }
}
    return C / (4 * xroughness * yroughness);
}
```

Figure 11.23 Anisotropic highlights using Ward's model.

Ashikhmin-Shirley Model

The Ashikhmin-Shirley BRDF contains a non-Lambertian diffuse term, an anisotropic term, and a Fresnel term (which can be used to obtain nice edge effects, such as an environment map that can be blended in based on its value). The anisotropic term uses a pair of values, nu and nv, for anisotropy (just like the anisotropic Ward model), in addition to the usual vectors L, N, H, and V. In contrast with the Ward model, higher (not lower) values for nu and nv create sharper highlights.

The code shown here was developed by user trb7 and posted on the Aqsis Web site www.aqsis.org. anisophong() contains code for the diffuse and specular terms, and the Fresnel calculation is done in a function called scaledschlick(). Figure 11.24 shows a render created with the shader.

```
// Shader based on the paper "An anisotropic Phong BRDF model", by
// Michael Ashikhmin and Peter Shirley, that you can find at
// http://www.cs.utah.edu/~michael/brdfs/jgtbrdf.pdf
// Fresnel compensation based on the paper:
// "Fresnel approximation terms for Metals", by Lazányi István and
// Szirmay-Kalos László, of the Department of Control Engineering and
// Information Technology, Budapest University of Technology and Economics,
// paper that you can find at :
// http://www.iit.bme.hu/~szirmay/fresnel.pdf
//
// Implementation by trb7, released under GNU GPL version 2 license
// details at: http://www.gnu.org/copyleft/gpl.html
//
// shader details:
//
// Ka = ambient coefficient;
// Kd = diffuse coefficient;
// Ks = specular coefficient;
// ior = IOR;
// nu = specularity coefficient for U direction;
// nv = specularity coefficient for V direction;
// extcoeff = extinction coefficient for IOR (fresnel spread)
//
// good starting values are nu = 10, nv = 1000, or vice-versa, ranges
// between 1 and 10000 work best, for a mix of soft/sharp highlights.

#define ALPHA 7 // second constraint for curve correction

float scaledschlick(
float theta;
float ior;
float extcoeff;
)
{
```

```
float out ;
out = ( pow(ior-1, 2)+4*ior*pow(1-theta, 5)+pow(extcoeff, 2) ) /
( pow(ior+1, 2)+pow(extcoeff, 2)) ; // the scaled Schlick term
// but now we need the compensation for high ior + k
// the deviation gets extreme if k > 1 and ior > 1.5, but even when k is
// > 0 and < 1, it's still there. (Question: when is the visual difference
// enough to trigger the compensation? We'll just compensate any extinction
// coefficient higher than 0, and IOR higher than 1.5, just to be safe)
if ( extcoeff > 0 || ior > 1.5 )
out = out - 2 * ior * theta * pow(1-theta, ALPHA) ;

return out ;
}


// cleaned up illuminance
color anisophong(
normal Nf;
vector Vf;
float nu;
float nv;
float Kd;
float Ks;
float sschlick;
color SurfaceColor;
color SpecularColor;
)
{
// we're going to clean things up a bit, and try to move out of the
// illuminance loop everything that can be moved.

extern vector dPdu;
vector u = normalize(dPdu);
vector v = Nf ^ u;

// we can keep everything, except the last part of the equation, out of the
// illuminance loop, since this last part needs to take into account the
// incoming light vector. We'll try to clean things up, to use only one
// loop for both diffuse and specular, instead of repeating things.
// 1st section, for diffuse term:
float secta, sectb, sectc, diffterm, specterm;
sectb = 1-pow( (1-( (Nf.Vf)/2)), 5);
secta = (((28*Kd) / 23 ) * (1-Ks)) * sectb; // ensuring energy conservation
// and no normaling factor PI, which i "forgot" to remove
```

```
// 2nd section for specular term:
sectc = sqrt( (nu + 1) * (nv + 1)) / 8;

extern point P;
color C = 0;

illuminance(P, Nf, PI/2)
{
vector Ln, Hv;

Ln = normalize(L);
Hv = normalize(Ln+Vf);

float hvu = Hv.u; // not passing hv.u/v angles previously, as specified
float hvv = Hv.v; // in page 5

diffterm = secta * (1 - pow( (1-( (Nf.Ln)/2)), 5) );

specterm = sectc * (pow( (Nf.Hv), ( (nu * pow( hvu, 2)) +
(nv * pow( hvv, 2)) )) /
( (Hv.Vf) * max( (Nf.Vf), (Nf.Ln) )) ) * sschlick;

C += ( (SurfaceColor * diffterm) + (SpecularColor * specterm) ) *
Cl * max(0, (Nf.Ln) );
}
return C;
}


// now for the test shader for the terms, arguments are quite obvious
surface
phonganiso(
float Ka = 0.05; // ambient coefficient
float Kd = 0.3; // diffuse coefficient
float Ks = 0.9; // specular coefficient
float ior = 1.5; // IOR
float extcoeff = 0; // extinction coefficient for IOR (high for metals)
float nu = 1000; // specularity along U direction surface tangent
float nv = 10; // specularity along V direction surface tangent
color SurfaceColor = color (.5, .5, .5);
color SpecularColor = color (1, 1, 1);
string envmap = ""; // pass your own envlatl environment map ...
// note, the paper mentions Kd being 0 for metals, and non zero for
// , quote: "polished surfaces, such as smooth plastics, there is both
// a diffuse and specular appearance and neither term is zero".
```

```
)
{
normal Nn, Nf;
vector Vf;

Nn = normalize(N);
Nf = faceforward(Nn, I, Nn);
Vf = -normalize(I);

float costheta = Nf.Vf; // cosine of angle between normal and viewer

float sschlick = scaledschlick(costheta, ior, extcoeff);
// (note: when using extremely high iors, we get negative values in the
// initial curve slope, which means that the 2nd constraint is causing
// problems, but the scaled fresnel paper isn't very clear about this, so
// we'll do an ugly thing, since when ior > 5 or 10, the 2nd constraint
// needs some verification)
if ( sschlick < 0)
sschlick = abs(sschlick);
else if ( sschlick > 1 )
sschlick = 1;

color aniso = anisophong( Nf, Vf, nu, nv, Kd, Ks, sschlick,
SurfaceColor, SpecularColor);

// this is temporary, just to map an reflection for test purposes
// the ideal would be to have proper anisotropic reflections, any ideas/
// suggestions for possible implementations, are welcome
if ( envmap != "") {
vector Rn = reflect( Vf, Nf);
color enviro = environment( envmap, Rn);
}
else
color enviro = 0;

Oi = Os;

// we'll multiply this test reflection by the rescaled schlick for grazing
// reflections
Ci = (Ka * ambient()) + aniso + (enviro * sschlick);
}
```

Figure 11.24 Ashikhmin-Shirley's anisotropic lighting model.

Lafortune—Simplified Model

The Phong specular model says that for a given light direction L and surface normal N, maximum reflection occurs along the mirror direction R. As we saw in a previous section, this is expressed as pow(R.V,n) where V is the view direction and n is a specular exponent. Another way of saying that the reflection is centered around R is to talk about a *cosine lobe* that occurs along this direction. (Lobes are commonly used to refer to concentration of electromagnetic waves along specific directions.)

The Lafortune BRDF is a generalization of the Phong cosine lobe model to arbitrary (non-R) reflection directions. You can find the full details in Lafortune's 1992 SIGGRAPH paper "Non-Linear Approximation of Reflectance Functions."

In brief, it works like this. Given an incident direction L and a surface (mirror) normal N, the reflection vector can be geometrically derived to be 2N(N.L)-L. Using a technique called *Householder transformation*, the reflection vector can be expressed as LM, M being the Householder matrix (2NN_transpose - I), where N_transpose is the transpose of N and I is the identity matrix. Loosely speaking, we are factoring out L from the two terms in 2N(N.L)-L.

Using the Householder matrix M, the Phong model pow(R.V,n) can now be expressed as pow(LM.V,n). Lafortune's generalization is that M can be an arbitrary 3×3 matrix, the Householder being just one of the possibilities. The 3×3 matrix plus the specular exponent gives us 10 free parameters in our lighting model. More commonly, a diagonal matrix (which has non-zero elements along the diagonal and zeros elsewhere) is used for M. If the diagonal matrix is expressed as (Cx,Cy,Cz), you can see that LM.V is equivalent to (LxCxVx+LyCyVy+LzCzVz). In other words, it is a scaled (or weighted) dot product of L and V, with (Cx,Cy,Cz) acting as the scale factors. Specifically, (Cx,Cy,Cz) can be regarded as scale factors for altering the incident direction L, the effect of which is to alter the length and orientation of the reflection vector R. In that sense, the Lafortune model generalizes the orientation as well as the scale of the original Phong lobe.

Figure 11.25 shows the Utah Teapot rendered using just the specular term (K1f is 0 in the shader below) on the left, and with the Lafortune model on the right (K1f is 0.7, and Cx,Cy,Cz,n are 4, -4, -0.6, and 2, respectively).

With appropriate values for (Cx,Cy,Cz), the Lafortune BRDF is able to capture several real-world phenomena such as non-Lambertian diffuse reflectance, increased specularity at grazing angles to a surface, off-specular reflection peaks, retroreflection, and anisotropy. Some choices for the coefficients include (Cx!=Cy), (-Cx=-Cy and >Cz), and so on. In addition, values for the coefficients can be obtained experimentally by fitting the cosine lobes to real-world BRDF measurements.

On the Web, you can find a more complete implementation of the Lafortune BRDF. It is called lafortune.sl, written by Steve Westin.

```
surface lafortune (
        uniform float Cx=1, Cy=1, Cz=1, n=1;
        uniform float Ka=.1, Kd=.2, Ks=1.0, K1f=1.0, roughness=0.2;
        )
{

  varying vector local_z;
  varying vector local_x, local_y;          /* Unit vector in "u" and "v"
                                                directions */

  varying vector V;                          /* Normalized eye vector */
  varying vector Ln;                         /* Normalized vector to light */

  local_x = normalize ( dPdu );
  local_z = faceforward (normalize(N), I);
  vector v = -normalize(I);
  local_y = local_z^local_x;

  Ci = (Kd*diffuse(local_z) + Ka*ambient()) * Cs;

  illuminance ( P, local_z, 1.570796326794889661923 /* Hemisphere */ )
    {
       vector u = normalize ( L );
       // Ci += ( Cl * color "rgb" ( fr, fg, fb ) ) * (local_z.Ln); //
```

```
local_z is Nf!

    float lf = Cx*xcomp(u)*xcomp(v) + Cy*ycomp(u)*ycomp(v) +
            Cz*zcomp(u)*zcomp(v);
    lf = pow(lf,n);
    Ci += Klf*Cs*Cl*color(lf,lf,lf)*(u.local_z);
  }

  Ci += Cs*Ks*specular(local_z,v,roughness);

  Ci *= Os;
}
```

Figure 11.25 Lafortune illumination model (simplified version).

Schlick's Model

Schlick's illumination model is inspired by the Cook-Torrance model. As with his approximations for specular reflection and Fresnel factor, this one also uses rational functions to simplify more elaborate computations. The BRDF features Lambertian diffuse reflectance, glossy specularity, anisotropy, and Fresnel edge effect. Here we will present a simplified version of the Schlick model to get the ideas across.

In the Schlick BRDF, there are no separate terms for diffuse and specular calculations. Instead, a rational function (ratio of polynomials) is used to create these as extremes of a continuum. Likewise, isotropy and anisotropy are also obtainable as extremes of a different rational function. To these two, we add a third function to smoothly vary the anisotropy direction from dPdu to dPdv. (You have encountered this function in the "Hair" section.)

The diffuse to specular continuous range is expressed as follows:

```
Z = = r/pow((1+r*t*t-t*t),2); // t is Nn.H
```

In the above, setting r=1 provides the diffuse case (Z is independent of t and is a constant) and when r is 0, we get the specular case (Z is 0 except in the perfect mirror direction, where t=1).

Likewise, the isotropy/anisotropy continuum is expressed as

```
A = sqrt(p/(p*p*(1-w*w)+w*w));
```

where p is a user-specified value (p=1 is isotropic, and p=0 is anisotropic) and w is the anisotropy factor. When p=1, A becomes a constant, and when p=0, A is 0 except where w=1.

The anisotropy direction is obtained as a blend between dPdu and dPdv using

```
vector anisoDir = 0.5*(T+B+(T-B)*cos(2*PI/180*theta));
```

where theta is a user-supplied angle between 0 and 90 degrees. Between these angles, anisoDir can be seen to vary between T and B.

Figures 11.26, 11.27, and 11.28 show the Schlick BRDF in action. The first figure illustrates the diffuse to specular transition, and the middle one shows the transition from isotropic to anisotropic specularity. The bottom image shows the result of varying the anisotropy direction.

```
color Schlick (normal Nn; vector V; float r,p,theta;)
{

  color C = 0;
  extern point P;
  // float v = V.Nn;
  extern vector dPdu;
  illuminance (P, Nn, PI)
    {
      extern vector L;
      vector Ln = normalize(L);
      extern color Cl;

      vector H = normalize(L+V);
      float t = Nn.H;

      // float vprime = normalize(L).Nn;
      // float multfac = 1.0/(4*PI*v*vprime);

      float Z = r/pow((1+r*t*t-t*t),2);
```

```
        Z = r*(Nn.Ln) + (1-r)*Z;

        // aniso. term
        vector H_perp_N = normalize(H-Nn*(H.Nn));
        vector T = normalize(dPdu);
        vector B = Nn^T;
        vector anisoDir = 0.5*(T+B+(T-B)*cos(2*PI/180*theta));
        // float w = T.H_perp_N;
        float w = anisoDir.H_perp_N;
        float A = sqrt(p/(p*p*(1-w*w)+w*w));

        //
        C += Cl*Z*A;
    }
  return C;
}// Schlick
```

Figure 11.26 Schlick's model: diffuse to specular transition.

Figure 11.27 Schlick's model: isotropic to anisotropic highlight transition.

Figure 11.28 Schlick's model: varying highlight orientation.

Banks

The Banks shading model is an ad hoc one; it is not based on physical principles. Here we look at the specular portion of the model. The tangent vector dPdv, passed into BanksFn() shown below as the variable t, is used to derive an anisotropic value for the specular highlight. Specifically, the angle between t and the view vector V and the angle between t and the light direction Ln (V.t and Ln.t, respectively) contribute to the anisotropy.

The render at the right of Figure 11.29 shows the Banks shading model, using Ks, Kd, Ka, and roughness values of 0.5, 0.3, 0.1, and 0.06, respectively, in the code below. For comparison, the left image shows the same values used in a standard plastic shader.

```
color BanksFn( normal N;  vector V; vector t; float roughness)
{
    color C = 0;
    extern point P;
    // extern normal N;
    // normal Nn = faceforward(normalize(N),V);
    illuminance (P, N, PI/2)
      {
        /* Must declare extern L & Cl because we're in a function */
        extern vector L;  extern color Cl;

        vector Ln = normalize(L);
        float ndotl = max(N.Ln,0);
        ndotl = pow(max(ndotl,0),1/roughness);

        float aniso = max((sqrt(1.0-V.t-V.t)*sqrt(1.0-Ln.t-Ln.t) -
        ((V.t)*(Ln.t))),0);
        C += Cl*ndotl*aniso;
      }
    return C;
}


surface Banks(float Ka=0.1, Kd = 0.5, Ks=0.5, roughness = .5)
{
  normal Nn = normalize(N);
  vector V = -normalize(I);
  normal Nf = faceforward(Nn,I);
  vector t = normalize(dPdv);
  Ci = Cs*(Ka*ambient() + Kd*diffuse(Nf)) + Ks*BanksFn(Nf,V,t, roughness);
}
```

Figure 11.29 Standard specular versus Banks lighting model.

Cook-Torrance Model

We have mentioned the Cook-Torrance model in some of the previous subsections. It is a physically based model that is based on the distribution of microfacets over a surface. Each microfacet is taken to be a flat, tiny, ideal Lambertian reflector. Light bounces around on the surface by reflecting off these microfacets. How these microfacets are oriented (in relation to the surface normal), masked (from the viewer by other facets), and shadowed (from the light, also by other facets) is what determines surface shading. The model is based on earlier work by Torrance and Sparrow that has to do with reflection of electromagnetic waves from a surface.

In the Cook-Torrance/Torrance-Sparrow model, three terms F, G, and D are involved, along with the usual L, N, and V directions:

`F*G*D/((L.N)*(N.V))`

F is the Fresnel factor, which takes into account the shading variation caused by the relative orientation of L and H, the halfway vector.

D, known as the "roughness term," expresses how the microfacets are distributed with respect to the geometric normal N. The Beckman exponential distribution function is commonly used for D:

`D = 1/(4*m*m*t*t*t*t) * exp((t*t-1)/(m*m*t*t));`

In the above, t is N.H and m is the root-mean-square (RMS) slope of the micro-facets. When m is large, the microfacets are scattered rather unevenly, so the surface appears rough. As m becomes small, the microfacets are all pretty much aligned with the macroscopic normal N, resulting in a smoother surface with a smaller, sharper highlight.

Blinn proposed the following simplified version for D:

`D = c*exp(-alpha*alpha/(m*m));`

In this equation, c is an arbitrary constant, m is now the RMS angle (not slope), and alpha is the angle between N and H, in other words, acos(N.H). For small angles, alpha approximately equals sin(alpha), so the Blinn version can be rewritten in terms of cos(alpha), which we have been calling t:

```
D = c*exp((t*t-1)/(m*m)); // since t*t + sin(alpha)*sin(alpha) = 1
```

As a third alternative for D, Schlick offers (as usual!) a rational function approximation of the Beckman distribution:

```
D = m*m*m*x/(t*(m*x*x-x*x+m*m)*(m*x*x-x*x+m*m)); // x=t+m-1
```

G is the geometry term that specifies the orientation of the microfacets. It is a function of (L,N,V) and is used to account for microfacet masking and self-shadowing.

The code shown here is a slight modification of an implementation by Brent Watkins. The built-in fresnel() call is used for the F term, and geom() and distro() functions implement the G and D terms, respectively. In distro() the tan() function is used, since sqrt(t*t-1)/t reduces to tan(beta) when t=cos(beta), where beta is the angle between N and H. Also, note that the geom() call uses four dot products between L, N, V, and H to account for masking and shadowing.

Figure 11.30 shows the Utah Teapot shaded using the Cook-Torrance model.

```
float distro( normal Nn;
              vector H;
              float m; )
    {
      float ndoth = Nn.H;
      float beta = acos( ndoth );
      float tanbeta = tan( beta );
      float tanbeta_over_m = tanbeta/m;
      float D = exp(-(tanbeta_over_m*tanbeta_over_m));
      D /= 4*m*m*pow(ndoth,4);
      return D;
    }


// geometric attenuation factor
float geom( normal Nn;
            vector H;
            vector L;
            vector V )
    {
      float ndoth = Nn.H;
      float ndotv = Nn.V;
      float ndotl = Nn.L;
```

```
          float vdoth = V.H;

          float masking = 2*ndoth*ndotv/vdoth;
          float shadowing = 2*ndoth*ndotl/vdoth;
          return min(1,min(masking,shadowing));
      }

float LocIllumCookTorrance(
normal N; vector V;
float eta, m;)
{
  extern vector I;
  extern point P;
  normal Nf, Nn;

  Nn = normalize(N);
  Nf = faceforward(Nn, I);

  float cook = 0;
  illuminance( P, Nf, PI/2 )
    {
      vector Ln = normalize(L);
      vector H = normalize(Ln+V);
      float D = distro( Nf, H, m );
      float G = geom( Nf, H, Ln, V );
      float F, Kt;
      // float F = fresnel_hack( Nf, V, IndexOfRefraction );
      fresnel(V,Nf,eta,F,Kt);

      cook += D*G*F;
    }
  float vdotn = V.Nf;
  cook /= vdotn;
  // normalize - preserves conservation of energy
  cook /= PI;

  return cook;

}
```

Figure 11.30 Cook-Torrance shading model.

Minnaert Illumination

The Minnaert shading model was originally proposed in 1941 to describe the reflectance of the moon. It is expressed as a product of L.N and N.V together with a "limb darkening" parameter k. For a given Ka and Kd, altering the k value can produce a variety of looks ranging from classic Lambert to a flattened one (first three images in Figure 11.31). k is usually in the 0..1 range, but giving it a negative value such as -9 (with an attendant increase in Kd to 6) creates a metallic, high-contrast look, as shown in the bottom right of Figure 11.31.

We use pow(ndotl*ndotv,1-k) for the Minnaert shading term, but in the literature you will come across these two alternate forms as well: pow(ndotl,k)*pow(ndotv,k-1) and pow(ndotl,1+k)*pow(1-ndotv,1-k). All three forms qualitatively produce similar results. Note also that in the first and second alternate versions, setting k=1 yields pure diffuse lighting (ndotl, which is the classic Lambert look, and ndotl*ndotl, respectively).

```
color MinnaertFunc(float k;)
{
  color C = 0;

  extern normal N;
  extern vector I;
  vector V = -normalize(I);
  extern point P;
```

```
normal Nn = normalize(N);
normal Nf = faceforward(Nn, I);
float ndotv = max(0, Nf.V); // same each time in the loop!
illuminance( P, Nf, PI/2 )
  {
     extern vector L;
     float ndotl = max(0, (normalize(L)).Nn);

     C += Cl*pow(ndotl*ndotv,1-k);
  }
return C;

}
```

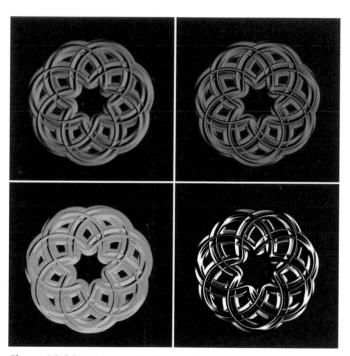

Figure 11.31 Minnaert shading.

We are now done looking at a wide variety of illumination models, some of which are more commonly used in CG production than others. For instance, the Seeliger, Banks, and Minnaert models can be considered almost "esoteric," and the Schlick, Ashikhmin-Shirley, and Lafortune models are not that commonplace. Likewise, a couple of non-photoreal models are thrown into the mix as well—the Gooch and Spirotropic ones. All of these have been included along with the more familiar models such as Oren-Nayar, Ward, Westin, and Cook-Torrance to illustrate the gamut of possibilities when it comes to designing your own illumination models.

Phosphor Under Blacklight

This example is a modified version of the blacklight/Phosphor example found in Pixar's RenderMan Artist Tools (RAT) documentation. It illustrates the use of a specific category of light source inside an illuminance() loop, which is done using a statement such as

```
illuminance ("blacklight", P) { ... }
```

or

```
illuminance ("blacklight", P,Nf,PI/2) { ... }
```

By including the blacklight category specifier string, we are restricting the illuminance loop to include only those lights whose category variable has been set to blacklight. Other lights (such as distantlights, for example) are ignored by such illuminance loops. You can use such a lightsource/surface shader pairing technique to achieve some special shading effects. Here, the blacklight shader (which is a modified spotlight) is used as a UV light to impart a phosphorescent glow to a surface to which a phosphor shader has been applied.

The phosphor shader calculates diffuse shading as usual and adds a phosphorescence value to the result. The phosphorescence comes from our phosfn(), which picks up blacklight in two back-to-back illuminance() loops. Every blacklight (regardless of orientation) is picked up by the illuminance("blacklight",P){} loop, whereas the illuminance("blacklight", P,Nf,PI/2){} loop only picks up blacklights inside its illumination cone. In other words, the second loop allows for orienting a blacklight in order to selectively increase the phosphorescence effect on specific parts of a surface. The result from phosfn() is scaled by a user-supplied Kp value and added to the matte calculation.

Figure 11.32 shows a progression of increasing Kp values of 0, .25, .5, and .75. Beyond Kp of .5, the phosphorescence takes over and masks the underlying surface color.

```
light blacklight(
        uniform float angle=30, penumbra=5;
        output uniform string __category="blacklight";
        output uniform float __nondiffuse=1;
        output uniform float __nonspecular=1;
        output varying float __inShadow=0;
)
{
  point from = point "shader"(0,0,0);
  vector axis = normalize(vector "shader"(0,0,1));
  uniform float ang = radians(angle);
  uniform float penum = radians(penumbra);
```

```
    uniform float cosoutside = cos(ang);
    uniform float cosinside = cos(ang-penum);
    illuminate(from, axis, ang) {
      varying float atten, cosangle;
      cosangle = L.axis / length(L);
      atten = smoothstep( cosoutside, cosinside, cosangle );
      atten *= 1 / pow(length(L), 0);
      Cl = atten * color(1);
      Cl = mix(Cl, color(0), __inShadow);
    }
}


color phosfn(color phoscol, fillcol)
{
  extern point P;
  extern color Cl;
  color result = color 0;
  extern normal N;
  extern vector I;
  normal Nf = faceforward(normalize(N),I);

  /* collect light from blacklights*/
  illuminance ("blacklight", P)
    {
      result += 0.5*phoscol*Cl;
    }


  illuminance ("blacklight", P,Nf,PI/2)
    {
      float ndotl = Nf.normalize(L);
      result += 0.5*phoscol*ndotl*Cl;
    }

  result = result + fillcol;

  return result;
}

surface phosphor(float Ka=0.1, Kd=0.4, Kp=0.5;
      color phoscol=color(.8,1,.8);
      color fillcol=color(0,0,0);
      )
{
```

```
color matte = Cs*Oi*(Ka*ambient() + Kd*diffuse(faceforward(normalize(N),I)));
color phosphorescence = phosfn(phoscol,fillcol);
Ci =  matte + Kp*(phosphorescence);

}// phosphor()
```

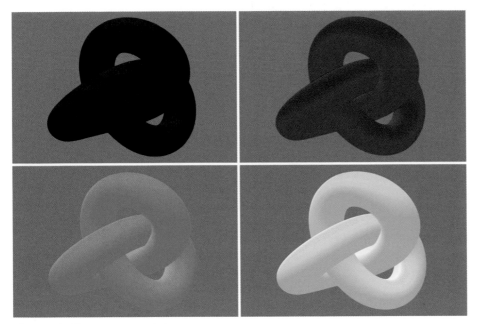

Figure 11.32 Use of a blacklight.

Scaling Lights

We conclude this chapter with a somewhat unusual illustration of the `illumi-nance()` function. Imagine that you have a scene that has been lit using several care-fully placed directional lights. You would like to increase or decrease the overall illumination level using a single control instead of doing it the tedious way, which would involve proportionately scaling each light source's intensity up or down.

The solution is to use a `scalinglight` shader, which is a directional light source that will be placed in the scene in order to trigger intensity-scaling in a corre-sponding `scaleddiffuse` shader that will look for a `scaledlight`.

The `scalinglight` shader is a modification of the standard `distantlight` shader, with an extra `slight` parameter that can be used to hide it from a regular diffuse calcu-lation and an extra `category` string variable, which is set to `scalinglight` to specify the light type. The `scaleddiffuse` surface shader has two illuminance loops. The first loop does a standard diffuse calculation, making sure to exclude `scalinglight` sources by querying the `slight` variable's value using the `lightsource()` call.

The second illuminance loop kicks in when the scene includes a scalinglight. In this loop, we scale (multiply) C, which was set in the previous illuminance() loop, using a constant uscale value, a direction-dependent (dscale*ndot1) one, and a global multiplier (Kls). It is the scaling of C that makes this loop unusual—most of the time the loop involves addition, not multiplication.

Figure 11.33 shows an example of using the scalinglight/scaleddiffuse pair of shaders. The scene contains two distantlights in addition to the scalinglight. At the top-left is the default case of no color scaling, obtained by setting Kls to 0. At the top-right, we brighten the scene by setting dscale and uscale to 0.375. At the bottom-left we darken the scene by setting dscale to -.75 and uscale to 0; notice that the darkening is directional, based on our scalinglight's orientation. Finally, at the bottom-right we set dscale to 0 and uscale to -.75 to uniformly darken the colors. The direction of the scalinglight is irrelevant for this last case. The key benefit is that in all the three scaling examples, the colors are maintained: There is no color shift because of scaling.

```
// Pixar's distantlight..
light scalinglight(
    float   intensity=1 ;
    color   lightcolor=1 ;
    point from = point "shader" (0,0,0) ;
    point to   = point "shader" (0,0,1) ;
    output float __slight=0;
    output uniform string __category="scalinglight";
)
{
    solar( to - from, 0.0)
      Cl = intensity * lightcolor;
}


color sdiffuse(float Kls; float dscale; float uscale;)
{
  extern point P;
  extern color Cl;
  color C = color 0;
  extern normal N;
  extern vector I;
  normal Nf = faceforward(normalize(N),I);

  // standard diffuse
  illuminance (P,Nf,PI/2)
    {
      float slight=0;
```

```
      lightsource("__sclight",sclight);
      if(0==sclight)
      {
        extern vector L;
        vector Ln = normalize(L);

        C += Cl*(Nf.Ln);
      }

   }


  // scale illum
  illuminance ("scalinglight", P)
    {
      extern vector L;
      vector Ln = normalize(L);
      float ndotl = Nf.Ln;
      C = C*(1+Kls*(dscale*ndotl + uscale));
    }

   return C;
}// sdiffuse()

surface scaleddiffuse(float Ka=0.1, Kd=0.4, dscale=1.0, uscale=0.0, Kls=1.0)
{
  Ci = Cs*Oi*(Ka*ambient() + Kd*sdiffuse(Kls,dscale,uscale));
}// scaleddiffuse()
```

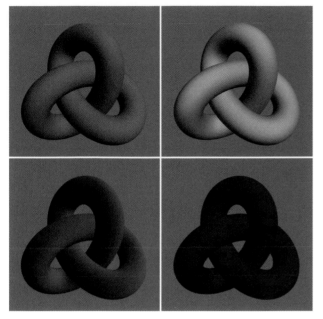

Figure 11.33 Scaling a pre-existing light distribution.

In this chapter, we have looked at a variety of ways to express illumination models using the illuminance() call. Having looked at these, you should have a good understanding of how to write custom illumination loops. In addition to the presented BRDFs such as Ashikhmin-Shirley, Schlick, and Anisotropic Ward, there are many more described in the CG literature. Implementing them using illuminance() would be a good way to improve your RSL programming skills. Here are some such BRDFs that you can look up:

- Poulin-Fournier
- Granier-Heidrich
- Lommel-Seeliger
- He-Torrance-Sillion-Greenberg
- Kelemen–Szirmay-Kalos

As mentioned at the beginning of the chapter, you could think about adapting elements from the preceding examples, as well as new ones you might implement, to come up with your own illumination models.

12

Procedural Patterns

In this chapter we examine how to use equations, formulae, and procedures to write pattern-generating shaders. The idea is to provide programmatic (that is, procedural) control over pattern parameters, thereby permitting limitless variations of the underlying designs (think of these as tunable patterns, or "patterns with knobs").

In the interest of keeping the discussion focused on pattern generation, most of the examples presented below do not include code for anti-aliasing, which would reduce "jaggy" artifacts stemming from the simpler code that we will encounter. We examine anti-aliasing in detail in Chapter 17. An exercise for you is to return to the examples in this chapter after reading the anti-aliasing material and outfit the example shaders with anti-aliasing code.

Why Procedural?

Imagine that you are creating a wood pattern shader to apply to a coffee table surface. Using the procedural approach, you would write a program to calculate the pattern (after carefully studying several photographs and real-world samples and coming up with an ad hoc formulation of wood pattern formation). You would have the full power of RSL at your disposal to do this—programming constructs, a rich library of built-in functions, user-defined add-ons, and so on. With RSL, your program would use equations, formulae, and calculation routines to synthesize the image you are after. In other words, with a procedural technique, you are essentially turning code into patterns.

Why not just use a texture map? In some cases, it is indeed possible to use one, for instance, if you are intent on creating a very specific pattern (for example, the oak wood pattern from your dining table) or if the pattern generation is a "one-off" that will not be reused. But the procedural approach is more flexible in general. You can write a shader that will create the pattern you want and countless more variations if you provide the appropriate "knobs" (parameters) to affect the pattern being generated. A procedural shader takes up a lot less storage space (mere kilobytes in most cases) compared to a high-resolution texture map. Also, with a procedural shader applied to a surface, you can zoom in arbitrarily close to it and still see crisp detail. If you try the same thing with a texture mapping shader, you are bound to experience fuzziness at some point because of the texture map's inability to generate unlimited detail from fixed resolution data.

Here is another way of saying this: Procedural shaders act as data amplifiers, calculating on-the-fly (instead of looking up) as much detail as needed. The calculations could be nontrivial and time consuming, but in the end you are guaranteed a good result. This justifies the effort spent in coding such shaders.

Yet another comparison between the procedural approach and a texture lookup approach is that the procedural shader is like a vector line, whereas a texture map shader is comparable to a bitmapped raster line. The vector line always generates crisp edges at any resolution because the line equation is evaluated to generate the pixels needed at that resolution. While it is possible to zoom into a raster line to a certain extent, excessive zooming eventually leads to loss of detail.

The procedural approach/mindset lets us specify our patterns with as much detail and care as we would use to specify our geometry, camera, and lights in a scene. We can create our patterns by using surface information at the current shading point (for instance, s,t texture coordinates, or normal N), other state information (the location of the camera, perhaps), or even space itself (for example, using point location P). The pattern generated could affect a variety of things—surface color, specularity, opacity, displacement, illumination, and so forth.

Design Philosophy

The most effective strategy to employ toward procedural pattern generation is to divide and conquer. When presented with a pattern to synthesize, the idea is to break the pattern into distinct layers, create each layer using an independent block of code, and then combine the layers to obtain the pattern sought.

Dividing up a pattern into different layers is usually done on the basis of frequency content or richness of detail, especially for naturally occurring patterns. Note that such layering is the signature technique of classic watercolor painting. A loose wash sets up broad areas and forms that are then refined using thin, transparent layers to build up progressive detail. After all the paint dries, final ("high frequency") details are added using a small-point dry brush to complete the painting.

Procedural patterns similarly progress from low- to high-frequency content that is added in successive layers (it doesn't make sense to do it the other way around). You can use temporary `color` type variables to generate these layers and use the `mix()` call (if you are mixing two layers) or `spline()` (for more than two) to combine the results. Alternately, you can simply accumulate partial results into a single color variable with something like this:

```
Cpatt += currentlayercol;
```

In addition to layering being useful for natural patterns such as rock, wood, and aging banana peel, it is equally effective in simulating imperfections in manufactured objects. After creating a base layer for a color/pattern, you can add a variety of markings such as blemishes, dents, spots, streaks, striations, and scratches in order to generate realistic-looking man-made objects. Without these imperfections, such objects tend to look clinically perfect, void of character, and ultimately fake ("too plasticky," in art director parlance).

With a good pattern in place, the last step in a (surface) shader is to add an illumination model. For instance, to simulate polished wood you need to add ambient, diffuse, and specular calculations that will be used to modulate the wood pattern.

Pattern Generation Toolbox

So far in this chapter we have looked at the motivation for using the procedural approach and an implementation methodology (layering). Here we will list a variety of items that you will find extremely useful in pattern generation. You can look these up in several other places (see the "Further Reading" section at the end of this chapter), so be sure to know these well—they form the basis of almost all procedural pattern synthesis. Note that many of these are RSL functions, others are macros, and yet others are just item names.

Thresholding and Interpolation

- `boxstep()`
- `step()`
- `clamp()`
- `pulse()`
- `mix()`
- `smoothstep()`
- `spline()`

Miscellaneous

- L-systems

- complex number fractals

- space-filling fractals

- chaos iterators

- ...

This is a (somewhat arbitrary) classification into 12 categories. In addition to these, there are several other operators, functions, curve equations, and such that are potentially useful in pattern synthesis. You can discover these in books on differential geometry, calculus, recreational math, group theory, signal processing, and so on. Every new generator or modifier you add to this "toolbox" collection can lead to a synergistic increase in your capability to generate procedural patterns.

Types of Patterns

Procedural patterns can be classified into the three broad categories discussed in the following sections. The first two are the stereotypical regular and irregular ones, and the third is a synthesis of the other two. In these sections, we will list examples of these classes of patterns to inspire you to study them and eventually create some of them yourself.

Regular Patterns

Nature hardly ever exhibits absolutely regular patterns, except maybe at the atomic/molecular levels. In other words, regular patterns are mostly man-made.

By definition, regular patterns tend to be repetitive or symmetric. Geometric examples include line groupings, groups of shapes such as rectangles and circles, tiling patterns, and so on. Regular patterns can be found in objects as diverse as a chessboard, a soccer ball, and graph paper. They can also be found in wallpaper and bathroom tiles used for ornamentation.

Logos of corporations often contain abstract design motifs that exhibit a regular pattern. Certain religious symbols also contain symmetrical motifs. Op art from the 1960s and certain classes of visual illusions employ highly regular patterns. Quilt patterns (and also rugs and baskets from indigenous cultures throughout the world) are composed of striking symmetric designs created from shapes and colors. More sources for inspiration include kirigami (the Japanese art of paper cutting), holiday decorations, and patterns on clothing, flags, and other insignia.

Stochastic Patterns

Stochastic patterns are characterized by absence of regularity and are variously referred to as "organic," "random," "disorderly," and "imperfect." Cloud shapes, flames, lava crust, marble, wrinkles on skin, markings on fruits/vegetables, mud distribution on an adobe wall, and coffee stains on a napkin are all examples of stochastic patterns.

Mixed Patterns

Sometimes a regular pattern can be perturbed (altered) in sometimes subtle and at other times quite obvious ways. Doing so gives rise to a third class of patterns that falls between the other two. For instance, a brick wall is hardly 100 percent regular due to imperfections in brick size, shape, and placement. Concentric rings can be warped a little to produce wood grain patterns, and simple water waves can be generated by distorting sine curves.

Mixed patterns are also generated via *bombing*, where stochastic formulations are used to derive locations for placement of detail over a surface (this is in contrast to starting with regular placement and then modifying locations). Bombing can also be used to decide whether to place the detail in the first place.

It is worthwhile to practice creating an assortment of shaders in these categories. In the following section, several sample procedural shaders are presented to get you started.

Examples of Procedural Shaders

This section contains examples of several procedurally derived patterns. Most examples are presented in the form of surface shaders, but there are two displacement shader examples: one light and one imager shader. You are advised to study each pattern without regard to the type of shader in which it occurs because the patterns are not shader-type specific and so can be mixed and matched with any of them.

Surface Shaders

You can synthesize a variety of patterns over surfaces. These patterns can be calculated using the (s,t) texture coordinates at the shading location, object/world/camera/shader space coordinates of the shading point itself, the relationship of the shading point to the camera, lights, and so on.

(s,t) Grid

Our first example is a very simple shader that simply colors the surface based on (s,t) at each point. The s and t values create the red and green values of our color, and blue is simply set to 0:

```
Ci = color(ss,tt,0);
```

ss and tt are obtained from (s,t) by rotating them about the center of the surface (assuming the surface contains texture coordinates ranging from 0 to1 in both s and t). In addition to rotating (s,t), we can also use the mod() function to create multiple rows and columns, thereby creating a grid of rotated squares. The mod() function is used in the repeat() call, which is defined in rmannotes.sl. Likewise, rotate2d() is also defined there.

```
#define rotate2d(x,y,rad,ox,oy,rx,ry) \
    rx = ((x) - (ox)) * cos(rad) - ((y) - (oy)) * sin(rad) + (ox); \
    ry = ((x) - (ox)) * sin(rad) + ((y) - (oy)) * cos(rad) + (oy)


#define repeat(x,freq)     (mod((x) * (freq), 1.0))
```

Figure 12.1 shows the results of using our shader. The leftmost image contains just a single (s,t) square with the rotation set to 0 and repetition set to 1. The middle image also shows no rotation, but the repeat value is now 5. The rightmost image shows both repetition and rotation.

```
// from Steve May's "rmannotes.sl":
/* rotate2d()
 *
 * 2D rotation of point (x,y) about origin (ox,oy) by an angle rad.
 * The resulting point is (rx, ry).
 *
 */
#define rotate2d(x,y,rad,ox,oy,rx,ry) \
    rx = ((x) - (ox)) * cos(rad) - ((y) - (oy)) * sin(rad) + (ox); \
    ry = ((x) - (ox)) * sin(rad) + ((y) - (oy)) * cos(rad) + (oy)


#define repeat(x,freq)     (mod((x) * (freq), 1.0))


surface showst(float freq=10, rot=45)
{
    float ss, tt, sss, ttt;

    rotate2d(s, t, radians(rot), 0.5, 0.5, ss, tt);
    ss = repeat(ss, freq);
    tt = repeat(tt, freq);
```

```
    Ci = color(ss,tt,0);
}
```

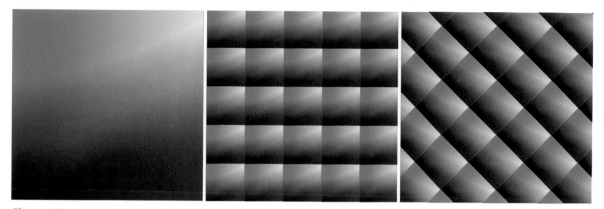

Figure 12.1 (s,t)-derived images over a square.

Visualizations of (s,t), N, P, and other global variables are often carried out for visual diagnostics. It is far better to see the values of such variables directly over a surface than to use the print() statement to have them printed out while the shader executes.

An Optical Illusion

We build on the idea of repetition and rotation to create an optical illusion pattern. In the optill shader below, we use rotate2d() and repeat() as before, but in addition we also use the pulse() macro to "constrict" our rotated squares into a thin grid. rmannotes.sl defines pulse() this way:

```
#define pulse(a,b,fuzz,x) (smoothstep((a)-(fuzz),(a),(x)) - \
    smoothstep((b)-(fuzz),(b),(x)))
```

The fourth parameter x is passed through only if it is between the two parameters a and b, transitioning to 0 outside that range. This creates a pulse of the x value. The falloff transition is handled by the third parameter, fuzz.

An unrotated grid of thin white lines on a black background appears to create an illusionary black grid diagonal to the original grid (see Figure 12.2, top left). This is not a strong illusion, however. As we rotate the white grid (Figure 12.2, top right and bottom left), the illusion is further weakened, but it reappears strongly when the white grid is rotated 45 degrees; now we see an imaginary black grid that is unrotated.

You can use shaders, such as optill, to create animated optical illusions. Note that you can also use JavaScript, ActionScript, and others to program such animations. RSL is still preferable because it lets you create a richer variety of patterns (which can also include lighting contributions) than the alternatives.

```
// the following four macros are from 'rmannotes.sl':
#define pulse(a,b,fuzz,x) (smoothstep((a)-(fuzz),(a),(x)) - \
    smoothstep((b)-(fuzz),(b),(x)))
#define repeat(x,freq)    (mod((x) * (freq), 1.0))
#define rotate2d(x,y,rad,ox,oy,rx,ry) \
  rx = ((x) - (ox)) * cos(rad) - ((y) - (oy)) * sin(rad) + (ox); \
  ry = ((x) - (ox)) * sin(rad) + ((y) - (oy)) * cos(rad) + (oy)
#define blend(a,b,x) ((a) * (1 - (x)) + (b) * (x))

surface optill(float freq=10, rot=45;color c1=color(1,1,1),c2=color(1,1,1))
{
  color surface_color, layer_color;
  color surface_opac, layer_opac;
  float fuzz = .025;
  float ss, tt, sss, ttt;

  surface_color = Cs;
  surface_opac = Os;

  /* repeat pattern in the following layers 'freq' times
      horizontally & vertically */
  rotate2d(s, t, radians(rot), 0.5, 0.5, ss, tt);
  ss = repeat(ss, freq);
  tt = repeat(tt, freq);

  float pw=.75*1.0/freq;

  layer_opac = pulse(0.5-pw, 0.5+pw, fuzz, ss);
  surface_color = blend(surface_color,c1, layer_opac);

  layer_opac = pulse(0.5-pw, 0.5+pw, fuzz, tt);
  surface_color = blend(surface_color,c2, layer_opac);

  /* output */
  Oi = surface_opac;
  Ci = surface_opac * surface_color;
 }
```

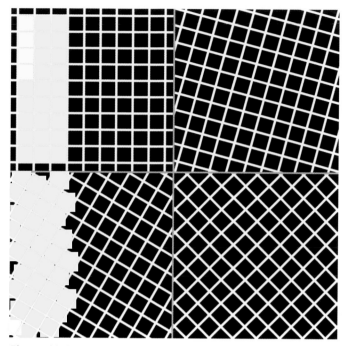

Figure 12.2 Optical illusion (appearance of a grid of black lines).

Anisotropic Hues

The `simpleaniso` shader is an example of using the normal vector N to create patterns. Since `normalize(N)` can range from -1 to 1 in each of the three components, we add 1 and multiply by 0.5 to obtain 0 to 1 values:

```
normal NNN = 0.5*(1+normalize(N));
```

Averaging the three components of NNN gives us a single 0 to 1 value that we can use to create a grayscale value or a hue. Here we use it as a hue value. To obtain colored fringes, the hue value can be repeated using a `huefreq` value:

```
h = mod(h*huefreq,1.0); // can also use 'repeat()' from rmannotes.sl
```

For extra interest, we can also use the h value to alter opacity:

```
Oi = .1+.9*h*Os; // 10% base opacity plus 90% variation
```

As the hue varies periodically across the surface, so does opacity, giving us bands of transparency that let us partially see through to the back of a surface (see Figure 12.3).

You can adapt the hue repetition idea to create rainbow patterns, oil slick or soap bubble interference patterns, and such. You can also use the point position P to create interesting fringe patterns.

```
surface simpleaniso(float Ka=.35,huemix=0.5,huefreq=1.0)
{
  // hue based on N
  normal NNN = 0.5*(1+normalize(N));
  float h = 0.333*(xcomp(NNN)+ycomp(NNN)+zcomp(NNN));
  h = mod(h*huefreq,1.0); // can also use 'repeat()' from rmannotes.sl
  color Cn = color "hsv" (h,1.0,1.0); // pure hue
  Oi = .1+.9*h*Os;
  // Oi = h*Os;
  Ci = Oi*Ka*mix(Cs,Cn,huemix);
}
```

Figure 12.3 Anisotropic color pattern.

Note Paper

Kendall Sor is the creator of the ruledpaper shader (see Figure 12.4 for a sample result). It is a good example of creating a commonly occurring pattern procedurally and also of using the layering methodology discussed in the "Design Philosophy" section at the beginning of this chapter. The paper is created first, followed by the horizontal ruled lines. The vertical margin comes last. The three holes are not colored circles, but rather they are transparent circles in order to let surfaces underneath the paper show through.

```
//-----------------------------------------------------------//
// Shader to emulate notepaper (ruled, with punched holes)
// Author: Kendall Sor
//-----------------------------------------------------------//

// checks if current s,t is where user wants to shade vertical pinkline
float checkVerticalLine (float sLocate,       // location along s to shade
lineThickness)                                // thickness of pink line
{
  float returnValue = 0;
  float thickness = lineThickness / 2;

  if ((s >= (sLocate - thickness)) && (s <= (sLocate + thickness)))
    returnValue = 1;

  return returnValue;
}


// checks if current s,t is where and within user-defined radius of
// where hole should be shaded
float checkHole(float  sLocate, // location along s for hole-origin
                       tLocate, // location along t for hole-origin
                       radius)  // radius of paper hole
{
  float sHole, tHole, sdist, tdist, dist;
  float newT = 1 - t;

  // top hole
  sHole = sLocate;
  tHole = tLocate;
  sdist = s - sHole;
  tdist = newT - tHole;
  dist = sqrt(sdist*sdist + tdist*tdist);
  float returnValue = 0;

  if (dist <= radius)
    returnValue = 1;
  return returnValue;
}

/* Layer approach:
   Paper color is shaded first.
   Horizontal blue lines are shaded on top of paper color.
```

```
      Vertical red line is shaded next and color-mixed with
      any colors in layers underneath. Holes are not shaded
      a certain color but instead their opacity is set to 0
      to mimic true paper holes.
*/
surface ruledpaper (float Ka=1,                 // user control ambient
                          Kd=1,                 // user control diffuse
                          Ks=1,                 // user control specular
                          roughness=.1,         // roughness for specular
                          highlite = 1,         // brightness of surface
                          gap = .1,             // horiz-line spacing gap
                          skipLines = 2,        // top of paper no lines
                          thickness = 1.0)      // thickness of lines
{
    color ambientcolor, diffusecolor, specularcolor;

    normal Nf = faceforward(normalize(N), I);
    vector V =  normalize(-I);

    float newT = 1 - t;
    color paperColor = color(1, 1, 1); // define paper color (white)

    // horizontal lines definitions
    float linesSpacing = mod (newT, gap);
    float lineThickness = gap / (10.0 / thickness); // thickness is % of gap
    float lineIndex = (newT/gap) - mod((newT/gap), 1);
    color lineColor = color (0, 169/256, 245/256); // define horiz line color

    // hole definitions
    float holeRadius = .02; // radius of paper hole
    float holeLocation = .075; // location along s of hole

    // lighting definitions
    ambientcolor = Ka*ambient();
    diffusecolor = Kd*diffuse(Nf);
    specularcolor = Ks*specular(Nf, V, roughness);

    // set apparent opacity
    Oi = Os;

    // shade white background
    Ci = Oi * paperColor * (ambientcolor + diffusecolor + specularcolor) *
        highlite;
```

```
// shade lines, skip n lines for the top header
if ((linesSpacing < lineThickness)  && (lineIndex > skipLines))
  Ci = Oi * lineColor * (ambientcolor + diffusecolor + specularcolor) *
      highlite;
// else

// shade vertical pink line, mix color with any layers underneath
if (checkVerticalLine (.13, lineThickness))
  Ci = mix (Ci, Oi * color (1, 0, 0) * (ambientcolor + diffusecolor +
      specularcolor) * highlite, .5);

// set mask for paper holes shading
Oi = 0.0;

// top hole
if (checkHole(holeLocation, .15, holeRadius))
  Ci = Oi * paperColor * (ambientcolor + diffusecolor + specularcolor) *
      highlite;

// middle hole
if (checkHole(holeLocation, .5, holeRadius))
  Ci = Oi * paperColor * (ambientcolor + diffusecolor + specularcolor) *
      highlite;

// bottom hole
if (checkHole(holeLocation, .85, holeRadius))
  Ci = Oi * paperColor * (ambientcolor + diffusecolor + specularcolor) *
      highlite;
}
```

Figure 12.4 Three-hole punched notepaper (shader by Kendall Sor).

Spirograph Curves

The spirofield shader is an example of drawing a curve given its equation. A Spirograph curve can be described in terms of the container wheel radius R, revolving wheel radius r, and offset b of the pen/pencil from the center of the moving wheel. Given these values and an angle a, the radial location can be computed:

```
rho = (sqrt((R-r)*(R-r)+ b*b + 2*(R-r)*b*cos((1+R/r)*a))));
```

After a certain number of revolutions, the curve closes in on itself, creating a nice, symmetric, closed-loop pattern. The LCM (Least Common Multiple) between R and r is what determines the number of revolutions. Note that even though our function is called LCM, it is actually returning LCM(R,r)/R, which is the number of revolutions the smaller wheel has to make.

The usual way to draw a Spirograph curve on the computer is to vary the angle a in small increments using a for() loop, calculate rho each time, and convert (rho,a) into an (x,y) value using the standard polar-to-Cartesian conversion formula. But in a shader, we cannot do this because we do not have access to the entire surface being shaded all at once. We can only color the current point over which our shader gets evaluated. We can still plot our curve by testing if our current shading point lies on or near the curve and use the test result to color the point accordingly. Since the Spirograph curve loops back on itself in general, it is a bit tricky to detect if our current point lies on/near a curve point. We obtain the polar angle for our current point (via a Cartesian-to-polar conversion), calculate all curve points that lie along that angle, find the distance to each from our current shading point, and sort the distances.

The sorted distance values help us color the surface (see Figure 12.5). In the two leftmost images, the maximum of the distances is used to obtain a color. At the top right, the closest distance is used, and at the bottom right, the average of all the distances is used. Each of these three variations yields a distinct, identifiable result.

```
float LCM(float R,rv)
{
  float i=0,cm=1.0;

  if (mod(R,rv)==0)
    {
      cm = 1;
    }
  else
    {
      i=1;
      while(mod(R*i,rv)!=0)
```

```
       {
       i=i+1;
       }
       cm = i;
     }
   return cm;
}


float calcspiro(float R, rv, b, a)
{
   float rho;
   rho = (sqrt((R-rv)*(R-rv)+ b*b + 2*(R-rv)*b*cos((1+R/rv)*a)));
   return rho;
}// calcspiro()


surface spirofield(float R=10,rv=5,b=2.5,hoff=0.0,freq=1.0, calctype=0,f=1.0)
{
   float i, theta, rho, nrev, a, rsp, ss, tt;

   ss=s-0.5;
   tt=t-0.5;
   theta = atan(tt,ss);
   theta += 3.1415;
   rho = 2*sqrt(ss*ss+tt*tt);
   if((rho>((R-rv+b)/R))||(rho<((R-rv-b)/R)))
     {
       Ci = 0.25;
     }
   else
     {
       float deltad;
       color Ch, Cg;

       nrev = LCM(R,rv);
       if(0==calctype)
         {
           float maxdist;
           maxdist = -2;
           for(i=0;i<nrev;i+=1)
             {
               a = theta + (i)*2*PI;
               rsp = calcspiro(R,rv,b,a)/R;
               deltad = abs(rsp-rho);
               if(deltad>maxdist) maxdist=deltad;
```

```
            }
          maxdist *= (nrev*freq);
          maxdist = mod((maxdist+hoff),1.0);
          Ch = color "hsv" (maxdist,1,1);
          Cg = color (maxdist,maxdist,maxdist);
        }
    else if(1==calctype)
      {
        float mindist;
        mindist = 2;
        for(i=0;i<nrev;i+=1)
          {
            a = theta + (i)*2*PI;
            rsp = calcspiro(R,rv,b,a)/R;
            deltad = abs(rsp-rho);
            if(deltad<mindist)
              mindist=deltad;
          }
        mindist *= (nrev*freq);
        mindist = mod((mindist+hoff),1.0);
        Ch = color "hsv" (mindist,1,1);
        Cg = color (mindist,mindist,mindist);
      }
    else
      {
        float avdist=0;
        for(i=0;i<nrev;i+=1)
          {
            a = theta + (i)*2*PI;
            rsp = calcspiro(R,rv,b,a)/R;
            avdist += abs(rsp-rho);
          }
        avdist *= freq;
        avdist = mod((avdist+hoff),1.0);
        Ch = color "hsv" (avdist,1,1);
        Cg = color (avdist,avdist,avdist);
      }
    Ci = mix(Cg,Ch,f);
  }
}// spirofield()
```

Hopefully, the math in the shader does not come across as intimidating. The idea we are trying to get across is that with a multiply self-intersecting curve, such as one from a Spirograph, we could generate interesting patterns by considering not just the closest curve point to an arbitrary point (our shading sample location), but also a set of them that lie along the radial line containing the point. Given a set of such curve points, we can use the closest of those to our shading location, the farthest, or the average of all of them to derive a color for our shading sample.

Figure 12.5 Spirograph patterns.

Colorful animations can be created by simply varying R, r, or b in small increments. Try creating one of these as an exercise. Also, try "plotting" several other curves such as sin(), an ellipse, and so forth using this idea of deriving shading color from distance(s) to curve point(s).

Mandelbrot Fractal

Fractal zooms create colorful, aesthetic imagery and are often coded as pixel routines. We can use (s,t) instead of pixel location (x,y) to compute fractal patterns over any surface.

The mandel shader contains the classic Mandelbrot fractal calculation. Starting with a location derived from the current shading point, we iteratively calculate new point locations. At the edges of the fractal, the successive new points tend to wander away from the starting location. After a certain number of iterations, a point is said to "escape" its neighborhood if it crosses a circle of preset radius centered at the starting location. We use the iteration count at the time of the escape to calculate a color for the starting point:

```
n=0; a=x; b=y;


while(n<maxiter)
   {
      aa = a*a;
      bb = b*b;
      twoab = 2*a*b;
      if((aa+bb)>escape)
      {
         break;
      }
      n=n+1;
      a = aa-bb+x;
      b = twoab+y;
   }
// convert n to a color value
h = 0.5*(1+sin(huefreq*n/maxiter));
Cmandel= color "hsv" (h,1,1);
```

Figure 12.6 shows representative images obtained from the shader. The first three images show three different "zoom" levels on a plane, while the fourth (bottom-right) image shows the fractal computed over a sphere. You can pan and zoom along the fractal's edges given a location (xc,yc) and zoom factor sz:

```
// convert s,t to (x,y)
xmin = xc-0.5*sz;
ymin = yc-0.5*sz;
x = xmin+sz*s;
y = ymin+sz*t;
```

(x,y) is now the starting point that gets iterated using the `while()` loop given above and in the shader below.

You can do a Web search for interesting coordinates (locations, zoom factors) on the Mandelbrot fractal that produce stunningly beautiful zooms. Like real terrain, such areas have been mapped out and even given names in some cases. Zooming into an interesting region produces nice animations. Be aware that after a certain magnification (small zoom factor `sz`), you start to reach the floating-point limit of your machine, at which point the zooms stop getting refined and instead start to become pixilated.

```
surface mandel(float xc=-.5, yc=0, sz=4, escape=256, maxiter=20,
               huefreq=1.0; float Ka=0, Kd=1, Ks=0,roughness=.1)
{
  float xmin,ymin,x,y,a,b,n,aa,bb,twoab,h;
  normal Nf;
  vector V;
  color Cmandel;

  // convert s,t to (x,y)
  xmin = xc-0.5*sz;
  ymin = yc-0.5*sz;
  x = xmin+sz*s;
  y = ymin+sz*t;


  n=0; a=x; b=y;

  while(n<maxiter)
    {
      aa = a*a;
      bb = b*b;
      twoab = 2*a*b;
      if((aa+bb)>escape)
      {
      break;
      }
      n=n+1;
      a = aa-bb+x;
      b = twoab+y;
    }

  // convert n to a color value
```

```
h = 0.5*(1+sin(huefreq*n/maxiter));
Cmandel= color "hsv" (h,1,1);

Nf = faceforward( normalize(N), I );
V = -normalize(I);
Oi = Os;
Ci = Os*Cs*Cmandel*(Ka*ambient() + Kd*diffuse(Nf)+ Ks*specular(Nf,V,
     roughness));
}// mandel()
```

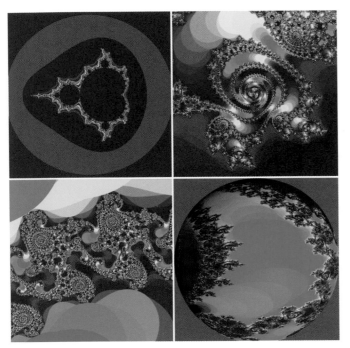

Figure 12.6 Mandelbrot fractals.

noise() Function

The noise() function is one of the most useful building blocks for procedural pattern generation because it can be used to mimic the look of a multitude of naturally occurring patterns, both inorganic and organic.

noise() simply associates a unique value (scalar, vector, or color) with every point in 1D, 2D, 3D, or 4D space (in 4D we usually take the fourth axis to be time). Figure 12.7 shows a 1D scalar noise pattern, where distance varies along the X axis and the corresponding noise() value is shown both as a grayscale value and as a curve. The noiseplot shader that was used to generate the figure is shown after it.

You can see that the noise plot, while being vaguely reminiscent of a sine curve, is "featureless"—there is no obvious pattern to the amplitude/frequency of the peaks and valleys. The function curve (also called *signal*) contains a "band limited" range of frequencies and amplitudes. The amplitude ranges from 0 to 1, with a mean of 0.5. The signal varies slowly, in the sense that there is no sudden change between two adjacent points. And yet the whole curve shows no identifiable pattern, which would be the case even when the signal is plotted for all 1D points ranging from negative to positive infinity. The curve is C1-continuous, which is to say that the slope varies smoothly all along the curve. If you plot the curve along a new axis obtained by translating or rotating the original axis, the function would still show identical characteristics; it is said to be invariant under translation and rotation.

The noise() function is repeatable, which means that the same input will always produce the same output. It is not appropriate to say that it produces a random value, which would imply that the output is different for different invocations on the same input.

While the default range for noise() is 0 to 1, it is often useful to shift/scale the range. For example, 1D signed noise is often defined this way to range from -1 to 1 with a mean of 0:

```
#define snoise(x)    (noise(x) * 2 - 1)
```

The noiseshader shader plots noise along a single dimension by considering just the X component of the current shading point P. A floating-point output is obtained by passing a 1D input to the noise() call:

```
float noiseval = noise(freq*xcomp(P));
```

We plot each noise() value as a vertical line of grayscale color, except at the height corresponding to noiseval; here we draw a white spot. The result is a band of gray values that denote noise, with an overlay of a white curve that shows the same noise variation as a function plot. The overlaid white signal plot is obtained using the pulse() macro. You can use this idea to plot any other function, such as sin() or log().

Note that the noise() function is polymorphic—the function's inputs and outputs are overloaded for multiple types. The following calls are listed in the RiSpec:

```
float noise (float v), noise (float u, v), noise (point pt) noise (point pt,
float t)
color noise (float v), noise (float u, v), noise (point pt), noise (point
pt, float t)
point noise (float v), noise (float u, v), noise (point pt), noise (point
pt, float t)
vector noise (float v), noise (float u, v), noise (point pt), noise (point
pt, float t)
```

As you can see, the input can be 1D (a float), 2D (a pair of floats), 3D (a point), or 4D (point, float). Likewise, the output of any of these can be assigned to a float, color, point, or vector variable, which would cause noise() to return a noise value of the appropriate type.

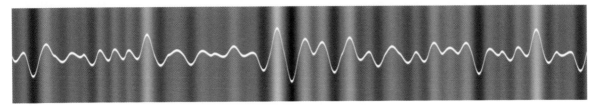

Figure 12.7 1D noise pattern.

```
// from rmannotes.sl
#define pulse(a,b,fuzz,x) (smoothstep((a)-(fuzz),(a),(x)) - \
  smoothstep((b)-(fuzz),(b),(x)))
float biasFunc(float t;float a;)
{
    return pow(t,-(log(a)/log(2)));
}

surface noiseplot(float freq=1.0)
{
  float delta=0.015;

  // consider just the x component of P.
  point PP = transform("shader",P);
  float noiseval = noise(freq*xcomp(PP));
  color noisecol = color(noiseval,noiseval,noiseval);

  float l = noiseval-2*delta*(noiseval);
  float u = noiseval+2*delta*(1-noiseval);
  float f = pulse(l,u,delta,t);
  color wh = color(1,1,1);
  f = biasFunc(f,.25);

  Ci = mix(noisecol,wh,f);
}// noiseplot()
```

The noise() function by itself is not very useful in pattern formation because it is featureless. We need to derive something from it that has more visual structure. This can be done via spectral synthesis by summing a set of noise values with specific frequencies and amplitudes. An analogy can be made as to how an orchestra produces a rich textured sound by layering instruments with different frequencies (pitch) and amplitudes (loudness). Specifically, the lower-frequency (bass) instruments provide the backdrop onto which higher-pitched instruments add their sound at reduced volumes (higher the pitch, lower the volume). Such a synthesis can be applied to noise() to produce what are termed "turbulence" patterns.

The turbsynth shader creates (scalar) turbulence values by summing together noise values inside a for() loop. The result is shown in Figure 12.8. From top left to bottom right, you can see a structure emerge. The top-left base image is a pure noise one, where the for() loop is run just once (no summations). At the top right, one extra layer of higher frequency noise is added to the base layer. You can see that the base layer's dark and bright areas are still preserved, but those flat areas now contain some structure (detail). The base layer's characteristics are still intact because the higher frequency layer is overlaid with a reduced amplitude. We do this two more times (bottom left, bottom right) to obtain even more detail at even finer scales. This cannot be carried out ad infinitum, of course, since the details eventually reach pixel scales with an attendant drop in amplitudes, making further modifications to the pattern unresolvable.

```
surface turbsynth (string sspace="shader";float nlevels=1, freq0=1, ampl0=1,
                   lacunarity=2, persistence=2,contrast=1)
{
    float t = 0,i, cumula=0;
    point PP = transform(sspace,P);

    // sum scaled frequencies
    for(i=0;i<nlevels;i+=1)
    {
        float f,a;
        f = pow(lacunarity,i);
        a = pow(persistence,-i);
        t += a*ampl0*noise(freq0*f*PP);
        cumula += a;
    }
    t/=cumula;
    t = pow(t,contrast);

    Oi = Os;
    Ci = Oi*Cs*color(t,t,t);
}
```

Note that our shader is subject to aliasing, since we are not limiting the high frequency content of noise(). In other words, if the base frequency freq0 or the per-loop frequency f is sufficiently high such that there is a lot of variation in noise() within a single micropolygon, we would not be able to capture all that finely varying detail without causing aliasing or "buzzing" artifacts when there is motion from frame to frame. We discuss two techniques to address such problems in Chapter 17, "Anti-aliasing."

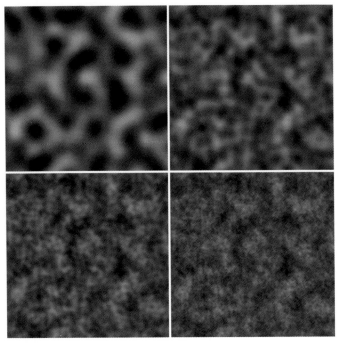

Figure 12.8 Synthesis of turbulence from noise.

We mentioned that in turbulence synthesis, noise() at increasingly higher frequencies and corresponding lower amplitudes is summed up. The amount of frequency change (usually an increase) between layers is called *lacunarity*. As with music, where a doubling of frequency occurs between successive octaves, a lacunarity of 2 is commonly used in turbulence summations. But using other values produces interesting results as well. Figure 12.9 shows turbulence patterns created with lacunarities of 1.5, 2.5, 3.5, and 4.5, from top left to bottom right. The image with the highest lacunarity is reminiscent of electron microscope images of biological specimens.

The amplitude change between successive levels is termed "persistence" to indicate how much of the original base layer persists with each successive addition of levels. Figure 12.10 shows comparisons between persistence values of 0.5, 1.0, 2.0, and 4.0. At the top right and top left, the base noise pattern is hardly recognizable because the higher frequency patterns are overlaid at large amplitudes, in effect, strongly mixing themselves with the original (see the turbsynth code listing). Conversely, the bottom-right image shows that at a persistence value of 4.0, detail that is hardly noticeable is all that is accrued over the base pattern.

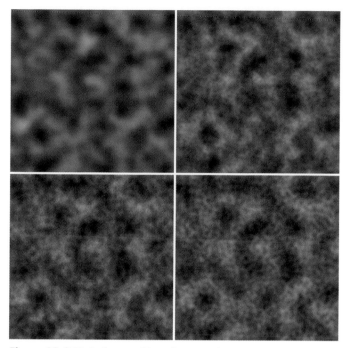

Figure 12.9 Turbulence: effect of varying lacunarity.

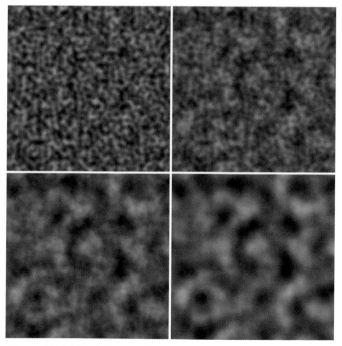

Figure 12.10 Turbulence: effect of varying persistence.

Next we illustrate a typical use of noise() to create a natural-looking formation. Figure 12.11 shows the development of a wood (or smooth rock) pattern. The rock shader creates the patterns. We start by creating a concentric set of rings on a blobby surface. The easiest way to create rings is to find the distance between each shading point and a fixed point in space and use the distance result in a mod() function:

```
C0 = transform("shader",c0);
newP = transform("shader",P);
PP = newP - C0;
dd = sqrt(abs(PP.PP));
alpha = mod(ringdensity*dd,1);
```

Another way to calculate distance between two points is to take their difference vector and dot it with itself.

Now we can use alpha to mix in a dark color with our Cs, creating bands of color (top left in Figure 12.11). We can control the spread of the mixed-in color in each band using a power function (middle image, top row):

```
alpha = pow(alpha,spread);
```

Since the alpha value results from a mod() remainder of 1.0, it will be in the range 0 to 1. So we can invert the color pattern (top-right image) by doing this:

```
alpha = 1-alpha;
```

Now we are ready to add noise to the pattern. First, we calculate turbulence using three layers of noise and add the result to the concentric ring distance value dd. This nicely distorts the rings (bottom-left image):

```
/* add some turbulence */
nn = swirl*noise(swirlfreq*newP);
nn += 0.5*swirl*noise(2.0*swirlfreq*newP);
nn += 0.25*swirl*noise(4.0*swirlfreq*newP);
dd += nn;
```

The ring pattern can be broken up even more by adding a few more noise layers (middle image, bottom row):

```
/* more turbulence */
nn = swirl*noise(swirlfreq*newP);
nn += 0.5*swirl*noise(2.0*swirlfreq*newP);
nn += 0.25*swirl*noise(4.0*swirlfreq*newP);
nn += 0.125*swirl*noise(8.0*swirlfreq*newP);
nn += 0.0625*swirl*noise(16.0*swirlfreq*newP);
nn += 0.03125*swirl*noise(32.0*swirlfreq*newP);
dd += nn;
```

At this point we pretty much have our pattern, but the light and dark regions are too regular (even though the boundaries are not). The last step is to add some noise to the alpha result:

```
alpha = 0.5*((1-alpha)+noise(alpha*dd));
```

This introduces some irregularity into the color mixing, thereby creating a more natural look.

```
surface rock(float Ka=1, Kd=.6, Ks=0.4, roughness=.2, ringdensity=2,
swirl=0.25, swirlfreq=1, spread=1; point c0=point "shader" (0,0,0); color
specularcolor = 1, darkcolor = 0.5;)
{
    point C0, PP, newP;
    normal Nf;
    vector V;
    float dd, alpha;
    color Cwood;

    Nf = faceforward( normalize(N), I );
    V = -normalize(I);

    C0 = transform("shader",c0);
    newP = transform("shader",P);
    PP = newP - C0;
    dd = sqrt(abs(PP.PP));

    alpha = mod(ringdensity*dd,1);
    Cwood = mix(darkcolor,Cs,alpha);

    Oi = Os;
    Ci = Oi * (Cwood* ( Ka*ambient() + Kd*diffuse(Nf) ) + Ks *
        specularcolor * specular(Nf,V,roughness));
}
```

In Figure 12.12 we apply four noise-based shaders to a blobby surface to illustrate a sampling of possible looks. These four shaders all ship with PRMan. The top row illustrates the cmarble and rmarble shaders (top left, top right). The bottom-left image is created using wood and the bottom-right with spatter. These four images hint at the diversity of patterns achievable by using noise().

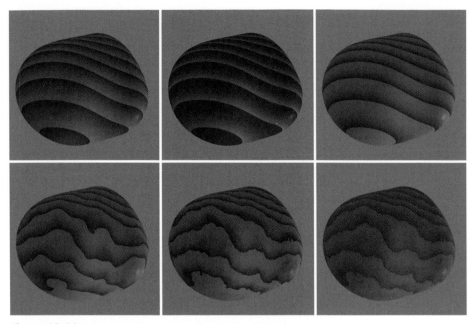

Figure 12.11 Progressive formation of a wood/rock pattern.

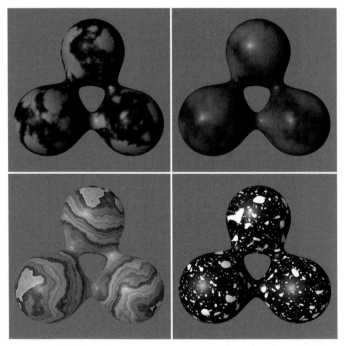

Figure 12.12 Marble (two kinds), wood, and spatter patterns over three blobs.

In Figure 12.11, you see that by layering noise, we are able to start with an initial regular pattern and evolve it into the look we are after. It is safe to assume that the noise() call forms the basis for thousands of shaders that use such an approach. Noise and turbulence values can be used on their own to create patterns, to mix colors (using the mix() function if there are just two colors or the spline() function to mix in more colors), or to randomize or "bump" directions/positions/colors/texture coordinates. In other words, they are used for adding variations to a surface, detail, visual realism, and so on. noise() is a truly versatile function—it is hard to imagine the world of procedural patterns without it!

RSL also has a periodic version of the noise() function called pnoise(). The value of pnoise() is periodic: Noise values in a limited range of inputs are tiled in order to produce values for inputs outside the range. It is as if the 1D/2D/3D/4D inputs are processed using a mod() function before being input to noise(). pnoise() behaves similarly to noise() and has the same output types. As for inputs, there is one extra argument (two for 4D cases), an integer-valued "periodicity" that specifies the range to be repeated (the "period"). The larger the period, the longer the range and hence the less the repetition. Here are some of the function signatures for pnoise():

```
float pnoise (float v, uniform float period)
color pnoise (float v, uniform float period)
pnoise (point pt, float t, uniform point pperiod, uniform float tperiod)
```

For our purposes, we used the noise() call with its default output range of 0 to 1 to create turbulence patterns. In other CG literature, you will encounter the more common form that uses the signed noise function for turbulence, where the noise ranges from -1 to 1 and has a 0 mean. Likewise, the absolute value of signed noise (where the values are all positive in 0 to 1, with abs()-derived "folds" occurring at places where signed noise is negative) can also be used to generate turbulence. This form of turbulence has a distinct look and is termed *fractal Brownian motion* or *fBm*. As an exercise, try to use signed noise and its absolute value to re-create variations of the wood/rock texture in Figure 12.11. Also, visualize these noise forms and their turbulence values in 1D by modifying the noiseplot shader presented at the beginning of this section. You can also use that shader to sketch the pnoise() call to see the periodicity inherent in that function.

cellnoise() Function

The cellnoise() function considers 1D/2D/3D/4D space to be made up of cells, and it outputs noise values that discontinuously vary from cell to cell while being constant throughout a cell (in 2D space a cell is a square; in 3D it is a cube). The cellnoise() call's inputs and outputs are identical to those of noise().

Figure 12.13 and the cn shader illustrate 2D cell noise. You can see that in each of the 6×6 grids of squares, the color output from cellnoise() is fixed, while color varies in an uncorrelated manner across cells.

```
surface cn(float freq=1.0)
{
  Ci = cellnoise(freq*P);
}// cn()
```

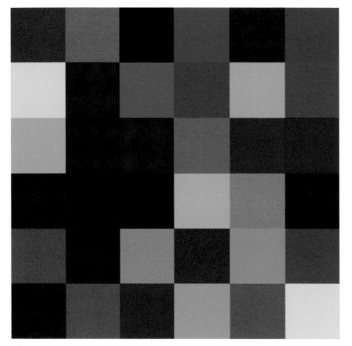

Figure 12.13 cellnoise() colors over a square.

What can we do with cellnoise()? An important use of this call is to create cellular patterns. Such patterns can be seen on froth, leather, giraffes, in polycrystalline materials, and so on and occur due to space partitioning when a group of "seed points" in 2D or 3D establish polygonal "territories." Each seed point is surrounded by a region inside which any point is closer to that seed point than to other seed points.

The cellnoise() function can be used to create such polygonal cells (termed *Voronoi regions*), as shown in Figure 12.14 for the 2D case. The Vor2D shader listed before the figure shows how the process works. The idea is to turn each cell color (output of cellnoise()) into a direction vector and displace the cell's midpoint along this direction. Doing so creates an uneven cluster of seed points, which will result in a typical Voronoi diagram. At each shading point, we calculate the distance between the shading point and nine seed points by considering our shading point's cell to be at the center of a 3×3 cell neighborhood. These nine values are sorted to obtain the shortest distance, which corresponds to the seed point closest to the shading location. The shading point is colored using the cellnoise() value of the cell containing the closest seed point. In the Vor2D shader, the vor_f1_2d() call does this closest distance calculation. The call returns four results via its argument list's "output" variables: distance to closest seed point, distance to shading point's cell center, location of closest seed point, and cellnoise() color result at the cell containing the closest seed point.

We can use a 0 to 1 value to displace cell centers fractionally along cellnoise() directions. For small fractions, the resulting seed points are almost undisplaced from their regular grid center locations, leading to an almost-regular Voronoi pattern. As the fraction approaches 1.0, the seed points are displaced farther away from cell centers, creating a more typical Voronoi diagram with convex polygonal edges. In Figure 12.14, you can see this progression from top left to bottom right (this would make for a good animation).

We used vor_f1_2d() to illustrate cell formation. A corresponding vor_f1_3d() function would carry out the computations in 3D space, using a 3×3×3 "Rubik's Cube" neighborhood of 27 cells for locating the nearest-neighbor seed point.

```
void vor_f1_2d (point P;
                float strength;
                output float f1;
                output float f2;
                output point pos1;
                output color col1;)
{
  point thiscell = point(floor(xcomp(P))+0.5, floor(ycomp(P))+0.5,0.0);
  f1 = 100000;
  uniform float i, j;
  for (i = -1;  i <= 1;  i += 1)
    {
      for (j = -1;  j <= 1;  j += 1)
        {
          point testcell = thiscell + vector(i,j,0);
          vector jitt = strength*((vector cellnoise(testcell))-0.5);
          point pos = testcell + vector(xcomp(jitt),ycomp(jitt),0);
          float dist = distance(pos,P);
          if (dist < f1)
            {
              f1 = dist;
              pos1 = pos;
              col1 = cellnoise(testcell);
            }
```

```
      }
    }

  // normalized distance of P to its closest point
  f1 /= 1.2;

  // distance of P from its own cell
  f2 = sqrt(2)*distance(P,thiscell);
}// vor_f1_2d()


surface Vor2D(float freq=1,strength=1.0)
{
  float d, f;
  point P1;
  color C1;

  point PP = transform("object",P);
  vor_f1_2d(freq*PP,strength,d,f,P1,C1);

  // white spot at the center of each cell
  float cen = smoothstep(.04,.05,d);
  Ci = mix(color(1,1,1),C1,cen);
}// Vor2D()
```

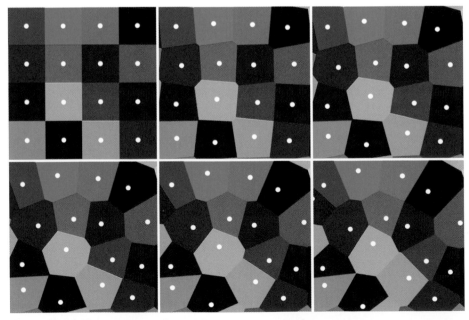

Figure 12.14 Voronoi regions derived from cellnoise() values.

The closest seed point distances are what create our convex cell patterns, and we can verify this by directly imaging those values. Small distances correspond to locations of seed points, while larger ones map out cell boundaries. Using contrasting colors for seed locations and boundaries (such as black and white) and using our distance values to mix() them should create cellular patterns. Further, we can non-linearly bias the distances using an S-curve gainFunc() call, which accepts a 0 to 1 gain parameter to do the nonlinear remapping. The relevant code chunks are as follows, and Figure 12.15 illustrates the results.

```
point PP = transform("shader",P);
vor_f1_3d(freq*PP,strength,d,f,P1,C1);


d = gainFunc(d,spread);
Ci = mix(colA,colB,d);


float biasFunc(float t;float a;)
{
    return pow(t,-(log(a)/log(2)));
}


float gainFunc(float t; float a;)
{
  float g;
  if (t <=0.5)
  {
    g = 0.5*biasFunc(2*t, a);
  }
  else
  {
    g = 1.0 - 0.5*biasFunc(2.0-2*t,a);
  }
  return g;
}
```

In Figure 12.15, the closest distance to each shading point is altered using gain values of .001, .25, .5, and .75, from top left to bottom right. The default gain value is 0.5, which leaves the distances unaltered. At smaller gain values, the central dark core is extended pretty much all the way to the boundaries. For gain values greater than 0.5, the opposite happens, and the dark core is confined to the seed point locations. Using such a gain value to alter distances gives us one more control for affecting the look of the cellular texture.

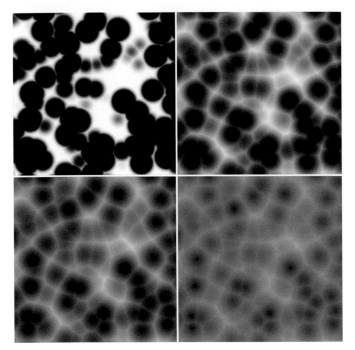

Figure 12.15 Visualization of distances to nearest Voronoi centers.

Nonlinear scaling of the Voronoi cells (extreme stretching, for example) can be used to create a fake ripple effect, as shown in Figure 12.16. The RIB block below shows the shader invocation. On the left of the figure, a small gain (spread) value of .05 is used to keep the ripples sharp, creating a satin look. On the right, a spread of .65 diffuses the ripples more, creating a wave-like appearance. The pattern can also be animated by translating/rotating the shader space that affects the cellnoise() result.

```
TransformBegin
Scale 25 2 40
# fake water ripples
Surface "Vor" "freq" 20 "strength" 1.0 "colA" [.1 .1 .4] "colB" [.64 .64
.95] "spread" .65
TransformEnd
```

Figure 12.16 Sharp and dissipated versions of "fake" ripples.

We observed that the vor_f1_2d() call outputs four results: two distances, a point, and a color (vor_f1_3d() outputs the same results). We can use the first three outputs to create some abstract patterns, as shown in Figure 12.17. Note that we use vor_f1_3d(), which makes it possible to create these patterns over surfaces in 3D. The figure shows the default "color cells" case on the top left for comparison with the three patterns shown in other panels. These patterns at the top right, bottom left, and bottom right correspond to pattern types 0, 1, and 2, respectively. The patterns are obtained as follows:

```
point PP = transform("shader",P);
vor_f1_3d(freq*PP,strength,d,f,P1,C1);
d = gainFunc(d,spread);
if(0==patttype)
   {
     point pd1 = point(d,d,d)-point(f,f,f);
     color Cnpd1 = color noise(mixfreq*pd1);
     Cnpd1 *= Cnpd1;
     Ci = mix(C1, Cnpd1, mixfrac);
   }
else if(1==patttype)
   {
     point pd2 = point(d,d,d)-P1;
     color Cnpd2 = color noise(mixfreq*pd2);
     Cnpd2 *= Cnpd2;
```

```
      Ci = mix(C1, Cnpd2, mixfrac);
   }
 else
   {
      point pd3 = point(f,f,f)-P1;
      color Cnpd3 = color noise(mixfreq*pd3);
      Cnpd3 *= Cnpd3;
      Ci = mix(C1, Cnpd3 ,mixfrac);
   }
```

The idea is to use differences between point(f,f,f), point(d,d,d), and P1 as inputs
to the standard color-valued noise() function to obtain color variations inside each
Voronoi cell. Concentric patterns in the cells result from using larger mixfreq values (we use 4 for the images shown). Also, the default color value C1 is mixed in
with the noise results in order to reintroduce the polygonal boundaries of the
Voronoi cells.

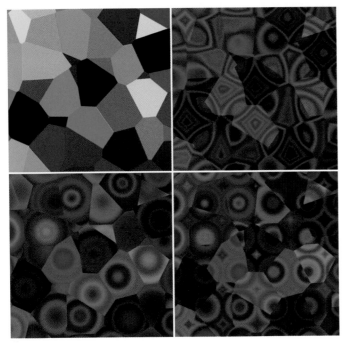

Figure 12.17 Ornamental patterns based on cellnoise().

Our last cellnoise() example uses alternate computations of distance. The standard Euclidean distance definition is one of several possible variations, though it
is by far more widely used than the alternatives. The Vor2Daltdist shader presents
four such alternatives, and you can see their effects in Figure 12.18.

The top-left image in Figure 12.18 shows the standard Euclidean case for comparison with the others. At the middle of the top row, we see that the "Manhattan distance" metric (also called "taxicab distance") leads to cell boundaries that are horizontal, vertical, and diagonal. The Manhattan metric replaces the "as the crow flies" shortest distance with an "along city blocks" distance, traveled on horizontal and vertical streets in a city grid. The top-right image in Figure 12.18 illustrates use of the "Canberra" distance calculation, while the bottom-left render shows the use of "max distance." (Definitions of these alternative distances can be found in image-processing/computer vision literature.)

The bottom-middle and bottom-right images illustrate Minkowski distance for parameter values of 0.5 and 1.5, respectively. The bottom-right case is especially interesting visually because it yields distorted boundaries of the Voronoi cells. The parameter value is an exponentiation factor in the Minkowski distance calculation, where a value of 2 reduces to the familiar Euclidean case.

```
float distance_manhattan(point A,B)
{
   float d;

   d = abs(xcomp(A)-xcomp(B)) + abs(ycomp(A)-ycomp(B)) + abs(zcomp(A)-
       zcomp(B));

   return d;
}// distance_manhattan()

float distance_canberra(point A,B)
{
   float d;

   d = abs(xcomp(A)-xcomp(B))/(abs(xcomp(A))+abs(xcomp(B))) + \
       abs(ycomp(A)-ycomp(B))/(abs(ycomp(A))+abs(ycomp(B))) + \
       abs(zcomp(A)-zcomp(B))/(abs(zcomp(A))+abs(zcomp(B)));

   return d;
}// distance_canberra()

float distance_max(point A,B)
{
   float d;

   d = max(max(abs(xcomp(A)-xcomp(B)),abs(ycomp(A)-ycomp(B))), abs(zcomp(A)-
       zcomp(B)));
```

```
  return d;
}// distance_max()

float distance_minkowski(point A,B;float k)
{
  float d;

  d = pow(abs(xcomp(A)-xcomp(B)),k) + pow(abs(ycomp(A)-ycomp(B)),k) +
      pow(abs(zcomp(A)-zcomp(B)),k);
  d = pow(d,1/k);

  return d;
}// distance_minkowski()

vvoid vor_f1_2d_alt_dist(
                    float disttype;
                    float mink_k;
                    point P;
                    float strength;
                    output float f1;
                    output float f2;
                    output point pos1;
                    output color col1;
     )
{
  point thiscell = point(floor(xcomp(P))+0.5, floor(ycomp(P))+0.5,0.0);
  f1 = 100000;
  uniform float i, j;
  for (i = -1;  i <= 1;  i += 1)
    {
      for (j = -1;  j <= 1;  j += 1)
        {
          point testcell = thiscell + vector(i,j,0);
          vector jitt = strength*((vector cellnoise(testcell))-0.5);
          point pos = testcell + vector(xcomp(jitt),ycomp(jitt),0);
          float dist=0;
          if(0==disttype)
          {
            dist = distance(pos,P); // standard case
          }
          else if(1==disttype)
          {
            // Manhattan metric :)
            dist = distance_manhattan(pos,P);
```

```
        }
        else if(2==disttype)
        {
          // Canberra
          dist = distance_canberra(pos,P);
        }
        else if(3==disttype)
        {
          // max
          dist = distance_max(pos,P);
        }
        else if(4==disttype)
        {
          // Minkowski
          dist = distance_minkowski(pos,P,mink_k);
        }

        // printf("P: %f %f %f\n",xcomp(P),ycomp(P),zcomp(P));

        if (dist<f1)
        {
          f1 = dist;
          pos1 = pos;
          col1 = cellnoise(testcell);
        }
      }
  }

// normalized distance of P to its closest point
f1 /= 1.2;

// distance of P from its own cell
if(0==disttype)
{
  f2 = sqrt(2)*distance(P,thiscell);
}
else if(1==disttype)
{
  f2 = sqrt(2)*distance_manhattan(P,thiscell);
}
else if(2==disttype)
{
  f2 = sqrt(2)*distance_canberra(P,thiscell);
}
```

```
  else if(3==disttype)
  {
    f2 = sqrt(2)*distance_max(P,thiscell);
  }
  else if(4==disttype)
  {
    f2 = sqrt(2)*distance_minkowski(P,thiscell,mink_k);
  }

}// vor_f1_2d_alt_dist()

surface Vor2Daltdist(float disttype=0,mink_k=2,freq=1,strength=1.0)
{
  float d, f;
  point P1;
  color C1;

  point PP = transform("object",P);
  vor_f1_2d_alt_dist(disttype,mink_k,freq*PP,strength,d,f,P1,C1);

  float cen = smoothstep(.04,.05,d);
  Ci = mix(color(1,1,1),C1,cen);
}// Vor2Daltdist()
```

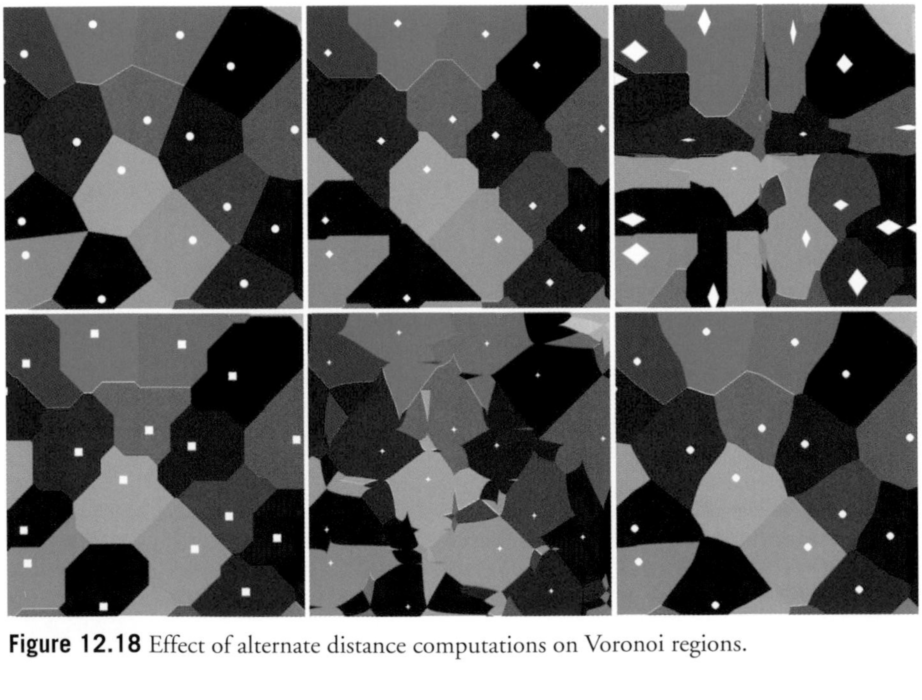

Figure 12.18 Effect of alternate distance computations on Voronoi regions.

For most CG production work, the discussion presented earlier that related to the standard Voronoi diagram should be quite adequate. If you found the math in the "alternate distances" section to be over your head, you can safely treat it as non-essential diversion. On the other hand, if you find the non-Euclidean distance formula intriguing, you can look up and experiment with even more alternatives, such as Chebychev, Mahalanobis, and Bray-Curtis. Also, in our discussion of cellnoise(), we used the closest seed point distances in our calculations. You can also experiment with second closest distances, magnitude difference between first and closest distances, and so on, which offer more possibilities for pattern generation.

The next shader (Mlcubes, originally by Matt Lewis of Ohio State) shows how the cellnoise() call can be used to generate a pretty pattern over a surface. The current shading point's location is perturbed by noise, and the result is used to derive a cell ID and color. The point is assigned the cell color only if its mod() fractional remainder (output of repeat()) lies within a user-specified distance r×r (small values of the r parameter will therefore cause less of the surface to inherit a colornoise() value). Also, it is the initial perturbation of the shading point before the cellnoise() and distance calculations are made that creates the amoeba-like shapes (see Figure 12.19). If you comment out the

```
PP += vector snoise(PP*10) * 0.1;
```

line or, even better, make 0.1 into an amplitude attribute and set it to 0, you can see that the pattern is comprised of regular circles evenly distributed over the sphere surface.

```
/* Slightly modified version of Matt Lewis' 'cubes.sl' */

// from rmannotes.sl:
#define repeat(x,freq)    (mod((x) * (freq), 1.0))
#define whichtile(x,freq) (floor((x) * (freq)))

surface MLcubes(float Ka = 0.2, Kd = 0.4, Ks = 0.6, roughness = 0.1,
                r = 0.5, freq = 6)
{
  color surface_color=1, layer_color, layer_opac;
  normal Nf = faceforward(normalize(N), I);
  vector V = -normalize(I);

  point PP = transform("shader", P); /* transform P to shader space */
  PP += vector snoise(PP*10) * 0.1;

  float x = xcomp(PP), y = ycomp(PP), z = zcomp(PP);
```

```
float xx = repeat(x,freq);
float yy = repeat(y,freq);
float zz = repeat(z,freq);

float col = whichtile(x,freq);
float row = whichtile(y,freq);
float pla = whichtile(z,freq);
color c = color cellnoise(point(col,row,pla));

float d = (xx-0.5)*(xx-0.5)+(yy-0.5)*(yy-0.5)+(zz-0.5)*(zz-0.5) - r*r;

if(d>0) { surface_color = Cs; }
else { surface_color = c; }

surface_color = surface_color * (Ka * ambient() + Kd * diffuse(Nf)) +
Ks * specular(Nf, V, roughness);

/* output */
Oi = Os;
Ci = Os * surface_color;
}
```

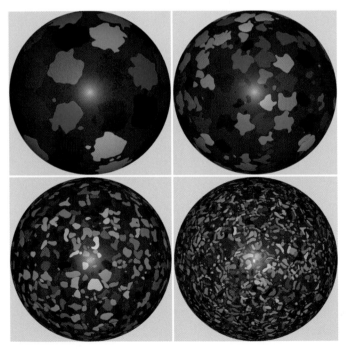

Figure 12.19 cellnoise()-based amoeba-like shapes.

Displacement Shaders

There is no reason why pattern synthesis should be used only inside surface shaders. Several real-world displacements can be computed procedurally, such as the rough mud texture on an adobe wall, fine capillary waves on a big ocean wave surface, cloth weave, threads on a screw, bumps on a rubber bath mat, or chip-carving patterns on wood. Procedural displacements can be combined with displacement and bump maps for even more pattern-generation possibilities.

Wireframe Cage

The following shader displaces a surface along its wireframe edges, creating a "webbed" look (see Figure 12.20). The (s,t) texture coordinates are used to derive "wireframe" edges, where the smult and tmult user-derived values are used to affect the spacing of the wires (displacements, in our case). Note that we use smooth-step() to transition between wireframe and no wireframe. This is done to prevent aliasing at the transition.

```
/* original by 'thaw'
 * equally spaced wires
 */
#define HALF 0.5
displacement wiredisp( float hwidth=0.0075,smult = 1.0,tmult = 1.0,disp-
scale=1.0)
  {
    float rim;
    float s_mid,t_mid,mid;
    float disp;

    rim = 2*hwidth;
    s_mid = length(dPdu)*(HALF - abs(mod(s*smult,1.0) - HALF))/smult;
    t_mid = length(dPdv)*(HALF - abs(mod(t*tmult,1.0) - HALF))/tmult;
    mid = (s_mid > t_mid) ? t_mid : s_mid;

    disp = 0.0;
    if (mid < hwidth)
      disp = 1.0;
    else if ( mid < (hwidth+rim))
      disp = (1.0-smoothstep(0,1.0,(mid-hwidth)/rim));

    P += faceforward(normalize(N),I)*disp*dispscale;
    N = calculatenormal(P);
  }// wiredisp()
```

Figure 12.20 Wireframe-like displacement pattern on the Utah teapot.

Ridged Multifractal

The next example presents the classic multifractal pattern discovered by Ken Musgrave. In a multifractal, sharp ridges are introduced inside an existing turbulence pattern (see Figure 12.21). The sharpness attribute controls the definition of those ridges. A ridged multifractal is especially good for generating mountainous-looking displacements.

```
/* Copyright notice from the original source: */
/*********************************
 * AUTHOR: Ken Musgrave.
 *    Conversion to Shading Language and minor modifications
 *    by Fredrik Brännbacka.
 *
 *
 * REFERENCES:
 *    _Texturing and Modeling: A Procedural Approach_, by David S. Ebert,
 *    ed.,
 *    F. Kenton Musgrave, Darwyn Peachey, Ken Perlin, and Steven Worley.
 *    Academic Press, 1998.  ISBN 0-12-228730-4.
 *
 *********************************/
#define snoise(x) (2.5*(noise(x)-0.5))
```

```
displacement RMFractalDisp(float freq=1., H = 0.8, lacunarity = 2.5,
                           octaves = 7, offset = 0.9,
                           sharpness = 4, threshold = 12, mfscale=0.5)
{
  float result, signal, weight, i, exponent;
  point PP =transform("shader",P*freq);
  normal Nn = normalize(N);
  for( i=0; i<octaves; i += 1 )
    {
      /* First octaves */
      if ( i == 0)
        {
        signal = snoise( PP );
        if ( signal < 0.0 ) signal = -signal;
        signal = offset - signal;
        signal = pow( signal, sharpness );
        /*This should give you a power function to control
          sharpness of the ridges. Or you can just use the
          original one -- signal *= signal;*/
        result = signal;
        weight = 1.0;
        }
      else
        {
        exponent = pow( lacunarity, (-i*H) );
        /*
          PP.x *= lacunarity;
          PP.y *= lacunarity;
          PP.z *= lacunarity;
        */
        PP = PP * lacunarity;
        /* weigh successive contributions by previous signal */
        weight = signal * threshold;
        weight = clamp(weight,0,1)    ;
        signal = snoise( PP );

        /* get absolute value of signal*/
        signal = abs(signal);

        /* invert and translate*/
        signal = offset - signal;
```

```
    /* sharpen the ridge*/
    signal = pow( signal, sharpness ); /* Or signal *= signal;*/

    /* weight the contribution*/
    signal *= weight;
    result += signal * exponent;
    }
  }
  result *= mfscale;

  P += normalize(N)*result;
  N = calculatenormal(P);
}// RMFractalDisp
```

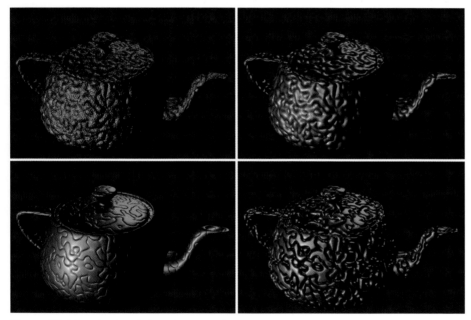

Figure 12.21 Ridged multifractal (RMF) displacements.

Light Shaders

Procedural patterns can also be used to create light shaders that are no less than light sources. This means that you can create custom shaders that emit light using any color/spatial pattern you create. Some possibilities include stripes, concentric rings, and noise-derived splotches.

Rainbow

A rainbow light shader does exactly what it sounds like: It emits light in the form of color fringes (see Figure 12.22). The main control is huefreq, which controls the spacing/width of the fringes.

A user-supplied `huedir` vector is used in conjunction with the light direction L (normalized versions are used for both) to derive a hue value. To obtain a 0 to 1 value given two normalized vectors, this is commonly done:

```
float lh = 0.5*(1+Ln.Hn);
```

Instead, we use a less-known approach:

```
vector lhcross = Ln^Hn;
float lh2 = (xcomp(lhcross)+ycomp(lhcross)+zcomp(lhcross)+3)/6.0;
```

Instead of the dot product, we take the cross product and then normalize the sum of the components to get an alternate 0 to 1 value compared to using the dot product to do the same.

The value of the light intensity is obtained by manually interpolating (as the `step()` function does) the length of the light ray between two user-supplied values d1 and d2 (as an exercise, try replacing the v calculation code with a call to `step()`).

The hue and value amounts are combined with a user-derived saturation value to generate the outgoing light ray's color:

```
Cl = intensity*color "hsv" (lh2,sat,v);
//////////////////////////////////////////////////////////////
light rainbowlight(
float intensity=1; vector huedir=0; float huefreq=1,
d1=0, d2=1, v1=1, v2=0, hfalloff=1.0, sat=1, vfalloff=1;
point from = point "shader" (0,0,0);
)
{
    illuminate( from )
      {
        vector Ln = normalize(L);
        vector Hn = normalize(huedir);
        float lh = 0.5*(1+Ln.Hn); // mention this

        vector lhcross = Ln^Hn;
        float lh2 = (xcomp(lhcross)+ycomp(lhcross)+zcomp(lhcross)+3)/6.0;

        lh2 = pow(lh2,hfalloff);
        lh2 = mod(huefreq*lh2,1.0);

        float v=1;
        float d = length(L);
        if (d<d1) v=v1;
        else if (d>d2) v=v2;
```

```
        else
        {
          d = pow((d-d1)/(d2-d1),vfalloff);
          v = v1 + (v2-v1)*d;
        }

        // 'rainbow' of colors
        Cl = intensity*color "hsv" (lh2,sat,v);
      }
}// rainbowlight()
```

Figure 12.22 Rainbow pattern created by a lightsource shader.

By using the hue value from the lh2 variable as a triplet in RGB space, mono-chrome (grayscale) fringes can be obtained:

```
Cl = intensity*color (lh2,lh2,lh2);
```

A pair of such lights is used to generate the rope-like abstract light pattern shown in Figure 12.23. Such an image can also be used as a texture or a displacement map elsewhere.

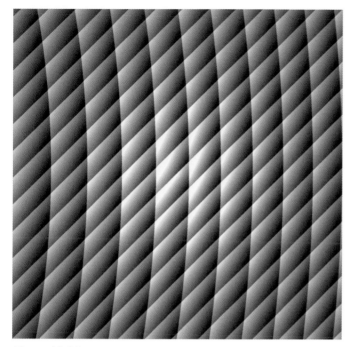

Figure 12.23 An abstract pattern created using a pair of rainbow light shaders.

Imager Shaders

As you might recall, imager shaders are used to "fill in the gaps" in an image where geometry does not occur. They can also be used to implement image-processing operations on all the pixels. This presents rich possibilities for pattern generation. For example, you can simulate a variety of art papers or create borders for your rendered images.

Sunburst

Here we show an example of an old-fashioned "sunburst" pattern, with rays of alternating color (see Figure 12.24).

Each pixel location is converted to an equivalent angular value and then to 0 to 1. After multiplying by n (the number of starburst rays), the result is passed through a mod() function to obtain the fractional part, which varies from 0 to 1.

If this repeating fractional part is clamped using a standard square wave, we get an alternating 0,1,0,1 pattern, which we can use with a mix() function to alternate between two colors. But doing so will cause "jaggies" at the edges between the rays because of the sharp transition from one color to another. So instead we use a fuzzysqwave() function, which slightly slopes the vertical steps at the beginning, middle, and end of a square wave. In these transition regions, the fuzzysqwave()

call produces a fraction between 0 and 1, which visually translates to a blend of the adjacent colors at the mating edges. We will study such "anti-aliasing" techniques in more depth in Chapter 17.

```
// mimics old-fashioned print ads that show rays in
// alternating colors

// a=0.5 is in=out
float bias (float t, a)
{
   return pow(t,-(log(a)/log(2)));
}


float fuzzysqwave(float a,fuzz)
{
  float fsw;

  if(a<fuzz)
    fsw=a/fuzz;
  else if((a>=fuzz)&&(a<(0.5-fuzz)))
    fsw=1.0;
  else if((a>=(0.5-fuzz))&&(a<(0.5+fuzz)))
    fsw = 1 + (0.5-fuzz-a)/fuzz;
  else if((a>(0.5+fuzz))&&(a<(1.0-fuzz)))
    fsw = -1.0;
  else
    fsw = -1 + (a+fuzz-1)/fuzz;

  return fsw;
}// fuzzysqwave();

imager retrorays
(
 color c1 = color(1,1,1);
 color c2 = color(0,0,0);
 float gam=1.0;
 float fuzz=0.05;
 float n = 10;
 )
{
 float curr_y;
 float rez[3];
 color rampcol=color(0,0,0);
 float mixf;
```

```
float s,t;
float ang;
point center = point(0.5,0.5,0), curr;
vector v;
float d;
float radius = 2., inDisk, ang2;

option("Format",rez);
s = xcomp(P)/rez[0];
t = ycomp(P)/rez[1];

s -= 0.5;
t -= 0.5;
ang = 3.14159278 + atan(t,s); // 0..2pi
ang /= (2*3.14159278);
ang = n*ang;
ang = mod(ang,1.0);
ang = 0.5*(1+fuzzysqwave(ang,fuzz));
rampcol = mix(c1,c2,ang);

Ci += (1-Oi)*rampcol;
Oi = 1.0;
alpha=1.0;
}// retrorays()
```

Figure 12.24 Old-fashioned sunburst pattern created using an imager shader.

Further Reading

As we have seen, procedural pattern synthesis is a powerful technique with algo-rithmic/mathematical underpinnings. Consult the following sources to learn more about this approach. (You can find links to relevant Websites at the online pages for this book, or you can do searches to locate them.)

The SIGGRAPH '92 course notes on shader writing offer a nice introduction to RSL shader writing, with the procedural approach discussed throughout. The RenderMan Interface Specification (version 3.3 as of this writing) contains a com-plete list of RSL functions along with some notes on each.

Steve May's "RmanNotes" is a classic introduction to the idea of layering patterns. Malcolm Kesson's "fundza" site is a rich resource for shaders, as is Tal Lancaster's "RMR" site.

Ken Perlin is the inventor of Perlin noise. His 1985 and 2002 papers on his `noise()` function and the 1989 "Hypertexture" paper (all presented during SIGGRAPH) are extremely well written. His NYU home page is packed with Java-based demos of a variety of procedural ideas that involve using noise in joint rotations to syn-thesize life-like gestures.

There are five RenderMan-related books in which you can find more information on procedural patterns. *Texturing and Modeling* by Ebert et al. is a classic, with 680+ pages that explore this topic. *The RenderMan Companion* has a chapter called "A Gallery of Shaders," which contains several procedural shaders. Likewise, *Advanced RenderMan* has two chapters, "Pattern Generation" and "A Gallery of Procedural Chapters." The book *Essential RenderMan Fast* has three relevant chap-ters: "Simple Patterns," "Tiling and Repeating Patterns," and "Noise." Finally, *Rendering for Beginners* contains a "Shading" chapter that discusses several proce-dural shaders, including nonphotoreal ones.

13

Texture Mapping

In Chapter 12, "Procedural Patterns," we looked at several ways to generate surface details algorithmically. In this chapter, we will explore the use of texture coordinates (s,t) to look up color and opacity in rectangular grids of data such as texture maps.

Basics

At each shading location, RenderMan provides a pair of coordinates (s,t), called *texture coordinates*. s and t both lie between 0.0 and 1.0 and therefore represent a point location inside a dimensionless image of unit size. In other words, (s,t) can be used to locate a point somewhere in a rectangular image, regardless of its resolution or aspect ratio.

The color looked up (or "indexed") at a given (s,t) location is referred to as the *texture value* at that location, or simply as *texture*.

In RenderMan, instead of using a raw image to look up texture, we use a texture map, which is a processed version of the image. This is done to provide high-quality lookups.

txmake is the program that converts TIFF images into "MIP-mapped" texture map files, which contain copies of the image at multiple resolutions. Depending on the situation (for example, distance from camera to the shading location), RenderMan will automatically determine the appropriate resolution(s) at which to index the texture. This scheme, along with good map filtering, results in high-quality texture lookups. txmake is discussed again at the end of the chapter, under the "Additional Details" section.

How do (s,t) values get associated with a shading point in the first place? There are several ways. For a spline (such as NURBS) surface, they come from the u and v isoparam values. Texture painting programs, UV editors, and such can also be used to associate texture coordinates with individual vertices in a polymesh. Regardless of how a shading location gets its texture coordinates, inside a shader, we will always be able to access the coordinates via the built-in s and t parameters.

As we will soon see, separating the texture coordinate assignment/generation from subsequent access in the shader comes with great flexibility—we can use the (s,t) coordinates to index into a texture map, modify it, or totally ignore it and generate our own (s,t) inside the shader and use those to look up texture values.

The following simpletex shader illustrates the use of the RSL texture() call, which is at the heart of the texture mapping process. In its most basic invocation, all it needs is the name (string value) of a texture file on disk. It uses the current shading sample's (s,t) value to look up an RGB color from the supplied map and outputs the value as a color type:

```
color texval = texture(texturemapname);
```

The fact that (s,t) is used can be made more obvious via this alternate version of the lookup:

```
color texval = texture(texturemapname,s,t);
```

It is customary to ensure that the string filename passed to the shader is not empty before using it to retrieve a texture result.

```
surface simpletex(
    string txnm="";
)
{
  Oi = Os;
  if(txnm!="")
    Ci = Oi*color texture(txnm);
    // more explicit version of the call:
    // Ci = Oi*color texture(txnm,s,t);
  else
    Ci = Oi*Cs;
}// simpletex()
```

Figure 13.1 shows the simpletex shader in use. At the top left is the colorful texture map that we use. At the top right, the texture is mapped onto a pair of rectangles connected along a single edge. The (s,t) values are supplied via the RIB file as follows:

```
PointsPolygons [4 4] [0 1 4 5 1 2 3 4] "P" [
0 1 0
.5 1 -.5
1 1 0
1 0 0
.5 0 -.5
0 0 0
]
"st" [
0 0 .5 0 1 0 1 1 .5 1 0 1
]
```

There are six vertices specified within "P" [ ]. There are six corresponding (s,t) values, which are supplied via "st" [ ] right below the vertex list. The (s,t) values are such that the four corner texture coordinates (0,0), (1,0), (1,1), and (0,1) are associated with the four corners of our bent, greeting card shape. This creates an exact fit between the two, as if our texture were a decal, sized just right to be pasted across the entire geometry.

At the bottom left is a single spline patch, again with our texture mapped across its entire surface. The RIB call is as follows:

```
Patch "bicubic" "P" [
-1 1 2   -.5 1 -.5   .5 1 2 1 1 -.5
-1 .5 -.5   -.5 .5 -3   .5 .5 -3  1 .5 .5
-1 -.5 .5   -.5 -.5 3   .5 -.5 3 1 -.5 -.5
-1 -1 1   -.5 -1 -.5   .5 -1 1   1 -1 -.5
]
```

Note that there is no mention of s and t. This is because the bicubic patch's own underlying (u,v) grid is used to generate (s,t) automatically. A single patch whose u and v range from 0 to 1 gets assigned texture coordinates across the patch that also range from 0 to 1 in s and t. So the default behavior is that no matter how the surface is shaped (flat, curved, noisy, or whatever), a texture maps across its entirety, with the texture map's four corners "pinned" to the four corners of the patch. Again, we imagine the texture to be printed on a thin decal that can be stretched over the surface for a tight, smooth fit.

The bottom-right image shows the "Gumbo" elephant model mapped with our texture. Because the model is comprised of multiple bicubic spline patches, and the texture is shrink-fitted across each, we see multiple copies of the texture mapped across the elephant geometry. This is for illustration only—in a real situation, the model would be assigned texture coordinates that make a single map stretch across multiple patches. Even so, a single map is often insufficient to texture an entire object such as Gumbo. Multiple maps are needed, with map boundaries carefully made to appear seamless across map transitions. Texture mapping is a vast topic and is both an art and a science. In this chapter, we will concern ourselves with just the low-level mechanics of the mapping process via the texture() call, not on mapping techniques, healing seams, and so on.

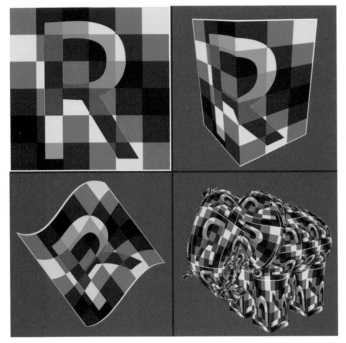

Figure 13.1 Basic texture mapping.

In Figure 13.1, the texture map that we used contains only R, G, and B channels (no alpha). Since not having alpha is equivalent to an alpha of 1.0 everywhere (uniformly solid matte), our texture applications cannot be limited to use just parts of a texture map. To remedy this, texture maps often contain four channels of data, with R, G, B, and A as well. The A alpha value can be used to modulate RGB resulting from color lookups. Specifically, we can do compositing (such as over) operations on a background by using the alpha value and texture RGB as foreground values.

The blendtex shader below illustrates how this is done, and Figure 13.2 shows the results. The top row of the figure shows the texture map we use. The patterned letter R on the left contains RGB, and the associated alpha channel is shown on the right. Note that the four channels are all stored in the same texture map file on disk. The alpha is shown as being separate in the figure, just for illustration.

We access the color value from the texture as before:

```
color Ct = color texture(txnm,s,t);
```

To retrieve the single channel alpha value, we use a modified syntax, with the channel number (0 for R, 1 for G, 2 for B, and 3 for A in a four-channel map) supplied with square brackets:

```
float a = float texture(txnm[3]);
```

Note that accessing a single channel makes the texture() call return a float value and not a color, as we would expect.

We want to overlay our texture on an existing background, as shown at the bottom left of Figure 13.2. We use the same bent shape as from the previous figure. For our background, we simply use Cs, the underlying body color passed in via RIB. In a more sophisticated example, the background could be another texture as well, a procedural pattern, and so on. The over compositing operation can now be carried out like so:

```
Ci = Oi*(Cs + a*(Ct-Cs));
```

When a is 0 (outside the letter R shape), Ci is simply Cs. Inside the textured region of our map, a is 1.0, so Ci becomes Cs+Ct-Cs, which equals Ct. At the edges of the texture, a is a grayscale value between 0 and 1, which creates a blend between Cs and Ct. Without a clean edge in the matte, our compositing operation would yield unsightly results with sharp jagged edges along the patterned shape, drawing unwanted attention to the compositing and destroying the illusion of seamless placement.

Our compositing equation above is a variation of this more standard version:

```
C_over = C_fg + (1-a_fg)*C_bg
```

This equation is also for doing an "over" compositing operation. We are placing a foreground image C_fg, which has an alpha channel a_fg, over a background image C_bg whose own alpha is unused (usually it is absent if the background is a photograph or live action plate). Further, the foreground image's alpha channel is premultiplied into the RGB color channels so that transparent areas where alpha is 0 appear black in the color image. As you can see, in regions where alpha is 1 (solid foreground), the result is C_fg. In other words, the foreground replaces the background. Likewise, at regions where the foreground is absent (a_fg is 0), the result is C_bg since C_fg is black in such regions due to premultiplication. At the edges of foreground regions, premultiplication ensures that the foreground is partially added to the background, producing a seamless composite.

A texture map can also be used to alter surface color in more subtle ways (for example, the map can contain color that slowly varies across the surface). This is known as *color mapping*, and the color-holding texture map is called a *color map*. Likewise, a texture map also can hold a "dirt" texture (scratches, blemishes, discoloration) to give a surface more liveliness and real-world feel. Such a map would then be a *dirt map*.

```
surface blendtex(
    string txnm="";
)
{
  if(txnm!="")
  {
      float a = float texture(txnm[3]);
      Oi = Os;
      color Ct = color texture(txnm,s,t);
      // Cs is background, Ct is foreground
      // when a=0, Ci=Oi*Cs; when a=1, Ci=Oi*Ct
      Ci = Oi*(Cs + a*(Ct-Cs));
  }
  else
  {
    Oi = Os;
    Ci = Oi*Cs;
  }
}// blendtex()
```

We can also use the alpha channel value from a texture map to alter the transparency of the surface being rendered. This is referred to as *transparency mapping* and is shown at the bottom of Figure 13.2. The shader we use is this:

```
surface simplealphatex(
    string txnm="";
)
{
  Oi = Os;

  if(txnm!="")
    {
      float a = float texture(txnm[3],s,t);
      Oi = a;
      Ci = Oi*color texture(txnm,s,t);
    }
  else
    Ci = Oi*Cs;
}// simplealphatex()
```

As you can see, the alpha value is used to set Oi, which means that the surface becomes transparent when alpha is 0. Since alpha is 0 outside the patterned shape, we see letter R textures tiling the Gumbo shape, with regions in between them that we can see through.

As an aside, the channel access number in texturemapname[channelnum] is not limited to being 0, 1, 2, or 3. The TIFF file format can hold an arbitrary number of channels, and so can the corresponding texture map. You can use this feature to store, for example, 16 frames of a grayscale animating sprite sequence (such as a water splash) in a single texture. You would then use indices 0 through 15 in a sprites shader to access each individual animating frame. Using this technique allows more compact storage of the maps on disk (a single file versus 16).

Also, a shader can access textures from multiple maps (more on this topic later). If the map names are stored in a string array, here is how you would access a different channel from each map.

```
string RGBfiles[3]; // contains names of three maps
// inner parentheses are NECESSARY!
float rval = float texture((RGBfiles[0])[0],s,t);
float gval = float texture((RGBfiles[1])[1],s,t);
float bval = float texture((RGBfiles[2])[2],s,t);
```

As you can see, we look up R, G, and B from maps in RGBfiles[0], RGBfiles[1], and RGBfiles[2], respectively. Because the square brackets are used to specify string array indices and also channel numbers, it is necessary to resolve the ambiguity by enclosing the map names in parentheses. In other words, the correct syntax is (RGBfiles[0])[0], not RGBfiles[0][0].

Figure 13.2 Use of a texture map that contains an alpha channel.

A given texture image can be mapped onto a surface using eight different confor-mations (orientations and flips) based on permuting and reflecting s and t. Again, we use the asymmetric `letter R` texture to illustrate this (see Figure 13.3), using the `texflips` shader below.

By swapping s and t, we can cause the texture to appear rotated by 90 degrees. By subtracting s and t from 1.0 (which will also yield a 0 to 1 value, since s and t are themselves 0 to 1), we can reverse the left/right or top/bottom orientations and cre-ate mirror images. These are all the variations (also used in the eight images in Figure 13.3): (s,t), (s,1-t), (1-s,t), (1-s,1-t), (t,s), (t,1-s), (1-t,s), and (1-t,1-s).

Doing these manipulations in the shader and providing flags for the user to turn them on/off is easier than having to go back to a TIFF image, doing the manip-ulation in an image editing program such as Photoshop, and re-creating the tex-ture map for use in the shader.

```
// 8 possible conformations of a texmap
surface texflips(
        string txnm="";
        float flips=0,flipt=0,swapst=0;
)
{
  Oi = Os;

  if(txnm!="")
    {
      float ss=s,tt=t;

      if(swapst==1)
      {
        ss = t;
        tt = s;
      }

      if(flips==1)
      ss = 1 - ss;
      if(flipt==1)
      tt = 1 - tt;

      Ci = Oi*color texture(txnm,ss,tt);
    }
  else
    Ci = Oi*Cs;
}// texflips()
```

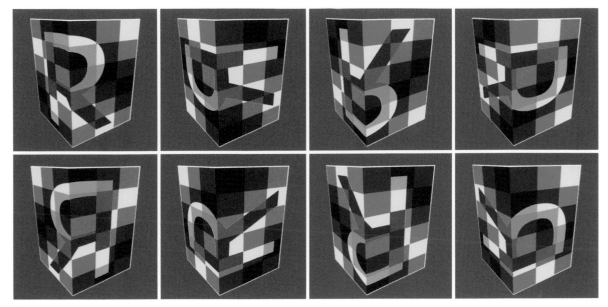

Figure 13.3 Eight permutations of texture coordinates s and t.

Image Processing

It should have started to occur to you by now that we can manipulate (s,t) values inside a shader and use the altered values to look up texture, as we did with the texture flips above. Indeed, we can perform arbitrary calculations on s and t themselves and then use the results to index texture. Likewise, we are not limited to using just the (s,t) that belongs to the current shading point. We can look up textures at any number of alternate (s,t) locations. In other words, we can perform image processing (IP) operations on the texture, effectively turning our shader into an image filter.

Figure 13.4 shows a letter A texture at the top left, which we will use for our IP examples. The IP_default shader shown below simply looks up a texture value at an (s,t) location. By applying this shader to a square that completely fills the image frame, we generate the image at the top left of Figure 13.4. (This rendered image would be the same as the input TIFF version of the letter A texture map.) We can effect image processing by applying our IP shaders over the same frame-filling square.

```
surface IP_default(
        string txnm="";
)
{
  Oi = Os;
```

```
if(txnm!="")
   Ci = Oi*color texture(txnm,s,t);
else
   Ci = Oi*Cs;
}// IP_default
```

The IP-ripples shader below creates concentric ripples over the texture, as shown in Figure 13.4's top right image. We first move the origin to the center of the image (the default origin is at the top left) via

```
ss = s-0.5;
tt = t-0.5;
```

Next, we convert the Cartesian pair (ss,tt) into their polar equivalents (r,theta):

```
float r = sqrt(ss*ss+tt*tt);
float theta = atan(tt,ss);
```

Sinusoidal ripples are applied using

```
float del_r = ampl*sin(r*freq);
r += del_r;
```

Applying the ripples was our goal (the IP operation), so now we need to convert back to Cartesian values and revert the origin:

```
sss = r*cos(theta);
ttt = r*sin(theta);
sss = sss + 0.5;
ttt = ttt + 0.5;
```

We get ripples on the map by using our new (sss,ttt) instead of the incoming (s,t). You can dream up many more ways to alter (s,t). Several of them are shown in subsequent examples.

```
surface IP_ripples(
        string txnm="";
        float ampl=1.0;
        float freq=1.0;
)
{
  Oi = Os;

  if(txnm!="")
    {
       float ss, tt, sss, ttt;

       ss = s-0.5;
       tt = t-0.5;
```

```
        float r = sqrt(ss*ss+tt*tt);
        float theta = atan(tt,ss);

        float del_r = ampl*sin(r*freq);
        r += del_r;

        sss = r*cos(theta);
        ttt = r*sin(theta);
        sss = sss + 0.5;
        ttt = ttt + 0.5;

        Ci = Oi*color texture(txnm,sss,ttt);
      }
   else
      Ci = Oi*Cs;
}// IP_ripples()
```

At the bottom left of Figure 13.4, we see that turbulence has been applied to our map. You could use such an effect (at a reduced strength) for creating heat shimmers, for example. The shader that is used to create the warp is this:

```
surface IP_turb(
        string txnm="";
        float ampl=1.0;
        float freq=1.0;
)
{
  Oi = Os;

  if(txnm!="")
    {
      float ss, tt;

      color Ct = noise(freq*P) - color(.5,.5,.5);
      ss = s + ampl*comp(Ct,0);
      tt = t + ampl*comp(Ct,1);

      Ci = Oi*color texture(txnm,ss,tt);
    }
  else
    Ci = Oi*Cs;
}// IP_turb()
```

We warp the texture coordinates before texture access. The warping is achieved by using P to obtain a color noise value with each component in 0 to 1, subtracting 0.5 from each to modify the range to -0.5..0.5:

```
color Ct = noise(freq*P) - color(.5,.5,.5);
```

R and G components of the result are now used to alter s and t. You can think of other ways of using the noise() call to warp s and t.

Rescaling an image is also an IP operation and is shown at the bottom right of Figure 13.4. We achieve rescaling by modifying the default 0 to 1 range of s and t into new user-supplied ranges (smin, smax) and (tmin, tmax), respectively, as shown in this IP_rescale_st shader:

```
surface IP_rescale_st(
        string txnm="";
        float smin=0, smax=1, tmin=0, tmax=1;
)
{
  Oi = Os;

  if(txnm!="")
    {
      float ss, tt;

      ss = smin + (smax-smin)*s;
      tt = tmin + (tmax-tmin)*t;

      Ci = Oi*color texture(txnm,ss,tt);
    }
  else
    Ci = Oi*Cs;
}// IP_rescale_st()
```

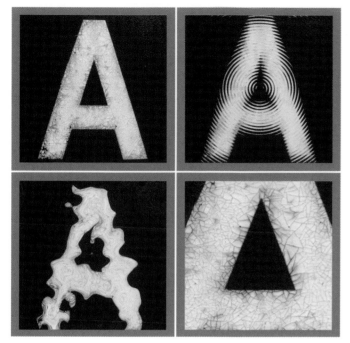

Figure 13.4 Image processing of texture maps.

Three more IP operations are illustrated in Figure 13.5. At the top left, the unaltered `strawberries` texture map is shown for comparison.

At the top right is a typical color tinting operation (for example, you might use it for sepia toning). The `sepia` shader below shows the details. We look up RGB color as usual at incoming (`s,t`) and convert it to an HSV triplet using the `rgb2hsv()` call. The `rgb2hsv()` function is presented here to show the details of the color space conversion. In practice we would use the built-in `ctransform()` call to convert between color spaces. Once we have our texture in HSV space, we alter all three components H, S, and V for the outgoing result. The varying hue component is replaced by a single hue value specified by the user—this is what leads to the monotone output. Saturation and value are scaled by user-supplied factors. The result is converted to `Ci`, which needs to be in RGB space, as follows:

```
Ci = Oi*color "hsv" (h,sat,val);
```

The `hsv` specifier is used to signal to the `color()` function that its three inputs are to be interpreted as being in HSV space, not in the usual RGB space.

```
// code for rgb2hsv() borrowed from Pixar's 'wood.sl' shader
point rgb2hsv(color Crgb)
{
  float red = comp(Crgb, 0);
  float grn = comp(Crgb, 1);
```

```
float blu = comp(Crgb, 2);

float hue, sat, val, x;
string spoke;

/* set val to largest rgb component, x to smallest */
if (red >= grn && red >= blu) {
  /* red largest */
  val = red;
  if (grn > blu) {
    x = blu;
    spoke = "Rb";
  } else {
    x = grn;
    spoke = "Rg";
  }
} else if (grn >= red && grn >= blu) {
  /* green largest */
  val = grn;
  if (red > blu) {
    x = blu;
    spoke = "Gb";
  } else {
    x = red;
    spoke = "Gr";
  }
} else {
  /* blue largest */
  val = blu;
  if (grn > red) {
    x = red;
    spoke = "Br";
  } else {
    x = grn;
    spoke = "Bg";
  }
}
hue = 0.;     /* default hue is red */
sat = 0.;     /* default saturation is unsaturated (gray) */

if (val > 0.0) {     /* not black */
  sat = (val - x)/val;     /* actual saturation */
  if (sat > 0.0) {   /* not a gray, so hue matters */
    /* now compute actual hue */
```

```
        if (spoke == "Rb") { /* red largest, blu smallest */
        hue = 1 - (val - grn)/(val - x);
        } else if (spoke == "Rg") {
        hue = 5 + (val - blu)/(val - x);
        } else if (spoke == "Gr") {
        hue = 3 - (val - blu)/(val - x);
        } else if (spoke == "Gb") {
        hue = 1 + (val - red)/(val - x);
        } else if (spoke == "Br") {
        hue = 3 + (val - grn)/(val - x);
        } else if (spoke == "Bg") {
        hue = 5 - (val - red)/(val - x);
        }
        hue *= 1/6.0;
     }
  }

  return point(hue,sat,val);
}// rgb2hsv


surface sepia(
        string txnm="";
        float h = 0.6, sscale=1, vscale=1;
)
{
  Oi = Os;

  if(txnm!="")
    {

      color Ct = color texture(txnm,s,t);

      // Convert our looked-up texture color to HSV and use its
      // saturation and value components for output.
      // We'll use incoming 'h' to set our outgoing hue, and incoming
      // sscale and vscale as multipliers for
      // outgoing saturation and value.
      point Phsv = rgb2hsv(Ct);
      float sat = sscale*comp(Phsv,1);
      float val = vscale*comp(Phsv,2);

      // Note that rgb2hsv's returning a color as a 'point'
```

```
      // type is non-standard. A modern alternative to use is this:
      // color Chsv = ctransform("hsv",Ct);
      // Also, Chsv's components h,s,v can simply be accessed using
      // array notation.
      // float sat = sscale*Chsv[1];
      // float val = vscale*Chsv[2];

      Ci = Oi*color "hsv" (h,sat,val);
    }
  else
    Ci = Oi*Cs;
}// IP_sepia()
```

The bottom left of Figure 13.5 shows how you can add "color turbulence" to an image. The colturb shader used to create the effect is presented below. By now you should be able to grasp the overall flow of using texture() for shading. We again use P to obtain a spatially varying turbulence value, which we add directly to the incoming texture's hue component. The hue component (and other color components for that matter) needs to stay in the 0 to 1 range, so the subsequent mod(hue,1.0) operation is done to ensure this. The hue-altered result is converted back to RGB-based Ci as usual, producing a band of hues across the image, reminiscent of tie-dye patterns. (Saturation and value are left unaltered.)

Note that the color tinting and color turbulence operations shown are examples of point operators, where the image processing is achieved by using just the color value at each sampling location. Brightness, contrast enhancement, posterization (quantization), and solarization are other examples of point operators. In contrast are area operators, typical examples being blurring and sharpening. For these, we need to know the color not just at the location of interest but also at neighboring locations. Since you can look up texture at any location in an image, such area operators are also able to be implemented as RSL shaders.

```
#define snoise(x) (2*noise(x)-1)
float turbulence(point Q)
{
  float turb=0, f;
  for(f=1;f<16;f*=2)
    {
      turb += abs(snoise(Q*f))/f;
    }
  return turb;
}
surface colturb(
        string txnm="";
        float hoff=0.0, freq=1.0, ampl=1.0;
```

```
)
{
  Oi = Os;

  if(txnm!="")
    {
      color Ct = color texture(txnm,s,t);

      // convert our looked-up texture color to HSV - code for rgb2hsv() is
      // given in the previous shader
      point Phsv = rgb2hsv(Ct);

      float hue = hoff + ampl*turbulence(P*freq);
      hue = mod(hue,1.0);
      float sat = comp(Phsv,1);
      float val = comp(Phsv,2);

      Ci = Oi*color "hsv" (hue,sat,val);

      // Ci = Ct;
    }
  else
    Ci = Oi*Cs;
}// colturb()
```

Finally, at the bottom right of Figure 13.5, a black-and-white `halftone` pattern is shown, generated using the `halftone` shader below. You can see from the image and from the code that only two colors—white and black—are used to generate perceived shades of gray. The idea is to divide the image into a grid of cells and draw a black circle (halftone dot) inside each cell, where the dot's radius is inversely proportional to the luminance at the center of the cell. So a very bright, almost white, luminance value leads to small dots, while dark values yield large dots. Note that we use an approximate version of the NTSC luminance formula to derive a float luminance value from an RGB triplet (br is a brightening scale factor):

```
float lum = br*(0.3*comp(Cc,0) + 0.6*comp(Cc,1) + 0.1*comp(Cc,2));
```

As you can see, the grid of halftone dots is aligned with the X and Y axes. As an exercise, given a rotation angle (called "screen angle" in the printing industry), you can try using it to rotate the dot grid about an axis perpendicular to the image plane. For example, an angle of 45 degrees will produce a more pleasing pattern than the one shown here by minimizing our perception of the individual dots that make up the image. You can also try creating color halftone images by overlaying multiple sets of colored dots, each with its own screen angle.

The use of equally spaced halftone dots and simulating grayscale by varying their radius is equivalent to amplitude modulation (AM) in radio broadcasting. There is a halftone analog of frequency modulation (FM) transmission as well, and that involves drawing fixed-size dots whose spacing varies in proportion to luminance (they cluster heavily in dark areas and are more sparse in light ones). You can try writing such an FM halftone shader as an exercise.

```
surface halftone(
               string txnm="";
               float n=10, br=1.0, gam=1.0, mixf=0;
               color bl=color(0,0,0),wh=color(1,1,1);
               )
{
  float ss=s, tt=t;
  color Ct = texture(txnm,ss,tt);

  float cellwidth=1/n;
  float sfrac = mod(ss,cellwidth);
  float tfrac = mod(tt,cellwidth);
  ss = ss-sfrac+0.5*cellwidth;
  tt = tt-tfrac+0.5*cellwidth;
  float sw = 0.5*cellwidth-sfrac;
  float tw = 0.5*cellwidth-tfrac;
  float d = sqrt(sw*sw+tw*tw);
  d /= (0.5*cellwidth);
  d = pow(d,gam);

  color Cc = texture(txnm,ss,tt);
  float lum = br*(0.3*comp(Cc,0) + 0.6*comp(Cc,1) + 0.1*comp(Cc,2));
  lum = 1-lum;

  if(d<lum)
     {
        Ci = bl;
     }
  else
     {
        Ci = wh;
     }


  Ci = mix(Ci,Ct,mixf);

}// halftone
```

Figure 13.5 Image processing of textures—more examples.

Our next example shows the use of `cellnoise()` to implement a crystallizing (also referred to as *stained glass*) filter. The `celltex` shader used to do this is shown below, followed by Figure 13.6, which displays the results for two different invocations of the shader.

First we divide up the image into a grid of cells, evaluate the `cellnoise()` function at the corner of each cell, and store the resulting colors' R and G values in a pair of arrays. The (R,G) pair, each value being 0 to 1, can be regarded as a 2D vector. If this 2D vector is imagined to be placed at a cell corner, the tip can be considered to be the corner's displaced location inside the cell. We now look up texture values at all these locations and store the resulting colors in another array. So instead of a uniform grid of cell corners that we began with, there is now a grid of randomized locations with an associated color value for each. The cellnoise and color storage operations are done using the nested pair of `for()` loops at the top of the shader.

To obtain our texture-based mosaic (Voronoi) cells, we compute the (squared) distance between our shading location and each stored location and pick the stored location that is closest to us. We then assign outgoing `Ci` to be the stored color corresponding to that closest location. In other words, the offset locations are centers of Voronoi cells. Each such center has a convex region of influence, inside which a point is closer to it than any other cell center. Accordingly, the entire convex region takes on the color at the cell center. A collection of cell centers creates a corresponding collection of nonoverlapping convex regions called *Voronoi poly-gons*, which tile the plane containing the centers. Strictly speaking, cell centers lying on the periphery of the collection create semi-infinite polygons, but for prac-tical purposes these are clipped by the boundary enclosing the centers, which in our case is the perimeter of our texture map. You can also see that points lying on cell edges are equidistant from two cell centers by definition, and points at the vertices are equidistant from three.

Figure 13.6 shows two applications of the celltex shader to the strawberries tex-ture map we used earlier. On the left, a coarse 10×10 grid is used, and the Voronoi cells are large as a result. The underlying texture map is faintly blended with the Voronoi cell pattern to help you see where the cell colors come from (as a reminder, each cell gets its color from the texture value at its center). On the right of the fig-ure, a finer 25×25 grid yields a network of smaller, more numerous cells. The influence of the red strawberry regions and the white cardboard box ones on the cell colors is more obvious in this image.

```
surface celltex(
                string txnm="";
                float m=5, n=5;
                float mixf=0;
                )
{
  float svals[2500], tvals[2500];
  float nrows=m, ncols=n;
  color CVor[2500];

  color Ct=texture(txnm,s,t);

  // limit user-supplied grid size to a max. of 50x50
  if(nrows>50)nrows=50;
  if(ncols>50)ncols=50;

  float i,j;
  for(i=0;i<nrows;i+=1)
     {
       for(j=0;j<ncols;j+=1)
       {
         float indx = i*ncols+j;

         color c = cellnoise(indx);
         float rands=comp(c,0), randt=comp(c,1);

         svals[indx] = rands;
```

```
            tvals[indx] = randt;
            CVor[indx] = texture(txnm,rands,randt);
          }


      }

  float mindist=1000000;
  for(i=0;i<nrows;i+=1)
    {
      for(j=0;j<ncols;j+=1)
      {
        float indx=i*ncols+j;
        float ss=svals[indx], tt=tvals[indx];
        float dsq = (ss-s)*(ss-s) + (tt-t)*(tt-t);

        if(dsq<mindist)
          {
            mindist=dsq;
            Ci = CVor[indx];
          }
      }

    }

  Ci = mix(Ci,Ct,mixf);

}// celltex
```

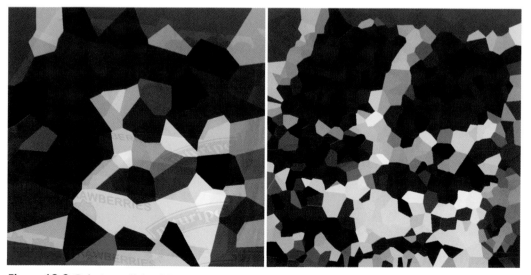

Figure 13.6 Coloring cellular (Voronoi) regions based on image content.

Image Warping

We now consider a pair of image-warping shaders. The first, `lensdewarp`, is shown below. The left image in Figure 13.7 shows our letter A shape, slightly "pinched" in the middle, reminiscent of the Eiffel Tower. This is an example of *pincushion distortion* exhibited by real-world zoom lenses with long focal lengths. Our shader undoes the distortion to produce straight sloping edges, as shown at the right of the figure. Conversely, we can modify the shader to correct for a "barrel" distortion (where the shape would appear to bulge in the middle) caused by wide angle lenses with short focal lengths.

As you can see below, the overall idea is to convert (s,t) to polar coordinates (as we did for the concentric ripples shader), do a nonlinear correction for the radial component using a cubic polynomial, and then convert the resulting (r,theta) pair back to Cartesian coordinates to produce a modified (s,t).

The dewarping is achieved using this cubic equation:

```
float rnew = r*(a*r*r*r + b*r*r + c*r + d);
```

The old value of r is multiplied by a cubic polynomial in r, with experimentally determined (usually via lens calibration) values for coefficients a, b, and c. For our example, we use 0, 0, 0.5, and 1.3 for a, b, c, and d, respectively. In other words, it turns out that for our example, the correction is first degree, not quadratic or cubic.

We are undoing the pinch distortion by creating a barrel distortion using the above equation. (This can be seen at the edges of the red background square.) To do this in reverse for undoing barrel distortion by introducing a pinch one, try a, b, c, and d values of 0, 0, -0.5, and 1.3.

```
surface lensdewarp(
                string txnm="";
                float a=0, b=0, c=0, d=1;
                )
{
  Oi = Os;

  if(txnm!="")
    {
      float ss, tt, sss, ttt;

      ss = s-0.5;
      tt = t-0.5;

      float ss2=ss*ss, tt2=tt*tt;
```

```
     float r = sqrt(ss2+tt2);
     float ang = atan(tt,ss);

     float rnew = r*(a*r*r*r + b*r*r + c*r + d);

     sss = rnew*cos(ang);
     ttt = rnew*sin(ang);

     sss += 0.5;
     ttt += 0.5;

     Ci = Oi*color texture(txnm,sss,ttt);
     }
  else
     {
     Ci = Oi*Cs;
     }
}// lensdewarp()
```

Figure 13.7 Dewarping a texture map containing pincushion ("pinching") distortion.

The next example shows how to create an anamorphically warped image for reconstruction on a cylindrical mirror placed at its center. Anamorphic art and viewers were popular parlor items (which were later mass produced as children's toys) during the Victorian era. Using the shader shown below on an animating sequence, you can create anamorphic animation as well as static images. Using a tablet display that lies flat and a cylindrical mirror made of Mylar, you can watch the animation come to life over the cylindrical surface.

The `cylmirror` shader shown below is particularly simple to write. As usual, we convert (s,t) into polar form such that both r and `theta` are in 0 to 1. Normalizing the angle is easy:

```
float ang = PI + atan(tt,ss); // atan() returns values in range -PI..PI
sss = ang/(2*PI);
```

r is normalized using `rmin` and `rmax`, which depend on the radius and height of the reconstructing cylinder:

```
ttt = gainFunc((r-rmin)/(rmax-rmin),rgain);
```

The `gain()` function is used for extra effect to nonlinearly alter the normalization, which in turn results in caricatured reconstruction over the cylinder.

```
float biasFunc(float t;float a;)
{
    return pow(t,-(log(a)/log(2)));
}
float gainFunc(float t; float a;)
{
  float g;
  if (t <=0.5)
  {
    g = 0.5*biasFunc(2*t, a);
  }
  else
  {
    g = 1.0 - 0.5*biasFunc(2.0-2*t,a);
  }

  return g;

}

surface cylmirror(
        string txnm="";
        float rmin=0, rmax=1;
        float rgain=0.5;
        )
{
  Oi = Os;

  if(txnm!="")
    {
```

```
    float ss, tt, sss, ttt;

    ss = s-0.5;
    tt = t-0.5;

    float ss2=ss*ss, tt2=tt*tt;
    float r = 2*sqrt(ss2+tt2); // to make it 0..1
    float ang = PI + atan(tt,ss);

    // use angle as 's', radial dist. as 't'
    sss = ang/(2*PI);
    if((r>=rmin)&&(r<=rmax))
    {
      ttt = gainFunc((r-rmin)/(rmax-rmin),rgain);
      Ci = Oi*color texture(txnm,sss,ttt);
    }
    else
    Ci = Oi*Cs;
  }
  else
    {
      Ci = Oi*Cs;
    }
}// cylmirror()
```

Figure 13.8 shows the anamorphically warped result of applying our `cylmirror` shader (right image) on a photograph (left image). As mentioned earlier, the photo can be seen reconstructed on the surface of a thin, shiny cylindrical mirror placed at the center of the anamorph image.

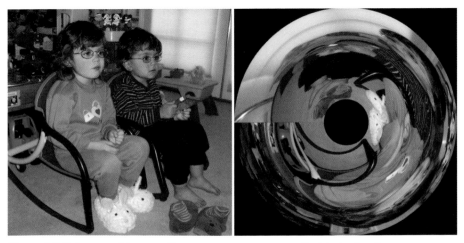

Figure 13.8 Anamorphic warp (for reconstructing over a cylindrical mirror).

As an exercise, try writing a shader to take as input an anamorphically warped image produced using the shader presented above and reconstructing it over a cylinder to recover the original image. (You will, of course, be able to see only the part of the image that is visible over your cylinder surface, not all of it at once.)

Texture Projection

We can ignore built-in (s,t) altogether and map a texture onto a surface using our own projection techniques. Four classic texture projection cases are shown in Figure 13.9: planar, spherical, cylindrical, and autoprojection. We use the letter R texture and a regular icosahedron in all four cases to allow comparison between them. The code for the four shaders presented below is derived from PRMan's maps.sl example shader.

The plnproj shader does planar projection (see Figure 13.9, top left), which works particularly well on a flat surface. The idea is to place a 2D coordinate system consisting of an origin, X-axis, and Y-axis over the flat surface, express each point on the surface in this coordinate system, and use the resulting 2D coordinates as (s,t) to assign a texture value to the point. Since our shader deals only with 2D points, it implicitly creates an orthographic view of the projection. As you can see from the figure, the 3D nature of the icosahedron is not at all evident in the projected result—instead, we see what appears to be a hexagon.

```
surface plnproj(
            string txnm="";
            point maporigin=point(0,0,0), xaxis=point(1,0,0),
            yaxis=point(0,1,0);
            )
{
  Oi = Os;
  if(txnm!="")
    {
      color Ct;
      float ss, tt;

      varying vector    V, XX, YY;
      point PP = transform("world",P);
      V = (PP - maporigin);

      XX = normalize(xaxis - maporigin);
      YY = normalize(yaxis - maporigin);
      ss = V.XX;
      tt = V.YY;
```

```
        // custom adj.
        ss = 0.5*(1+ss);
        tt = 0.5*(1+tt);

        Ct = color texture(txnm,ss,tt);
        Ci = Oi*Ct;
      }
  else
    {
      Oi = Os;
      Ci = Cs* Oi;
    }


}// plnproj()
```

Spherical projection is next, as seen in the sphproj shader below and at the top right of Figure 13.9. Here we convert each surface point to a spherical coordinate (r,theta,phi) and use the two angles to look up corresponding texture values in our 2D map—this type of projection is used in cartography to map a flat atlas of the earth onto a globe (and vice versa). The polar angles are derived as follows:

```
tt = acos(-zz)/PI;
ss = 1.0 - 0.5*(1+atan(yy,xx)/PI);
```

With spherical projection, horizontal lines in a texture map (latitude lines) appear to curve upward and downward near the poles, as can be seen in our figure.

```
surface sphproj(
            string txnm="";
            point maporigin=point(0,0,0),
            xaxis=point(1,0,0), yaxis=point(0,1,0), zaxis=point(0,0,1);
            )
{
  Oi = Os;
  if(txnm!="")
    {
      color Ct;
      float ss, tt;

      point PP = transform("shader",P);
      // point PP = transform("world",P);


      varying vector    V,Vn, XX, YY, ZZ;
      varying float     xx, yy, zz;
      V = PP - maporigin;
```

```
        Vn = normalize(V);

        XX = normalize(xaxis - maporigin);
        YY = normalize(yaxis - maporigin);
        ZZ = normalize(zaxis - maporigin);
        xx = Vn.XX;
        yy = Vn.ZZ;
        zz = Vn.YY;

        tt = acos(-zz)/PI;

        ss = 1.0 - 0.5*(1+atan(yy,xx)/PI);

        ss = 1-ss; // adjustment

        Ct = color texture(txnm,ss,tt);
        Ci = Oi*Ct;
    }
  else
    {
        Oi = Os;
        Ci = Cs* Oi;
    }

}// sphproj()
```

Next is cylindrical projection, shown at the bottom left of Figure 13.9. The cyl-proj shader below does the projection. Conceptually, the cylindrical case is quite similar to the spherical one. The polar triplet is now (r,theta,z), where z is the height along the cylinder. The texture coordinates are arrived at as follows:

```
tt = 0.5*(1+tt);
ss = 1.0 - 0.5*(1+atan(yy,xx)/PI);
```

The visual appearance of cylindrical mapping is quite similar to that of the spherical case, except that the latitude lines no longer bend toward the poles—they are left undistorted in the z calculation step.

```
surface cylproj(
            string txnm="";
            point maporigin=point(0,0,0),
            xaxis=point(1,0,0), yaxis=point(0,1,0), zaxis=point(0,0,1);
            )
{
  Oi = Os;
  if(txnm!="")
```

```
  {
    color Ct;
    float ss, tt;

    point PP = transform("shader",P);
    // point PP = transform("world",P);

    varying vector    V,Vn, XX, YY, ZZ;
    varying float     xx, yy;
    V = PP - maporigin;
    Vn = normalize(V);

    XX = normalize(xaxis - maporigin);
    YY = normalize(yaxis - maporigin);
    ZZ = normalize(zaxis - maporigin);
    xx = Vn.XX;
    yy = Vn.ZZ;

    tt = V.YY;
    tt = 0.5*(1+tt);
    ss = 1.0 - 0.5*(1+atan(yy,xx)/PI);
    ss = 1-ss; // adjustment
    Ct = color texture(txnm,ss,tt);
    Ci = Oi*Ct;
  }
else
  {
    Oi = Os;
    Ci = Cs* Oi;
  }

}// cylproj()
```

Finally, auto-projection maps a copy of the texture onto each polygon in a polymesh so that the projection (mapping) is locally flat (see Figure 13.9, bottom right, and the autoproj shader below). As a result, of the four examples in Figure 13.9, this is the only one that makes the underlying icosahedral surface (with its 20 equilateral triangles) explicit.

The idea here is to create a local coordinate system for each polygon and do planar projection using the local axes.

```
surface autoproj(
            string txnm="";
            point maporigin=point(0,0,0), yaxis=point(0,1,0);
            )
{
  Oi = Os;
  if(txnm!="")
    {
      color Ct;
      float ss, tt;

      point PP = transform("shader",P);
      normal NN = transform("shader",N);


      varying vector    V, XX, YY, ZZ;
      varying float     xx, yy, dot;
      uniform vector yvector, zvector;


      /*
       * The yvector and zvector are the axes of
       * shader space, but expressed
       * in shader space coordinates, not in current coordinates, so no
       * space conversion is required.  Everything else has already been
       * put into shader space coordinates by the callers of this routine.
       */

      yvector = vector (0,1,0);
      zvector = vector (0,0,1);

      V = PP - maporigin;

      ZZ = normalize(NN);
      YY = normalize(yaxis - maporigin);
      dot = ZZ . YY;
      /* if "up" (YY) vector parallel to "at" (ZZ) vector, find new "up" */
      if ((dot > (1-0.01))||(dot < (-1+0.01))) {
         dot = ZZ . yvector;
         if ((dot > (1-0.01))||(dot < (-1+0.01))) YY = zvector;
         else YY = yvector;
      }
```

```
      /* get orthogonal coordinate system */
      XX = YY ^ ZZ;
      YY = ZZ ^ XX;

      ss = V.XX;
      tt = V.YY;

      ss -= 0.5;
      tt -= 0.5;

      ss = 1-ss;

      Ct = color texture(txnm,ss,tt);
      Ci = Oi*Ct;
    }
  else
    {
      Oi = Os;
      Ci = Cs* Oi;
    }

}// autoproj()
```

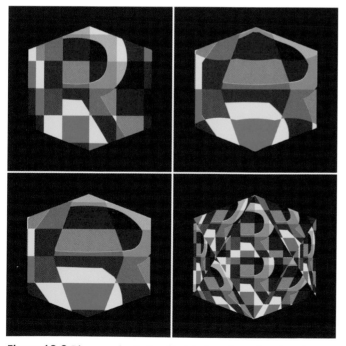

Figure 13.9 Planar, spherical, cylindrical, and per-face (auto) texture projection.

In addition to the four most common projections already discussed, there are other projection types, such as shrinkwrap and box, which you can look up and implement as an exercise. Note that all these projections, including the four above, are "hands off" techniques in which we use mapping math to associate shading points with texture coordinates. In typical CGI production, interactive texture editing tools are used in addition to such projection techniques. With such tools, it is possible to create much better mappings by interactively minimizing unsightly warps, achieving continuous mapping by stretching texture regions across contiguous surfaces, eliminating seams by overlapping texture regions, and maximizing texture map use by laying out regions such that there is minimal gap (unused areas of the map) between them. All this makes interactive texture mapping as much art as it is science.

The "automap" idea from the previous discussion can be generalized to the notion of camera projections, where a texture map can be projected onto a surface or a group of surfaces, analogous to a slide being projected onto the surface(s). A surface shader can be used for this purpose, but it is more advantageous to use a light-source shader—you can project multiple textures this way and combine them in unique ways in your surface shader.

Four variations of this technique are shown in Figure 13.10. In the first (top-left) version, the rendering camera is used as the projector, headlight-style. A single texture map containing a pattern of colored bands in star formations is projected on to a set of four evenly spaced, nonplanar star shapes hovering over a plane. A matte shader is applied to each surface, which has its own color and opacity. The texture projection occurs via the camProj light shader. As you can see, we operate in camera space. We are creating a directional light that is located at the camera origin and is oriented along the view direction (in other words, a headlight). The headlight's color is different at each surface location being shaded, coming from a texture lookup. The (s,t) for the lookup is derived from the shading point's location Ps, which is transformed to camera space and subjected to a perspective projection:

```
point PP = transform("camera",Ps);
float x = xcomp(PP), y=ycomp(PP), z=zcomp(PP);
x = (x/z)*0.5*h_apert/tan(fov*PI/180);
y = (y/z)*0.5*v_apert/tan(fov*PI/180);
```

The result of perspective projection is that points that lie farther from the camera (larger z values) produce smaller (x,y) projected values. In the limit, z tends to infinity, so (x,y) become (0,0). Conversely, closer points with smaller z values produce bigger projected (x,y) values. This is why parallel lines receding from a camera appear to converge toward a far-off vanishing point. The aperture and field-of-view (FOV) values act as zoom factors that scale the projected values and are usually chosen so that the entire texture map gets projected on to the scene, exactly filling the rendered image. In that case, the projected (x,y) will be in the range -0.5 to 0.5, so we apply a (0.5,0.5) offset via xc and yc to bring them into the 0 to 1 range and mirror/flip the coordinates if necessary before using them to look up the texture.

```
light camProj (
                float intensity = 1;
                string txname = "";
                float fov = 45;
                float h_apert = 1;
                float v_apert = 1.;
                float xc=0.5, yc=0.5;
                float flipx=0, flipy=0;
                )
{

  point from = point "camera" (0,0,0);
  vector axis = normalize(vector "camera" (0,0,1));
  color lcol = color(1);

  if(txname!="")
    {
      point PP = transform("camera",Ps);

      float x = xcomp(PP), y=ycomp(PP), z=zcomp(PP);

      x = (x/(z+0.0001))*0.5*h_apert/tan(fov*PI/180);
      y = (y/(z+0.0001))*0.5*v_apert/tan(fov*PI/180);

      x += xc;
      y += yc;

      if(flipx)x=1-x;
      if(flipy)y=1-y;

      lcol = color texture(txname,x,y);
    }

  illuminate (from,axis,fov)
    {
      Cl = intensity * lcol;
    }

}// camProj
```

Instead of applying our texture map as a headlight, we can project it from an arbitrary position and orientation, just as a gobo/cukaloris would be used in theater or movie sets. Such a "slide projector" light can be used to project leaf patterns, snow, or color variations to break up a monotonous background. The slideProj shader does this, as you can see in Figure 13.10, top right (the shader is an adaptation of the slideprojector shader from *The RenderMan Companion*). We are creating a spotlight that will be used to project the texture, but it is not always necessary to do so—a directional light will also work. The light is tilted downward so that you can see its extent on the top two stars, which are only partially illuminated by the texture projection. Our example uses a single slide projector, but you can also use multiple slide projectors to create visually complex, aesthetically pleasing patterns over your surfaces.

Code-wise, the shader is very similar to the previous one. Here, the cone angle for the spotlight is calculated from the aperture and FOV settings:

```
/* horizontal camera half-cone tangent */
float h_tan = (h_apert / 2) / (focal / 25.4);
float v_tan = (v_apert / 2) / (focal / 25.4); /* vertical one */
/* solid angle, for illuminate() only */
float angle = atan(sqrt(h_tan*h_tan + v_tan*v_tan));
```

(xslide,yslide) result from perspective projection (as before) and are used to look up the slide texture.

```
light slideProj (
float intensity = 1;
string slidename = "";
float focal = 55;
float h_apert = 1.260;
float v_apert = 0.945;
)
{
  point from = point "shader" (0,0,0);
  vector axis = normalize(vector "shader" (0,0,1));
  /* horizontal camera half-cone tangent */
  float h_tan = (h_apert / 2) / (focal / 25.4);
  float v_tan = (v_apert / 2) / (focal / 25.4); /* vertical one */
  /* solid angle, for illuminate() only */
  float angle = atan(sqrt(h_tan*h_tan + v_tan*v_tan));
  point Pslide = transform("shader", Ps);
  color lcol = color(1);
  if (slidename != "")
    {
      float zslide = zcomp(Pslide);
```

```
    float xslide = 0.5 - 0.5 * xcomp(Pslide) / h_tan / zslide;
    float yslide = 0.5 - 0.5 * ycomp(Pslide) / v_tan / zslide;
    lcol = color texture (slidename, xslide, yslide);
  }
  // spotlight
  illuminate (from, axis, angle)
    {
      Cl = intensity * lcol;
    }
}// slideProj
```

Texture projection can be done on a per-surface basis by placing the source of projection near the surface and orienting it appropriately. Such a customProj surface shader is presented below, and the bottom-left image in Figure 13.10 shows how it is used. The same striped pattern is projected on the four stars, but each star has its own customProj shader instance, which is passed in a custom coordinate system for the source of projection. For instance, the RIB chunk for the first star A is as follows:

```
# Star1
AttributeBegin
Attribute "identifier" "name" ["|polySurface1|polySurfaceShape6"]
ConcatTransform [1 0 0 0 0 1 0 0 0 0 1 0 0 0 0 1]
Translate -1.1 1.1 0
TransformBegin # rel. to star1
Translate 0 0 -3
CoordinateSystem "star1CoordSys"
TransformEnd
ShadingInterpolation "smooth"
Color [1 1 1]
Opacity [1 1 1]
Surface "customProj" "txname" "PenTex.tex" "coordSys"
"star1CoordSys" "fov" 30
ReadArchive "Star.dat"
AttributeEnd
```

The projectors' offset from the stars is identical for the top two stars, and the right star's projector is turned upside down. The bottom two stars also have identical offsets (different from the top stars' offsets), and the right star's projector is turned upside down here, too. As a result, we see four variations in projection. The shader logic again is nearly identical to that of the two previous shaders.

```
surface customProj (
            string txname = "";
            string coordSys="";
            float fov = 45;
```

```
                    float h_apert = 1;
                    float v_apert = 1.;
                    float xc=0.5, yc=0.5;
)
{
  if(txname!="")
    {
      point PP;
      if(coordSys!="")
      {
        PP = transform(coordSys,P);
      }
      else
      PP = transform("shader",P);

      float x = xcomp(PP), y=ycomp(PP), z=zcomp(PP);

      x = (x/(z+0.0001))*0.5*h_apert/tan(fov*PI/180);
      y = (y/(z+0.0001))*0.5*v_apert/tan(fov*PI/180);

      x += xc;
      y += yc;

      x = mod(x,1.0);
      y = mod(y,1.0);

      Ci = color texture(txname,x,y);
    }
  else
    {
      Oi = Os;
      Ci = Os*Cs;
    }
}// customProj
```

Our last example is technically not a projection, but we include it for completeness. Rendered images are often composited over a live-action background. The compositing occurs as a post process. The bgfill shader fills the unrendered background (which is usually black, unless a background color is specified via the background imager shader) during rendering, thereby making the over operation part of the rendering step. The bottom-right image in Figure 13.10 shows the shader in action. Here we use our striped pattern to fill the background instead of using it to project over the star surfaces.

The shader is extremely simple. We use P (which in an imager shader will be in pixel units) and the passed-in resolution values to derive (s,t) and use it to look up texture for filling the background. Instead of passing the resolution into the shader, you can also use the option() RSL call with Format to retrieve the resolution values.

```
imager bgfill(
string txnm="";
float xres=1024.0;
float yres=1024.0;
)
{
    color bgcol = color(.5,.5,.5);
    float s,t;
    if(""!=txnm)
    {
        s = xcomp(P)/xres;
        t = ycomp(P)/yres;
        bgcol = color texture(txnm,s,t);

    }
    Ci+=(1-Oi)*bgcol; // fill just bg
    Oi=1;
}// bgfill()
```

Figure 13.10 More forms of texture projection.

Environment Mapping

So far we have been using the texture() function to look up colors. RSL also provides an environment() call that takes the name of a map, as usual, as its primary input. But instead of requiring (s,t) for looking up the texture, this call needs a direction vector for the lookup. This form of specialized texture mapping is known as *environment mapping*.

We idealize a scene to be contained in a cuboidal environment if it is an indoor scene, or a spherical environment if it is an outdoor one. The scene is imagined to be enclosed by the (cuboidal/spherical) volume, with the environment textured on the inside walls of the cube or the inner surface of the sphere.

Given this setup, any ray fired off from a shading point on a surface in the scene will continue outward till it intersects with a cube wall/edge/corner or the sphere. In either case, we can look up the texture color at the intersection and use it to texture our shading point. We are using the ray direction to index the texture on the enclosing surfaces. This is the idea behind environment mapping.

While you can manually set up an enclosing cube/sphere, texture it appropriately, and do the ray intersection and lookup yourself, it is much easier to use the environment() call instead, where there is no need for an explicit enclosing surface or ray intersection calculations. You simply supply a map and a direction and get back a color, like so:

```
color envColor = environment(envTexmap,rayDirection);
```

The texture map used for the lookup is not an ordinary .tex map of the kind we've used so far. Instead, it is a specially constructed map meant specifically for ray-based lookup. In PRMan you would create such a map using the txmake program as usual, but with an additional -envlatl flag to create a spherical environment map or a -envcube flag for a cubical environment map. For creating the spherical version, a single TIFF file is input as usual, whereas for the cubical one you need to supply six TIFF images as input—one for each inner wall of the enclosing cube. The cube environment map is also called a *cross map* because the six sides of a flattened cube can be laid out in the shape of a cross. Visit www.debevec.org (Paul Debevec's site on image-based lighting) for more details.

The envmap shader does spherical mapping, and Figure 13.11 shows the results. At the left of the figure is the image we use for creating a spherical environment map. (As an aside, environment maps are usually given an .env extension to tell them apart from regular texture maps.) The right image in the figure shows a torus and the Utah teapot environment mapped using the map via our shader. As you can see, the shader does an ambient, diffuse, and specular calculation first and then overlays the environment texture on top using a user-supplied Kr reflection strength value:

```
color Crefl = Kr*refl(envname);
Ci += Crefl;
```

The environment texture lookup is done inside our refl() function, where the view direction V is reflected about the surface normal using the built-in reflect() RSL call, and the resulting vector Rray is used for the map lookup inside environment().

Environment mapping is an easy way for you to add some extra lighting effects to surfaces in your scene. You can reflect trees, clouds, sky, and so forth on outdoor objects (a car, for instance) to add realism. Likewise, indoor surfaces can benefit from reflections of light fixtures, wall hangings, and such to make them appear more realistic. *Chrome mapping* is a version of environment mapping where 100 percent of the coloring comes from the environment() lookup. This makes the surface ultra shiny, like the T-1000 chrome surfaces in *Terminator 2*.

```
color refl(string envname)
{
    color Cr=0;

    if(envname!="")
    {
      vector Nf = faceforward(normalize(N), I);
      vector V = -normalize(I) ;
      vector Rray = reflect(-V,Nf);
      Rray = vtransform("shader",Rray);
      Cr = color environment(envname,Rray);
    }
    return Cr;
}//refl()


surface envmap(float Ka=0, Kd=0, Ks=.6, Kr=0.5, roughness=.025;
               color specularcolor=1; string envname="";)
{
    vector Rray;
    normal Nf;
    vector V;
    color highlight;

    Nf = faceforward( normalize(N), I);
    V = -normalize(I) ;

    highlight = specularcolor*Ks*specular(Nf,V,roughness);
    Ci = Cs * (Ka * ambient() + Kd * diffuse(Nf)) + highlight;
```

```
    color Crefl = Kr*refl(envname);
    Ci += Crefl;

    Oi = Os;
    Ci *= Oi;

}//envmap()
```

Figure 13.11 Spherical environment mapping, standard technique.

For fun, we can also experiment with another variation of spherical mapping that uses a regular texture map, performing its lookup inside a circular region of the map. Figure 13.12, top left, shows the aloe photo we are using as our environment map. This image is preprocessed to produce the image on the top right, which resembles a warped panoramic image obtained with a hemispherical "fisheye" lens. Such a lens creates a circular image, inside which is packed the entire hemispherical environment that is in front of the lens. For our purposes of creating a map for spherical lookup, we approximate the hemispherical panorama using the hemipano shader. In our preprocessing RIB file, we apply this shader onto a hemisphere, with the aloe texture map as input. The result is the fisheye image on the top right of Figure 13.12. Incidentally, we color the nonrendered region around the hemisphere to be red (using the background imager shader) to make it explicit that texture lookup should not occur in this region; the presence of this red in the environment mapped outputs (bottom row, Figure 13.12) will alert us if this happens.

The hemipano shader uses a circular region in the center of our texture map and an annulus region around it to create the fisheye image. The extent of the circle and annulus is set by the user via R1 and R2, which are used to control the stretching at the center of the circular result and the compression at the periphery.

```
// Wraps a centered circular region on to the
// central part of a hemisph, and the remaining annulus
// on to the reminder of the hemisph.
// Result: "360 deg" fisheye img. from a single
// img, suitable for Haeberli-style refl. mapping


surface hemipano(float R1 = 0.5, R2=0.5, warp=1; string tx="")
{
    // R1 is used to index the texmap and R2, for img.
    // coords

    point PNDC = transform("NDC",P);
    Oi = Os;
    Ci = Cs;

    float x = (xcomp(PNDC)-0.5);
    float y = (ycomp(PNDC)-0.5);

    float d = sqrt(x*x+y*y);
    float r, ang, ss,tt,at;
    if(d<=(0.5*R2))
    {
      r = R1*pow(d/(0.5*R2),warp);
    }
    else
    {
      // the excess d - 0.5*R2 needs to start at R1 on the texmap..
      r = R1 + (1-R1)*(d-0.5*R2)/(0.5-0.5*R2);
    }
    r *= 0.5;
    ang = atan(y,x);
    ss = 0.5 + r*cos(ang);
    tt = 0.5 + r*sin(ang);

    Ci *= texture(tx,ss,tt);
}// hemipano
```

Now that we have a pseudo-fisheye panorama, we can treat it as a regular texture map, using (s,t) to do environment mapping with it. The sphrefl shader does this, and the resulting images are the bottom row of Figure 13.12. In the refl() function in the shader, we first obtain a reflected ray as before. But instead of using it in an `environment()` call as we did earlier, we use its z component to calculate a radial distance for a regular (s,t) texture lookup and use the ray's (x,y) values to calculate an angular offset.

```
Rray = vtransform("camera",Rray);
// map z to r, and (x,y) to theta
float rho = 0.5*(1+zcomp(Rray));
rho = biasFunc(rho,bias);
float ang = atan(ycomp(Rray),xcomp(Rray));
```

Now you can see why the texture lookup will be confined to a circular region in our map. Our math causes every possible reflection vector to map to an (r,ang) value inside the circle. We then convert such an (r,ang) polar form to Cartesian (s,t) as usual and look up the texture, which will serve as the outgoing environment-mapped value:

```
float ss = 0.5*(1+rho*cos(ang));
float tt = 0.5*(1+rho*sin(ang));
Cr = color texture(envname,1-ss,1-tt,"width",0);
```

The two variations shown at the bottom of Figure 13.12 are the result of two different values for the `bias` parameter in the shader, which nonlinearly alters the radius variable `rho`. The result is that we are able to control the apparent enlargement of the mapping at the center of our render.

The panorama technique is a variation of a clever idea by Paul Haeberli. At Paul's delightful Grafica Obscura site (www.graficaobscura.com), you will find a wealth of unusual CG ideas, techniques, and hacks, among which is a section on environment mapping. Here, Paul uses a full spherical panorama (not just a hemisphere) for the mapping. He creates the panorama using the circle/annulus regions as discussed above, with the difference that a front hemispherical fisheye image is mapped to the circle, and a back one is mapped to the annulus. In other words, his circular region contains a full view of the environment resulting from two hemispherical images stitched together. The equations in his note show how to map a reflection vector to a location inside the full panorama.

As an exercise, you can try modifying our pair of `hemipano`/`sphrefl` shaders to implement Paul's version. You need to feed your panorama creation shader two maps instead of one (use one for the circular region and the other for the annulus). Unless your pair of maps is actual hemispherical panoramas of a scene, you will notice a seam in your output between the circle and annulus. This is not a showstopper. If the seam bothers you, "cheat" by using a single image twice, taking care to reflect one about the circular boundary between the circle and annulus. Remember also to alter the lookup math in your reflection shader to use Paul's formulae in place of the ones we used.

```
float biasFunc(float t;float a;)
{
    return pow(t,-(log(a)/log(2)));
}


color refl(string envname;float bias)
{
    color Cr=0;

    if(envname!="")
    {
        vector Nf = faceforward(normalize(N), I);
        vector V = -normalize(I) ;
        vector Rray = reflect(-V,Nf);
        Rray = vtransform("camera",Rray);

        // map z to r, and (x,y) to theta
        float rho = 0.5*(1+zcomp(Rray));
        rho = biasFunc(rho,bias);
        float ang = atan(ycomp(Rray),xcomp(Rray));
        float ss = 0.5*(1+rho*cos(ang));
        float tt = 0.5*(1+rho*sin(ang));
        Cr = color texture(envname,1-ss,1-tt,"width",0);
    }
    return Cr;
}//refl()


surface sphrefl(float Ka=0, Kd=0, Ks=.6, Kr=0.5, roughness=.025;
                color specularcolor=1; string envname="";
                float bias=0.7071;)
{
    vector Rray;
    normal Nf;
    vector V;
    color highlight;

    Nf = faceforward( normalize(N), I);
    V = -normalize(I) ;

    highlight = specularcolor*Ks*specular(Nf,V,roughness);
    Ci = Cs * (Ka * ambient() + Kd * diffuse(Nf)) + highlight;
```

```
      color Crefl = Kr*refl(envname,bias);
      Ci += Crefl;

      Oi = Os;
      Ci *= Oi;

}// sphrefl()
```

Figure 13.12 Alternate form of spherical projection using a fisheye image.

As noted above, the environment() call is a variation of the standard texture() function that uses a ray direction instead of (s,t) for texture lookup. Likewise, shadow() is another variation, one that looks up a floating-point shadow value in a specialized texture map called a *shadow map* (also known as *depth map*). For texture access, we specify a point in the same coordinate system that was used when creating the shadow map. The returned value is typically multiplied with an existing surface color value to darken it, thereby creating a shadow. Depth mapped shadows are an alternative to the more contemporary raytraced shadows.

Displacement Mapping

The technique of using texture maps for displacements is called *displacement mapping*. The idea is to use the looked up texture(s) at each shading location to displace the surface. As with regular texture mapping, this offers a wealth of possibilities for using maps for this purpose.

The texdisplace displacement shader is an example of displacement mapping (Figure 13.13 contains the shader application's result, where we use a photo of a coin to create an embossed gold leaf effect). In the shader, we look up texture in the passed-in map as usual, using an additional blur factor specified by the user (more on the blur factor later). The R,G, and B values of the texture are combined into a single luminance grayscale result as before. This is so that we can use the luminance as the magnitude for our displacement.

```
r = float texture(txnm[0],s,t,"blur",blur);
g = float texture(txnm[1],s,t,"blur",blur);
b = float texture(txnm[2],s,t,"blur",blur);
float lum = 0.3*r + 0.6*g + 0.1*b;
```

The luminance value is now used to displace the current point P along its normal direction N, after transforming both to a user-specified space:

```
point PP = transform(space,P);
normal NN = ntransform(space,N);
PP += dispscale*lum*NN;
```

As you know, because of the displacement, the existing normal vector is not valid anymore, so we ask to recalculate it:

```
PP = transform(space,"current",PP);
N = calculatenormal(PP);
```

The last part of the shader optionally sets the outgoing current point P to the displaced value PP, if the user specifies displacement mapping (as opposed to bump mapping; with this option we do not modify P, leaving it to the normal recalculation to result in an apparent look of displacement).

```
// bump or true displacement
if(1==bumpordispl)
  {
    P = PP;
  }
```

As an alternative to displacing along a single normal vector direction by a single luminance value, you can try using R, G, and B for three separate displacements, along dPdu, dPdv, and N, respectively (or even along three directions input to the shader). This variation is somewhat related to the discussion that follows.

```
displacement texdisplace(
              string txnm="";
              float dispscale=1.0;
              float blur=0, bumpordispl=1;
              string space="shader";
          )
{
  // look up colors, calc. luminance
  float r,g,b;
  r = float texture(txnm[0],s,t,"blur",blur);
  g = float texture(txnm[1],s,t,"blur",blur);
  b = float texture(txnm[2],s,t,"blur",blur);
  float lum = 0.3*r + 0.6*g + 0.1*b;

  // apply along normal
  point PP = transform(space,P);
  normal NN = ntransform(space,N);
  PP += dispscale*lum*NN;

  // back to current space
  PP = transform(space,"current",PP);
  N = calculatenormal(PP);

  // bump or true displacement
  if(1==bumpordispl)
    {
      P = PP;
    }
}// texdisplace()
```

Figure 13.13 Texture-based displacement.

Our next example (see Figure 13.14) illustrates the very useful idea of normal mapping. The top row of the figure illustrates the classic bump and displacement techniques, while the bottom row shows the relatively new technique of using a normal map. Normal mapping involves looking up a surface normal vector at each shading point in a map and simply setting N to that value. Instead of using scalar values to displace along surface normals, we use vector (derived from RGB) values to replace existing normals. You can see that the normal map results are superior to those of bump/displacement mapping.

We first generate a displacement map to use for our bump/displacement/normal mapping comparisons. This is done using the gen_dispmap surface shader. We create Voronoi cells using cellnoise() just as we have done a couple of times before, and at the current shading location, use the nearest feature point (Voronoi seed) and its distance to derive a grayscale value:

```
//////////////////////////////
vor_f1_3d(freq*P,jitter,d,Pf);
//////////////////////////////
d = pow(d,gamma);
d = mix(d,1-d,mixf);
float vordisp = length(d*normalize(Pf-P));
```

The grayscale is what is returned by the shader via Ci. By varying the mixf mixing factor, we can cause the feature points to be dark and the cell "walls" to be brighter, or vice versa. This causes a pock-marked or bubble-like appearance, respectively. We apply this shader to a frame-filling square, looking down orthographically at it. The generated displacement map image is shown at the top left of Figure 13.14.

```
void vor_f1_3d (point P;
        float jitter;
        output float f1;
        output point pos1;
    )
{
  point thiscell = point (floor(xcomp(P))+0.5, floor(ycomp(P))+0.5,
                       floor(zcomp(P))+0.5);
  f1 = 10000;
  uniform float i, j, k;
  for (i = -1;  i <= 1;  i += 1) {
    for (j = -1;  j <= 1;  j += 1) {
      for (k = -1;  k <= 1;  k += 1) {
        point testcell = thiscell + vector(i,j,k);
        point pos = testcell +
        jitter * (vector cellnoise (testcell) - 0.5);
        vector offset = pos - P;
```

```
          float dist = offset . offset; /* actually dist^2 */
          if (dist < f1) {
             f1 = dist;  pos1 = pos;
          }
       }/* for k */
    }/* for j */
  }/* for i */
  f1 = sqrt(f1);
  f1 /= (1.732);
}


surface gen_dispmap(float freq=1,gamma=1,jitter=0,mixf=0;)
{
  float d;
  point Pf;

  ////////////////////////////////
  vor_f1_3d(freq*P,jitter,d,Pf);
  ////////////////////////////////

  d = pow(d,gamma);
  d = mix(d,1-d,mixf);


  float vordisp = length(d*normalize(Pf-P));

  Ci = color(vordisp,vordisp,vordisp);

}// gen_dispmap()
```

We now generate a normal map, which encodes surface normals as RGB colors. We use a Vordisp displacement shader together with a gen_normmap surface shader.

The Vordisp shader produces the same displacements as the gen_dispmap surface shader we used for creating a displacement map. The difference is that we cause actual displacements on our square geometry, causing new surface normals to be computed for the bumps and grooves. These normals are what are encoded in the normal map that will result from rendering our square using the Vordisp/gen_normmap combination.

```
void vor_f1_3d (point P;
                float jitter;
                output float f1;
                output point pos1;
            )
{
```

```
    point thiscell = point (floor(xcomp(P))+0.5, floor(ycomp(P))+0.5,
                      floor(zcomp(P))+0.5);
    f1 = 10000;
    uniform float i, j, k;
    for (i = -1;  i <= 1;  i += 1) {
      for (j = -1;  j <= 1;  j += 1) {
        for (k = -1;  k <= 1;  k += 1) {
            point testcell = thiscell + vector(i,j,k);
            point pos = testcell +
            jitter * (vector cellnoise (testcell) - 0.5);
            vector offset = pos - P;
            float dist = offset . offset; /* actually dist^2 */
            if (dist < f1) {
              f1 = dist;  pos1 = pos;
            }
        }
      }
    }
    f1 = sqrt(f1);
    f1 /= (1.732);
}

displacement Vordisp(float freq=1,gamma=1,jitter=0,disp=0.0, mixf=0;)
{
    float d;
    point Pf;

    /////////////////////////////
    vor_f1_3d(freq*P,jitter,d,Pf);
    /////////////////////////////

    d = pow(d,gamma);
    d = mix(d,1-d,mixf);


    P += disp*d*normalize(Pf-P);
    N = calculatenormal(P);

}// Vordisp()
```

The gen_normmap shader is very simple: It converts normals into RGB colors as
follows:

```
normal NN = normalize(N);

float nmapx = 0.5*(1+xcomp(NN));
float nmapy = 0.5*(1+ycomp(NN));
float nmapz = 0.5*(1+zcomp(NN));

Ci = color(nmapx,nmapy,nmapz);
```

Our version of the resulting normal map (shown at the bottom left of Figure 13.14) is called an *object space normal map*. In contrast, you can also try creating a tangent space normal (UVN) map by encoding magnitudes of dPdu, dPdv, and N in the R, G, and B channels. If you do this, you need to alter the map-usage code correspondingly (our version will be presented shortly).

```
surface gen_normmap()
{
  normal NN = normalize(N);

  float nmapx = 0.5*(1+xcomp(NN));
  float nmapy = 0.5*(1+ycomp(NN));
  float nmapz = 0.5*(1+zcomp(NN));

  Ci = color(nmapx,nmapy,nmapz);
}// gen_normmap()
```

Now that we have a displacement map and a normal map, we can apply them to a simple square in order to evaluate their relative merits. The normalmapper displacement shader performs displacement/bump mapping and normal mapping, too. These can be separately turned on/off using their scale factors Kdisp and Knorm, respectively. Additionally, the bumpordisp flag allows us to switch between bump and displacement mapping. These lead to six variations: bump only, displacement only, normal only, normal+displacement, normal+bump, and nothing at all. The last choice is there just for completeness, and of the remaining five, we compare the first four (normal+bump is not a useful variation).

The middle image in the top row of Figure 13.14 shows our Voronoi map used just as a bump map. As you are aware, the main problem here is that the clean, undisturbed silhouette gives away the fact that we are not truly displacing geometry. Additionally, some of the detail in the Voronoi cell arrangements is not captured when we use bump (or displacement) mapping, since the perturbations are always along the local normal.

The image at the top right of Figure 13.14 shows the displacement-mapping–only variation. The silhouette appropriately rises and falls in line with the bumps and grooves that lead up to it, creating more realism than bump mapping.

At the middle of the bottom row in Figure 13.14, you can see what applying just the normal map looks like. Compared to the bump-only version above it, you can see a heightened (pun intended) level of realism: The cells seem more rounded, as do the boundaries between them. For added measure, our choice of surface shader causes highlights to appear, something that was missing in the bump/displacement versions. As a reminder, normal mapping looks better than bump mapping because we retrieve from our map and directly set actual surface normals (which get stored in the form of a normal map from a prior operation). As good as the interior of the normal-mapped square looks, we have the same problem as with bump mapping, which is that the look of the silhouette does not match the rest of the surface.

To remedy the silhouette situation, we apply both displacement and normal mapping in concert. This produces the best outcome of all, as shown in the bottom right of Figure 13.14. The interior, as well as the silhouette, appears correctly displaced and shaded, too.

The bottom line is this. Normal+displacement mapping on a low-resolution surface can create a convincing alternative to using a corresponding high resolution surface. For instance, you could use a low-resolution version of a character's head and apply a suitable normal and displacement map to it, generating a look that can only be replicated by directly rendering (without maps) an impossibly high-resolution surface. This is what makes normal mapping attractive to game developers in particular and in movie-related CG as well. A variety of tools and techniques exist to generate normal/displacement map combinations, starting with a high-resolution and low-resolution pair of surfaces. These are outside the scope of this book, but a Web search will come up with useful links.

```
displacement normalmapper(
  float    Knorm = 1.0;
  float bumpordisp=0, reverse=0;
  float Kdisp=0;
  string   nmapnm = "", dmapnm="")
{


  if((dmapnm!="")&&(Kdisp!=0))
    {
      float ss=s, tt=t;
      if(tt==1)tt=0.999;
      if(ss==1)ss=0.999;
      color Cdisp = texture(dmapnm,ss,tt);
      float vdisp = 0.3333*(comp(Cdisp,0)+comp(Cdisp,1)+comp(Cdisp,2));
      if(reverse)vdisp=-vdisp;
```

```
      point PP = P + Kdisp*vdisp*normalize(N);
      N = calculatenormal(PP);
      if(bumpordisp==1)
      P=PP;
   }


if((nmapnm!="")&&(Knorm!=0))
   {
      color Ct=texture(nmapnm,s,t,"width",0);

      // the normal is assumed to be encoded in object space
      // (not 'tangent', aka UVN space)
      float nx = 2*comp(Ct,0)-0.5;
      float ny = 2*comp(Ct,1)-0.5;
      float nz = 2*comp(Ct,2)-0.5;
      if(reverse)
      {
        nx = 1-nx;
        ny = 1-ny;
        nz = 1-nz;
      }
      normal NN = normalize(normal(nx,ny,nz));
      N = mix(normalize(N),NN,Knorm);
   }
}// normalmapper()
```

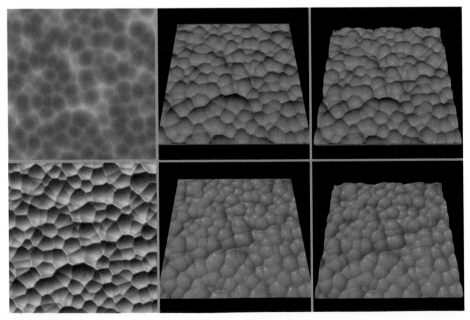

Figure 13.14 Normal mapping.

In addition to the use of normal mapping for increasing photorealism, there is also parallax mapping (also called *offset mapping*), where (s,t) coordinates are displaced in accordance with a displacement map before being used for texture access. Woven cloth, rocky walls, floorboards, and such can be made to display more apparent depth using this idea, which leads to enhanced realism. Another enhancement technique is called *polynomial texture mapping* or *PTM*, which is an image-based method that uses multiple maps (such as photographs) of a surface under varying lighting conditions. PTM helps portray surface deformations (similar to bump/displacement mapping) and also more subtle self-shadowing and inter-reflection effects, all of which again create a better sense of realism.

Multiple Maps

So far we have been using a single texture map in our shader examples, but this is not an RSL restriction—we are free to look up textures from more than one map via multiple texture() calls. We can combine the results of the lookups any way we want in order to derive a composite value. Four possibilities are shown in Figure 13.15.

The crossfade shader is used to create the image at the top left of Figure 13.15. At a given (s,t), it looks up textures in two different maps and then uses the t value as a blending fraction to transition from one texture to another:

```
Ci = Oi*mix(CtB,CtA,gainFunc(t,gain));
```

The t value is nonlinearly altered using the gainFunc() function before being used as the blend factor. This lets us control the width of the transition region.

```
float biasFunc(float t;float a;)
{
    return pow(t,-(log(a)/log(2)));
}


float gainFunc(float t; float a;)
{
  float g;
  if (t <=0.5)
  {
    g = 0.5*biasFunc(2*t, a);
  }
  else
  {
    g = 1.0 - 0.5*biasFunc(2.0-2*t,a);
  }
```

```
  return g;

}

surface crossfade(
    string txA="", txB="";
    float gain=0.5;
)
{
  Oi = Os;

  if((txA!="")&&(txB!=""))
    {
       color CtA = color texture(txA,s,t);
       color CtB = color texture(txB,s,t);

       // blend from top to bottom, using 't'
       Ci = Oi*mix(CtB,CtA,gainFunc(t,gain));
    }
  else
     Ci = Oi*Cs;
}// crossfade()
```

Our next example (top right of Figure 13.15 and `variblend` below) shows variable blending across the image. We look up textures from three maps and use the third value to blend the first two:

```
color CtA = color texture(txA,s,t);
color CtB = color texture(txB,s,t);
color CtBl = color texture(txBl,s,t);
float lum = 0.3*comp(CtBl,0)+0.6*comp(CtBl,1)+0.1*comp(CtBl,2);
lum = gainFunc(lum,gain);
Ci = Oi*mix(CtA,CtB,lum);
```

Here we are blending images of white and yellow flowers using luminance from a `letter S` texture map. You can use this shader to create transition image sequences between two still frames. Use a sequence of textures for the third (blender) input where the luminance of the map starts out as all black and gradually transitions to all white over a series of frames. Depending on what happens in between as black becomes white, you can create transitions between the first two inputs, ranging from simple dissolves and wipes to more complex, imaginative ones.

```
float biasFunc(float t;float a;)
{
```

```
     return pow(t,-(log(a)/log(2)));

}


float gainFunc(float t; float a;)
{
  float g;
  if (t <=0.5)
  {
    g = 0.5*biasFunc(2*t, a);
  }
  else
  {
    g = 1.0 - 0.5*biasFunc(2.0-2*t,a);
  }

  return g;

}


surface variblend(
    string txA="", txB="", txBl="";
    float gain=0.5;
)
{
  Oi = Os;

  if((txA!="")&&(txB!="")&&(txBl!=""))
    {
      color CtA = color texture(txA,s,t);
      color CtB = color texture(txB,s,t);
      color CtBl = color texture(txBl,s,t);

      float lum = 0.3*comp(CtBl,0)+0.6*comp(CtBl,1)+0.1*comp(CtBl,2);
      lum = gainFunc(lum,gain);

      Ci = Oi*mix(CtA,CtB,lum);
    }
  else
    Ci = Oi*Cs;
}// variblend()
```

At the bottom left of Figure 13.15 is another example that uses more than one map. In this case, we perform a two-level or indirect texture lookup. In other words, (s,t) is used to look up a color from a first map, and the (r,g) values of the color serve as a modified (s,t) to look up texture in a second map. This second lookup gets output from the shader. If the first texture map is generated via a shader with a Ci = color(s,t,0); assignment, you can see that the first-level indirection will have no effect: Looking up (r,g) at a given (s,t) in such a map will result in the same (s,t) for output. In other words, the two-level lookup reduces to a direct lookup of the second texture, which makes this a "no op" or default case.

If this default map is progressively distorted using a paint program, for example, the indirect lookup using the resulting textures will now cause the second map to undergo the same distortions. You can reuse the first map's progressive distortion sequence as a template to warp arbitrary images in an identical way.

In our "indirect" shader that does this two-level lookup, ss and tt are the texture coordinates that are used for the indirect lookup. As an extra control that lets us set the extent of the indirect lookup, we use a mixf blending factor to transition between the original incoming (s,t) and our (ss,tt).

```
ss = ss + (s-ss)*mixf;
tt = tt + (t-tt)*mixf;
Ci = Oi*color texture(txB,ss,tt);
```

You can also experiment with treating the (r,g) from the indirect texture result as yet another set of texture coordinates to look up texture back in the first image.

```
float biasFunc(float t;float a;)
{
   return pow(t,-(log(a)/log(2)));
}

float gainFunc(float t; float a;)
{
  float g;
  if (t <=0.5)
  {
    g = 0.5*biasFunc(2*t, a);
  }
  else
  {
    g = 1.0 - 0.5*biasFunc(2.0-2*t,a);
  }
```

```
    return g;


}

surface indirect(
    string txA="", txB="", txBl="";
    float mixf=0,gain=0.5;
)
{
  Oi = Os;

  if((txA!="")&&(txB!=""))
    {
       color Ctransfer = color texture(txA,s,t);

       float ss = gainFunc(comp(Ctransfer,0),gain);
       float tt = gainFunc(comp(Ctransfer,1),gain);

       ss = ss + (s-ss)*mixf;
       tt = tt + (t-tt)*mixf;

       Ci = Oi*color texture(txB,ss,tt);


    }
  else
     Ci = Oi*Cs;
}// indirect()
```

The last example that illustrates use of multiple maps is at the bottom right of Figure 13.15. The texcombine shader shows what is going on. We use the incoming (s,t) as is, but we derive outgoing color by looking up values in three different texture maps. (We are combining channels from multiple maps.) Each looked up value is itself a triplet (RGB), so we can either use just a single value from the triplet (R from the first lookup, G from the second, and B from the third) or combine the three values into a float. Here we choose to combine them using an approximation for the NTSC luminance formula via the lum() function. For extra effect, these luminance values are subjected to mod() and pow() functions. For example, with the first lookup we do this:

```
float r = lum(color texture(txA,s,t));
r = mod(r*rfreq,1.0);
r = pow(r,rgam);
```

While deriving Ci from the (r,g,b) triplets, we use a colspace string input to interpret the triplets either as R,G,B or as H,S,V.

```
float lum(color c)
{
  return 0.3*comp(c,0) + 0.6*comp(c,1) + 0.1*comp(c,2);
}// lum()
surface texcombine(
    string txA="", txB="", txC="";
    string colspace="rgb";
    float rfreq=1.0, gfreq=1.0,bfreq=1.0;
    float rgam=1, ggam=1, bgam=1;
)
{
  Oi = Os;

  if((txA!="")&&(txB!="")&&(txC!=""))
    {
      float r = lum(color texture(txA,s,t));
      r = mod(r*rfreq,1.0);
      r = pow(r,rgam);

      float g = lum(color texture(txB,s,t));
      g = mod(g*gfreq,1.0);
      g = pow(g,ggam);

      float b = lum(color texture(txC,s,t));
      b = mod(b*bfreq,1.0);
      b = pow(b,bgam);

      if("rgb"==colspace)
          Ci = Oi*color(r,g,b);
      else
          Ci = Oi*color "hsv" (r,g,b);
    }
  else
    Ci = Oi*Cs;
}// texcombine()
```

You can experiment with bringing multiple texture maps into a shader and combining them using Photoshop-like layer combination modes, such as add, multiply, darken, dodge, and so on. As you combine textures you can also rotate, scale, and translate them over a surface and restrict them to parts of it (using the alpha channel). Such techniques let you break up the pristine look of typical CG surfaces to give them a "dirty" or weathered appearance.

Figure 13.15 Ways of combining multiple texture maps.

Additional Details

We have used the texture() call numerous times in shaders throughout this chapter, and almost all of them have been of the form

```
color c = texture(texmapname);
```

or

```
color c = texture(texmapname,s,t);
```

This section points out additional/optional parameters you can pass to the texture() call to exercise more control over the texture access.

The first of the additional parameters is blur, which specifies an extra area (expressed in texture coordinate space units) to be added to the default area being filtered in both s and t directions. This additional lookup area causes the texture result to appear that much more blurry. A value of 1.0 means that the entire texture would be blurred in order to produce our result, while a value of 0.001 when applied to a 1000×1000 pixel texture map would mean the addition of a single pixel along s and t (0.001×1000=1).

The texture_blur shader that follows shows how to specify blur, and Figure 13.16 shows the results. From top left to bottom right, the blur values used were 0, 0.01, 0.1, and 1.0.

```
surface texture_blur(
    string txnm="";
    float blurval=0.0;
)
{
  Oi = Os;

  if(txnm!="")
    Ci = Oi*color texture(txnm,s,t,"blur",blurval);
  else
    Ci = Oi*Cs;
}// texture_blur()
```

Figure 13.16 Varying the blur parameter in the texture() function call.

Another parameter used to fine-tune texture access is width (with a default value of 1.0), which acts as a multiplier for the area being filtered. The width value is multiplied with the width of the filtered area along both s and t.

The following texture_width shader shows the use of this parameter, and Figure 13.17 shows the results. The image used to create the texture map for this example is pixilated on purpose for illustration purposes. In the figure, from top left to bottom right, the width values employed were 0, 1, 2 and 5. The top-right "control" image results from using the default value of 1.0 for width. The bottom images appear blurrier, resulting from larger width multiplier values of 2 and 5.

At the top left is a crispier result due to a width of 0—using 0 for the width parameter turns off texture anti-aliasing. In some cases, we do need unfiltered access to a texture, and that is when 0 is used as the width value.

```
surface texture_width(
    string txnm="";
    float wdval=0.0;
)
{
  Oi = Os;

  if(txnm!="")
    Ci = Oi*color texture(txnm,s,t,"width",wdval);
  else
    Ci = Oi*Cs;
}// texture_width()
```

Figure 13.17 Varying the filter width parameter in the texture() function call.

The texture() call also supports an optional filter attribute to specify the type of filter used while looking up texture values. The following texture_filter shader illustrates the use of the attribute, and Figure 13.18 shows a comparison between the box and Gaussian filter types. The box filter is quick but inaccurate, while the

Gaussian filter is more computer intensive and produces better results. The list of filters supported varies with RenderMan implementations. PRMan offers box, disk, Gaussian, Lagrangian, and radial-bspline filters.

```
surface texture_filter(
    string txnm="";
    string filternm="box";
)
{
  Oi = Os;

  if(txnm!="")
    // use "filter" to specify the type of filter via the filternm variable
    Ci = Oi*color texture(txnm,s,t,"filter",filternm,"blur",.1);
  else
    Ci = Oi*Cs;
}// texture_filter()
```

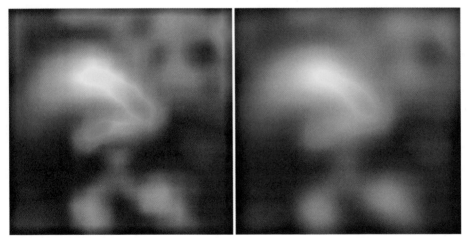

Figure 13.18 Use of box versus Gaussian filter types in the texture() function call.

Note that multiple optional parameters can occur in the same texture() call, in any order. This is demonstrated in the texture() call in the above texture_filter shader.

In addition to the blur, filterwidth, and filter type options discussed above, the texture() function usually has more implementation-dependent parameters that you can use to make better use of texture maps. Consult your renderer's documentation to find out what these extra flags are. For example, PRMan provides sblur, tblur (in addition to blur), swidth, twidth (in addition to width), and fill parameters.

Also, textureinfo() is a call you can use to query a texture map to find out its type (texture, shadow, or environment), resolution, number of channels, and so on.

For instance, you can use the resolution information to set an appropriate value of the `blur` parameter for accessing texture.

So far in this chapter, we have looked at a variety of ways in which texture maps are used, but we have not talked about what the maps themselves contain. In PRMan, the `txmake()` call takes as input a TIFF file and outputs a texture file (for which we use a customary `.tex` or `.tx` extension). This texture file is a MIP map, which is a collection of images derived from the input TIFF file. The idea is to represent the texture at smaller and smaller resolutions with attendant loss of detail. This mimics the way the eye or a physical lens system would perceive the texture as it recedes from the camera. Conceptually this is an "image pyramid," as pictured at the right of Figure 13.19. At the bottom of the pyramid is the original image. As we go up the levels, the resolution is halved. If the parent image is a square image with power-of -2 resolution for its side (such as 512 or 2,048), the topmost level of the pyramid will contain just a single pixel whose color represents the zoomed out average of the entire image.

The MIP map conceptualized at the right of Figure 13.19 is stored in a clever, efficient format shown at the left of the figure. The R,G, and B channels of the square parent image are laid out adjacent to each other, creating a square hole at the top-right quadrant. This hole can be used to lay out the next level (smaller) image's R, G, and B channels, and so on. Again, because of the power-of-2 resolution, the very last image's single pixel R, G, and B values will fit in a 2×2 square at the top-right corner, leaving the very last corner pixel blank. The entire MIP map fits in a next-higher power-of-2 square compared to the parent image and takes up one-third more size compared to the parent (not counting the alpha channel).

For the purposes of creating the MIP map representation shown in the left of Figure 13.19, the following shader was used to look up single-channel texture values from the texture map. As mentioned earlier, the `texturename[channel_number]` syntax is used to retrieve float values for a single channel, as opposed to an RGB color value.

```
surface onechantex(
                    string txnm="";
                    float chan=0;

)
{
  Oi = Os;

  if(txnm!="")
    {
      if(chan==0)
      {
        float r = float texture(txnm[0],s,t);
```

```
        Ci = Oi*color(r,0,0);
      }
      else if(chan==1)
      {
        float g = float texture(txnm[1],s,t);
        Ci = Oi*color(0,g,0);
      }
      else if(chan==2)
      {
        float b = float texture(txnm[2],s,t);
        Ci = Oi*color(0,0,b);
      }
    }
  else
    Ci = Oi*Cs;
}// onechantex()
```

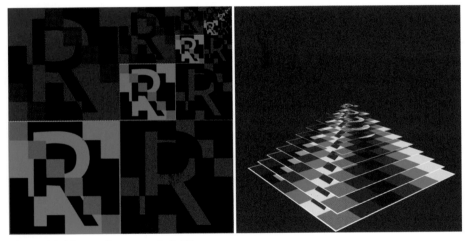

Figure 13.19 Visualizations of a MIP map.

We have also not talked about what happens when (s,t) values used to index into a texture map lie outside the 0 to 1 range. In other words, regardless of the resolution of the texture map, the dimensionless (s,t) pair of texture coordinates guarantees that a valid color is returned if both the coordinate values lie between 0.0 and 1.0, representing a point "somewhere inside the texture map." Outside the default 0 to 1 range, there are several possibilities for what color to return. Four of these are illustrated in Figure 13.20.

The first three (black, clamp, and periodic) are supported by all RenderMan implementations and can be specified during texture creation. For instance, the periodic mode is specified in PRMan this way:

```
txmake -mode periodic LetterR.tiff LetterR.tex
```

At the top left of Figure 13.20, you can see that the black mode simply returns black when (s,t) fall outside 0 to 1. At the top right is the clamp mode, where the edge values (white, in our texture map) are extended out. At the bottom left is the periodic mode, where the texture is tiled (this is equivalent to doing a mod(s,1.0) and mod(t,1.0) and using the resulting 0 to 1 values to look up the texture). At the bottom right, the mirrortex shader is used to mirror the texture at each of the four edges. Such mirroring works only when s and t lie between 1.0 and 2.0. You can also invent your own ways to deal with nondefault texture coordinate values (such as fade-out colors) depending on the needs of your application.

```
surface mirrortex(
        string txnm="";
)
{
  Oi = Os;

  if(txnm!="")
    {
      float ss,tt;
      if((s>=0)&&(s<=1))
      ss = s;
      else if (s<0)
      ss = abs(s); // mirror about '0'
      else if(s>1)
      ss = 1-(s-1); // mirror about '1'

      if((t>=0)&&(t<=1))
      tt = t;
      else if (t<0)
      tt = abs(t);
      else if(t>1)
      tt = 1-(t-1);

      Ci = Oi*color texture(txnm,ss,tt);
    }
  else
    Ci = Oi*Cs;
}// mirrortex()
```

Figure 13.20 Various texture access modes (black, clamp, periodic, and mirror).

PRMan's txmake() call was mentioned above when we talked about MIP map creation and texture access modes. This call has several other options, such as for specifying resizing and compression. Consult the documentation for particulars.

14

Raytracing

In this chapter, we will look at the RSL calls that enable us to add raytracing to our scenes. Raytracing involves following the path of rays that originate at the camera (reverse of real world rays that originate at light sources) and interact with surfaces in the scene, accumulating colors and opacities as they do so. Tracing rays allows us to obtain realistic effects such as reflection, refraction, and shadows in a straightforward, intuitive manner. In addition, we can also use the raytracing calls to create unusual effects such as the ones shown at the end of this chapter.

If you want to get a quick taste of raytracing, you can turn to the end of this chapter (to the "Miscellany" section) where we describe a way to get certain legacy shaders (even those from the very early days of RenderMan!) to raytrace. Feel free to experiment with that technique before returning here to resume reading.

Reflection, Refraction, Shadowing

Reflections, refractions, and shadows are ubiquitous in the real world. It is possible to add these phenomena to our RenderMan scenes without raytracing, but it is tedious to do so. For example, to add reflections to a surface, we need to do a pre-pass to render a reflection or environment map and then use the map in the actual pass to add in the reflections. Likewise, shadows are created using a shadow map, which is a depth map rendered from a light's point of view. In addition to necessitating multiple passes, these techniques are also limiting; for instance, it is very difficult to create multiple inter-reflections where several reflective surfaces in close proximity are seen reflecting each other. As we will see in this section, raytracing is a more natural method for creating reflections, refractions, and shadows.

The following one-line shader does raytraced reflection:

```
surface simpletrace()
{
  Ci = Cs + trace(P,reflect(I,N));
}
```

Figure 14.1 shows the shader applied to the blue ground plane to make it reflect the heap of spheres over it. A pair of directional lights and an ambient light illuminate the scene. The spheres themselves have a simple plastic shader applied to them, which creates two specular spots on each sphere—one for each directional light that illuminates it.

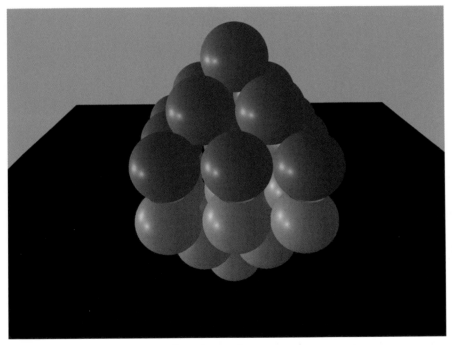

Figure 14.1 Raytraced spheres reflected on a plane.

If the ground plane had a matte, plastic, or some other simple shader applied to it, the spheres would not be reflected on it. But in our simpletrace shader, we enable raytracing using this expression:

```
trace(P,reflect(I,N))
```

The trace() call originates a single ray at a given location and along a given direction. In our case, the location is the current shading location P, and the direction is the reflection vector reflect(I,N). The ray continues along a straight path until one of two things happens. If the ray does not "hit" anything at all in the scene, the trace() call returns black. This is called a "ray miss." If the ray impinges upon a surface, this is a "ray hit." When a ray hits a surface, that surface's shader is invoked, and the resulting color produced by that shader is what is returned as the output of the trace() call. In this case, the ray hits return with the color from the shiny plastic spheres. In our simple shader, these raytraced colors are added to the surface color Cs via this statement:

```
Ci = Cs + trace(P,reflect(I,N));
```

At the edges of the base plane, the trace() call returns black, so the color of the surface is simply Cs. The traced sphere reflections make the surface rather bright at the middle. A useful addition would be a scale factor that controls the amount (strength) of reflection:

```
// Kr controls how much of the reflection is layered onto the base surface
Ci = Cs + Kr*trace(P,reflect(I,N));
```

This simple example was intended to show how easy it is to add raytracing capability to a surface shader. It also shows the hybrid nature of the scheme, where a scene can contain a mix of raytracing and ordinary (nonraytracing) shaders. Such a hybrid mix makes for very efficient rendering, where ray operations, which are rather expensive to compute, are deliberately invoked by the shader writer as needed.

Also, note that raytracing is recursive. If there were other objects that surrounded the spheres, and the spheres had a raytracing shader applied to them, the rays originating from our plane would kick off raytracing on the spheres as well, causing them to reflect the surrounding objects, as well as neighboring spheres. These complex reflections would all be reflected on the base plane. Further, if the surrounding objects also had raytracing shaders applied to them, the results would be that much more visually rich. The simplicity of the raytracing paradigm makes all this intuitively easy to understand, and the trace() call makes it equally easy to create such rich, detailed imagery.

The rt_refl shader shown below is a slightly more elaborate version of the simple shader that we just discussed. Here, a colorful base pattern is first computed using the sin() function, and raytracing is added to it via the statement

```
Ci += Kr*trace(P,R);
```

where Kr is a scale factor for the reflection, and R is the vector along which rays are traced.

Figure 14.2 shows the shader applied to a trefoil knot surface. In the absence of other surfaces in the scene, the raytracing causes parts of the surface to be reflected onto other parts. At the top left, the base pattern is shown without any raytracing, for reference.

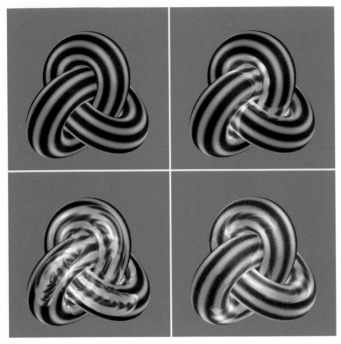

Figure 14.2 Raytraced reflections.

The top right image is calculated using the usual value of R, which is

```
vector R = reflect(In,Nf);
```

We can also experiment with alternate directions along which rays can be traced. The bottom left image in Figure 14.2 is obtained with values of R taken to be

```
R = reflect(Nf,In);
```

In other words, we reflect the surface normal about the camera vector (instead of the other way around) and use the result to trace rays. Likewise, the noisy image at the bottom right of Figure 14.2 results from this value of R:

```
R = normalize(vector(P)^Nf);
```

Here we use a physically meaningless vector obtained by crossing P with Nf. This quantity does not vary smoothly along the surface, even though the surface itself is smooth, resulting in grainy-looking, incoherent reflections. The point of such experimentation is that unusual patterns are easy to obtain using creative choices for the ray direction. You might use such patterns at a low strength to add interest to an otherwise dull surface.

```
surface rt_refl(float Kr=1.0;)
{
  vector In = normalize(I);
  vector Nf = faceforward( normalize(N), In);

  Ci= 0.75*color(0.5*(1+sin(s*50)),0.5*(1+sin(t*50)),1);

  if(Nf.-In>0)
  {
    // reflect I about N - "proper" way
    vector R = reflect(In,Nf);

    // expt.
    R = reflect(Nf,In);

    // expt
    R = normalize(vector(P)^Nf);

    Ci +=  Kr*trace(P,R);
  }
}
```

Note that you can also modify the reflection vector using noise to make the reflection look warped. For example:

```
R *= noise(R);
or
vector noiseP = noise(P);
R += 0.5*(vector(-1,-1,-1)+2*noiseP);
```

Next, we consider refractions, where light rays appear to "bend" (deviate from their original path) as they enter and exit translucent materials such as glass. The illustration at the top right of Figure 14.3 shows a ray undergoing refraction twice, as it enters and exits the spherical surface.

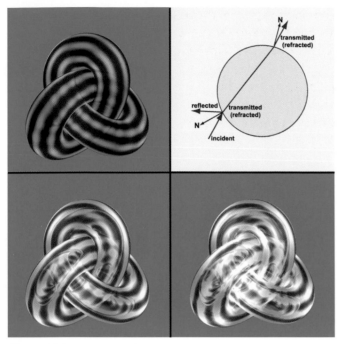

Figure 14.3 Raytraced refractions.

Snell's Law is used to calculate the refraction angle given the incident angle and index of refraction. Index of refraction is a material property that is defined to be 1.0 for air and is greater than 1.0 for denser materials. In RSL, we use the refract() call to calculate the refraction direction given an incident direction. In the rt_refr shader below, refraction direction is calculated as follows:

```
vector Refr = refract(In, Nf, (Nf.-In)>0 ? eta : 1/eta );
```

We pass the function either the user-defined eta index of refraction value or its inverse, depending on whether the incident ray In enters the surface or exits it. Whether In enters or exits the surface is determined by the sign of (N.-In), where -In points from the surface toward the camera. More precisely, eta is of relative index of refraction—it is the ratio of the *refractive* index of the incident volume to that of the entered volume. That is the reason why we use eta as-is or its inverse, depending on which we consider the entering versus exiting medium (eg., air-to-glass or glass-to-air).

Note that as an alternative to using refract() and reflect() separately for calculating the reflection and refraction vectors, we could use the fresnel() call to obtain both the vectors as its output. As a bonus, fresnel() also returns the relative strengths of the reflected and transmitted (refracted) rays. We can use these as scale factors to modulate reflected and refracted colors, thereby adding more realism to our renders.

The rest of the images in Figure 14.3 show the application of rt_refr to the tre-foil surface we used in the previous example. Again, the top left image shows just the sin()-derived pattern on a translucent surface without reflection or refraction. The bottom left image shows what refraction looks like for an eta value of 1.5. Finally, at the bottom right, both refraction and reflection are applied using strength values of 0.5 for both Krefr and Krefl. Even with absence of nearby sur-faces, you can see that the combination of reflection and refraction creates a glass-like appearance of the surface.

```
surface rt_refr(float Krefl=1.0, Krefr=1.0, eta=1.5)
{
  vector In = normalize(I);
  vector Nn = normalize(N);
  vector Nf = faceforward(Nn, In);

  // base
  Ci= 0.75*color(0.5*(1+sin(s*50)),0.5*(1+sin(t*50)),1);

  // refr.
  vector Refr = refract( In, Nf, (N.-In)>0 ? eta : 1/eta );
  Ci += Krefr * trace(P,Refr);

  // refl
  if(Nf.-In>0)
  {
    vector Refl = reflect(In,Nf);
    Ci +=  Krefl*trace(P,Refl);
  }

  Oi=Os;
  Ci *= Oi;
}
```

Given two points A and B, the transmission() RSL call is used to calculate the degree of visibility between the points. The transparency of intervening surfaces (if any) is used to calculate the degree of obstruction, so the result of transmis-sion() is a color value where (1,1,1) signifies no obstruction and (0,0,0) is total obstruction. This call can be used in light shaders to calculate shadows, which obviates the need for using depth maps for shadow calculations. The spotlight_rts light shader shown below is a modification of Pixar's spotlight shader. After cal-culating spotlight's outgoing color Cl using

```
Cl = strength*atten*intensity*lightcolor;
```

we scale it using the result of a transmission() call as follows:

```
Ct = transmission(Ps, from, "samples", samples, "samplecone", blur);
Cl *= Ct;
```

In this case, from is the location of the light, and Ps is the shading point location. The left image in Figure 14.4 shows raytraced shadows of a stellated polyhedron obtained using our spotlight_rts shader.

```
light spotlight_rts(
    float intensity = 1;
    float falloff=2.0;
    color lightcolor = 1;
    point from = point "shader" (0,0,0);
    point to = point "shader" (0,0,1);
    float coneangle=radians(30);
    float conedeltaangle=radians(5);
    float samples=1;
    float blur=0;
    float bias=0;
    )
{
  uniform vector A = (to-from)/length(to-from);
  uniform float cosoutside= cos(coneangle);
  uniform float cosinside = cos(coneangle-conedeltaangle);
  float atten, cosangle;
  float strength, ldist;
  color Ct;

  illuminate(from,A,coneangle)
  {
    cosangle = L.A / length(L);
    atten = smoothstep( cosoutside, cosinside, cosangle );
    ldist=length(L);
    strength = pow((1+ldist),-falloff);
    Cl = strength*atten*intensity*lightcolor;  // light

    Ct = transmission(Ps, from, "samples", samples, "samplecone", blur);
    Cl *= Ct;
  }
}//spotlight_rts
```

The soft shadows are obtained by specifying multiple samples and a non-zero "samplecone" angle parameter in our transmission() call. In this case, a sampling cone is set up with the first argument to transmission() as the apex, and visibility is computed as the average of multiple sample paths in this cone, which approximates the effect of a broad light source (hence the soft shadows). To obtain the image shown, eight samples and a cone angle of 0.075 radians were used.

Given that transmission() computes visibility between points, it is ideal for creating colored, transparent shadows as would result from stained glass. The right image in Figure 14.4 shows an example.

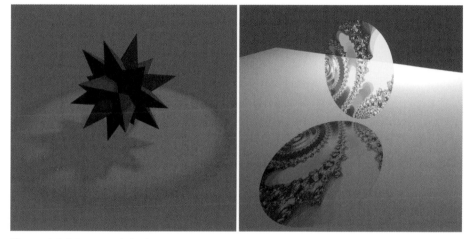

Figure 14.4 Raytraced shadows.

Here, a pointlight raytracing shader is used to obtain the shadows. The surface is colored using the stainedglass shader shown below. The shader looks up color in a texture map and saturates it using the powcol() function:

```
color Ctx = texture(texnm,ss,tt);
...
Ci = powcol(Ctx,colsat);
```

It also sets the opacity Oi to be

```
Oi = opascale*(1 - Ctx);
```

This makes the darker colors opaque and the lighter ones transparent. The pointlight_rts shader lights the stained glass surface and also creates a colored, transparent shadow on the ground plane under it:

```
// code snippets from Pixar's 'pointlight_rts' shader:
...
Cl = intensity * lightcolor * pow(dist, -falloff);
...
Cl *= transmission(Ps, from, "samples", s);
```

Just like with `spotlight_rts`, the output of `transmission()` is used to scale outgoing light color Cl, thereby generating shadows where the points being illuminated are fully/partially blocked by other surfaces.

```
color powcol(color c;float p)
{
  float r = pow(comp(c,0),p);
  float g = pow(comp(c,1),p);
  float b = pow(comp(c,2),p);

  return color "rgb" (r,g,b);
}

surface stainedglass(string texnm="";float opascale=1.0;float colsat=1.0)
{
  if (texnm != "")
  {
    point Po = transform("object",P);
    float ss = 0.5*(1+xcomp(Po));
    float tt = 0.5*(1+ycomp(Po));

    color Ctx = texture(texnm,ss,tt);
    Oi = opascale*(1 - Ctx);
    Ci = powcol(Ctx,colsat);

  }
}
```

Distributed Tracing

As we saw in Figure 14.2's bottom right image, tracing single rays can sometimes give rise to "noisy" (grainy) renders. The issue is one of adequate sampling. A single ray impinging on a surface is inadequate for capturing the richness of detail in the neighborhood where the ray hits the surface. This is somewhat analogous to trying to infer the entire concentric bulls-eye pattern on a dartboard by throwing a single dart on it and reading off the color at the point where the dart pierces the board. Using just a single dart will simply not do. But we get better results by using more and more darts to cover the surface of the dartboard in an even manner. Likewise, with raytracing, using a collection of rays instead of a single one helps to sample the surface better, leading to a less noisy image.

The top row of Figure 14.5 shows the difference between using single rays (left) and a distribution of them (right). The distributed raytracing version is much better.

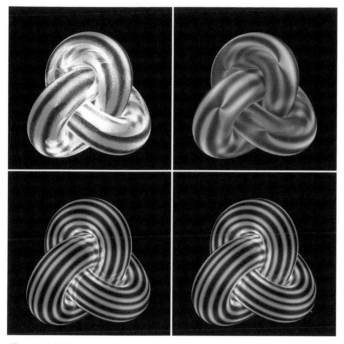

Figure 14.5 trace() versus gather() calls.

The left image is very similar to the noisy image in Figure 14.2. The simplegather shader shown next is used to obtain the images at the top of Figure 14.5. At the top of the shader we see the now-familiar formula for the sin()-based pattern we have been using. Following that, we calculate a physically unreal R vector just as we did earlier in Figure 14.2.

The gather() call that follows is what enables distributed raytracing. Technically, gather() is not a traditional function call, but is rather a loop with conditions inside parentheses and a loop body within curly braces. By way of comparison, illuminance(), illuminate(), and solar() are loops, too. These formulations, along with the traverse() loop that we will encounter in the next section, are called *block statement constructs*.

The gather() statement needs at least five parameters: sampling category (in the shader below, this is illuminance), origin and direction for the distributed rays (these are P and R, respectively, in our shader), a half-angle for a sampling cone whose apex is at the specified origin and is centered along the specified sampling direction. The fifth required parameter is the number of samples, the number of distributed rays to generate inside the sampling cone. The gather() loop can also contain a number of additional inputs, several of which you will encounter in subsequent shaders. In our simplegather shader, we specify a ("surface:Ci",hitcol) pair, where `surface:Ci` instructs `gather()` to use the distributed rays to fetch the surface shader's `Ci` value at locations where the rays hit a surface, and `hitcol` is our own local color variable, which we pass in for fetching the `Ci` result.

Each distributed ray hit fetches a value via the `hitcol` variable and causes the body of the loop to execute. This gives us a way to use the resulting `hitcol` values any way we want. The most common thing to do is to accumulate the values and average them, which is what our shader does.

The top left image in Figure 14.5 is obtained by setting the sampling cone angle to 0 degrees. Degrees are converted to radians via the `radians(coneangle)` call and setting the sample count to 1.

Used this way, the `gather` loop reduces to a single `trace()` call. The better image at the top right results from using a cone angle of 10 degrees and a sample count of 10. This simple example illustrates the dramatic difference between distributed raytracing versus tracing single rays. Where possible, you should use `gather()` instead of `trace()`. Also, as mentioned above, `gather()` allows several additional inputs which provide a great deal of control over the tracing process. This is another reason to prefer it over `trace()`.

Speaking of distributing rays, you can specify one of two types of distributions in the `gather` call:

```
gather(.....,"distribution","cosine",...)
{

}
or
gather(.....,"distribution","uniform",...)
{


}
```

A `uniform` distribution generates rays that uniformly fill the sampling cone from the apex to the periphery, whereas a `cosine` distribution uses the `cos()` function to concentrate most of the sample rays around the apex.

```
surface simplegather(float nsamp=1, coneangle=0)
{
  vector In = normalize(I);
  vector Nf = faceforward( normalize(N), In);

  Ci= 0.75*color(0.5*(1+sin(s*50)),0.5*(1+sin(t*50)),1);

  if(Nf.-In>0)
  {
```

```
    vector R = normalize(vector(P)^Nf);
    color hitcol=0;
    float nhits=0;
    gather("illuminance", P, R, radians(coneangle), nsamp, "surface:Ci",
    hitcol)
    {
      Ci += hitcol;
      nhits += 1;
    }
    Ci /= nhits;
  }
}
```

The ray distribution mechanism used in the gather() loop results from a sophisticated implementation (which is not exposed to the shader writer). In the gathersim below, we show a relatively crude way to generate distributed rays, just to provide a feel for the process. The gathersim shader is used to generate the pair of images at the bottom of Figure 14.5. In this shader, we use the standard reflection direction to trace rays.

```
vector R = normalize(reflect(I,Nn));
```

We need to create distributed rays inside a cone whose axis is R, so we create an orthogonal (mutually perpendicular) coordinate system R-X-Y using R and the normalized surface normal Nn:

```
vector X = normalize(R^Nn);
vector Y = normalize(Nn^X);
```

The ray sampling directions are generated inside the subsequent for() loop. We use a pair of uniformly distributed random numbers e1 and e2 to generate each ray direction:

```
e1 = conesize*random();
e2 = random();
// reflDir lies in a cone, with R being the cone axis. e1
// determines R's contribution, while e2 determines relative
// contributions of X and Y
vector refldir = normalize((X*(sqrt(e1)*cos(2*PI*e2)))
+(Y*(sqrt(e1)*sin(2*PI*e2))) +(R*sqrt(1-e1)));
```

As an exercise, you can try to derive the above equation for reflDir, or at least convince yourself that it produces meaningful directions inside the sampling cone by substituting different values for e1 and e2 in it.

Another thing to try is to use a "low discrepancy sequence," such as the Sobol, Halton or Hammersley sequence, to create evenly distributed sampling ray directions (see Chapter 16, "Beyond RSL: DSO Shadeops" for a way to calculate points of the Halton sequence).

The image at the bottom left of Figure 14.5 is created using a sample cone angle of 0.02 radians and a sample count of 10, whereas the bottom right image results from a broader cone angle of .1 radians and a sample count of 10 again. You can see that using a wider cone broadens the boundary regions between reflecting and non-reflecting areas, as expected. It also makes the image noisier, since we are using the sample count for the bigger and smaller cones. You can experiment with using a larger count for the bigger cone to study its impact on the resulting image quality.

```
surface gathersim(float nsamp=1, conesize=0, Kr=0.5)
{
  Ci= 0.75*color(0.5*(1+sin(s*80)),0.5*(1+sin(t*80)),1);

  normal Nn = faceforward(normalize(N), I);
  float e1, e2;
  color Crt=0;
  float nhits=0;
  float i;

  // form an orthogonal system R-X-Y
  vector R = normalize(reflect(I,Nn));
  vector X = normalize(R^Nn);
  vector Y = normalize(Nn^X);

  for(i=0;i<nsamp;i+=1)
  {
    // note: 'e1' and 'e2' are more commonly referred to
    // as 'eta1' and 'eta2' in mathematical literature
    // describing such random processes, but we
    // use 'e1' and 'e2' instead, to avoid potential confusion related to
    // the use of 'eta' in fresnel() or refract()
    e1 = conesize*random();
    e2 = random();
    // reflDir lies in a cone, with R being the cone axis. e1
    // determines R's contribution, while e2 determines relative
    // contributions of X and Y
    vector refldir = normalize((X*(sqrt(e1)*cos(2*PI*e2)))
    +(Y*(sqrt(e1)*sin(2*PI*e2))) +(R*sqrt(1-e1)));
    Crt += trace(P,refldir);
    nhits += 1;
```

```
    }

    Crt /= nhits;
    Ci += Kr*Crt;
}
```

Ray Continuation

When a ray hits a semitransparent surface, that surface's color and transparency get evaluated as usual, and the ray is automatically continued through the surface in order to reach a surface that might lie behind it. If there is a surface, its shader gets evaluated, and the results are combined with those of the first surface. If the second surface is also semitransparent, the ray continues further, and so on. This is convenient for the user because the right thing (accumulation of encountered colors and opacities) happens automatically. But what if we need explicit control over the ray's continuation? In this section, we'll show two different ways to achieve this.

The vignette shader is used to create the three semitransparent disks shown in Figure 14.6.

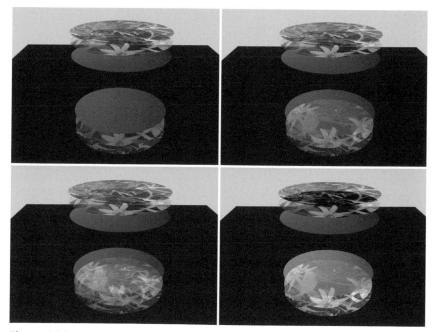

Figure 14.6 Ray continuation through semitransparent surfaces.

The shader cuts out circular regions on the surface over which it is applied (squares in this case) using texture coordinates:

```
float d = sqrt((ss-0.5)*(ss-0.5)+(tt-0.5)*(tt-0.5));
Oi = Os;
Ci = Cs;

if(txnm!="")
{
  Ci *= color texture(txnm,ss,tt);
  if(d>vig_rad)
  {
    Oi=0;
  }
}
```

The shader is shown in its entirety below, but its workings are secondary to the discussion that ensues. You should be able to use your own shaders if you like and still follow along.

```
float scale_coord(float u, sc)
{
  float rslt;

  rslt = u-0.5;
  rslt *= sc;
  rslt += 0.5;
  return rslt;
}// scale_coord

void rot_coord(float ss,tt,rot; output float sr,tr)
{
  float sss, ttt, s2, t2;

  sss = ss-0.5;
  ttt = tt-0.5;

  float ra = rot*PI/180.0;
  float cra = cos(ra), sra=sin(ra);

  s2 = sss*cra - ttt*sra;
  t2 = sss*sra + ttt*cra;

  s2 += 0.5;
  t2 += 0.5;
```

```
  sr = s2;
  tr = t2;
}// rot_coord


float tr_coord(float u, tr)
{
  return (u+tr);
}// tr_coord

surface vignette(
    string txnm="";
    float flip_s=0, flip_t=0;
    float tx=0, ty=0, rot=0, scale=1.0;
    float srep=1., trep=1.;
    float vig_rad=0.5;
    color bg=1;
    float falloff=1;
)
{
  float ss, tt;
  color wh=color(1,1,1);

  if(flip_s!=0)
    ss = 1-s;
  else
    ss = s;

  if(flip_t!=0)
    tt = 1-t;
  else
    tt = t;

  // scale
  ss = scale_coord(ss,scale);
  tt = scale_coord(tt,scale);

  // rotate
  rot_coord(ss,tt,rot,ss,tt);

  // translate
  ss = tr_coord(ss,tx);
  tt = tr_coord(tt,ty);
```

```
// repeat
ss = mod(ss*srep,1.0);
tt = mod(tt*trep,1.0);

ss = clamp(ss,0,1);
tt = clamp(tt,0,1);

float d = sqrt((ss-0.5)*(ss-0.5)+(tt-0.5)*(tt-0.5));

Oi = Os;
Ci = Cs;

if(txnm!="")
{
    Ci *= color texture(txnm,ss,tt);
    if(d>vig_rad)
    {
        Oi=0;
    }
}

    Ci *= Oi;
}
```

The first three images (top left, top right, and bottom left) in Figure 14.6 are created using the traversetrace shader shown below. As you can see from the images, there are three semitransparent disks with textures on them that hover over a reflective plane. The three images differ as to how much the plane reflects. In the top left image, only the bottommost disk (closest to the plane) is reflected fully. In the reflection it appears opaque and therefore obscures the other two disks behind it. In the top right image, the bottommost disk is not opaque, so the second disk is visible through it. However, that second disk is now opaque, obscuring the third disk. Finally, in the bottom left image, the second disk is also transparent and therefore makes the third visible.

In the traversetrace shader, we are able to control how far the ray reflected from the plane is able to continue through the three disks. We do so by enclosing a gather() call inside a for() loop that can run up to 100 times (which is overkill since we only need it to run at most three times). At the start of the loop, the ray origin for gather() is simply the surface point P on the plane (rayPt=P). Each time gather() runs, it fetches the surface color, opacity, and also the location on the surface where the ray hits it (note that we are sending out a single ray):

```
gather("illuminance",rayPt,R,0,1,
       "othreshold",color(.001,.001,.001),
       "surface:Ci", hitcol,"surface:Oi",hitopa,
       "primitive:P",hitpt)
{
}
```

The "primitive:P",hitpt specification is where we request gather() to return us the point location via our variable hitpt. Also, note the "othreshold", color(.001,.001,.001) specification, which tells gather() to treat any surface with an opacity greater than (0.001,0.001,0.001) to be opaque. Our low threshold guarantees that the three disks, though semitransparent, will be deemed opaque by our gather() loop. An opaque surface will cause ray continuation to terminate. Without this specification, gather() will continue to advance rays through all our three surfaces, frustrating our attempt to do so manually.

Inside the gather() loop, we accumulate both the color and opacity. When the opacity exceeds a user-defined threshold, we terminate the loop. The three images in Figure 14.6 were generated using thresholds of 0.5, 0.75, and 1.5. In the body of the loop, we also set the rayDir variable's value to the location of the current hit point, thereby enabling the next gather() ray to originate there. This is how we effect our own ray continuation by propagating rays from one surface to the next, along a fixed direction.

```
surface traversetrace(float othresh=0.5)
{

  vector In = normalize(I);
  vector Nn = normalize(N);
  vector Nf = faceforward( normalize(N), In);

  Ci = Cs;
  if(Nf.-In>0)
  {
    vector R = reflect(In,Nn);

    color Caccum=0, Oaccum=0., hitcol=0, hitopa=0, wh=color(1,1,1),
    bl=color(0,0,0);
    point hitpt=0, rayPt=P;
    float nhits=0;
```

```
Ci = Cs;
Oi = Os;
float i;
float tmpo=0;

for(i=0;i<100;i=i+1)
{
  gather("illuminance", rayPt, R, 0,1,"othreshold",color
  (.001,.001,.001),"surface:Ci", hitcol,"surface:Oi",
  hitopa,"primitive:P",hitpt)
  {
    Oaccum += (hitopa);
    Caccum += (hitcol*hitopa);
    rayPt=hitpt;

    if(comp(Oaccum,0)>othresh) // .5, .75, 1.5
    {
      i=100; // break;
    }


  }
  else
  {
    Ci = Cs;
    i=100; // break;
  }
}// next intersection

Ci += 1.*Caccum;
Ci *= Os;
  }
}
```

As an alternative to using a for() loop around gather(), we can use traverse(), which is a loop construct provided specifically to take control of ray continuation. The shader that uses this, raytraverse, is shown below. We use it to generate the bottom left image in Figure 14.6, which resembles the top left one (examine traversetrace and raytraverse to see why the images are not identical, and try to make them so).

The shader resembles the previous one a lot, except for the obvious replacement of for() and gather() with traverse(). The body of the traverse() loop is executed each time a ray hit occurs (there is no need to force it to do so as we did using othreshold in the previous shader):

```
traverse("illuminance", P, R,"surface:Ci", hitcol,"surface:Oi", hitopa)
{
  ...
}
```

For each ray hit, we are asking traverse() to provide Ci and Oi at the hit location. We accumulate the color and opacity inside the loop and break out of it when the accumulated opacity exceeds a user specified threshold. (In this case, it is the same threshold value of 0.75 that we used with the previous shader to generate the comparable image.)

```
surface raytraverse(float othresh=0.5)
{

  vector In = normalize(I);
  vector Nn = normalize(N);
  vector Nf = faceforward( normalize(N), In);

  Ci = Cs;
  if(Nf.-In>0)
  {
    vector R = reflect(In,Nf);

    color Caccum=0, Oaccum=0, hitcol=0, hitopa=0, wh=color(1,1,1),
    bl=color(0,0,0);

    float n=0;
    traverse("illuminance", P, R,"surface:Ci", hitcol,"surface:Oi",
    hitopa)
    {

      Oaccum += (hitopa);
      if(comp(Oaccum,0)>othresh)
      {
        Oaccum -= (hitopa);
        break;
      }
      else
      {
        Caccum += (hitcol);
      }
    } // traverse

    Ci += Caccum;
```

```
    Ci *= Os;

   }
}
```

Collaborative Shading

In the early days of RenderMan and RSL, shader execution took place in a restricted environment. Predefined global variables brought into a shader the graphics state it needed to do its calculations, and additional user-settable parameters were specified in RIB files and were passed to the shader via its argument (parameter) list. Other than these, shaders ran "blind," not being aware of neighboring surfaces, extra attributes such as surface names, or options set for the rendering. But with today's RenderMan the blinders have come off, so to speak, and a shader has access to a rich environment, including attributes and options and even values output by other shaders. Such an expanded "awareness" in a shader makes it possible for us to achieve creative shading effects that were simply not available before. In this subsection, we show five examples of how gather() can work together with the shaders that it invokes during its ray hits. We will see that the gathering shader and hit shader can work in concert via message-passing.

Our first example is shown at the left of Figure 14.7. The pair of teapots shown have identical raytracing (reflective) shaders applied to them, and the ground plane on which they sit has a different raytracing shader applied to it. The teapots are seen reflected on each other in the usual way, but their reflections on the ground appear desaturated, which is by design. We are using "ray labeling" to achieve this desaturating effect.

Figure 14.7 Use of ray label and primitives' name to compute shading.

The teapots' uselabel shader is shown below. It uses the rayinfo() call to obtain the name (label), if any, of the incoming ray that invoked it. rayinfo() fills an input string variable passed to it, with a ray label:

```
string raylabel = "";
rayinfo("label",raylabel);
```

The shader then does its own raytracing call using gather() as usual. Since this shader is applied to both teapots, it makes the teapots' reflections appear on each other as expected. As always, the Ci variable contains the outgoing color. By way of added functionality, the raylabel variable is now checked to see if the shader-invoking ray has a label called desatmirror (not all rays need to have labels), and if it does, the outgoing color in Ci is desaturated by working in HSV space and then transforming back to RGB:

```
// process Ci based on raylabel
if(raylabel=="desatmirror")
{
  color Cihsv = ctransform("rgb","hsv",Ci);
  setcomp(Cihsv,1,0); // saturation is component#1, set it to 0
  Ci = ctransform("hsv","rgb",Cihsv);
}
```

The uselabel shader can be considered to contain two parts—a generic one that invokes raytracing to produce output color, and an additional processing section that kicks in only for incoming rays labeled desatmirror.

```
surface uselabel(float Ka=1, Kd=1, Kr=1)
{
  vector Nn = normalize(N);
  vector In = normalize(I);
  vector R = reflect(In,Nn);
  vector Nf = faceforward(Nn,I);

  color rt=0, hitc=0;
  float nhits=0;

  string raylabel = "";
  rayinfo("label",raylabel);

  gather("illuminance",P,R,0,1,"surface:Ci",hitc)
  {
    rt += hitc;
    nhits += 1;
  }
```

```
  rt /= nhits;


  Oi = Os;
  Ci = Oi*Cs*(Ka*ambient() + Kd*diffuse(Nf) + Kr*rt);

  // process Ci based on raylabel
  if(raylabel=="desatmirror")
  {
    color Cihsv = ctransform("rgb","hsv",Ci);
    setcomp(Cihsv,1,0); // saturation is component#1, set it to 0
    Ci = ctransform("hsv","rgb",Cihsv);
  }
  // else leave Ci as-is
}
```

The obvious question is, where does the desatmirror label get assigned to incoming rays to uselabel? That happens in the gather_by_label shader shown below. This shader is applied to the ground plane that contains the pair of teapots. It also uses gather() to do its raytracing and labels rays inside that call:

```
gather("illuminance",P,R,0,1,"label","desatmirror","surface:Ci",hitc)
{
  rt += hitc;
  nhits += 1;
}
```

The "label", "desatmirror" token-value pair is what does the ray labeling. All the rays generated by this gather() call are labeled desatmirror, and the shaders that are invoked when these rays hit other surfaces can optionally use rayinfo() to discover this label and compute outgoing color appropriately. In this case the receiving uselabel shader simply desaturated the outgoing color when it was invoked by these desatmirror rays. The ground plane can be considered the "caller" surface, and the teapots are the "called" surfaces. Such caller/called surface pairs can communicate via ray labels, which is one way for them to do so.

```
surface gather_by_label(float Ka=1, Kd=1, Kr=1)
{
  vector Nn = normalize(N);
  vector In = normalize(I);
  vector R = reflect(In,Nn);
  vector Nf = faceforward(Nn,I);

  color rt=0, hitc=0;
  float nhits=0;
```

```
gather("illuminance",P,R,0,1,"label","desatmirror","surface:Ci",hitc)
{
  rt += hitc;
  nhits += 1;
}
rt /= nhits;
Oi = Os;
Ci = Oi*Cs*(Ka*ambient() + Kd*diffuse(Nf) + Kr*rt);
}
```

Another way the caller/called surface pair can communicate is for the called surface to return its own name to the caller. The caller can then use this information to modify the returned color/opacity as appropriate.

The right image in Figure 14.7 shows how this works. The teapots are then called surfaces and return their names via an ID to the caller, which is the ground plane. The calling shader modifies the teapots' colors based on their surface ID—the left teapot's color is partly desaturated, while the right teapot's color is fully desaturated.

The useattrname shader below, which is applied to the teapots, does raytracing as before using gather(). It also outputs an object ID based on the name of the surface to which it is applied. In a RIB file, a surface can be named as follows:

```
AttributeBegin
Attribute "identifier" "name" ["rightTeapot"]
ConcatTransform [-0.5 0 -0.866025 0 0 1 0 0 0.866025 0 -0.5 0 1 0 1 1]
Color [1 .65 0 ]
Surface "useattrname" "Ka" .4 "Kd" .6
# geometry specification
PointsGeneralPolygons [1 1 1 1 1 1 1 1
# ...
```

The Attribute "identifier" "name" mechanism is used to name the surface. This name can be queried inside a surface shader using the attribute() call:

```
// set objid, for caller (gather() to use)
string objname="";
attribute("identifier:name",objname);
if(objname=="leftTeapot")
  objid=1;
else if(objname=="rightTeapot")
  objid=2;
```

The name of the surface is returned via our objname string variable and is used to set the outgoing objid float variable. Other than returning the surface name coded as an ID, the shader does not do anything special. Note that the attribute() call can be used to retrieve a variety of attributes related to the graphic state of elements in the scene, such as surfaces and lights (these include *user-defined attributes*). Likewise, the option() call can be used to query standard implementation and user-defined options. The gather() call also be used to retrieve attributes:

```
float propval = 0;
gather(..., "attribute:user:someproperty", propval, ...)
{
  // now use propval
  // ...
}
```

Here is the useattrname shader:

```
surface useattrname(float Ka=1, Kd=1, Kr=1;output varying float objid=-1)
{
  vector Nn = normalize(N);
  vector In = normalize(I);
  vector R = reflect(In,Nn);
  vector Nf = faceforward(Nn,I);

  // set objid, for caller (gather() to use)
  string objname="";
  attribute("identifier:name",objname);
  if(objname=="leftTeapot")
    objid=1;
  else if(objname=="rightTeapot")
    objid=2;

  color rt=0, hitc=0;
  float nhits=0;

  gather("illuminance",P,R,0,1,"surface:Ci",hitc)
  {
    rt += hitc;
    nhits += 1;
  }
  rt /= nhits;
  Oi = Os;
  Ci = Oi*Cs*(Ka*ambient() + Kd*diffuse(Nf) + Kr*rt);
}
```

The gather_by_attrname shader below is applied to the ground plane containing the teapots. It makes a gather() call to fetch raytraced results from the teapots. In addition to fetching the surface color as usual via Ci, it also specifies that the called shader's outgoing objid also be returned:

```
gather("illuminance",P,R,0,1,"surface:Ci",hitc,"surface:objid",objid)
{
  ...
```

The surface:objid specification will result in the called shader's outgoing objid value being returned in a variable also called objid, which we pass to the gather() call. Note that if a shader does not output this variable, the surface:objid specification is ignored, and the objid variable's value will remain 0, which is the value that we use to initialize that variable. If the returned objid value is 1 or 2 (leftTeapot and rightTeapot, respectively), we modify the gathered Ci value by desaturating it by 50% or 100%.

Compared to the ray label-based approach, the variation here is that we let the called surface return a regular color and an additional surface ID and then modify the color based on the ID. If the ray label approach is a "push based" one where we send in a label for the called surface to use, the surface name approach can be thought to be a "pull based" one where the caller gets back additional data from the called surface and uses it to modify the called shader's result.

```
color desat(color c;float f)
{
  color chsv = ctransform("rgb","hsv",c);
  setcomp(chsv,1,f*comp(chsv,1));
  return ctransform("hsv","rgb",chsv);
}
surface gather_by_attrname(float Ka=1, Kd=1, Kr=1)
{
  vector Nn = normalize(N);
  vector In = normalize(I);
  vector R = reflect(In,Nn);
  vector Nf = faceforward(Nn,I);

  color rt=0, hitc=0, white=color(1,1,1);
  float nhits=0;
  float objid=0;

  gather("illuminance",P,R,0,1,"surface:Ci",hitc,"surface:objid",objid)
  {
    // process hitc, based on objid
    if(objid==1) // "leftTeapot"
    {
      hitc = desat(hitc,.5);
    }
    else if(objid==2) // "rightTeapot"
    {
```

```
        hitc = desat(hitc,0);
    }
    // else do nothing to hitc
    rt += hitc;
    nhits += 1;
  }
  rt /= nhits;
  Oi = Os;
  Ci = Oi*Cs*(Ka*ambient() + Kd*diffuse(Nf) + Kr*rt);
}
```

Figure 14.8 illustrates a couple more ways by which shaders can obtain extra information about the environment in which they are running. At the left of Figure 14.8 is again shown our teapot pair and ground plane. You can see that the reflections of the teapots appear desaturated to a smaller extent (50%) on the ground plane as well as to a larger extent (75%) on each other. The traced rays' depth value is used to desaturate reflected colors. Note that ray depth refers to the number of "bounces" a ray has undergone as it originates on one raytraced surface and is further propagated because of raytracing on the called surfaces. It is not a physical quantity. A ray depth of 0 signifies camera rays that originate at the image plane and have not yet been subjected to additional bounces.

Figure 14.8 Use of ray level (depth) and ray length to compute shading.

The useraydepth shader shown next shows how this works. It is the shader that is applied to the teapots. It uses the rayinfo() call with a depth argument to fetch ray depth:

```
float raydepth=-1;
rayinfo("depth",raydepth);
```

It does a `gather()` to compute reflection and then uses the ray depth value to desaturate the result:

```
if(raydepth==0) // camera rays
{
  Ci = desat(Ci,0.75);
}
else if(raydepth==1)
{
  Ci = desat(Ci,0.5);
}
else if(raydepth>=2)
{
  Ci = desat(Ci,0);
}
```

The primary interreflections of the teapots are caused by camera rays that impinge on the teapots, so they are desaturated by 75%. The rays emanating from the ground plane have a ray depth of 1, so they are desaturated 50%. The `gather_by_raydepth` ground plane shader shown below does nothing special at all. It simply calls `gather()`, which fetches the already desaturated teapot reflections.

```
color desat(color c;float f)
{
  color chsv = ctransform("rgb","hsv",c);
  setcomp(chsv,1,f*comp(chsv,1));
  return ctransform("hsv","rgb",chsv);
}

surface useraydepth(float Ka=1, Kd=1, Kr=1)
{
  vector Nn = normalize(N);
  vector In = normalize(I);
  vector R = reflect(In,Nn);
  vector Nf = faceforward(Nn,I);

  color rt=0, hitc=0;
  float nhits=0;

  float raydepth=-1;
  rayinfo("depth",raydepth);

  gather("illuminance",P,R,0,1,"surface:Ci",hitc)
  {
    rt += hitc;
```

```
      nhits += 1;
  }
  rt /= nhits;

  Oi = Os;
  Ci = Oi*Cs*(Ka*ambient() + Kd*diffuse(Nf) + Kr*rt);

  // process Ci based on raydepth
  if(raydepth==0) // camera rays
  {
    Ci = desat(Ci,0.75);
  }
  else if(raydepth==1)
  {
    Ci = desat(Ci,0.5);
  }
  else if(raydepth>=2)
  {
    Ci = desat(Ci,0);
  }
}

surface gather_by_raydepth(float Ka=1, Kd=1, Kr=1)
{
  vector Nn = normalize(N);
  vector In = normalize(I);
  vector R = reflect(In,Nn);
  vector Nf = faceforward(Nn,I);

  color rt=0, hitc=0;
  float nhits=0;

  // straightforward gather
  gather("illuminance",P,R,0,1,"surface:Ci",hitc)
  {
    rt += hitc;
    nhits += 1;
  }
  rt /= nhits;
  Oi = Os;
  Ci = Oi*Cs*(Ka*ambient() + Kd*diffuse(Nf) + Kr*rt);
}
```

On the right side of Figure 14.8, a different idea is used to fade out teapot reflections on the ground plane. Here, the teapots have a straightforward `simplegather` shader applied to them. This shader is the same as the `gather_by_raydepth` shader shown previously, where it was applied to the ground surface.

The ground plane now has a `gather_by_raylength` shader applied to it, which uses a variation of the `gather()` call that will fetch the total length of each traced ray. This length can be used to modify the called shader's `Ci` value, which is also fetched by `gather()`:

```
gather("illuminance",P,R,0,1,"ray:length",raylength,"surface:Ci",hitc)
{
  // fade hitc based on raylength
  float fade = fadescale*exp(-fadeexp*raylength);
  hitc *= fade;
....
```

The `ray:length` specification instructs `gather()` to return ray length in addition to the usual color resulting from `surface:Ci`. This length is returned via a `raylength` float variable that we pass in. The length is then used to derive an exponential falloff value as shown. We use the falloff to scale the hit color resulting from `gather()`. Longer rays result in a bigger falloff and hence a darker reflection, which is what causes the fading out of the reflection as can be seen in the figure.

As an aside, note that in addition to `ray:length`, you can also use `ray:origin` and `ray:direction` to obtain the origin and the direction, respectively, of a traced ray.

```
surface simplegather(float Ka=1, Kd=1, Kr=1)
{
  vector Nn = normalize(N);
  vector In = normalize(I);
  vector R = reflect(In,Nn);
  vector Nf = faceforward(Nn,I);

  color rt=0, hitc=0;
  float nhits=0;

  gather("illuminance",P,R,0,1,"surface:Ci",hitc)
  {
    rt += hitc;
    nhits += 1;
  }
  rt /= nhits;

  Oi = Os;
```

```
  Ci = Oi*Cs*(Ka*ambient() + Kd*diffuse(Nf) + Kr*rt);
}

surface gather_by_raylength(float Ka=1, Kd=1, Kr=1, fadeexp=1.,
fadescale=1.)
{
  vector Nn = normalize(N);
  vector In = normalize(I);
  vector R = reflect(In,Nn);
  vector Nf = faceforward(Nn,I);

  color rt=0, hitc=0;
  float nhits=0, raylength=0;

  gather("illuminance",P,R,0,1,"ray:length",raylength,"surface:Ci",hitc)
  {
    // fade hitc based on raylength
    float fade = fadescale*exp(-fadeexp*raylength);
    hitc *= fade;

    rt += hitc;
    nhits += 1;
  }
  rt /= nhits;
  Oi = Os;
  Ci = Oi*Cs*(Ka*ambient() + Kd*diffuse(Nf) + Kr*rt);
}
```

Our last example of gather()-based collaborative shading is shown in Figure 14.9. The teapots have a non-raytracing R_out shader applied to them. As shown below, R_out returns a reflection vector as output in addition to calculating Ci.

```
surface R_out(float Ka=1, Kd=1;output varying vector R=0)
{
  vector Nn = normalize(N);
  vector Nf = faceforward(Nn,I);

  vector In = normalize(I);
  R = reflect(In,Nn); // this is output

  Oi = Os;
  Ci = Oi*Cs*(Ka*ambient() + Kd*diffuse(Nf));
}
```

Figure 14.9 Fetching arbitrary shader output using a gather() call.

The gather_AO (AO stands for "arbitrary output") shader employs a version of gather() where we request the called shader's N value using primitive:N, and its outgoing R value via surface:R. We then normalize the resulting Nout and Rout vectors and turn them into positive 0..1 quantities so we can derive a color from them:

```
gather("illuminance",P,R,0,1,"primitive:N",Nout,"surface:R",Rout)
{
  vector Np = 0.5*(1+normalize(Nout));
  vector Rp = 0.5*(1+normalize(Rout));
  color C = mix(color(xcomp(Np),ycomp(Np),zcomp(Np,
  color(xcomp(Rp),ycomp(Rp),zcomp(Rp)),.5);
....
```

The primitive specification can be used to fetch global variables such as P, N, s, I, and so on without causing the hit surface's shader to run (we are not requesting a result color). Note that in our gather_AO shader, we cause the called R_out shader to run since we are requesting its surface:R value.

This example demonstrates that a surface's reflection does not have to match its look at all: We can request arbitrary values and/or global variables from a hit surface's shader and use these results to create the reflection.

```
surface gather_AO()
{
  vector In = normalize(I);
```

```
vector Nn = normalize(N);
vector Nf = faceforward(Nn,I);

Ci = Cs;
if(Nn.In >= 0)
{
  color hcol=0;
  vector Nout=0, Rout=0;
  vector R = reflect(In,Nn);
  float nhits = 0;
  // gather() N and computed 'R' from surf. shader
  gather("illuminance",P,R,0,1,"primitive:N",Nout,"surface:R",Rout)
  {
    vector Np = 0.5*(1+normalize(Nout));
    vector Rp = 0.5*(1+normalize(Rout));
    color C = mix(color(xcomp(Np),ycomp(Np),zcomp(Np)),
    color(xcomp(Rp),ycomp(Rp),zcomp(Rp)),.5);
    Ci += C;
    nhits += 1;
  }
  Ci /= nhits;
}


  Oi = Os;
  Ci *= Oi;
}
```

In this section we looked at several ways by which calling/called shaders can collaborate to create custom shaded results. You can try to think of even more creative uses for this extremely powerful mechanism.

Miscellany

We conclude this chapter with three somewhat unusual examples. The first is a fisheye lens shader, useful in creating spherically warped panoramic imagery. The idea is to place a square parallel to the camera, just past the clipping plane so that it fills the entire view. A raytracing shader applied to the square sends out rays into the scene, and the resulting image is entirely derived from the results of this shader. It is in this shader that we can simulate the use of a hemispherical lens to image the scene.

The fjs_fisheye shader shown below illustrates the process. The idea is to trace rays starting from the camera origin along directions calculated using shading point P in camera space:

```
// refer to the 'fjs_fisheye' shader for full source
varying point Pcam = transform("camera", P);
varying float ss = 0.5*xcomp(Pcam)/scale;
varying float tt = 0.5*ycomp(Pcam)/scale;
varying float r = sqrt(ss*ss + tt*tt);
varying float polar_angle = radians(lens_angle)*r;
varying float z = cos(polar_angle);
varying float x = sin(polar_angle)*ss/r;
varying float y = sin(polar_angle)*tt/r;
varying vector tracedir = vector "camera" (x, y, z);
```

At the center of the image where ss and tt are 0, the trace direction is simply (0,0,1). As we move away from the center, the direction diverges from (0,0,1), creating a cone of sampling rays. This is what creates the effect of a fisheye lens.

```
/*
 *----- fjs_fisheyelens.sl
 *
 * Description:
 *    A near clip-plane shader that uses raytracing to provide
 *    a simple fisheye lens for the camera.
 *
 * Usage:
 *    User must define a square polygon just beyond the
 *    near clip-plane distance. Generally, this polygon
 *    fills the entire viewing frustum.
 *
 *    This shader is applied to the polygon, and the user
 *    should specify the polygon placement and the maximum
 *    angle of the lens.
 *
 *    The result is a circular lensed image on the square
 *    polygon, with black corners. The angular distribution
 *    is like polar graph paper, with angle increasing
 *    linearly with distance from the center.
 *
 *    Corners of polygon are assumed to be (in camera space):
 *       [ scale,  scale, zdistance]
 *       [-scale,  scale, zdistance]
 *       [-scale, -scale, zdistance]
 *       [ scale, -scale, zdistance]
 *
 *    RIB example:
 *       Clipping 0.099 1000.0
 *       Declare "lens_angle" "uniform float"
```

```
 *       Declare "zdistance" "uniform float"
 *       Declare "scale" "uniform float"
 *       Surface "fjs_fisheyelens" "lens_angle" [180] "zdistance" [0.1]  *
 *       "scale" [0.1]
 *       Polygon "P" [0.1 0.1 0.1 0.1 0.1 0.1 0.1 0.1 0.1 0.1 0.1 0.1]
 *
 * History:
 *    12/17/01 - 1.0 - Cleaned up and documented - Frank Summers,
 *                         summers@SpamSucks_stsci.edu
 *
 */
surface fjs_fisheyelens (float lens_angle = 180.0;
                         float zdistance = 0.1;
                         float scale = 0.1)
{

/* Do not shade near clip-plane polygon more than once
 *
 *    The code below will begin the fisheye raytrace from the
 *    camera. The near clip-plane polygon will then be hit a
 *    second time by those rays.  Checking raylevel ensures
 *    that only rays originally from the camera will be shaded.
 */

  float d;
  rayinfo("depth",d);
  if (d> 0) {
    Oi = 0.0;
    Ci = color(0,0,0);
  /* Otherwise, shade with fisheyelens */
  } else {
    /* Transform the point being shaded into camera coordinates */
    varying point Pcam = transform("camera", P);
    /* Generate coordinates relative to the center of the polygon */

    varying float ss = 0.5*xcomp(Pcam)/scale;
    varying float tt = 0.5*ycomp(Pcam)/scale;

    /* Calculate distance from center of the polygon */
    varying float r = sqrt(ss*ss + tt*tt);
    /* If point is outside of polygon filling circle,
       paint it opaque and black */
    if (r > 0.5) {
      Oi = 1.0;
```

```
    Ci = color(0,0,0);
  /* Otherwise, calculate ray to trace */
  } else {
    /* Angle increases linearly with distance from center */
    // r =pow(r,.3);
    varying float polar_angle = radians(lens_angle)*r;
    /* Direction is calculated from angle and shade point coordinates */
    varying float z = cos(polar_angle);
    varying float x = sin(polar_angle)*ss/r;
    varying float y = sin(polar_angle)*tt/r;

    /* Set trace direction and start point (at camera) */
    varying vector tracedir = vector "camera" (x, y, z);
    varying point startpoint = point "camera" (0, 0, 0);

    /* Call trace function to perform the raytrace */
    Oi = 1.0;
    Ci = trace(startpoint, tracedir);
  }
 }
}
```

The left image in Figure 14.10 shows the result of using the lens shader to render a stellated polyhedron. For comparison, a regular undistorted image is shown on the right. Notice in the fisheye image the magnification at the center and the slightly curved edges of the polyhedron.

You can write similar lens shaders to create/undo barrel, pincushion, and keystone distortions or simulate other kinds of warps exhibited by real-world lenses. Such a lens-based warp is an alternative to the map-based technique discussed in

Figure 14.10 Simulation of a fisheye lens warp (left image).

Chapter 13, "Texture Mapping." You can also try to create a kaleidoscope lens shader or simulate micro lens arrays (such as "bug's-eye kaleidoscope"). Finally, you can experiment with generating the equivalents of lens assemblies by placing multiple lens-bearing planes parallel to the view axis. All these allow for creative image synthesis possibilities beyond those obtainable using the standard camera model built into RenderMan.

The artistic image in Figure 14.11 shows the raytraced interior of a sphere. The core of this idea is due to Kevin Suffern, who presented a sketch at SIGGRAPH 2002 called "Painting with Light." His technique involves using a noise-based bump map to scatter highlights and their reflections on the inside surface of the sphere.

In the rtspecul shader shown below, we perturb the view vector V before using it for highlight calculations:

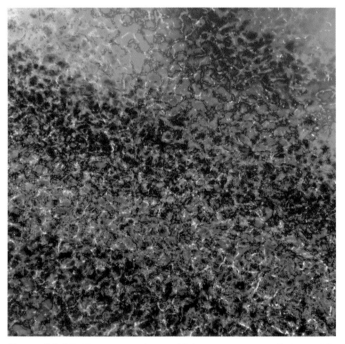

Figure 14.11 Abstract art obtained by raytracing specularity inside a sphere.

```
V = -normalize(I);
...
V += namp*turbulence(V*nfreq,space);
```

```
Ci = Oi*Cs*Ks*specularcolor*specular(Nf,normalize(V),roughness);
```

A nonstandard ray direction is used to trace rays for artistic effect:

```
vector H = normalize(normalize(N) + normalize(L) - normalize(P));
c = trace(P,H);
```

The resulting color is converted to a grayscale value from 0 to 1, which is used to look up an interpolated color:

```
lum = (0.333*comp(c,0)+0.333*comp(c,1)+0.333*comp(c,2));
Crts += splinecol(lum);
```

In addition to perturbing V, you can also experiment with procedurally modifying the ray direction. You could also affect these using maps, try alternate coloring schemes, experiment with tracing the interiors of more complex surfaces, and so on.

```
#define snoise(x) (2*noise(x)-1)

vector turbulence(vector Q;string space)
{
  float f;
  vector turb=0;
  vector VV = vtransform(space,Q);
  for(f=1;f<16;f*=2)
    {
      turb += abs(snoise(VV*f))/f;
    }
  return turb;
}

color splinecol(float f)
{
  color out = ;
  color spline(f,
    color (1,0,0),
    color (1,0,0),
    color (1,0,0),
    color (0,1,0),
    color (0,0,1),
    color(1,1,0),
    color(1,0,1),
```

```
        color(0,1,1),
        color(0,1,1),
        color(0,1,1)
    );
    return out;
}


surface rtspecul(
float Ks=0.6, roughness=1.5;
float nfreq=30,namp=8;
float  Krts=1.0;
color specularcolor=1;
string space = "shader";
)
{
    normal Nf;
    vector V;
    color Ct;

    Nf = faceforward( normalize(N), I );
    V = -normalize(I);
    // vector R = reflect(Nf,V);

    Oi = Os;
    V += namp*turbulence(V*nfreq,space);
    Ci = Oi*Cs*Ks*specularcolor*specular(Nf,normalize(V),roughness);

    color Crts=0;
    float lum;
    color c;
    illuminance(P,(N),PI/2)
    {
        vector H = normalize(normalize(N) + normalize(L) - normalize(P));
        c = trace(P,H);
        lum = (0.333*comp(c,0)+0.333*comp(c,1)+0.333*comp(c,2));
        Crts += splinecol(lum); // alternative: Crts += c;
    }
    Ci += Krts*Crts;
}
```

We conclude this chapter by pointing out that legacy shaders that look up values in an environment map or a shadow map can be tricked into carrying out ray-tracing in order to compute those values—no maps are required. This is achieved by specifying the special keyword string raytrace in place of an actual map name. For instance, the envtrace shader looks up environment color from a map specified in the RIB file via the envmapnm string.

If the value of that variable is specified to be raytrace instead, raytracing is used instead of a map lookup:

```
# RIB

Surface "envtrace" "Kr" 0.5 "envmapnm" "raytrace"
```

The thing to note is that the envmap shader itself does not need to be altered (or even recompiled) to get it to trace rays. Likewise, light shaders that normally compute shadows using a depth (shadow) map can be made to compute raytraced shadows instead by specifying raytrace for the shadow map name. In summary, the raytrace keyword is able to breathe new life into old shaders that normally perform environment and shadow map lookups.

```
surface envtrace(float Kr=1.; string evnmapnm="")
{
  vector In = normalize(I);
  normal NN = normalize(N);
  vector Nf = faceforward(NN, In);

  vector posNorm = 0.5*(vector(1,1,1)+NN);
  Ci = color(comp(posNorm,0),comp(posNorm,1),comp(posNorm,2));

  if(Nf.-In>0)
  {
    if(envmapnm!="")
    {
      vector R;
      // reflect I about N - "proper" way
      // R = reflect(In,Nf);
      // experiment with a non-standard ray direction!
      R = reflect(Nf,(dPdu+dPdv+In));
      Ci += Kr*environment(envmapnm,R);
    }
  }
}
```

The right image in Figure 14.12 shows the result of our envtrace shader applied to a set of Borromean rings. The reflections seen on the surface are a result of raytracing. The left image for comparison contains no raytracing. As a side note, the reflections in the right image look unusual because of our arbitrary choice of ray direction:

```
R = reflect(Nf,(dPdu+dPdv+In));
```

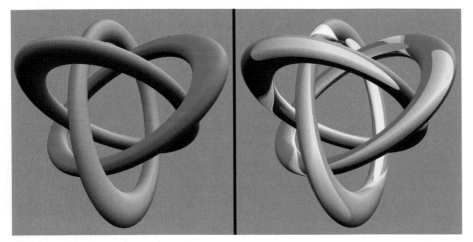

Figure 14.12 Enabling raytracing on legacy shaders using the raytrace keyword.

PART V

ADVANCED SHADING

15

Global Illumination

Light is energy. As light travels through space, its energy is slowly lost with distance, usually in an inverse square falloff. As light rays hit an object, some of its energy is absorbed, and the rest is bounced back into the world. This is a condensed version of the description of the properties of lights as described in Chapter 8. For those of us working in computer graphics, this description can be different depending on what algorithms we are using to try to replicate light phenomena.

As you might recall, the REYES rendering algorithm was designed to be fast and memory efficient. For this reason, it is extremely aggressive in how it hides and discards geometry that is not directly visible to the camera. This design made it impossible to use raytracing within the algorithm, and it is for this reason that in earlier versions of Pixar's PRMan all objects had a local illumination model. This means that an object had no notion of what surrounded it. Each object assumed it lived in its own little world—just it and some lights. In this context, when light traveled and hit an object, that light ray died right then and there, and no energy was bounced back into the environment.

This old limitation made lighting photorealistic CG scenes a very arduous job. Thus, lighting artists had devised several techniques to replicate how light moved through the scene. Among these tricks were dome lights, object lights (objects that emit light), and spinning lights. However, as raytracing techniques evolved and became more memory efficient and computers became faster and cheaper, developers began to incorporate global illumination capabilities into their renderers. *Global illumination* (GI) refers to the calculation of light as it bounces around in the scene.

For PRMan, global illumination rendering came about in version 11, simultaneously with raytracing. Most users would like to be able to make three to five clicks and have GI enabled and their images look prettier immediately. That might work with closed-box renderers that give you a set number of parameters to control GI quality and materials that can compute GI, but with a renderer as customizable as PRMan, things are somewhat more complicated. We will use this chapter to go over the steps necessary to make PRMan calculate GI and other tricks to simulate GI.

Occlusion

The latest "trick" to fake the visual effects of GI to take over the CG rendering world is known as *occlusion* or *ambient occlusion* (AO). We call it a "trick" because the process involves checking whether a shading point is occluded from the environment by other surfaces. This technique does not evaluate light transmission from one surface to another, so effects such as color bleeding are not achievable using AO. But being as simple a trick as it is, it does wonders for rendered images and allows users to replicate lighting environments quite fast and to bring out details that usually would not be visible.

Ambient occlusion is a very simple concept. All the technique requires is for an X number of rays to be shot from every shading point. If the point hits another geometric primitive, it returns 1, and if it doesn't, it returns 0. To get a visually pleasing effect that is free of artifacts, you will need to shoot a larger number of (256 or more) rays into the environment. Before you use these hit values, they need to be averaged by dividing the sum of all the values by the number of rays (or samples) cast into the environment.

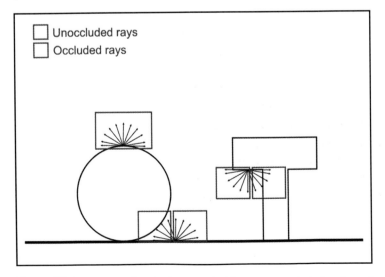

Figure 15.1 Diagram of occlusion: rays in blue are unoccluded and rays in red are occluded. Final occlusion value for each point is the average of all the rays.

The original way to write a shader that could compute AO was to use the raytracing call gather(). The simplest AO surface shader would look something like this:

```
#include "pixar/pixarutils.h"

surface s_RP_aogather(
          uniform float samples = 16;
          uniform float hemiangle = 90;
          )
{
  /* Use Pixar's shadingnormal() function to properly initialize Ns for
     raytracing */
  normal Ns = shadingnormal(N);

  /* Use gather to compute occlusion */
  float hits = 0;
  float occlusion;
  gather ("illuminance",P,Ns,radians(hemiangle),samples){
    hits +=1;
  }
  /* assign to occlusion the average of the sampled hits */
  occlusion = hits / samples;

  Ci = (1 - occlusion);
  Oi = 1 ;
}
```

As you might recall, gather() is a mix between a while loop and an if...then statement. It will shoot X number of rays (controlled by the samples parameter) randomly into the environment using the shading cone defined by hemiangle. If the ray hits something (other objects or itself), the next block of code is executed, and if it doesn't hit anything, then an optional else {} block is executed. In our shader, we care only about the hits, so we don't declare an else block. At the end of the shader, we invert the value of occlusion because so far the value of a hit is 1 and no hit is 0. In occlusion, we want "no hit" to be 1 (nothing occludes it) and "hit" to be 0 (it is occluded). One problem with the previous implementation is that the gather() call is a very powerful function that allows you to submit all kinds of queries to the environment around the object. For what we need to do, it is actually a bit of overkill because the only thing we really care about is whether the ray is hitting another surface or not.

It is for this reason that the folks at Pixar came up with the `occlusion()` call, which is specifically designed and optimized to do occlusion, and is a lot faster than `gather()`. The `occlusion()` call has the following syntax and can take any of the parameters listed in Table 15.1:

```
float occlusion( point P, normal N, float samples, [.. parameter pairs ])
```

Table 15.1 Parameters Accepted by Occlusion

Parameter Name	Type	Description	Default Value
adaptive	float	Indicates if the shading hemisphere should be sampled adaptively (more samples where they are needed).	1
minsamples	float	Minimum number of samples for adaptive sampling. If sample is > 64, the default value will be `samples/4`; otherwise, just `samples`.	samples/4 or samples
coordsystem	string	Name of the coordinate system the object is in.	current
maxdist	float	The maximum distance used for calculating ray hits. If the ray hits nothing within this distance, it returns 0.	infinity
falloffmode	float	Selects whether to use exponential falloff [0] or falloff through a power (^) call [1].	0
falloff	float	The rate at which the occlusion will fall off. 0 = no falloff.	0
coneangle	float	Specifies the size of the hemisphere to be considered when shooting rays for testing. Value is in radians.	PI/2
samplebase	float	Specifies whether the rays will be emitted from the center of the micropolygon or jittered over the area of it.	0
Default	string	Specifies how opacity should be computed at hit point. `Default` = Object will be shaded using the object's `shade diffusemode` attribute. `Primitive` = Opacity read from the object's `Os` value. `Shader` = Surface shader executed to get the opacity default.	
hitsides	string	Specifies which side of a single-sided surface can be hit by rays. Allowed values are `front`, `back`, and `both`.	both
subset	string	Limits the occlusion calculation to objects in the given trace subset (created using grouping).	none
label	string	A name to give to the spawned rays.	none

The `occlusion()` call takes more parameters than specified above. We will cover the rest in the next section of this chapter. With our knowledge of the `occlusion()` call, we can rewrite the previous shader and avoid using `gather()`.

One thing to consider is that the `occlusion()` call can also be made from a light. This brings forth a pipeline design decision: Do we want the occlusion to be set and calculated per object or through a light? From a performance point of view, it makes no big difference if you calculate the occlusion in the surface or in the light, but from a user's perspective it can make a big difference in how you work. If the occlusion is calculated on a per-object basis, things will quickly go out of control when you have a decent number of objects in your scene. Imagine setting up the parameters for 100 objects and then having to edit them to get the result you want.

Calculating the occlusion in the light makes tweaking the occlusion for all objects a breeze, but you lose some control because there might be some objects in which the current global settings don't give you a good result. On top of that, occlusion is something that you will usually want to render to a separate render pass, and in RenderMan renderers, only surface shader variables can be written into AOV (render pass) files. We can get around this problem by calculating the occlusion in the light and then using message-passing to query that value from the surface shader.

That leaves us with the problem of controllability. One solution is to use a two-way message-passing technique in which `occlusion()` is calculated in the surface shader, and we use a light shader to control all of the parameters for such an `occlusion()` call. A similar implementation would be to use "user attributes" to control the call. In that approach, we would need to use a RenderMan exporter, which allows us to add inline statements to the RIB stream. This feature is usually referred to as *RIB boxes*. One problem that arises from calculating occlusion in the surface shader is that you will need to update all the shaders in your production to include the new occlusion routines.

To implement this technique, we first need to write a light shader that will allow us to control the AO parameters from a single location. This light will be very simple; all it's designed to do is enable AO in a scene. Without one of these lights in the scene, AO won't be computed. Here is the code for the light:

```
light l_RP_ao(
        uniform float dissable_ao = 0;
        uniform float samples = 16;
        uniform float coneangle = 90;
        uniform float maxvariation = 0.02;
        color envcolor = color(0.9,1,1);
        string __category = "occlight";
        )
{
```

```
  normal Ns = shadingnormal(N);
  /* this light only passes parameters down to the surface */
  illuminate(Ps + Ns){
    Cl = 1;
  }
}
```

As you can see, the light does nothing but define a set of parameters you will use to control the occlusion lookup on the surface shaders of the scene's objects. The illuminate() call is absolutely necessary because otherwise this would be an ambient light, and therefore the illuminance() or solar() loop would not be invoked from the surface shaders. The surface shader designed to interact with this light and calculate occlusion is also very simple. You usually wouldn't have a shader do only occlusion. You would usually have a custom calculateocclusion() function that would allow you to insert occlusion into any shader. The shader code for such calculations is as follows:

```
surface s_RP_ao_MP(
        uniform float overridemode = 0;
        uniform float samples = 16;
        uniform float coneangle = 90;
        uniform float maxvariation = 0.02;
        color envcolor = (1,1,1);
        )
{
  /* Use Pixars shadingnormal() function to properly initialize Ns for
     raytracing */
  normal Ns = shadingnormal(N);

  float occlusion = 0;
  uniform float f_samples = samples,
     f_coneangle = coneangle,
     f_maxvariation = maxvariation;
  color f_envcolor = envcolor;

  illuminance("occlight",P){
    /*define the variables to be used by the AO controls */
    uniform float li_dissable_ao, li_samples,
       li_coneangle, li_maxvariation;
    color li_envcolor;

    /*use message passing to get the proper values from the light */
    lightsource("dissable_ao",li_dissable_ao);
    lightsource("samples",li_samples);
```

```
      lightsource("coneangle",li_coneangle);
      lightsource("maxvariation",li_maxvariation);
      lightsource("envcolor",li_envcolor);

   if (li_dissable_ao == 0){
      /* Use occlusion() */
      /* set the values to be used on the occlusion call based on the
   override mode */
      if (overridemode == 0){
   f_samples = li_samples; f_coneangle = li_coneangle;
   f_maxvariation = li_maxvariation;
   f_envcolor = li_envcolor;
      }
      if (overridemode == 2){
   f_samples *= li_samples; f_coneangle *= li_coneangle;
   f_maxvariation *= li_maxvariation;
   f_envcolor *= li_envcolor;
      }

      occlusion = occlusion(P,Ns,f_samples,"coneangle",radians(f_coneangle),
            "maxvariation",f_maxvariation);
   }
}
/*set the final values */
Ci = (1 - occlusion)* f_envcolor;
Oi = 1 ;


}
```

This shader is an expansion of the original s_ao.sl we wrote before. We first initialize the "final" variables (f_samples, f_coneangle, and such) to the value provided by the shader parameters. We then call an illuminance loop that will only run lights that have a _category value of occlight. This ensures that the occlusion calculations, which are somewhat expensive, are not called unless there is a light of that category in the scene. It also prevents other lights from making the surface shader calculate occlusion. Note that if you create more than one l_RP_ao light, the illuminance loop will calculate occlusion() as many times as you have lights in the scene. This will be very expensive, so make sure you create only one occlusion light per scene.

Next in our shader, we define the "light parameter" variables (li_samples and such), which will be used in our message-passing section. The lightsource() call allows shaders to communicate with the current light being evaluated inside the illuminance loop. With these calls, we get all the parameters from the l_RP_ao light shader. If `ambient_ao` is not disabled, then we make some decisions based on the `overridemode` parameter. If `overridemode` is 0, we are not overriding values, so we set the "final" variables to be the values queried from the light. If `overridemode` is 1, we leave the "final" values untouched because they are already set to the local shader parameter values. An `overridemode` of 2 means that all the values of the local shader become scalars (or multipliers) of the values read from the light shader. So if the light shader has a `samples` value of 128, the surface shader has `overridemode` = 2, and `samples` = 2, then `f_samples` will be 256.

Image-Based Lighting (IBL)

It is true that ambient occlusion helps enormously in making images look richer and more detailed, but without the use of some type of environment map to provide variation, the images will look quite plain. The process of using an environment map to illuminate the scene is known as *image-based lighting* (IBL), and it is a very quick way to get an approximation of the environmental conditions of the scene. It is for techniques such as IBL that those shiny chrome spheres in the set of a VFX shoot can be so useful. The chrome sphere can be used to capture a snapshot of the lighting conditions on the set. That image can be turned into an environment map. Combine the values of that map and an occlusion pass, and you are probably 25 to 50 percent on the way to matching an element to a background plate. To gather information about the environment, we could use the `gather()` call and then do an environment call on the else portion of the function, something like this:

```
/* Compute average color of ray misses */
        vector dir = 0;
        color irrad = 0;
    float hits = 0;
        gather("illuminance", Ps, Ns, PI/2, samples,
                "distribution", "cosine", "ray:direction", dir) {
          hits +=1;
        } else { /* ray miss */
          /* Lookup in environment map */
          irrad += environment(envmap, dir);
        }
        irrad /= samples;
    hits /= samples;
```

Fortunately, the `occlusion()` call was also expanded to provide this type of functionality. When an environment map is provided to the `occlusion()` function, PRMan will perform importance sampling based on the brightness of the map.

This means that there will be more samples evaluated where the map is brighter. The environment parameters supported by occlusion are shown in Table 15.2.

Table 15.2 Environment Parameters Accepted by Occlusion

Parameter	Type	Description	Default
environmentmap	string	Name of an environment texture to use where there is no occlusion.	none
environmentspace	string	The coordsys used to access the environmentmap.	current
environmentcolor	color	Defines the output value of the environmentmap lookup plus the occlusion. If no environmentmap is provided, it returns 0.	0
brightnesswarp	float	Enables or disables importance sampling based on the environmentmap.	1

We will modify our surface and light shaders to support IBL. First, we start with the light because the change is as trivial as things get.

```
light l_RP_IBL(
        uniform float dissable_ao = 0;
        uniform float samples = 16;
        uniform float coneangle = 90;
        uniform float maxvariation = 0.02;
        color envcolor = color(0.9,1,1);
        string environmap = "";
        string __category = "occlight";
        )
{
  normal Ns = shadingnormal(N);
  /* this light only passes parameters down to the surface */
  illuminate(Ps){
    Cl = 1;
  }
}
```

Our surface shader has somewhat more changes than the light since we now must account for different behaviors based on whether an environment map is provided to the shader. Here is the code, which is an extension of s_RP_ao_MP:

```
#include "pixar/pixarutils.h"

surface s_RP_ao_MP_IBL(
        uniform float overridemode = 0;
        uniform float samples = 16;
        uniform float coneangle = 90;
        uniform float maxvariation = 0.02;
        string environmap = "";
        color envcolor = (1,1,1);
        )
{
  /* Use Pixars shadingnormal() function to properly initialize Ns for
     raytracing */
  normal Ns = shadingnormal(N);

  float occlusion = 1;
  uniform float f_samples = samples,
            f_coneangle = coneangle,
                 f_maxvariation = maxvariation;
  color f_envcolor = envcolor;
  string f_environmap=environmap;
  color outenv = 1;

  illuminance("occlight",P){
    /*define the variables to be used by the AO controls */
    uniform float li_dissable_ao, li_samples,
      li_coneangle, li_maxvariation;
    color li_envcolor;
    string li_environmap;


    /*use message passing to get the proper values from the light */
    lightsource("dissable_ao",li_dissable_ao);
    lightsource("samples",li_samples);
    lightsource("coneangle",li_coneangle);
    lightsource("maxvariation",li_maxvariation);
    lightsource("envcolor",li_envcolor);
    lightsource("environmap",li_environmap);

    if (li_dissable_ao == 0){
      /* set the values to be used on the occlusion call based on the
    override mode */
      if (overridemode == 0){
    f_samples = li_samples; f_coneangle = li_coneangle;
```

```
   f_maxvariation = li_maxvariation;
   f_envcolor = li_envcolor;
   f_environmap = li_environmap;
       }
     if (overridemode == 2){
   f_samples *= li_samples; f_coneangle *= li_coneangle;
   f_maxvariation *= li_maxvariation;
   f_envcolor *= li_envcolor;
       }
     if (f_environmap != "")
   occlusion = occlusion(P,Ns,f_samples,"coneangle",radians(f_coneangle),
               "maxvariation",f_maxvariation,
               "environmentmap",f_environmap,
               "environmentcolor",outenv);
     else {
   occlusion = occlusion(P,Ns,f_samples,"coneangle",radians(f_coneangle),
               "maxvariation",f_maxvariation);
   outenv = (1- occlusion);
       }
     }
   }
   /*set the final values */

   Ci = outenv * f_envcolor;
   Oi = 1 ;

}
```

The following images (Figures 15.2 and 15.3) were created with the IBL shader using the standard environment maps street.env and desert.env. Note the difference in the lighting tonality and how easy it is to get a foundation to match lighting to background plates.

Figure 15.2 Environment lit with a street environment map.

Figure 15.3 Environment lit with a desert environment map.

Transmission

In the past, shadow calculations were usually done exclusively with depth-based shadow maps. With the need for more believable shadowing, soft shadows and deep shadow maps were introduced. Soft shadows allowed users to fake penumbral shadows by using four shadow maps and interpolating the values between them. Deep shadow maps were designed to help shadow very small detail in objects such as hair or fur, to shadow objects with partial opacity (tinted shadows or smoke), and to provide map-based support for motion-blurred shadows. With the integration of raytracing into PRMan, the possibilities for shadowing effects increased dramatically.

As explained in Chapter 8, any light shader that supports shadow maps can be forced to raytrace shadows by passing the keyword `raytrace` as the name of the map. This works very well, but the shadows that you create will not be as controllable as the ones that can be obtained using the `transmission()` function. The `transmission()` function is similar to the `occlusion()` function in that it is a highly specialized raytracing function designed to deal specifically with shadows. When a surface shader is being evaluated and an illuminance loop finds a light shader that uses transmission, a ray is traced from the light position to the current surface shading point. If no object intersects with the ray, the shading point is in full intensity, and if there is an intersection, the shading point is inside a shadow. This is how raytraced shadows are evaluated.

The `transmission()` returns a color that represents the value of light as it flows between two points. The color value can change based on the object's opacity and its `visibility transmission` setting. The transmission call will continue to evaluate the color value of the ray until it reaches a shading point with an opacity of 1. This function also allows you to define a shading cone or hemisphere similar to the one used in `occlusion()`. Within this cone, X number of samples will be fired, evaluated, and averaged to return the shadowed color value. This single feature allows you to re-create penumbral shadows very easily. Figure 15.4 demonstrates what happens to transmission rays as they spawn from the light. If a ray hits an opaque surface, the ray dies, and everything behind it is in opaque shadows. A ray that hits a semi-transparent object continues with the new opacity color shadow. That ray will continue until the opacity of the ray is set at 1.

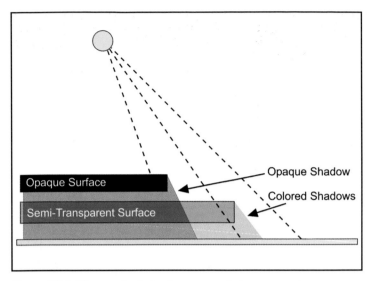

Figure 15.4 Diagram depicting how transmission rays work.

Just like gather() and occlusion(), the transmission() function supports several optional parameters that can be used to control the behavior of the call and to optimize the calculations. The syntax for the transmission() function is shown below, followed by Table 15.3 with the optional parameters it accepts.

```
color transmission( point Psrc, point Pdst, [.. parameter pairs ])
```

For transmission to be properly calculated, the following two attributes need to be assigned to the objects that you want to cast shadows:

Attribute "visibility" "transmission": When calculating shadow intersection tests, transmission rays will intersect only with objects that are visible to transmission. The default value for all objects in a scene is transmission [0]. By default, no objects will cast shadows. This allows you to optimize the scene by giving a transmission [1] value only to the objects that require it.

Attribute "shade" "transmissionhitmode": This attribute allows you to control what the transmission() function will do when it finds an intersection with an object. Two values are accepted by this attribute: primitive and shader. If primitive is used, then the uniform value of the object's Os will be used. If shader is selected, then the whole shader will be evaluated to get a final opacity value. As expected, the cost of using shader is higher than using primitive.

One final note on how transmission() performs adaptive sampling. If samples and minsamples are declared, and minsamples is greater than 0 but less than samples, the renderer will first fire minsamples number of rays. If a variation is detected within those rays, then the difference between samples and minsamples will be fired (at the end, the value of samples will be used) to get the proper transmission value of an object.

Table 15.3 Parameters Accepted by Transmission

Parameter	Type	Description	Default
samples	float	Number of sample rays to shoot per each shading sample.	1
minsamples	float	Minimum number of sample rays to shoot for adaptive sampling.	0
samplecone	float	Radians value that defines the size of the shading hemisphere.	PI/2
samplebase	float	Jittering value for the origin of the sample rays on the shading point.	0
bias	float	Controls the distance to offset hemisphere sample origins. If not specified, the global trace bias value is used.	none
label	string	An identifier name used to label the rays shot by transmission.	none
subset	string	A set of objects to be considered by the rays fired.	none
hitmode	string	How the value of the ray hit point is to be calculated. If default, the value of the "shade" "transmissionhitmode" attribute is used. If the objects have not defined transmissionhitmode, the shader will be used.	shader
hitsides	string	Specifies which sides of a surface can be hit by shadow rays. Possible values are front, back, and both.	Both

Let's take a look at how transmission can be used to create penumbral and tinted shadows. We will create a spotlight shader that supports shadowing using transmission. The code of the light shader is very straightforward, and you can refer to Chapter 8 for an explanation of how the spotlight shader works.

```
light l_RP_transmissionSpot(
        float intensity = 1;
        color lightcolor = color(1);
        point from = point "shader" (0,0,0);
        point to   = point "shader" (0,0,1);
        float coneangle =30;
        float conedeltaangle = 5;
        float beamdistribution = 2;
        uniform float doShadows = 1;
        uniform float samples = 1;
        uniform float minsamples = -1;
        uniform float shadowblur = 0;
        uniform float bias = 0.0001;
        )
{
  /* Init variables */
  color Ctrans;
```

```
float cosangle;
uniform vector A;
uniform float outcircle, incircle;

/* Create a unit vector using the to and from parameters */
A = (to - from)/length(to-from);
outcircle = cos(radians(coneangle));
incircle  = cos(radians(coneangle) - radians(conedeltaangle));

illuminate(from,A,coneangle){
  cosangle = L.A/length(L);
  /* Initialize the value of the light to a inverse square falloff */
  Ctrans = pow(cosangle,beamdistribution)/ (L.L);
  /* clip the light by the shape of the cone angle */
  Ctrans *= smoothstep(outcircle,incircle,cosangle);

  if (doShadows == 1){
    Ctrans *= transmission(Ps, from,"samples",samples,
            "minsamples",minsamples,
            "samplecone", shadowblur,
            "bias",bias);
  }
  Cl = Ctrans * intensity * lightcolor;
  }
}
```

The important part of this shader is where we decide if shadows are to be calculated. We filter the value of the transmission() function with the attenuation and shaping that have already been stored in Ctrans. The use of the samples and the shadowcone is what allows us to replicate penumbral soft shadows. The bigger the coneangle is, the more samples needed, with a value between 256 and 512 usually delivering smooth results.

A simple stainedglass shader that will allow us to demonstrate the effect of the transmission call looks like this (see Figure 15.5).

```
surface s_RP_stainedglass (
            color opacityFilter = color (1);
            string texturename = ""; )
{
  color opactex ;
  if (texturename != "")
    opactex = color texture(texturename);
  else
    opactex = color(1);
```

```
    Oi = (1 - opactex) * opacityFilter;
    Ci = Oi * opactex ;   /* pleasantly saturated */
}
```

Figure 15.5 Stained glass-tinted shadows effect through transmission().

Indirect Diffuse

Moving upward on the scale of advanced shading techniques for GI simulation, we need to simulate how the light that bounces from one object has the capability to tint other objects in its proximity. This is an extremely important effect. Photographers have taken advantage of this effect for ages. They place cleverly positioned cards to bounce light onto the subject to be photographed, effectively softening shadows and tinting areas. Because of the lack of energy transmission that was the norm for most renderers in the past, CG lighting artists had to add clever lights to replicate light bouncing within a scene.

Since version 11, PRMan has been able to compute *indirect diffuse calculation*, which is also known as *single bounce GI* or *final gathering*. It is a simple computation in theory, but it can be very expensive (depending on the complexity of your scene). In the first implementations, indirectdiffuse() worked, but not many people considered it useful for production because the rendering times were exorbitant. Today, the rendering in PRMan has been optimized significantly from version 11, and even though indirectdiffuse() is still more expensive to use than regular local illumination, it is not out of reach for production schedules and budgets. It is a lot more expensive to have an artist spend 20 hours tweaking a scene so it renders in 10 hours than it is to have an artist work for two hours and have the scene render in 20 hours. Also, for the cost of those extra 18 hours of an artist's salary, one new rendering server can be purchased to speed up the process. On the other side, there are some scenes in which adding indirectdiffuse() will make the rendering jump up to four times longer or more. In such cases, it might be worthwhile to spend more time tweaking the scene and creating raytracing subsets or groups and then cheat with extra lights to reduce the rendering times.

Just as with the occlusion() call, indirectdiffuse() can be called from the surface or the light shader. It is somewhat more convenient to do it from the light shader so that you won't have to update all of your shaders to support the feature. As long as the shader has an illuminance loop, indirect diffuse will be contributed to the output. Here is the code for our indirect diffuse light (the BF at the end of the shader stands for "brute force").

```
light l_RP_indirectdiffuse_BF(
                float intensity = 1;
                /* Indirect Diffuse Controls */
                uniform float doIndirectDiffuse = 0;
                uniform float samples = 64;
                uniform float minsamples = 4;
                uniform float bias = 0.0001;
                uniform float maxvariation = 0.02;
                string __category = "indirectdiffuse";
)
{
  /* Variables */
  color lc = 1;
  normal Ns = shadingnormal(N);

  illuminate( Ps + Ns ){
  if (doIndirectDiffuse != 0){
     Cl = intensity * indirectdiffuse(Ps,Ns,samples,"maxvariation",maxvaria-
tion,
                "minsamples",minsamples,"bias",bias);
   }
  }
}
```

Below to the left is a typical Cornell box scene in which we have one single spotlight shining down from the ceiling (see Figure 15.6). Note how many areas of the image are completely black; this is because no light is reaching them. Figure 15.7 shows the same scene with our l_RP_indirectdiffuse_BF light added to it. Observe how rich the image becomes and how the color bleeds and transfers from one surface to another, all with the inclusion of one single shader to the scene, which took less than a minute to do.

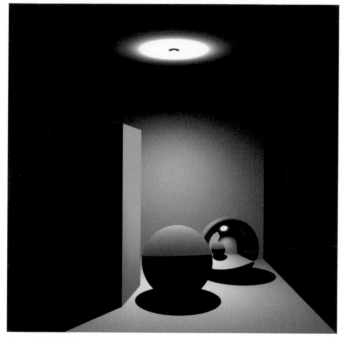

Figure 15.6 Cornell box using only local illumination.

Figure 15.7 The same scene but with `indirectdiffuse()` on.

Photon Map GI

Indirect diffuse by default calculates only single-bounce GI. It can be made to calculate more bounces by increasing the value of the trace `maxdiffusedepth` attribute. The problem with this technique is that the rendering times will go through the roof. If you ever find yourself in a situation where single-bounce GI is not enough, you might want to take a closer look at photon map GI in RenderMan.

A photon map is a special kind of point cloud data file that stores in each point the light power and the incident direction. Rendering scenes with multiple-bounce GI involves a three-step process known as baking. We will touch on *baking* here and go into more detail by the end of this chapter.

First, you need to render out a photon map file. Then the photon map file is processed into a set of files that PRMan can use efficiently at render time. Finally, the image is rendered using the processed files. To render a photon map, we use a RIB file that is virtually the same as the one we will use for the final image file, with the following differences:

- We don't need to specify any of the typical image quality options or an output driver.

- The following two calls are necessary:

```
Hider "photon" "emit" 30000  #emit represents the number of photons to fire
Attribute "photon" "globalmap" "mymap.gpm" # The name for the photon map to write
```

- These controls are optional but very useful:

```
Attribute "trace" "maxdiffusedepth" [5]  # maximum number of diffuse bounces
Attribute "trace" "maxspeculardepth" [5] # maximum number of specular bounces
```

- `maxdiffusedepth` limits the amount of times a ray can bounce when it hits either a diffuse or a specular calculation; `maxspeculardepth` controls the limit for reflections and refractions.

- A `shading model` to be used on the photon calculation:

```
Attribute "photon" "shadingmodel" "matte"
```

We can use the `shadingmodel` attribute to accelerate the calculation of the photon map; if the user provides an empty string as the `shadingmodel` parameter, the attached shader to the surface will be evaluated. Here is an example of a simple RIB file used to output a photon map.

```
Attribute "trace" "maxspeculardepth" [ 5]
Attribute "trace" "maxdiffusedepth" [ 5]
FrameBegin 1
# Photon map generation
 Hider "photon" "integer emit" [2000000] "jitter" [1]
```

```
Attribute "photon" "globalmap" [ "globalmap.gpm" ]
#position the camera
Transform [1 0 0 0 0 1 0 0
  0 0 -1 0 0 0 17 1]
WorldBegin
Attribute "trace" "bias" 0.0001    # to avoid bright spot under sphere
Attribute "identifier" "string name" ["/obj/light1"]
Transform [1 0 0 0 0 6.12303176911189e-017 -1 0
  0 -1 -6.12303176911189e-017 0 0 4.38956022262573 0 1]
LightSource "cosinelight_rts" 1 "intensity" 40
 Identity # Make sure space is well defined

 # Object: /obj/cornell_box_red
 AttributeBegin# {
   Color [1 0 0]
   Opacity [1 1 1]
   Attribute "photon" "shadingmodel" "matte"
   Transform [1 0 0 0 0 1 0 0
  0 0 1 0 0 0 0 1]
# Geometry /obj/cornell_box_red
PatchMesh "bilinear" 4 "nonperiodic" 4 "nonperiodic"
   "P" [ -5 -5 5 -5 -5 2 -5 -5 -2 -5 -5 -6 -5 -2 5 -5 -2 2 -5 -2 -2 -5 -2
-5
   -5 2 5 -5 2 2 -5 2 -2 -5 2 -5
   -5 5 5 -5 6 2 -5 5 -2 -5 5 -5]
 AttributeEnd

 # EndObject: /obj/cornell_box_red
 AttributeBegin# {
   Color [0 0 1]
   Opacity [1 1 1]
   Attribute "photon" "shadingmodel" "matte"
   Transform [1 0 0 0 0 1 0 0
  0 0 1 0 0 0 0 1]
# Geometry /obj/cornell_box_blue
NuPatch 4 4 [ 0 0 0 0 1 1 1 1] 0 1
  4 4 [ 0 0 0 0 1 1 1 1] 0 1
   "Pw" [ 5 -5 -5 1  5 -5 -2 1 5 -5 2 1  5 -5 5 1 5 -2 -5 1  5 -2 -2 1
   5 -2 2 1  5 -2 5 1 5 2 -5 1  5 2 -2 1 5 2 2 1  5 2 5 1 5 5 -5 1  5 5
2 1
   5 5 2 1  5 5 5 1]
 AttributeEnd
# Object: /obj/greencube
 AttributeBegin
```

```
    Color [0 1 0]
    Opacity [1 1 1]
    Attribute "photon" "shadingmodel" "matte"
    Transform [1.32200869664572 0 0.219516898943099 0 0 1.94010996818542 0 0
   -0.219516898943099 0 1.32200869664572 0 -2.90748000144959 -
2.34198999404907 1.15246999263763 1]
# Geometry /obj/greencube
Declare "Cs" "vertex color"
# Starting polys
PointsGeneralPolygons
    [1 1 1 1 1 1]
    [ 4 4 4 4 4 4]
    [ 0 4 5 1 1 5 6 2 2 6 7 3 3 7 4 0 3 0 1 2 4 7 6 5]
    "P" [ -1 -2 -1 1 -2 -1 1 -2 1 -1 -2 1 -1 2 -1 1 2 -1 1 2 1 -1 2 1]
    "Cs" [ 0 1 0 0 1 0 0 1 0 0 1 0 0 1 0 0 1 0 0 1 0 0 1 0]
  AttributeEnd
# Object: /obj/matte_ball
  AttributeBegin# {
    Color [0.5 0.5 0.5]
    Opacity [1 1 1]
    Attribute "photon" "shadingmodel" "matte"
    Transform [1.36693000793457 0 0 0 0 1.36693000793457 0 0
   0 0 1.36693000793457 0 0.182960003614426 -3.62385988235474 1.5299299955368
1]
# Geometry /obj/matte_ball
TransformBegin
    ConcatTransform [1 0 0 0 0 -4.371139e-008 -1 0
   0 1 -4.371139e-008 0 0 0 0 1]
    Sphere 1 -1 1 360
TransformEnd
  AttributeEnd
# Object: /obj/chrome_ball
  AttributeBegin
    Color [1 1 1]
    Opacity [1 1 1]
    Attribute "photon" "shadingmodel" "chrome"
    TransformBegin # {
   Transform [1.36693000793457 0 0 0 0 1.36693000793457 0 0
   0 0 1.36693000793457 0 2.5661199092865 -3.63286 -1.35608005523682 1]
    Surface "s_RP_chrome" "__instanceid" "/obj/chrome_ball:surf"
    TransformEnd # }
    Transform [1.36693000793457 0 0 0 0 1.36693000793457 0 0
   0 0 1.36693000793457 0 2.5661199092865 -3.62385988235474 -1.35608005523682
1]
```

```
# Geometry /obj/chrome_ball
TransformBegin
    ConcatTransform [1 0 0 0 0 -4.371139e-008 -1 0
  0 1 -4.371139e-008 0 0 0 0 1]
    Sphere 1 -1 1 360
TransformEnd
  AttributeEnd
# Object: /obj/cornell_box_white
  AttributeBegin# {
    Color [0.8 0.8 0.8]
    Opacity [1 1 1]
    Attribute "photon" "shadingmodel" "matte"
    Transform [1 0 0 0 0 1 0 0
  0 0 1 0 0 0 0 1]
# Geometry /obj/cornell_box_white
PatchMesh "bilinear" 2 "nonperiodic" 2 "nonperiodic"
    "P" [ -5 5 -5 5 5 -5 -5 5 5 5 5 5]
PatchMesh "bilinear" 2 "nonperiodic" 2 "nonperiodic"
    "P" [ -5 -5 5 5 -5 5 -5 -5 -5 5 -5 -5]
PatchMesh "bilinear" 2 "nonperiodic" 2 "nonperiodic"
    "P" [ -5 -5 -5 5 -5 -5 -5 5 -5 5 5 -5]
  AttributeEnd
# EndObject: /obj/cornell_box_white
WorldEnd
FrameEnd
```

You can render this file with the regular command (use render instead or prman if in Linux). You can use the -p:2 flag only if you have a dual processor machine.

```
prman -progress -p:2 photonfile.rib
```

This command will output a file named globalmap.gpm that will be stored in the location where prman was called from. To send the file to a specific place, you must modify the photon globalmap attribute in the RIB file. To use this file, you need to filter the values stored in the photon map and store those values in an irradiance file. This is done by calling this command:

```
ptfilter -photonmap -nphotons 100 globalmap.gpm globalmap.irr
```

This command will make the ptfilter program process the values in the photon map using a special algorithm designed to handle photon maps. -nphotons tells the program how many photons can affect the value of the current photon being calculated. A value of 100 means that the 100 photons closest to the current one will be used to determine the amount of energy that arrives at that point. The default value is 50. The last two parameters are the sourcemap and the outputmap. You can view the output of the irradiance file with the ptviewer utility, which should output something similar to what you see in Figure 15.8.

```
ptviewer -multiply 4 globalmap.irr
```

Figure 15.8 The irradiance file viewed through ptviewer.

This file could be used as it is within the renderer using the texture3d() call, but PRMan supports a new texture map type known as a *brickmap*. A brickmap is a three-dimensional texture map that is mipmapped much like PRMan's texture files, but with a third dimension added. To convert globalmap.irr to a brickmap, we use the brickmake command. To view the map, we can use the brickviewer command.

```
brickmake globalmap.irr globalmap.bkm
brickviewer globalmap.bkm
```

This will output a texture file that can be read into the shader easily and quickly.

Before we continue to how to use this map in a shader, let's look at how you can automate the brickmap generation. You can use any scripting language, such as Python or Perl, to do this. For simplicity we will use a very straightforward bash script named makephotonmap, which can be run from where the photon-generating RIB file is stored. To run this script, you must be using the CYGWIN environment described in Chapter 4, and you must change the file's mode to executable. Save the file somewhere in your system's PATH variable and just type **makephotonmap** at the location where you stored the photon-generating RIB file.

```
#! /usr/bin/bash

echo "Rendering rib file"
prman -progress -p:2 myribfile.rib
echo "Generating irr file"
ptfilter -photonmap -nphotons 100 globalmap.gpm globalmap.irr
echo "Making brickmap"
brickmake globalmap.irr globalmap.bkm
#comment the following 2 lines if you don't want to display the brickmap at
the end
echo "Displaying brickmap"
brickviewer globalmap.bkm
echo "Done!"
```

Some programs, such as Houdini and Maya, allow you to define a script that will be run at the end of a frame. You can use a script similar to the one provided here to automate the generation of the brickmap. A clear upgrade to this script would be to provide support for an input variable, because at the moment the name of the files, myribfile.rib, globalmap.gpm, globalmap.irr, and globalmap.bkm, are hard-coded into the script.

We will now write a shader that is capable of reading the information stored in this map. The simplest shader to read the photon information would look something like this.

```
surface read_photons(
   string filename = "";
)
{
  color irrad = 0;
  normal Nn = normalize(N);
  texture3d(filename, P, Nn, "_radiosity", irrad);
  /* Set Ci and Oi */
  Ci = irrad;
  Ci *= Os; /* premultiply opacity */
  Oi = Os;
}
```

If we render the image with this shader, the output image will look something like what you see in Figure 15.9. As you can see, the light transmission is visible, but the image is extremely noisy. To generate an image with acceptable (unperceiv-able) levels of noise, you would have to use a prohibitive number of photons, which is not possible in production schedules.

Figure 15.9 Cornell box rendered with only photon contribution.

To get around this issue, we will perform an indirectdiffuse() call that will be called if the depth of the current diffuse ray is less than the diffuse limit provided to the scene. Once the depth has been reached, the shader will not do indirect-diffuse() anymore, but will send a call to our photon map, which already has mul-tiple bounces calculated in it. This means that as a ray travels from the camera and hits a surface (ray depth is 0 at this point), the shader will perform an indirect-diffuse() call. The rays spawned by indirectdiffuse have a depth value of 1, which means that when a shader is queried from those secondary rays, the shader will use the photon map. Here is the code, followed by Figure 15.10, where the Cornell box is using only indirectdiffuse(), and Figure 15.11, a render of the Cornell box with multiple-bounce GI.

```
surface s_RP_matte_FG(uniform string filename = "";
                      float Kd = 1, samples = 64,
            maxvariation = 0.02,
            maxdistance = 5000,
            bias = 0.0001;)
{
```

```
color irrad = 0;
normal Nn = normalize(N);
uniform float maxddepth, ddepth;

attribute("trace:maxdiffusedepth", maxddepth);
rayinfo("diffusedepth", ddepth);
color diff = diffuse(Nn);

if (ddepth == maxddepth) { //max diffuse depth reached
  /* lookup in 3d irradiance texture*/
  texture3d(filename, P, Nn, "_radiosity", irrad);
  } else {   //compute direct illum and shoot final gather rays
  irrad = indirectdiffuse(P, Nn, samples,
          "maxvariation", maxvariation,
          "maxdist",maxdistance,
             "bias",bias);
    }

/* Set Ci and Oi */
Ci = Kd * Cs * (diff + irrad);
Ci *= Os; /* premultiply opacity */
Oi = Os;
}
```

Figure 15.10 Cornell box with only indirectdiffuse().

Figure 15.11 Cornell box with `indirectdiffuse()` + photon map.

Subsurface Scattering—Irradiance

The final effect that we will cover in this chapter is the calculation of subsurface scattering. If you have been an active practitioner of CG arts during the last three years, you are more than likely familiar with the term. For a lot of people, sub-surface scattering (referred to as SSS) is the miracle ingredient that was missing from most images years ago. Its introduction was so revolutionary and important to the art of visual effects that in 2003 Henrik Wann Jensen, Stephen R. Marschner, and Pat Hanrahan received a Scientific and Technical (Technical Achievement Award) by The Academy of Motion Picture Arts and Sciences for their paper "A Practical Model for Subsurface Light Transport." That same year, Christophe Hery, Ken McGaugh, and Joe Letteri also received an Academy Award for their groundbreaking implementations of practical methods for rendering skin based on Jensen's, Marschner's, and Hanrahan's paper. Without SSS, creatures such as *Gollum*, *Dobby*, and *Davy Jones* would have been almost impossible to create with such incredible realism. What exactly is subsurface scattering?

As light rays hit a surface, those rays can be affected in several ways. The whole light ray can be reflected in its entirety as in a mirror. Some of the light might be absorbed and the rest reflected, as with matte objects. Light can go through (either straight or bent) as with glass objects. For all of these situations, CG renderers had a solution to re-create the effect. But there is one very common effect for light rays in nature that until 2001 most CG renderers could not re-create. This property is known as *subsurface light transport*, and it is what happens when light rays penetrate a surface, scatter within that surface (change directions more than once), and then come out of the surface in a different location with different intensity and color values. The resulting appearance of this phenomenon is that a surface looks softer, more organic, and less like plastic. Figure 15.12 illustrates the differences between a mirror BRDF (chrome), a diffuse BRDF (typical CG matte shader), and a BSSRDF (subsurface scattering shader).

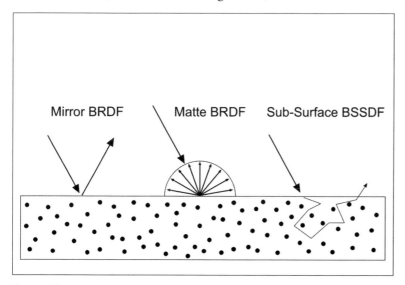

Figure 15.12 Differences between a light interaction of a mirror, a matte BRDF, and a BSSRDF.

Most raytracers should be able to compute SSS, but a brute force method is usually very expensive and not viable for production work. To get around this limitation, Pixar expanded the capabilities of the ptfilter program so that it could calculate irradiance values to simulate SSS. Once again, it will be a three-step process to render SSS efficiently in PRMan. Since the next section will describe baking in detail, we will touch on the steps briefly here.

For ptfilter to calculate SSS contribution, a very strict set of rules must be followed. Here are the rules:

■ Your shader must bake out a point cloud with two data channels stored in it. They must be in the following order and with these names and data types:

`"float _area"` and `"color _radiance_t"`

This is usually done with a call similar to this:

```
bake3d(filename,displaychannels,P,Nn,"interpolate",1,   "_area",ar,"
    _radiance_t",irrad);
```

- You must add the following statements to the RIB file:

```
DisplayChannel "float _area"
DisplayChannel "color _radiance_t"
Attribute "cull" "hidden" 0    # don't cull hidden surfaces
Attribute "cull" "backfacing" 0    # don't cull backfacing surfaces
Attribute "dice" "rasterorient" 0 # turn viewdependent gridding
```

- Finally, your shader that will read the SSS data must make a call similar to this:

```
texture3d(filename, P, N, "_ssdiffusion", ssdiffusion);
```

To put things into a better perspective, let's write a shader that will bake and read SSS. Let's start by looking at the shader parameters. The following parameters will be provided to our shader:

```
surface s_RP_sss(
    float bake = 0;
    string filename = "";
    string displaychannels = "_area,_radiance_t";
    color surfacecolor = color (1);
    )
```

bake represents a switch to enable or disable baking. If baking is disabled, then the shader will attempt to read the SSS from the provided texture. filename is the name of the file to write to disc or to read at render time. The string displaychannels is a comma-separated list of the channels that will be written into the point cloud. Only those names provided in this parameter that match the names provided in the bake() RSL call will be written into the point cloud. The final parameter, surfacecolor, is just a simple color that will be used for the surface. For the sake of clarity, we have omitted several parameters that would be very useful, such as Kd and Kss, and maybe some filtering color for the SSS value read. Next, we will move to the body of our shader.

```
normal Nn = normalize(N);
color irrad, rad_t;
float ar = area(P,"dicing");
color ssdiffusion = 0;
irrad = ambient() + diffuse(Nn) * surfacecolor;

/* if the filename and displaychannels are not "" then write
    out the value */
if ((filename != "") && (displaychannels != "")){
  if (bake == 1)
    bake3d(filename,displaychannels,P,Nn,"interpolate",1,
      "_area",ar,"_radiance_t",irrad);
```

```
       else
           texture3d(filename, P, N, "_ssdiffusion", ssdiffusion);
   }
   Ci = (irrad + ssdiffusion) * Os;
   Oi = Os;
```

The body starts by initializing a set of variables for our shader. A variable of particular interest is the ar value, which is initialized to the area of P using the dicing value. This ensures that the accurate size of the micropolygon at P is used and not a smoothed value, which is what area() returns by default. We then store the contribution of ambient lights and the diffuse component into the irrad value. The shader then makes a decision whether to bake the calculated values into a point file or read the values from a brickmap. It is very important when writing a point cloud for SSS calculation that the display channels are stored in the right order in the point cloud, and they must have the right names. The following call should usually be left as is:

```
bake3d(filename,displaychannels,P,Nn,"interpolate",1,
    "_area",ar,"_radiance_t",irrad);
```

Further down in our shader, we see the texture3d() call, which uses the filename provided and extracts the _ssdiffusion values from the brickmap into the ssdiffusion parameter of the shader. The SSS information on a brickmap that has been generated with the point data of ptfilter (using the ssdiffusion method) will always be named _ssdiffusion. The final step of our simple shader is to add the ambient and diffuse components plus the sss value, which will be 0 if no brickmap has been provided. Here is the final shader source code:

```
surface s_RP_sss(
        float bake = 0;
        string filename = "";
        string displaychannels = "";
        color surfacecolor = color (1);
        )
{
  normal Nn = normalize(N);
  color irrad, rad_t;
  float ar = area(P,"dicing");
  color ssdiffusion = 0;
  irrad = ambient() + diffuse(Nn) * surfacecolor;

  /* if the filename and displaychannels are not "" then write
     out the value */
  if ((filename != "") && (displaychannels != "")){
    if (bake == 1)
```

```
        bake3d(filename,displaychannels,P,Nn,"interpolate",1,
          "_area",ar,"_radiance_t",irrad);
    else
        texture3d(filename, P, N, "_ssdiffusion", ssdiffusion);
  }
  Ci = (irrad + ssdiffusion) * Os;
  Oi = Os;
}
```

Using the proper rendering attributes, we generate the image in Figures 15.13 and 15.14 using the sss_baking.rib file from the rib directory. Below the image is the point cloud that was written to disk by the bake() call. The soldier model was provided by Christophe Desse.

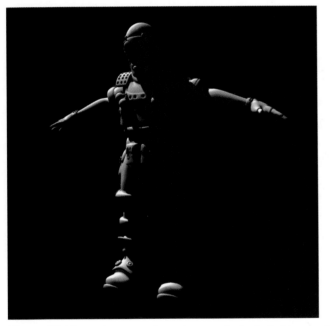

Figure 15.13 Result image of running our shader in baking mode.

Figure 15.14 The resulting point cloud when viewed with ptviewer.

With our beautiful irradiance point cloud ready, we will move to the second step of our three-step process, which corresponds to filtering the radiance values and calculating SSS contribution. We perform this operation by calling this command from a shell window:

```
ptfilter -ssdiffusion -material cream -unitlength 0.1 ssmap3.ptc
    ssdiffusion.ptc
```

`-ssdiffusion` tells ptfilter to calculate `ssdiffusion` contributions. `-material` indicates what type of material the calculated SSS should simulate. These are based on very extensive research performed by Henrik Wann Jensen, Stephen R. Marschner, Marc Levoy, and Pat Hanrahan. The materials supported by ptfilter are `apple`, `chicken1`, `chicken2`, `ketchup`, `marble`, `potato`, `skimmilk`, `wholemilk`, `cream`, `skin1`, `skin2`, and `spectralon`. You can use anything you think resembles your object the most.

The next parameter is `-unitlength`, which tells ptfilter the native unit in the current scene. If no unit length is provided, ptfilter will assume that the scene units are expressed in millimeters. Your scene must be expressed in millimeters, so if it uses centimeters, you need a value of 10; if it's meters, you need a value of 1,000. Using the previous call, we get a new point cloud named `ssdiffusion.ptc`, which will look like Figure 15.15. Changing the material to `skin1` will look like Figure 15.16.

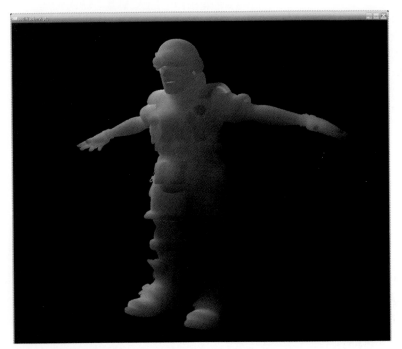

Figure 15.15 SSS computed using the cream model.

Figure 15.16 SSS computed using the skin1 model.

There are other parameters that are supported by ptfilter when performing SSS computations. Please read "The ptfilter Utility" section later in this chapter for a more detailed description. It is important to note that the filtering time for a point cloud is directly proportional to how many points are stored in the point cloud file, which in turn is derived by the resolution and the shading rate used on the render that performed the baking. Sometimes, you can get away with using a lower shading rate for SSS than a final image.

The final step is to convert point data into a brickmap, which is a lot more efficient to use at render time. We need to use the `brickmake` command, and for this exercise we will call it with its simplest form.

```
brickmake sssmap2.ptc sssdiffusion.bkm
```

We can now pass `sssdiffusion.bkm` as the `filename` parameter to our `s_RP_sss` shader. Make sure you turn off baking by setting it to 0. If you render the same scene as the one used for baking, you will have an image that looks like Figure 15.17.

Figure 15.17 Soldier rendered with SSS read from the brickmap.

Baking Rendered Data

Most of the high-end phenomena rendering introduced in this chapter will add a large amount of detail and richness to a scene. It will also add a lot more time to your renders, which creates an interesting conundrum: "We want the richness of the images, but we can't afford the rendering times." Since PRMan is used extensively in production, Pixar knows that telling a client that *rendering GI is expensive, and that's just the way it is* was never really an option. Considering that Pixar is one of its own biggest clients, it was in their interest to come up with a way to reduce rendering times. At the beginning, they came up with a technique for irradiance catching, followed by point cloud baking and reading. These solutions worked, but the amount of data stored was quite large, and the rendering times were still high because filtering and value lookup were performed on a point cloud that had thousands of points.

Eventually, Pixar came up with a sound solution: Why not use the same concept used for texture mipmaps, which are extremely efficient, and apply it to a 3D texture? That is pretty much what a brickmap is—a three-dimensional texture that is prefiltered and can be accessed with extraordinary efficiency. We will not go into the technical details of how brickmaps are created or filtered, but we do need to explain how they are accessed.

To understand brickmaps, we first need to take a closer look at point clouds. Point clouds are files that contain 3D data such as a point's position and its normal, plus whatever other channels the user saves in those points. These points and normals are stored in the object's local coordinate system (just like the points from the mesh). This makes baking ideal for objects that will not deform but will have rigid transformations. When you read a point cloud into a shader with the texture3d() call, you must provide a surface point and a normal. The texture3d() call will then go into the file provided, which can be a point cloud or a brickmap, and it will return the value of the queried channel stored at the point that matches the provided surface point and has a normal similar to the provided normal. This means that if your mesh changes for any reason (deformation or displacements), your point cloud might include bad lookups (which usually render as black) if you didn't take the proper steps in your shader to access the point cloud.

Baking Point Cloud Files

To bake out point cloud files in PRMan, the TD must take the proper steps to ensure that the data written is correct. There are several attributes that need to be set, and there needs to be a shader that can properly output the necessary data. Let's take a look at the attributes that need to be inserted into the RIB stream.

```
DisplayChannel "[class] type channelName"
```

You need to define a DisplayChannel for every channel you are planning to store into the point cloud. It is always advisable to include this directive before you declare any geometry objects in your scene. This tells PRMan that it needs to prepare a new display channel, which will be written to a display driver or as part of the channels stored using a bake3d() call. The class of the variable is optional, but the type and channelName must match those of the data that you are trying to write out.

```
Attribute "cull" "hidden" 0   # don't cull hidden surfaces
```

This attribute tells the renderer to disable the culling (dumping) of hidden surfaces. The default behavior for most renderers is to cull such surfaces to speed up time. If you don't disable the culling of hidden surfaces, all points that are hidden from the camera will not be stored in the point cloud, so if you move the object or your camera around, the surface will render black in those areas where it was invisible to the camera before.

```
Attribute "cull" "backfacing" 0   # don't cull backfacing surfaces
```

This attribute is similar to the previous attribute, but it disables the culling in backfacing surfaces. Backfacing surfaces are those in which the normal of a surface is pointing more than 90 degrees away from the incident vector I. So the difference between hidden and backfacing is that hidden is when a surface is not visible to the camera because other objects are blocking it, while backfacing is when a surface is not visible because it is blocking itself, such as the back side of a sphere. If you don't disable backfacing culling, all the parts of your object that face away from the camera in your baking pass will be rendered black.

```
Attribute "dice" "rasterorient" 0 # turn off view dependent dicing
```

This attribute allows you to control how a surface will be diced into micropolygons. Older versions of RenderMan always used a screen-aligned measure to decide how much a surface needed to be diced. This means that the surface's shading rate would change in the object based on its position in relation to the camera. By disabling this attribute, we make sure that each shading point is of the same size when it is stored in the point cloud. No matter how close to or far from the camera it is, the points will be constant. A clear example is when you are baking data for a model of a long table—a ridiculously long table. The shading rate on the points that are farthest away from the camera will be larger (fewer shading points) than those that are closest to the camera. If you use such a point cloud in a scene where the camera happens to be closer to the other end, you will see that the shading becomes splotchy with the loss of detail as the surfaces are farther from the camera.

Those are the attributes that need to be declared to ensure a good point cloud. There are many ways to ensure that these attributes are inserted only into the RIB stream in a baking pass. The method varies from program to program, and there are too many to list here.

The ptfilter Utility

Earlier in this chapter, we briefly skimmed the surface of this powerful utility, which ships with PRMan. This utility is needed because when we use bake3d() to store data in a point cloud, that point stores only information that was calculated at that particular point. There are certain lighting effects, such as final gathering and ssdiffusion, that need to be calculated based on an area of influence, taking into consideration adjacent points. To do these types of calculation in the 3D scene would be very memory and processor intensive. Using ptfilter, you can use optimized algorithms to calculate those lighting effects. Here is the API description as listed in PRMan's manual.

```
ptfilter [-filter photonmap|ssdiffusion|mergeicf] [-nphotons n] [-material
apple|chicken1|chicken2|ketchup|marble|potato|skimmilk|wholemilk|cream|skin1|
skin2|spectralon] [-unitlength length] [-scattering r g b] [-absorption r g
b] [-albedo r g b] [-diffusemeanfreepath r g b] [-ior ior] [-maxsolidangle
m] [-progress p] inputfiles outputfile
```

On the above statement, all parameters in square brackets [] are optional, and the values within those brackets are the values that can be passed to the parameter. A | separates the different values that can be used and only one of those can be used at a time. The -filter flag allows you to specify what filtering algorithm you would like to use. The most-used ones are photonmap and ssdiffusion. The mergeicf filter exists mostly for backward compatibility and allows you to merge several ICF (or OCF) files into a single ICF file. When using photonmap as your filter, the algorithm will calculate the contribution of the light at the current point based on a given number of points around it. When you use this filter, -nphotons becomes available. It allows you to define how many points around the current shading point should be evaluated for the GI calculations. The default value for -nphotons is 50; the higher this value, the more accurate your GI will be (and your calculation times will be longer, too).

When using -ssdiffusion as the filter, a lot more parameters are exposed to the user to control how the points are processed. The -material parameter allows you to define a preset material that has been implemented using the extensive research of [Jensen01.]. The -unitlength parameter allows you to tell the ptfilter utility what unit was used to store the data in the point cloud. If this is not provided, ptfilter will assume the units are millimeters. To change the value, you would need to provide the unit value in millimeters, so to use centimeters you must type **-unitlength 10**. If you would like to simulate other materials, you can use either of the following combinations to try to achieve the necessary look:

- -scattering (a color), which is a color that will be used to tint the scattering of the light

   -absorption (a color), which represents how much light is absorbed by the surface

   -ior (a float), which represents the index of refraction of the material

   or

- -albedo (a color)

   -diffusemeanfreepath (a color), which represents how deep into the surface the rays can enter (or how thick the surface is).

   -ior (a float) index of refraction.

One final parameter that we must cover is the -maxsolidangle parameter. This parameter acts like a speed/quality knob through which the lower the value, the longer it will take to compute.

Using ptfilter with the -ssdiffusion filter will create a new brickmap that will have a channel named _ssdiffusion, which is the name of the channel you must query to extract the SSS calculations stored in the brickmap.

The brickmake Utility

Point clouds are usable by themselves because texture3d() accepts them as input files. However, there are several problems attached to using point clouds:

- When a point cloud is accessed by the renderer, the entire point cloud is read into memory, even if only a few points will actually be used in the render.

- The entire point cloud file will remain in memory until the whole frame has finished.

- A point cloud file does not provide methods for level of detail representation, which makes filtering and blurring quite difficult.

This is where brickmaps save the day. Being a 3D version of the typical 2D mipmap texture, brickmaps are easily filtered, can be loaded and culled in segments just like 2D textures, and have level of detail methods that will make the renderer load only the necessary data to provide a smooth result based on the shading rate. To create a brickmap, use this syntax:

```
brickmake [-maxerror eps] [-radiusscale scale] [-maxdepth depth] [-ignorenor-
mals 0|1] [-progress 0|1|2] [-newer 0|1] pointcloudfiles brickmapfile
```

-maxerror allows you to control the amount of error that can be tolerated inside the brickmap. The smaller this value is, the more accurate the brickmap will be and the larger the texture file will be. -radiusscale allows you to specify the scaling value that will be applied to the radius of each point. The default value is 1, and values greater than 1 will result in a more blurred and smaller (file size) brickmap. The -maxdepth parameter takes an integer that specifies the maximum depth for a brickmap. This can be used to reduce the file size of the brickmap. The default value is 15, but the brickmake utility might not store that many levels if there is not enough detail to store them. If -ignorenormals is set to 1, then all data will be stored in the brickmap as if its normal were (0,0,0). The default value is 1 (use the provided normals). The -progress parameter prints out the progress of the operation, while -newer will only perform the operation if the point cloud is newer than the brickmap. The newer operation is useful for automation scripts through which you can generate the brickmap.

For a more technical description on brickmaps, refer to Per Christensen and Dana Batali's "An Irradiance Atlas for Global Illumination in Complex Production Scenes" available at http://graphics.pixar.com/.

ptviewer and brickviewer

PRMan ships with a couple of extra utilities that can be used to visualize the information stored on a point cloud or a brickmap. These utilities are ptviewer and brickviewer, used for viewing point clouds and brickmaps, respectively. The brickviewer utility takes the following parameters:

```
brickviewer [-minDepth x] [-maxDepth y] [-approximate] [-window W H] [-info]
brickmapfile
```

-minDepth and -maxDepth represent the minimum and maximum depths to display in the utility. Brickviewer will load all available levels by default. If you want the display to be faster but less accurate, you can use the -approximate parameter. The -window parameter allows you to define the width and height of the window, and -info displays the brickmap bounding box and camera information when loading the file. When the window is open, the following controls are provided:

- s switches between fast approximation and accurate display.

- up/down arrows switch between levels

- left/right arrows adjust the point size in approximate mode

- t toggles frames per second (fps) display

The ptviewer takes these parameters:

```
ptviewer [-help] [-info] [-onlyinfo] [-window W H] [-cropbbox x y z x y z]
[-multiply f] filename
```

If -info is used, then the bounding box of the point cloud is printed to the screen before the viewer is displayed. If -onlyinfo is used, then the info will be printed, and the program will exit without displaying the window. The -window allows you to provide the size of the viewing window. If the -cropbox parameter is defined, then only the points that are within the given bounding box (notice that the parameter takes 2 points) will be displayed. Finally, the -multiply parameter allows you to provide a scaler value that will be applied to all the values in the point cloud.

To navigate within the brickviewer or the ptviewer window, you can use the following combinations:

Rotate: Left button

Zoom: Shift+left button

Dolly: Right button

r: Resets the view

f: Centers the bounding box of points on the screen

q: Quit

16

Beyond RSL: DSO Shadeops

In this chapter, we will look at extending RSL's functionality via custom plug-ins written in C/C++. Such RSL plug-ins (which have been referred to as *DSO shadeops*, where DSO stands for Dynamic Shared Object) can significantly improve shading capability by allowing you to create powerful routines that simply cannot be implemented using RSL calls alone.

Need for RSL Plug-Ins

RSL calls offer rich functionality for carrying out a variety of shading calculations that include math calls, vector/matrix operations, space transformations, and lighting and pattern computations. Additional calculations can be expressed in the form of function calls, such as conversion to/from a new color space, a prototype for a new noise algorithm, and so on. But RSL functions are not very efficient because they are inlined by the shading compiler when they are called. This means that their invocations are not shared, be it from a single shader or multiple shaders (even when these shaders share an RSL function in source form via the #include statement).

Even so, combinations of built-in RSL calls alone are not sufficient to express arbitrary shading schemes than can be conjured up by developers. To address the need for developing custom functionality, PRMan has included the capability for creating DSO shadeops since version 3.8. The need for such DSOs arose during the production of *A Bug's Life*, when a rayserver DSO from PRMan was able to invoke BMRT (a now-defunct RenderMan implementation created by Larry Gritz) to carry out raytracing calls and return with RGBA values.

You can make a DSO shadeop do anything that a regular C/C++ program can do: create complex objects, allocate dynamic memory, link to external libraries for leveraging even more functionality, make system calls, read/write files, query databases, open pipes to other processes, embed a scripting language, interface with arbitrary hardware, do networking, create graphical user interfaces, draw to the screen, and so on. These capabilities are practically nonexistent in built-in RSL calls. In spite of all their power, there are a few limitations of DSO shadeops: They cannot call other shadeops or built-in RSL calls; the plug-in API defines a formal way of passing data back and forth between the renderer and DSOs, so they cannot hook into arbitrary points in the core of the renderer; they have no knowledge of a shading point's neighborhood topology; and they cannot make use of RSL globals such as P and N except when explicitly passed in via the defined interface.

Old-Style versus New-Style Plug-Ins

Prior to PRMan version 13.5, these DSOs have been referred to as DSO shadeops. With version 13.5, the RenderMan development team at Pixar has significantly enhanced the way these shadeops work, and has begun referring to them as *RSL plug-ins/SIMD plug-ins*. We will informally continue to use either term to talk about our plug-ins.

"SIMD" stands for *Single Instruction Multiple Data* and is a popular form of parallel processing. With regards to PRMan, SIMD makes it possible to run the same shader code over several data points (such as all points on a shading grid) at once, which is more efficient than doing so sequentially for each shading point. Further, with multithreading or parallel processing, several of these calculations can happen simultaneously, resulting in even more efficiency.

The difference between the older shadeops and the newer plug-ins is illustrated in Figure 16.1. On the left is shown the old interface, where within a shader, built-in RSL calls were run in SIMD fashion while DSO shadeops were not—they were invoked separately for each shading point on a grid. As you can imagine, this obviated some of the speed gains obtained by running compiled C/C++ code in the shadeops. In contrast, the new architecture brings SIMD invocation to DSOs as well, resulting in significant efficiency. For the first time, DSOs can be considered to be first-class citizens on par with RSL built-ins, keeping in mind their limitations mentioned at the end of the previous section. In addition to SIMD, our DSO plug-ins can now be run in multiple threads (more on threading at the end of the chapter).

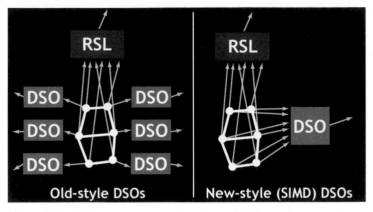

Figure 16.1 Difference between old and new DSO plug-in invocations

To illustrate the change between the old and new interface further, consider this sample RSL statement:

```
P = P + noise(P) + customnoise(P);
```

Here, `noise()` is, of course, a built-in call, while `customnoise()` would come from a DSO. With the pre–PRMan-13.5 interface, `noise()` was called in SIMD fashion while `customnoise()` was run sequentially for each point to be shaded on a grid. With the modern version of the interface, both `noise()` and `customnoise()` would run as SIMD invocations.

Creating and Using DSO Shadeops

In this section we are about to see 10 complete examples of RSL plug-ins. Before we do so, it is instructive to consider the workflow for developing and invoking a DSO plug-in. Here are the six steps involved:

1. Write C/C++ code to express the desired functionality. The header file `RslPlug-in.h` (which ships with the PRMan Developer's Kit) needs to be included, and the code needs to be linked with the library file `prman.lib`, which also ships with the Developer's Kit. Together, the header and library file contain the plug-in API that our DSOs need. In addition, the code can call functions and methods from additional libraries, use system calls, and so on, just like a regular C/C++ program.

2. Compile the plug-in into a DSO (`.so` extension under Linux/UNIX or `.dll` extension under Windows). You can either use the makefile mentioned in the PRMan Application Note that discusses RSL plug-ins or use a development platform (IDE) such as Eclipse or Windows-based Visual Studio. Figure 16.2 shows a snapshot of a successful plug-in compilation using Visual C++ 2005 Express Edition, which is a free download from Microsoft.

3. Place the plug-in .so/.dll (whose filename must be the same as the name of the function you are developing) in a known directory in the shader search-path that PRMan uses. Alternate locations can be communicated to the shader compiler using the -I flag.

4. In the shader, usually at the top, use a plug-in directive to declare your DSO function, such as this:

```
plug-in "customnoise"; // customnoise() from customnoise.so or .dll
```

5. Create the rest of the RSL shader as usual, calling your new DSO function as appropriate. Compile the shader.

6. Associate the shader with a RIB file as normal and render. During render time, your DSO will be loaded and run by PRMan when it encounters the shader that contains the DSO call.

Figure 16.2 Compiling a shadeop plug-in using Visual C++.

Example Shadeops

In this section, we look at 10 DSO shadeops. Full C++ code for each DSO is provided, as is a sample RSL shader for each that makes use of the DSO call(s). Looking at them, you should be able to see that writing these DSOs is pretty straightforward. There are pitfalls to watch for when it comes to multithreading and shared/global data, but we choose to ignore aspects related to that and instead focus on simpler examples that show the mechanics of DSO construction.

As you examine each DSO, it is instructive to see that, in some cases, equivalent functionality could not be achieved using built-in RSL calls alone, and in other cases, doing so would be tedious or would result in slow shader execution.

Parts of each example are used to explain API features which make the DSO creation possible. The section following these 10 DSO examples summarizes the plug-in API calls encountered throughout, and fills in others for the sake of completeness.

Our first example creates a DSO function called tod(), which uses the time of day (hour, minutes, seconds) to create a color (or as a variation, three floats) result.

The DSO is below. At the end of the source is this code:

```
static RslFunction myFunctions[] =
 {
   {"color tod()", timeOfDay, NULL, NULL },
   NULL
 };
```

The above creates an array called myFunctions of type RslFunction, which contains an entry for each call the DSO contains. In this example, there is just a single call, so there is only one entry. It specifies that the call (which we will make from RSL) is tod(), which will take no input and will return a color. The corresponding C++ function which we need to implement will be called timeOfDay. The last two arguments contain names of per-frame initialization and cleanup functions for this call, which in our case are NULL. So each entry declares an RSL function prototype and corresponding C++ function names to implement the RSL function.

The DSO function array needs to be declared as an RslFunctionTable, which should **always** be called RslPublicFunctions, like so:

```
RSLEXPORT RslFunctionTable RslPublicFunctions(myFunctions);
```

The rest of the code implements the timeOfDay call, whose function prototype looks like this:

```
RSLEXPORT int timeOfDay(RslContext* rslContext, int argc, const RslArg* argv[]);
```

Every DSO call will have the exact same prototype. An int value is returned (0 for success, others to denote errors), and the inputs are an RslContext (useful to retrieve the function call invocation's context, for example, for gaining access to data storage locations for purposes for handling multithreading properly), an RslArg argument's array, and argument count. The arguments array is what we use to retrieve inputs (if any) from the RSL call and also output return values (either as proper function returns for RSL calls or modifications of output arguments in their parameter list).

Once we have compiled the above plug-in code and have placed the resulting DSO (tod.dll on Windows or tod.so on Linux, for example), we can write a shader to call the DSO's timeOfDay function via a tod() RSL call:

```
// The 'plugin' directive tells the compiler which DSOs
// to search for finding plugin functions.
plugin "tod";
surface tod()
{
 Ci = tod();
}// tod()
```

Our shader is very simple. The plug-in statement at the top is what tells the RSL compiler which files to examine for locating subsequent DSO calls. In our example, tod.dll (or tod.so) is what will be searched. The shader body is just a single line, where the color output from tod() is directly used to set outgoing Ci. The result is shown at the left of Figure 16.3.

An alternative version of the tod() call is shown below. This implementation of timeOfDay sets three individual values, one each based on hour, minutes and seconds, via float array pointers called h, m, and s. These h, m, and s variables are of type RslFloatIter and are used to output values via argv[1], argv[2], and argv[3], respectively. argv[0] is not used. The RslFunction array element

```
{"void tod(output float h, output float m, output float s)",
          timeOfDay, NULL, NULL }
```

correspondingly has been declared to be able to receive the three floats from timeOfDay() call via the parameter list. The RSL call will not receive an actual return value, which is signified by the void return type in the above declaration.

```
#include <stdlib.h>
#include <stdio.h>
#include <string>
#include <math.h>
#include <time.h>
#include "RslPlugin.h"

using std::string;

extern "C" {
  RSLEXPORT int timeOfDay(RslContext* rslContext,
                          int argc, const RslArg* argv[])
  {
    RslFloatIter h(argv[1]);
    RslFloatIter m(argv[2]);
    RslFloatIter s(argv[3]);
```

```
    time_t raw;
    time(&raw);
    struct tm* timeInfo = localtime(&raw);
    // the print statement is here just so you can see what is being output
    printf("%02d:%02d:%02d\n",timeInfo->tm_hour,timeInfo->tm_min,
            timeInfo->tm_sec);

    int numVals = RslArg::NumValues(argc,argv);
    for(int i=0;i<numVals;i++) {
      (*h) = ((float)(timeInfo->tm_hour))/23;
      (*m)  = ((float)(timeInfo->tm_min))/59;
      (*s)  = ((float)(timeInfo->tm_sec))/59;
      ++h;++m;++s;
    }

    return 0;
  }// timeOfDay()

  static RslFunction myFunctions[] =
  {
    {"void tod(output float h, output float m, output float s)",
     timeOfDay, NULL, NULL },
    NULL
  };
  RSLEXPORT RslFunctionTable RslPublicFunctions(myFunctions);
}; /* extern "C" */
```

Note that to get our iteration loop count, we are using a static form of NumValues().
The reason is explained when we discuss the cmix DSO below.

The shader that makes use of this alternate DSO call is shown below. We simply
call tod(h,m,s) and have the DSO set h, m, and s for us. Just for variation, we use
the three values as hue, saturation, and value (instead of R,G,B) by specifying hsv
color space in the color construction call. The result is shown at the right of Figure
16.3. Notice that we would obtain the same functionality as the first version of
the DSO if we simply use color (h,m,s) instead.

```
plugin "tod";
surface tod()
{
 float h,m,s;
 tod(h,m,s);
 Ci = color "hsv" (h,m,s);
}// tod()
```

Figure 16.3 Using time-of-day to shade.

In the HSV version at the right of Figure 16.3, you can notice a color change from top to bottom of the image—the color gets brighter. This is because with HSV, the seconds value changes by a few units between the time the grids at the top of the image and those at the bottom were shaded by RenderMan. In our shader we are using seconds to set value (brightness) in HSV color space. To have all the grids be the same color so that we get a completely flat image, we need to make our DSO return a single value for all points on all grids. This can be done by creating a per-frame initialization call for timeOfDay() where the current time is retrieved just once for each frame and stored. Inside the per-grid shading loop in timeOfDay(), we would simply set outgoing hour, minutes, and seconds value to this previously-stored set of values. You can try to create such a DSO as an exercise. The "API Support" section later in this chapter has more information relevant to this.

A more elaborate version of the tod() DSO was presented by Mach Kobayashi at the "Stupid RenderMan/RAT Tricks" event (part of the RenderMan User Group meeting) held during SIGGRAPH 2007. Julian used the retrieved time values to color appropriate parts of 7-segment LED numerals, creating a digital-clock representation. Something like this might be useful for watermarking renders with time-stamp values. Incidentally, Mach's DSO used the old style API to obtain time values.

Our next example colors all incoming grid points using a single, random color value. This is very similar to the built-in randomgrid() RSL call. In the variation shown in the code below and at the top row of Figure 16.4, random values for r, g, and b variables are generated outside the grid point loop and are used to set out-going color in the loop over incoming grid points. This makes all points in a grid the same color, which would be different for adjacent grids. That is what creates a colorful patchwork over the rendered surface, visualizing for us what the grid extents look like.

Alternately, as shown at the bottom of Figure 16.4 and in the commented out sections below, we could come up with a single random value outside the grid sample loop to serve as a gray value for the whole grid, and use another "coin flip" random value 'flip' inside the loop to decide whether to multiply the gray value by 0.25 or 0.75. The result is that we can tell grids apart based on their overall gray value, and can discern individual micropolygons in each grid based on the random light/dark distribution within each grid.

Codewise, there is nothing new to point out. The function declaration shows that the RSL gridcol call takes no inputs and returns a color value and the corresponding C++ call is called gridCol(). There is one thing to note—the color result is set via an RslPointIter type rather than an RslColorIter type just to show that internally these are equivalent. (This is probably not a good idea when future versions of the API/compiler might perform more strict type checking.)

```
#include <stdio.h>
#include <string>
#include <ctime>
#include <cstdlib>
#include <iostream>
#include <iomanip>
#include "RslPlugin.h"

using namespace std;

extern "C" {
  RSLEXPORT int gridCol(RslContext* rslContext,
                        int argc, const RslArg* argv[])
  {
    RslPointIter result(argv[0]);
    int numVals = argv[0]->NumValues();

    // either use the r,g,b values from the stmt. below, or comment it
    // out and uncomment the 'darken' line and 'flip' block below
    float r = ((float)rand())/RAND_MAX, g = ((float)rand())/RAND_MAX,
          b = ((float)rand())/RAND_MAX;

    // used with 'flip' below
    // float darken = (float)(0.25 + 0.5*((float)rand())/RAND_MAX);

    for(int i=0;i<numVals;i++) {
```

```
      // used with 'darken' above
      /*float flip = ((float)rand())/RAND_MAX;
      float r,g,b;
      if(flip>0.5)
      {
        r = g = b = (float)(darken*0.25);
      }
      else
      {
        r = g = b = (float)(darken*0.75);
      }*/
      (*result)[0] = r; (*result)[1] = g; (*result)[2] = b;
      ++result;
    }
    return 0;
  }// gridCol()

  static RslFunction myFunctions[] =
  {
    {"color gridcol()", gridCol, NULL, NULL },
    NULL
  };
  RSLEXPORT RslFunctionTable RslPublicFunctions(myFunctions);
}; /* extern "C" */
```

Here is the RSL shader that uses gridcol():

```
plugin "gridcol";

surface gcol()
{
  Ci = gridcol();
}
```

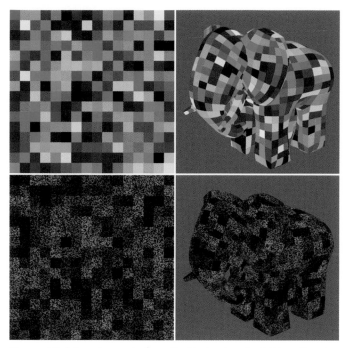

Figure 16.4 Random coloring of grids (top) and additionally micropolygons (bottom).

The next example shows how to implement a pair of RSL calls, bias() and gain(), which nonlinearly modify their inputs (Figure 16.5). This functionality is very useful in a variety of situations ranging from color correction to modifying noise distribution frequencies. The functions' domain, as well as range, is 0..1.

The RslFunction array now contains two elements, one for bias() and the other for gain(). The corresponding C++ calls are biasFloat and gainFloat. Both RSL calls need two inputs—the value to modify, and a parameter to control the extent of modification. They return with a single output, which is the modified value.

Both the biasFloat and gainFloat calls in turn invoke the same bias calculation formula, encapsulated in biasfunc below. x is the incoming value, which is non-linearly modified based on a. Note that a=0.5 is the "no op" value, where the return value is x (output is the same as input).

```
#include <stdlib.h>
#include <stdio.h>
#include <string>
#include <math.h>
#include "RslPlugin.h"

using std::string;

extern "C" {
```

```
float biasfunc(float x, float a) {
  return powf(x,-logf(a)/logf(2));
}

RSLEXPORT int biasFloat(RslContext* rslContext,
                        int argc, const RslArg* argv[])
{
  RslFloatIter result(argv[0]);
  RslFloatIter x(argv[1]);
  RslFloatIter a(argv[2]);

  int numVals = argv[0]->NumValues();

  for(int i=0;i<numVals;i++) {
    *result = biasfunc(*x,*a);
    ++x; ++a;
    ++result;
  }
  return 0;
}// biasFloat()

RSLEXPORT int gainFloat(RslContext* rslContext,
                        int argc, const RslArg* argv[])
{
  RslFloatIter result(argv[0]);
  RslFloatIter x(argv[1]);
  RslFloatIter a(argv[2]);

  int numVals = argv[0]->NumValues();

  for(int i=0;i<numVals;i++) {
    *result = (float)(0.5*((*x<0.5)?
    biasfunc(2*(*x),1-*a):(2-biasfunc(2*(1-*x),1-*a))));
    ++x; ++a;
    ++result;
  }
  return 0;
}// gainFloat()

static RslFunction myFunctions[] =
{
  {"float bias(varying float, varying float)", biasFloat, NULL, NULL },
  {"float gain(varying float, varying float)", gainFloat, NULL, NULL },
```

```
      NULL
  };
  RSLEXPORT RslFunctionTable RslPublicFunctions(myFunctions);
}; /* extern "C" */
```

The RSL shader below uses the bias() or gain() call to plot a curve to visualize the nonlinear nature of the calls. Since we have no way to trace a continuous line across a surface, we render closely spaced antialiased spots instead that are sampled along the curve, in order to approximate it.

```
plugin "biasgain";
#define BIGNUM 1000000

surface bgain(string bg="bias"; float a=0.5, th=0.01)
{
  float xpts[1000+1], ypts[1000+1];
  float cldist = BIGNUM;
  float i;
  for(i=0;i<1000;i+=1)
    {
      float x = i/1000;

      xpts[i] = x;
      if(bg=="bias")
        ypts[i] = bias(x,a);
      else
        ypts[i] = gain(x,a);
    }

  for(i=0;i<1000;i+=1)
    {
      float ss=s, tt=t;
      float dsq = (xpts[i]-ss)*(xpts[i]-ss)+(ypts[i]-tt)*(ypts[i]-tt);

      if(dsq<cldist)
      {
        cldist = dsq;
      }
    }
  Oi = Os;
  Ci = Os*Cs*smoothstep(0,th,cldist);
}// bgain
```

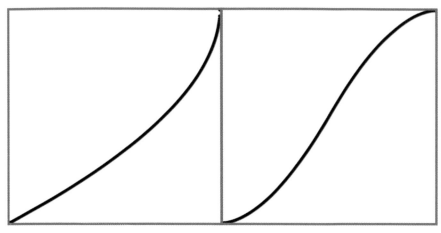

Figure 16.5 Visualization of bias() and gain() DSO calls.

In the above shader, we calculate 1,000 bias/gain values (the count being chosen arbitrarily) and locate the closest one to our current shading point by calculating and tracking the distance between our point and the bias/gain function samples. We then use smoothstep() along with a user-specified threshold to use the closest distance value to render a spot. The results are shown in Figure 16.5 (where the left image shows a bias() curve and the right, a gain() one).

An alternate way to implement the curve-drawing functionality would be to calculate the array of function values as a DSO call. As an exercise, add such a pair of calls to the DSO, one for bias and one for gain. Given a user-specified count, the calls would calculate that many values for bias or given, along evenly-spaced values between 0..1. This will significantly speed up the curve rendering. Note that you will be returning an array of values at each grid point, instead of a single value at each.

The next DSO makes it possible to mix a pair of colors A and B, given a mix fraction f and the mode of mixing: arithmetic, geometric, or harmonic. As you might recall, given two numbers A and B, their arithmetic, geometric, and harmonic means AM, GM, and HM are

```
AM = (a+b)/2
GM = sqrt(a×b)
HM = ab/(a+b)
```

The above can be generalized to calculate not just the mean (where their mix fraction is always 0.5) but any arbitrary mix proportion with a mix factor of f:

```
amix = (1-f)×A + f×B
gmix = exp((1-f)×log(A) + f×log(B))
hmix = 1/((1-f)/A + f/B) = AB/((1-f)×B+f×A)
```

Note that the built-in mix() call calculates the amix value above for colors, floats, points, normals, and vectors. Our DSO is a generalization of mix() for the color and float types (you can add the other types as an exercise) to handle the geometric and harmonic cases, too.

The two function calls are declared in the function table as

```
{"float cmix(varying float, varying float, varying float, uniform string)",
cmixFloat, NULL, NULL},
```

```
{"color cmix(varying color, varying color, varying float, uniform string)",
cmixTriple, NULL, NULL}
```

In each call, the first two values specify either A and B floats or colors, and the third value specifies the mix fraction f. Because these can vary across the grid, they are declared as varying float or varying color. In contrast, the mix type string specifier (whose value is either AM or GM or HM) is a uniform string. The uniform qualifier means that the value is the same across the grid for all shading points.

Note that our float result is varying float by default (likewise for color). We can explicitly specify the RSL function result to be uniform if that is appropriate. In that case, our shading points loop will run exactly once, as opposed to the varying result case where the loop runs for each active shading point.

If the result is varying and the incoming arguments are a mix of varying and uniform types, the shading loop will run once for each active point on the grid. But if the result is uniform and the incoming arguments are a mix of varying and uniform types, the shader compiler will generate an error because of the presence of varying parameters. In other words, uniform result calls can only have uniform arguments.

Also, if our call has no formal return and only returns values via output parameters in the RSL argument list, we need to explicitly examine each argument whether it is varying or uniform. The IsVarying() method of the RslIter iterator class is used for this purpose. If we know that a parameter is uniform, we can retrieve its value outside the shading points loop, which is more efficient than fetching the same value repeatedly inside the loop. If we just want the loop iteration count, that is easily obtained using the static method

```
int numVals = RslArg::NumValues(argc, argv);
```

instead of the version used when there is a formal return value, which is

```
int numVals = argv[0]->NumValues();
```

The code below shows the whole plug-in, with implementations of both the float and color variations.

```
#include <stdlib.h>
#include <stdio.h>
```

```cpp
#include <string>
#include <math.h>
#include "RslPlugin.h"

using std::string;

extern "C" {
  RSLEXPORT int cmixFloat(RslContext* rslContext,
                          int argc, const RslArg* argv[])
  {
    RslFloatIter result(argv[0]);
    RslFloatIter f1(argv[1]);
    RslFloatIter f2(argv[2]);
    RslFloatIter mix(argv[3]);
    RslStringIter mixtype(argv[4]);

    int numVals = argv[0]->NumValues();
    string mxtype(*mixtype);
    if (mxtype == "AM") {
      for (int i = 0; i < numVals; ++i) {
        (*result) = (1-*mix)*(*f1) + (*mix)*(*f2);
        ++f1; ++f2; ++mix; ++mixtype;
        ++result;
      }
    }
    else if (mxtype == "GM") {
      for (int i = 0; i < numVals; ++i) {
        if((((*f1))==0)||(((*f2))==0))
          (*result) = 0;
        else
        {
          (*result) = expf((1-*mix)*logf((((*f1)))+(*mix)*logf((((*f2))));
        }
        ++f1; ++f2; ++mix; ++mixtype;
        ++result;
      }
    }
    else if (mxtype == "HM") {
      for (int i = 0; i < numVals; ++i) {
        if((((*f1))==0)||(((*f2))==0))
          (*result) = 0;
        else
        {
```

```
             (*result) = (((((*f1))*((*f2)))/((1-*mix)*((*f2))+(*mix)*((*f1)))));
        }
        ++f1; ++f2; ++mix; ++mixtype;
        ++result;
     }
  }
  return 0;
}// cmixFloat()


RSLEXPORT int cmixTriple(RslContext* rslContext,
                          int argc, const RslArg* argv[])
{
  RslPointIter result(argv[0]);
  RslPointIter col1(argv[1]);
  RslPointIter col2(argv[2]);
  RslFloatIter mix(argv[3]);
  RslStringIter mixtype(argv[4]);

  int numVals = argv[0]->NumValues();
  string mxtype(*mixtype);
  if (mxtype == "AM") {
    for (int i = 0; i < numVals; ++i) {
      (*result)[0] = (1-*mix)*(*col1)[0] + (*mix)*(*col2)[0];
      (*result)[1] = (1-*mix)*(*col1)[1] + (*mix)*(*col2)[1];
      (*result)[2] = (1-*mix)*(*col1)[2] + (*mix)*(*col2)[2];
      ++col1; ++col2; ++mix; ++mixtype;
      ++result;
    }
  }
  else if (mxtype == "GM") {
    for (int i = 0; i < numVals; ++i) {
      if(((((*col1)[0])==0)||(((*col2)[0])==0))
        (*result)[0] = 0;
      else
      {
        (*result)[0] = expf((1-*mix)*logf(((*col1)[0]))+
        (*mix)*logf(((*col2)[0])));
      }
      if(((((*col1)[1])==0)||(((*col2)[1])==0))
        (*result)[1] = 0;
      else
      {
```

```
          (*result)[1] = expf((1-*mix)*logf((((*col1)[1]))+
          (*mix)*logf((((*col2)[1]))));
        }
      if(((((*col1)[2])==0)||((((*col2)[2])==0))
        (*result)[2] = 0;
      else
      {
        (*result)[2] = expf((1-*mix)*logf((((*col1)[2]))+
        (*mix)*logf((((*col2)[2]))));
      }
      ++col1; ++col2; ++mix; ++mixtype;
      ++result;
    }
  }
  else if (mxtype == "HM") {
    for (int i = 0; i < numVals; ++i) {
      if(((((*col1)[0])==0)||((((*col2)[0])==0))
        (*result)[0] = 0;
      else
      {
        (*result)[0] = (((((*col1)[0])*((*col2)[0])))/
        ((1-*mix)*((*col2)[0])+(*mix)*((*col1)[0]))));
      }
      if(((((*col1)[1])==0)||((((*col2)[1])==0))
        (*result)[1] = 0;
      else
      {
        (*result)[1] = (((((*col1)[1])*((*col2)[1])))/
        ((1-*mix)*((*col2)[1])+(*mix)*((*col1)[1]))));
      }
      if(((((*col1)[2])==0)||((((*col2)[2])==0))
        (*result)[2] = 0;
      else
      {
        (*result)[2] = (((((*col1)[2])*((*col2)[2])))/
        ((1-*mix)*((*col2)[2])+(*mix)*((*col1)[2]))));
      }
      ++col1; ++col2; ++mix; ++mixtype;
      ++result;
    }
  }
  return 0;
```

```
  }// cmixTriple()

  static RslFunction myFunctions[] =
  {
    {"float cmix(varying float, varying float, varying float,
               uniform string)", cmixFloat, NULL, NULL },
    {"color cmix(varying color, varying color, varying float,
               uniform string)", cmixTriple, NULL, NULL },NULL
  };
  RSLEXPORT RslFunctionTable RslPublicFunctions(myFunctions);
}; /* extern "C" */
```

Here is a shader that exercises the plug-in. We interpolate between two colors across a square, varying the interpolation type down the square from AM to GM to HM, ending with AM again. The result is seen in Figure 16.6. Each interpolation type is distinct, which is what generates the three sharp borders at the interfaces between the four regions (AM/GM, GM/HM, and HM/AM).

```
plugin "cmix";

surface colmix(color A=0, B=1)
{
  if (t<0.25)
    Ci = cmix(A,B,s,"AM");
  else if (t<0.5)
    Ci = cmix(A,B,s,"GM");
  else if (t<0.75)
    Ci = cmix(A,B,s,"HM");
  else
    Ci = cmix(A,B,s,"AM");
}// colmix
```

Figure 16.6 Arithmetic, geometric, and harmonic blending of two colors.

2D Halton sequence computation is the topic for the next DSO we will consider. Halton, Hammersely, Sobol, and so on are examples of quasi-random (or low discrepancy) sequences, which can serve as alternatives for random or pseudorandom number sequences. Although numbers in a quasi-random sequence appear to be random, mathematically speaking they are not—the sequence values are computed using deterministic algorithms (where the next number in the sequence is available by iterating the algorithm one more time).

The Halton sequence is probably the easiest quasi-random sequence we can construct. It uses a prime number as a basis for construction. For example, we use the prime number 2 as a base to express natural numbers 1,2,3... , adding a ".0" at the end of each resulting "base2" (binary) value. We then reverse the binary digits (starting with "0.") and express the result back in base10. In other words:

```
1: 1.0 -> 0.1 -> 1/2
2: 10.0 -> 0.01 -> 1/4
3: 11.0 -> 0.11 -> 3/4
4: 100.0 -> 0.001 -> 1/8
5: 101.0 -> 0.101 -> 5/8
```

So the first five values of the Halton sequence that uses 2 for its generator base are $1/2, 1/4, 3/4, 1/8$ and $5/8$. Likewise, we can use other prime numbers such as 3, 5, 7, 13, and so on to generate more Halton sequences.

To construct a 2D Halton sequence, we simply create two independent 1D Halton sequences using two different primes, and pair up values from the two sequences to obtain 2D (x,y) points that lie within the unit square. Well-chosen prime number pairs result in a good sequence of 2D points, which will fill the unit square uniformly yet randomly—the square always appears well filled, with an even distribution of points such that there are no vacant areas or overcrowding of points. This makes it unnecessary to have to do point rejection while filling the plane or point repulsion after the plane is filled, as might be required if a pseudorandom number generator is used instead.

The following DSO call takes a point on the unit square (we will use texture coordinates (s,t) for these in RSL), two primes, and a count that specifies how many Halton (x,y) points to generate. It tracks the distance of each of these generated Halton points to the given point, and outputs the closest distance. The results are shown in Figure 16.7, which visualizes the same set of Halton points in different ways (see below).

```
#include <stdlib.h>
#include <stdio.h>
#include <string>
#include <math.h>
#include "RslPlugin.h"

using std::string;

extern "C" {
  RSLEXPORT int haltonCalc(RslContext* rslContext,
                           int argc, const RslArg* argv[])
  {
    RslFloatIter result(argv[0]);
    RslFloatIter p1(argv[1]);
    RslFloatIter p2(argv[2]);
    RslFloatIter n(argv[3]);
    RslFloatIter s(argv[4]);
    RslFloatIter t(argv[5]);

    int numVals = argv[0]->NumValues();
    for(int i=0;i<numVals;i++) {
      float hx,hy;
      float p, ip, k, kk, a;
      float mindist = INT_MAX;
      for (k=0;k<(*n);k++)
      {
        hx = 0;
```

```
        ip = 1.0f/(*p1);
        p=ip;
        for (kk=k ; kk>0 ;kk=floor(kk/(*p1)))
        {
          a = fmod(kk,(*p1));
          if(a>0)
            hx += a*p;
            p = p*ip;
        }

        hy = 0;
        ip = 1.0f/(*p2);
        p=ip;
        for (kk=k ; kk>0 ; kk=floor(kk/(*p2)))
        {
          a = fmod(kk,(*p2));
          if(a>0)
            hy += a*p;
            p = p*ip;
        }

        float dist = sqrt((*s-hx)*(*s-hx)+(*t-hy)*(*t-hy));
        if(dist<mindist) mindist = dist;
      }
      *result = mindist;
      ++p1; ++p2; ++n; ++s; ++t;
      ++result;
    }// next i
    return 0;
  }// haltonCalc()

  static RslFunction myFunctions[] =
  {
    {"float haltondist(uniform float, uniform float, uniform float,
      varying float, varying float)", haltonCalc, NULL, NULL },NULL
  };
  RSLEXPORT RslFunctionTable RslPublicFunctions(myFunctions);
}; /* extern "C" */
```

Let us look at the shader that uses the 2D Halton sequence to shade a unit square. As you can see, the call to haltondist() sends in (s,t) as the value for the free-standing point which we use to compute a closest distance to some Halton (x,y).

To obtain Figure 16.7's images, we use prime numbers 2 and 3 for the two independent sequences, and generate 50 Halton points. The resulting d values will lie between 0 and 1 since we operate in a unit square in the RIB file. Values close to 0 indicate that the (s,t) in question lies close to a Halton point, so it is a good way to visualize where the points lie on the square (the corresponding locations will be black). Values farther from Halton points get brighter, resulting in a Voronoi cell pattern (top right, Figure 16.7). By scaling the d value using a dmult value such as 60, we brighten the interior of the cells which leads to isolated black dots, which depict Halton point centers (top left, Figure 16.7).

The commented-out lines in the code below show two other possibilities. By inverting the scaled distance, we are able to obtain bubble-like shading, as seen in the bottom left of Figure 16.7. Finally, doing the grayscale inversion on the fractional distance remainder (which is obtained by mod(d*dmult,1)) produces concentric dark/light rings in place of the smooth bubbles. This is shown at the bottom right of Figure 16.7.

```
plugin "halton";

surface halton(uniform float p1=2, p2=3, n=10, dmult=1)
{
  float gray;

  float d = haltondist(p1,p2,n,s,t);

  // black dots on white bg!
  gray = d*dmult;

  // bubbles
  // gray = 1-d*dmult;

  // rings
  // gray = 1-mod(d*dmult,1);

  Ci = color(gray,gray,gray);
}// halton
```

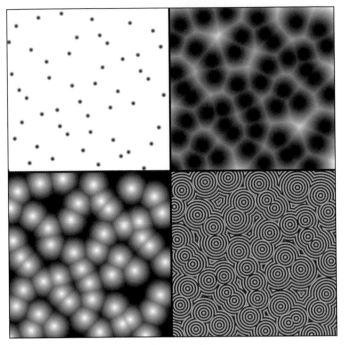

Figure 16.7 Visualizations of a 2D Halton point sequence.

In the DSO above, we calculate the same set of Halton points repeatedly inside the shading points loop in order to track the closest one to each shading point. A more efficient version (which is left as an exercise for you to implement) would calculate the point set just once in a per-frame initializer call, and will simply look it up inside the grid point iteration loop.

The following DSO shows how to plot arbitrary analytical plane curves, which can exist in parametric, implicit, or explicit form, in Cartesian or polar space. Such functionality could come in handy in a variety of situations.

Specifically, we draw Pendulum Harmonograph curves, which are pretty curves resulting from damped oscillations of a double conical pendulum—hence the call dcp() below. The curves are described by a parametric equation in Cartesian coordinate space. An astonishing variety of curves can result from varying the 12 parameters that control them. The parameters relate to frequency, amplitude, and damping of circular oscillations.

The curve drawing follows the same technique we used to plot bias() and gain() curves earlier. We calculate an array of points on the curve (whose count is specified by tmax and tincr below, where we step from 0 to tmax in steps of tincr using the result as our parametric variable). From this collection of points, we track the one closest to an incoming point (in the shader we use (s,t)) and output the distance to it as the DSO function result.

Two examples of these curves are shown in Figure 16.8. The one on the left has
its parameter increment value tincr set to a large value on purpose to show the
point-wise nature of the curve building technique. For the curve on the right, the
increment is finer, resulting in a smoother curve.

Both the RSL function dcp() and the corresponding dcp_eval() call that implements it take 14 parameters related to curve construction, in addition to an arbitrary point passed in. As you can see below, this leads to verbose, repetitive code
where the 14 parameters are retrieved and their pointers updated in lock-step. As
a variation, we can use a float array in RSL to send in these 14 arguments as a set,
and handle it correspondingly in dcp_eval().

```
#include <stdlib.h>
#include <stdio.h>
#include <string>
#include <math.h>
#include "RslPlugin.h"
#include <limits.h>

using std::string;

extern "C" {
  RSLEXPORT int dcp_eval(RslContext* rslContext,
                         int argc, const RslArg* argv[])
  {
    RslFloatIter result(argv[0]);

    RslFloatIter a1(argv[1]);
    RslFloatIter a2(argv[2]);
    RslFloatIter b1(argv[3]);
    RslFloatIter b2(argv[4]);
    RslFloatIter c1(argv[5]);
    RslFloatIter c2(argv[6]);
    RslFloatIter d1(argv[7]);
    RslFloatIter d2(argv[8]);
    RslFloatIter e1(argv[9]);
    RslFloatIter e2(argv[10]);
    RslFloatIter f1(argv[11]);
    RslFloatIter f2(argv[12]);
    RslFloatIter tmax(argv[13]);
    RslFloatIter tincr(argv[14]);
    RslFloatIter x(argv[15]);
    RslFloatIter y(argv[16]);
```

```
float *xpts, *ypts;
xpts = (float *) malloc(((((*tmax)/(*tincr))+1)*sizeof(float));
ypts = (float *) malloc(((((*tmax)/(*tincr))+1)*sizeof(float));

int numVals = argv[0]->NumValues();
float a;
int n;

for(int i=0;i<numVals;i++) {
  float xmin=INT_MAX,xmax=-INT_MAX,ymin=INT_MAX,ymax=-INT_MAX;
  for(a=0,n=0;a<(*tmax);a+=(*tincr),n++)
  {
    float r1 = (float)exp(-(*a1)*.01*a);
    float r2 = (float)exp(-(*a2)*.01*a);
    float s1 = r1*sin((*f1)*a);
    float s2 = r2*sin((*f2)*a);
    float t1 = r1*cos((*f1)*a);
    float t2 = r2*cos((*f2)*a);
    xpts[n] = ((*b1)*s1 + (*b2)*s2 + (*c1)*t1 + (*c2)*t2);
    ypts[n] = ((*d1)*s1 + (*d2)*s2 + (*e1)*t1 + (*e2)*t2);

    if(xpts[n]<xmin) xmin = xpts[n];
    if(xpts[n]>xmax) xmax = xpts[n];
    if(ypts[n]<ymin) ymin = ypts[n];
    if(ypts[n]>ymax) ymax = ypts[n];
  }

  float rangex = (xmax-xmin), rangey=(ymax-ymin);
  for(n=0;n<((*tmax)/(*tincr));n+=1)
  {
    // rescale points to shrink them so they don't touch frame edges
    xpts[n] = 0.025+0.95*(xpts[n]-xmin)/rangex;
    ypts[n] = 0.025+0.95*(ypts[n]-ymin)/rangey;
  }
  float cldist = INT_MAX;
  for(n=0;n<((*tmax)/(*tincr));n++)
  {
    float dsq = (xpts[n]-(*x))*(xpts[n]-(*x))+
    (ypts[n]-(*y))*(ypts[n]-(*y));
    if(dsq<cldist)
    {
      cldist = dsq;
    }
```

```
      }
      *result = cldist;

      ++a1;++a2;++b1;++b2;++c1;++c2;++d1;++d2;++e1;++e2;++f1;++f2;
      ++tmax;++tincr;++x;++y;
      ++result;
    }
    free(xpts);
    free(ypts);
    return 0;
  }// dcp_eval()

  static RslFunction myFunctions[] =
  {
    {"float dcp(uniform float, uniform float, uniform float,
               uniform float, uniform float, uniform float,
               uniform float, uniform float, uniform float,
               uniform float, uniform float, uniform float,
               uniform float, uniform float, varying float,
               varying float)", dcp_eval, NULL, NULL },NULL
  };
  RSLEXPORT RslFunctionTable RslPublicFunctions(myFunctions);

}; /* extern "C" */
```

The dcp surface shader that plots the curves is shown next. As already mentioned, it passes 14 curve-related parameters and (s,t) to the dcp() call, and uses the returned distance value along with a threshold distance to create anti-aliased spots via smoothstep(). This creates a continuous-looking curve if the spots are overlapped closely enough.

The shader also contains, in comment form, parameter sets that result in pretty curves. You can use these as starting points, modify one parameter at a time in small increments, and discover more pleasing curves.

As usual, another assignment for you is to create a per-frame initializer call that computes the curve once, making it available for subsequent lookup inside the shading samples loop.

```
plugin "dcp";
// The following groups of parameters describe lovely curves.
// Each set shows a1,a2,b1,b2,c1,c2,d1,d2,e1,e2,f1,f2,tincr,tmax.
// Classic_1, rounded rect.
// dcp .3 .1 1.5 1.55 1.5 1.55 -1.5 1.55 1.5 1.55 2.8 2.864 0.01 100;
// Classic_2, 5-fold flower
```

```
// dcp .4 1 1.4 -1.5 1.4 1.5 -1.4 1.5 1.4 1.5 2.0 3.0 0.05 200;
// Classic 3, spiralling spiral
// dcp 1. 1. 3. 0. 0 .3 0 -.3 3. 0 .2 5. .01 100;
// dcp 1. 1. 2.5 0. 0 .312 0 -.3 2.5 0 .2 4. .1 200;  // variation_1
// dcp 1. 1. -2.5 0. 0 .312 0 -.3 2.5 0 .2 4. .1 200; // variation_2
// Classic_4, double burritos
// dcp 1. .3 2. -.65 2. .65 -2 .65 -2 .65 1. 3.01 .05 200;
// Classic_5,butterfly
// dcp .25 2. 4. 0. 0 0 0 4 0 0 1 2.03 .05 200;
// Classic_6, spider web
// dcp 1 3 2 -1 2 1 2 -1 -2 -1 .5 5 .05 200;
// Classic_7.dat, another b'fly
// dcp .25 2 4 0 0 0 0 4 0 0 1 2 .01 100;
// More:
// dcp 1 2 -2 1 0.5 -0.25 0 0 1 -2 2 4.0 0.025 100; // nice1, fun owl
// dcp 1 2 -2 1 0.5 -0.25 0 0 1 -2 2 4.0 0.02 120;  // nice2
// dcp 1 1.1 -1 2.1 3.14 1.2 0 1 -1 1 2 3. .05 200; // nice3 - broken disk
// dcp 1 2.01 -1 2.1 3.14 1.2 0 1 -1 1 2 3. .05 200;n // nice4 - like nice3
// dcp -.1 2.005 -.099 2.1 3.14 1.2 0.4 1.2 -1 1 2 3. .05 200; // manta ray
// dcp -.075 2.005 -.099 2.1 3.14 1.2 0.4 1.2 -1 1 2. 4. .1 200; //  plane
// dcp -.075 2.005 -.099 2.1 3.14 1.2 1.4 1.2 -1.1 1.1 2. 3. .1 200;
// dcp 0.08 2.005 -.099 2.1 3.14 1.2 1.4 1.2 -1.1 1.1 2. 3. .01 100;
// dcp 0.08 2.005 -.099 2.1 3. 1.2 1.4 1.2 -1.1 1.1 2. 3..05 200; // fish2


// Given 12 coeffs, eval curve, then smoothstep() for shading
surface dcp(float
a1=1,a2=1,b1=1,b2=1,c1=1,c2=1,d1=1,d2=1,e1=1,e2=1,f1=1,f2=1,
tmax=100, tincr=0.1, th=0.0001)
{
   float cldist = dcp(a1,a2,b1,b2,c1,c2,d1,d2,e1,e2,f1,f2,tmax,tincr,s,t);
   Oi = Os;
   Ci = Os*Cs*smoothstep(0,th,cldist);
}//dcp
```

Figure 16.8 Pendulum Harmonograph curves.

From double conical pendulum curves, we now turn our attention to Spirograph™ curves. We used the Spirograph equation in a couple of earlier chapters for lighting calculations and for illustrating procedural pattern generation.

In the procedural pattern version, at any point specified as (rho, theta), we considered the multiple curve points for that angle theta, and use the rho value to calculate maximum, minimum, or average distance to the set of curve points. Below is a DSO that re-creates the same field calculations as the procedural patterns example. It calculates the average distance from the current point to Spirograph curve points lying along the same angle as the point. The mindist output is shown in commented-out form.

Note that unlike the Pendulum Harmonograph curve plotting, precalculating Spirograph curves outside the shading grid loop will not help us. That is because we are not plotting the curves themselves (you can easily implement that as an exercise). Rather, we are performing distance calculations specific to each shading point location.

The returned (average) distance to each shading point is used in an RSL shader to create a continuous field of colors (Figure 16.9).

```
#include <stdlib.h>
#include <stdio.h>
#include <string>
#include <math.h>
#include "RslPlugin.h"
#include <limits.h>

#define PI 3.141592653589f;
```

```
extern "C" {
  int LCM(float R, float r) {
    int i=0,cm=1;
    if (fmod(R,r)==0)
      cm = 1;
    else
    {
      i=1;
      while (fmod(R*i,r)!=0)
        i++;
      cm = i;
    }
    return cm;
  }// LCM()

  float calcspiro(float R, float r, float b, float a)
  {
    return (sqrt((R-r)*(R-r)+ b*b + 2*(R-r)*b*cos((1+R/r)*a)));
  }// calcspiro()

  RSLEXPORT int spirofield_eval(RslContext* rslContext,
                                int argc, const RslArg* argv[])
  {
    RslFloatIter result(argv[0]);

    RslFloatIter R(argv[1]);
    RslFloatIter r(argv[2]);
    RslFloatIter b(argv[3]);
    RslFloatIter theta(argv[4]);
    RslFloatIter rho(argv[5]);

    int nrev = LCM(*R,*r);
    int numVals = argv[0]->NumValues();
    for(int i=0;i<numVals;i++) {
      float mindist=2;
      float avdist=0;
      for(int j=0;j<nrev;j++)
      {
        float a = (*theta) + j*2*PI;
        float rsp = calcspiro(*R,*r,*b,a)/(*R);
        float deltad = fabs(rsp-(*rho));
        if(deltad<mindist)
          mindist=deltad;
```

```
            avdist += fabs(rsp-(*rho));
        }

        avdist /= nrev;
        // *result = mindist;
        *result = avdist;

        ++R;++r;++b;++theta;++rho;
        ++result;
    }
    return 0;
}// spirofield_eval()

static RslFunction myFunctions[] =
{
    {"float spirofield(uniform float, uniform float, uniform float,
        varying float, varying float)", spirofield_eval, NULL, NULL },NULL
};
RSLEXPORT RslFunctionTable RslPublicFunctions(myFunctions);
}; /* extern "C" */
```

The `spirofield` shader that uses our new DSO call is shown below. It converts (s,t) into (rho, theta) centered at a unit square, and passes the polar coordinate into the `spirofield()` plug-in call along with user-specified Spirograph curve parameters. The resulting distance is turned into a set of repeating colors using `mod` (mdst×freq,1.0) to obtain a hue value for an HSV color sample, which is a useful trick that works with any scalar value stored in `mdst`.

```
plugin "spiro";

surface spirofield(float R=10,rv=5,b=2.5,hoff=0.0,freq=1.0, calctype=0,f=1.0)
{
    float i, theta, rho, nrev, a, rsp, ss, tt;

    ss=s-0.5;
    tt=t-0.5;
    theta = atan(tt,ss);
    theta += 3.1415;
    rho = 2*sqrt(ss*ss+tt*tt);
    if((rho>((R-rv+b)/R))||(rho<((R-rv-b)/R)))
        Ci = 0.25;
    else
    {
        float mdst = spirofield(R,rv,b,theta,rho);
```

```
    float hue=mod(mdst*freq,1.0);
    Ci = color "hsv" (hue,1,1);
  }
}// spirofield()
```

Figure 16.9 Color fields resulting from Spirograph curves.

Our next DSO example shows how to plot 2D slices of quaternion Julia fractals. A traditional Julia fractal is a pattern generated by iterating a complex number z over the complex number plane like this:

```
z = z^2 + c
```

where c is a constant complex number. A Julia fractal is therefore a 2D fractal since it lies on the 2D complex plane. Likewise, a quaternion Julia fractal is a 4D one. Whereas a complex number can be thought of as a 2D number with a real and an imaginary component, a quaternion can be considered to have one real and three imaginary components:

```
q = r + ai + bj + ck
```

where q is the quaternion, and components (r,a,b,c) define a single point in 4D space. The point can be imagined to lie in 4D space defined by mutually perpendicular axes (x,y,z,w).

Analogous to complex Julia fractals, quaternion Julia fractals are obtained using this quaternion iteration:

```
q = q^2 + c
```

where q and c are quaternions.

Given two quaternions q1 and q2 with components (r1,a1,b1,c1) and (r2,a2,b2,c2), multiplication q1×q2 is defined to be

```
r1r2-a1a2-b1b2-c1c2, r1a2+r2a1+b1c2-c1b2,
r1b2-a1c2+b1r2+c1a2, r1c2+a1b2-b1a2+c1r2)
```

Note that the multiplication is not commutative, for example, q1×q2 does not equal q2×q1. In any case, we can use the multiplication formula to obtain one for squaring a quaternion. Given quaternion q as (r,a,b,c), its square q×q works out to be

```
(r×r-a×a-b×b-c×c, 2×r×a, 2×rb, 2×r×c)
```

The quatfract() call shown below takes a quaternion (x,y,z,w) to iterate, (r,a,b,c) as the constant quaternion to use for adding during the iteration, an escd escape value to use for early terminating the iteration, and n value as the maximum iteration count. It then performs the iteration and outputs the count when iteration terminates, which is either n if the iteration did not terminate early, or a smaller value than n if it did.

After each iteration, the square of the quaternion's current magnitude is compared against escd to determine if iteration should terminate:

```
float d = (rn*rn+an*an+bn*bn+cn*cn);
if(d>*escd)
{
  *result = j;
  break;
}
```

The resulting count output by the DSO function is used by the RSL caller to color the current shading point appropriately.

```
#include <stdlib.h>
#include <stdio.h>
#include <string>
#include <math.h>
#include "RslPlugin.h"
#include <limits.h>

extern "C" {
  RSLEXPORT int quatfract(RslContext* rslContext,
                          int argc, const RslArg* argv[])
  {
    RslFloatIter result(argv[0]);

    RslFloatIter x(argv[1]);
```

```
    RslFloatIter y(argv[2]);
    RslFloatIter z(argv[3]);
    RslFloatIter w(argv[4]);
    RslFloatIter r(argv[5]);
    RslFloatIter a(argv[6]);
    RslFloatIter b(argv[7]);
    RslFloatIter c(argv[8]);
    RslFloatIter escd(argv[9]);
    RslFloatIter n(argv[10]);

    int numVals = argv[0]->NumValues();
    for(int i=0;i<numVals;i++)
      {
        // Q = r + ai + bj +ck
        // Q <- Q^2 + c

        float j;
        float ro=*x, ao=*y, bo=*z, co=*w;
        *result = *n;
        for(j=0;j<*n;j++)
        {
          float rn = ro*ro-ao*ao-bo*bo-co*co + *r;
          float an = 2*ro*ao + *a;
          float bn = 2*ro*bo + *b;
          float cn = 2*ro*co + *c;

          float d = (rn*rn+an*an+bn*bn+cn*cn);
          if(d>*escd)
          {
            *result = j;
            break;
          }
          // prep for next iteration
          ro=rn; ao=an; bo=bn; co=cn;
        }

      ++x;++y;++z;++w;++r;++a;++b;++c;++escd;++n;
      ++result;
      }
    return 0;
}// qfractal()

static RslFunction myFunctions[] =
{
```

```
  {"float qfractal(varying float, uniform float, varying float,
     uniform float, uniform float, uniform float, uniform float,
     uniform float, uniform float, uniform float, )", quatfract,
     NULL, NULL },NULL
  };
  RSLEXPORT RslFunctionTable RslPublicFunctions(myFunctions);
}; /* extern "C" */
```

Here is the RSL shader that invokes the plug-in call. It uses (s,t) as part of the quaternion to iterate. After scaling and shifting (s,t) to get (ss,tt), the iteration quaternion is constructed to be (ss,inity,tt,initw) where inity and initw are user-defined values which stay constant throughout the image. Since only ss and tt vary, we are in effect rendering a 2D slice of the 4D result. By varying either inity or initw in small quantities, we can advance the 2D slice along the y or w dimension, respectively. Playing back the resulting sequence of slices as an animation provides a glimpse of such 2D slicing through 4D space.

Once we get back an iteration count from the DSO, we use it to create a hue component for an HSV color value. The saturation component is provided by the user. We use hue and saturation to create a value like so:

```
float val = hue + sat*(1-hue);
```

The resulting (hue,sat,val) is used to set outgoing color.

```
plugin "qfractal";

surface revjulia(float smult=0.01, sshift=0, tmult=0.01, tshift=0,
                 inity=0.01, initw=-0.01, cr=-.2, ca=-.8, cb=0.06, cc=0,
                 escd = 2, n=1000, hmult=1, sat=1)
{
  float ss, tt, esc, hue;

  ss = sshift+(s*smult);
  tt = tshift+(t*tmult);
  esc = qfractal(ss,inity,tt,initw,cr,ca,cb,cc,escd,n);
  if(esc==n)
    hue = 1;
  else
  {
    hue = 1-log(esc)/log(n);
  }
  hue = mod(hmult*hue,1);
  float val = hue + sat*(1-hue);
  Ci = color "hsv" (hue,sat,val);
}// revjulia
```

Figure 16.10 shows four slices through the quaternion Julia fractal. In addition to varying inity to create the slicing, we also vary the saturation sat to change the coloring from vivid (sat=1) to black-and-white (sat=0). The RIB statement for the shader looks like this:

```
Surface "revjulia"
"smult" 1 "sshift" -.5 "tmult" 1 "tshift" -.5
# inity is .05, .06, .07, .08 for a four-frame anim seq.
# vary sat to be 1, .666, .333, 0 for the four frames
"inity" 0.08 "initw" 0.05 "sat" 0
"cr" -.745 "ca" .113 "cb" 0.01 "cc" 0.01 "n" 1500 "escd" 10 "hmult" 2.5
```

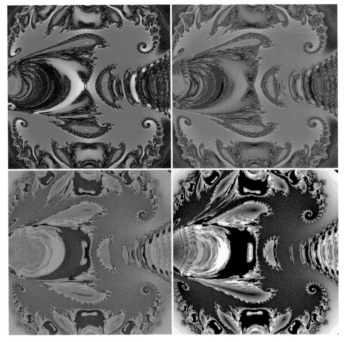

Figure 16.10 Slices through a quaternion (4D) Julia fractal.

Data amplification is the topic of the next DSO. We present a technique origi-nally due to Stefan Gustavson, who described it in a paper called "Beyond the pixel: towards infinite resolution textures." The data for Figure 16.11 was derived from material presented in a Website associated with the above paper.

The idea is very simple but powerful: to draw complex patterns such as the Celtic knot shown at the bottom-left of Figure 16.11 at arbitrary resolution, analyze its contours in terms of conics (or higher order curves such as cubic Bezier), and store curve coefficients in the form of colors in low resolution texture maps. To re-create the vector patterns, simply access the textures, retrieve colors, unpack to pro-duce coefficients, and use them to draw curve segments.

The conics_eval() call below takes two colors and a point (x,y) in 0..1 local space, creates conics coefficients A,B,C,D,E,F from the two incoming color values, and evaluates the general conic equation at the incoming point (x,y). The value of the conic curve at a given (x,y) is a good approximation to the orthogonal distance from (x,y) to the curve. To render anti-aliased contours, this evaluated value needs to be divided by the magnitude of the gradient at (x,y):

```
float Fxy = A*x*x + B*x*y + C*y*y + D*x + E*y + F;
float gradFxy_x = 2*A*x+B*y+D, gradFxy_y = B*x+2*C*y+E;
float len = sqrtf(gradFxy_x*gradFxy_x + gradFxy_y*gradFxy_y);
*result = Fxy/len;
```

The resulting output distance is used in RSL inside a smoothstep() statement as usual, to draw anti-aliased contours.

```
#include <stdlib.h>
#include <stdio.h>
#include <string>
#include <math.h>
#include "RslPlugin.h"
#include <limits.h>

extern "C" {

  RSLEXPORT int conics_eval(RslContext* rslContext,
                            int argc, const RslArg* argv[])
  {
    RslFloatIter result(argv[0]);

    RslColorIter C1(argv[1]);
    RslColorIter C2(argv[2]);
    RslFloatIter xval(argv[3]);
    RslFloatIter yval(argv[4]);

    int numVals = argv[0]->NumValues();
    float midgray = 0.50196f;
    for(int i=0;i<numVals;i++)
    {
      float A=((*C1)[0]-midgray)/midgray;
      float B=((*C1)[1]-midgray)/midgray;
      float C=((*C1)[2]-midgray)/midgray;
      float D=((*C2)[0]-midgray)/midgray;
      float E=((*C2)[1]-midgray)/midgray;
      float F=((*C2)[2]-midgray)/midgray;
      float x = *xval, y=*yval;
```

```
      float Fxy = A*x*x + B*x*y + C*y*y + D*x + E*y + F;
      float gradFxy_x = 2*A*x+B*y+D, gradFxy_y = B*x+2*C*y+E;
      float len = sqrtf(gradFxy_x*gradFxy_x + gradFxy_y*gradFxy_y);
      *result = Fxy/len;

      ++C1;++C2;++xval;++yval;
      ++result;
    }
    return 0;
  }// conics_eval()

  static RslFunction myFunctions[] =
  {
    {"float conics(varying color, varying color, varying float,
      varying float)", conics_eval, NULL, NULL},NULL
  };
  RSLEXPORT RslFunctionTable RslPublicFunctions(myFunctions);
}; /* extern "C" */
```

The conics shader given below performs the pattern generation. It first divides the 0..1 unit square into a grid of resolution (texw,texh), where textw and texh are the horizontal and vertical resolutions of the texture maps where we store curve coefficients. For the example shown in Figure 16.11, these are both 32. The top-left and top-right images in that figure show the texture maps that hold the conics coefficients (the 32×32 maps are shown magnified for clarity).

Once we have the binned versions of our (s,t) texture coordinate, we can use it to retrieve a pair of colors, one from each texture map that contains the coefficients. We need to point-sample these low-resolution maps at these precise locations, so we pass the same texture coordinates four times in order to effectively set texture access filter width to 0:

```
color cABC = texture(ABCtex,ss,tt,ss,tt,ss,tt,ss,tt);
color cDEF = texture(DEFtex,ss,tt,ss,tt,ss,tt,ss,tt);
```

The looked-up colors, along with a local space (x,y) relative to the current texel, are then sent to the plug-in call. The resulting distance d is used in smoothstep(), along with a reasonable filter width derived from the current micropolygon area (more on this in Chapter 17, "Antialiasing"). This creates the smooth transitions between our pattern and the background, as seen in the pretty knot work at the bottom left of Figure 16.11.

At the bottom right of Figure 16.11 is shown a superposition of the underlying low resolution `texels` that encode coefficient data and the corresponding curve contours generated from the coefficients. The region shown lies in the top-right quadrant of the pattern. You can see that a given `texel` color always gives rise to the same curve contour.

```
plugin "conics";

surface contours(string ABCtex="", DEFtex="";float texw=32, texh=32)
{
  float A, B, C, D, E, F;

  // 'bin' s into 0,1,2,3...(texw-1), likewise for t
  float ss = (s*(texw)) - mod(s*(texw),1.0);
  float tt = (t*(texh)) - mod(t*(texh),1.0);
  ss *= (1.0/(texw));
  tt *= (1.0/(texh));
  ss += 0.5/(texw);
  tt += 0.5/(texh);

  color cABC = texture(ABCtex,ss,tt,ss,tt,ss,tt,ss,tt);
  color cDEF = texture(DEFtex,ss,tt,ss,tt,ss,tt,ss,tt);

  float x = mod(s*texw,1.0);
  float y = mod(t*texh,1.0);
  float  d = conics(cABC,cDEF,x,y);

  float stepwd = 2*sqrt(area(P));
  Oi = Os;
  color cpatt = Os*Cs*smoothstep(-stepwd,stepwd,(d));

  Ci = cpatt;
}// contours
```

Figure 16.11 Conic curves (Celtic knot) from coefficient lookups in texture maps.

For our very last DSO example, we consider the calculation of `curl noise`, which was the topic of a paper in SIGGRAPH 2007 by Robert Bridson, Jim Hourihan, and Marcus Nordenstam. Their idea is to create convincing fluid flows (which are incompressible, for example, divergence-free) simply by taking the curl of a potential field derived from the `Perlin noise()` function.

In the DSO below, we use a simple implementation of `noise()` to calculate curl. The noise values are obtained from coefficients stored in the `rndx`, `rndy`, and `rndz` arrays, along with a `perm` array to permute indices.

The `snoise()` function takes a point as input and returns a scalar noise value at the location. It does so by situating the point in an appropriate cell in the noise lattice, retrieving four corner values from the stored tables, and performing three linear interpolations to arrive at the noise at the given point. Note that the function is only doing a 2D lookup based on `x` and `y`. It is left to you as an exercise to implement a full 3D version. (You would need to locate eight corners and perform seven interpolations.)

The `curl` value at any point (x,y,z) is obtained from a vector potential $(F1,F2,F3)$ as follows:

```
curl = (dF3/dy-dF2/dz, dF1/dz-dF3/dx, dF2/dx-dF1/dy)
```

Since snoise() does not output vector values, we simply obtain a vector value by taking scalar values at three different locations. Likewise, the partial derivatives are approximated by finite differences. You can see all this in the code below.

```
#include <cstdlib>
#include <stdio.h>
#include <string>
#include <math.h>
#include "RslPlugin.h"
#include <limits.h>
#include <cmath>


extern "C" {

  class vec
  {
  public:
    float x,y,z;

    vec(float a, float b, float c) {x=a;y=b;z=c;}
    vec operator+(vec v)
    {
      return vec(x+v.x, y+v.y, z+v.z);
    }
    vec operator-(vec v)
    {
      return vec(x-v.x, y-v.y, z-v.z);
    }
    vec operator*(float s)
    {
      return vec(x*s, y*s, z*s);
    }
  };// vec


float perm[256] =
{125,182,133,214,154,99,21,242,45,222,110,235,51,189,111,50,41,147,241,221,
253,161,135,120,84,145,19,150,44,13,107,137,165,79,75,34,8,230,158,48,29,
157,238,131,86,246,213,70,95,33,186,184,46,159,68,20,36,220,11,225,64,54,38,
130,171,23,77,155,132,97,205,250,136,245,76,112,168,169,67,30,193,87,206,200,
216,2,14,104,144,93,199,249,72,156,103,16,252,89,105,49,198,134,236,175,192,
```

```
92,119,211,239,58,167,85,113,160,151,180,181,22,7,26,52,234,174,0,228,226,91,
185,18,188,179,152,243,232,122,139,203,123,187,210,118,172,121,60,177,102,98,
6,3,223,217,35,142,195,237,202,196,127,108,141,101,31,163,82,1,233,12,240,47,
143,71,10,69,55,162,88,109,219,194,231,90,190,209,212,153,173,178,114,78,81,
191,40,15,224,128,204,254,5,57,94,176,215,124,53,126,9,17,229,65,138,37,4,25,
129,227,164,56,247,96,251,28,42,170,32,183,66,140,27,100,244,80,208,24,106,
255,62,117,115,218,146,39,61,59,166,201,149,248,116,43,63,74,148,83,73,207,
197};
float rndx[256] = {0.634684,0.943947,-0.784834,0.335621,-0.769104,0.293177,
0.123174,-0.033229,-0.345652,-0.337625,-0.184900,-0.361281,0.252918,0.519241,
-0.331445,-0.563336,-0.536267,0.995926,0.667489,-0.697762,0.942124,0.274294,
-0.750986,0.169621,-0.659082,0.037860,-0.891200,0.007589,-0.261716,0.951287,
-0.516900,-0.627032,0.895234,-0.301734,0.708589,-0.873870,0.991443,-0.168237,
0.092902,-0.354209,0.494138,0.908001,0.284510,-0.252943,0.427243,0.953065,
0.183721,0.890976,0.948992,-0.148790,-0.806787,0.891115,-0.874496,-0.557773,
0.060736,-0.533578,0.480087,0.169536,0.474011,-0.781628,0.120824,0.957112,
-0.408660,0.016058,-0.344622,-0.700071,0.142188,-0.353179,0.131692,-0.764910,
0.292612,-0.374170,-0.856908,-0.422878,0.372886,0.570334,-0.469813,-0.443393,
0.461310,-0.520821,0.407817,0.654523,-0.629706,0.533321,-0.903250,0.431030,
0.999743,0.576837,-0.399433,0.473755,0.795209,0.721390,0.430866,-0.613451,
-.262552,-.913756,-.313522,.879637,-.266935,.818169,-.885273,-.974324,
-0.556001,-0.742182,-0.397202,0.816886,0.828153,0.132985,-0.626507,0.289462,
0.612164,0.781310,-0.056015,0.982458,0.314631,0.040736,0.413488,0.314375,
-0.382427,-0.985945,-0.211871,-0.587218,0.735445,-0.781005,-0.200669,
-0.527107,-0.694761,0.485809,-0.647470,0.038304,0.303978,-0.532743,0.063980,
0.747977,-0.274925,0.666778,0.564863,-0.446772,-0.200237,0.938356,0.842690,
-0.588073,0.719666,-0.213325,-0.605615,0.034298,0.827411,0.807873,-0.651328,
-0.555016,0.821928,0.136801,-0.142234,0.557373,0.355797,0.657098,-0.969734,
0.661036,0.142907,-0.617204,-0.300660,-0.553115,-0.149948,0.763320,-0.805137,
0.575127,0.430099,0.759726,-0.871645,-0.770138,0.698082,0.971045,-0.358211,
0.417748,-0.242280,0.036174,-0.547954,-0.414869,-0.155953,-0.199282,0.030115,
-0.334025,0.937519,0.887882,-0.776652,0.293316,0.544980,-0.746387,-0.045648,
-0.312114,-0.363591,0.653692,0.134772,0.486461,0.417012,0.329634,0.061589,
-0.152889,0.089360,0.189944,0.076973,-0.212558,0.160988,0.718762,-0.794810,
0.918708,-0.245063,-0.342765,-0.496161,0.598984,0.457953,0.533955,-0.735041,
0.395472,0.421836,-0.511693,-0.311213,-0.033184,-0.258080,0.643139,0.654702,
0.378330,0.296831,-0.210526,-0.135209,-0.286157,-0.880892,0.926380,0.560954,
0.208468,0.116323,-0.362073,0.995909,-0.722689,-0.643311,-0.798901,-0.803980,
.111626,-.141666,-.300141,-.289390,-.683713,-.766186,-.024430,.711758,
```

```
0.655650,0.463877,-0.599454,-0.377534,-0.794203,-0.956315,-0.722832,0.584127,
-0.784834,.943947,0.634684};

float rndy[256]={0.181774,-0.991805,0.367250,0.601245,0.554657,0.491876,
-0.609906,0.976655,0.948175,-0.517662,0.511952,-0.302132,-0.540234,-0.408729,
0.628504,0.390981,0.782640,0.451893,-0.248958,-0.225675,-0.336551,-0.078348,
-0.014980,0.822931,-0.985959,0.457572,-0.699059,-0.723987,0.191296,0.397440,
0.325333,-0.626929,0.405635,-0.307417,0.974315,-0.039708,-0.815542,-0.635591,
-.063053,-.867367,-.153253,-.551101,-.169499,.306512,.040170,-.540994,
-0.302507,-0.177190,0.910899,0.448535,0.597135,-0.425652,-0.629813,-0.417845,
-.602721,-.615772,-.960273,-.301781,-.339759,.231023,-.904341,.985574,
0.604093,0.501294,-0.321843,0.578408,-0.538414,-0.137385,0.942817,0.398533,
-.004751,-.210436,.847432,.825750,-.903924,-.112397,-.715244,-.206432,
0.710413,-0.804345,-0.757897,0.307548,-0.229997,-0.387710,0.889703,0.167282,
-0.003482,0.929430,0.865501,0.656759,0.160452,0.961160,0.642333,-0.235454,
0.462454,-0.679510,-0.657046,0.924040,0.183106,-0.714229,0.322573,-0.821646,
0.075335,0.170006,-0.995896,0.171411,-0.942392,-0.711140,0.964979,0.768021,
-0.515484,-0.792918,0.075570,0.254519,-0.180628,-0.034727,-0.578199,0.815890,
-0.105298,-0.712698,0.472649,-0.944845,-0.751538,0.114982,-0.180299,0.710916,
0.435473,0.162655,0.634956,-0.381422,0.448426,-0.042471,-0.203067,-0.476239,
-0.872465,-0.198963,0.695171,-0.814857,0.089898,0.660150,0.953165,0.574413,
0.867232,0.028734,-0.171068,-0.313396,0.994007,0.250733,-0.497506,-0.111291,
0.538035,0.975143,-0.056136,0.786497,0.090125,0.763565,0.497413,-0.474402,
-0.073780,0.132369,0.144177,-0.625354,-0.910102,0.941109,-0.101594,-0.782567,
-.257853,-.406422,-.597424,.832045,-.746272,-.644259,.406458,-.879040,
0.384476,-0.764610,-0.192435,0.378483,0.486124,0.310059,-0.732808,0.024159,
0.285202,0.211056,-0.189344,-0.624673,-0.025379,-0.691931,-0.099075,0.900841,
0.440438,-0.954898,-0.724514,0.530336,0.986211,0.173893,0.747769,-0.271642,
0.767470,-0.849654,-0.439597,-0.978802,-0.493913,0.966861,-0.857841,0.890563,
-0.797749,-0.050277,0.269045,0.688375,-0.740218,0.536237,-0.287467,0.544984,
-0.252707,0.523189,0.920311,0.721914,0.831258,-0.178763,0.622755,0.271696,
-0.133661,0.898241,-0.197968,-0.147450,0.072134,-0.450199,0.580908,-0.160396,
-0.299853,-0.858689,-0.139197,0.206234,-0.891828,0.002961,0.096796,-0.689577,
0.952685,-0.634158,0.998798,-0.787533,0.902079,-0.288669,0.757451,-0.350628,
-0.765480,0.677762,-0.628713,-0.934222,-0.501001,0.994042,0.337474,.367250,
-.991805,0.181774};

float rndz[256]={0.623662,-0.169139,0.304542,-0.773112,-0.547269,0.613448,
0.896751,-0.450885,0.199973,0.977116,-0.818435,-0.643385,0.852926,0.620739,
```

```
-0.143182,-0.044675,-0.800102,0.532213,-0.041337,0.832636,0.325241,0.415345,
0.532000,0.134712,0.753865,-0.414280,-0.432513,0.039542,0.986253,-0.095935,
-0.796807,0.609915,0.734926,0.507735,0.836804,-0.812343,0.121183,0.733555,
-0.263228,-0.678844,0.710671,-0.081663,-0.322229,0.563597,-0.460925,0.534588,
-.481078,-.261027,.066802,.477585,-.428390,-.607957,-.107070,-.896390,
0.526756,-0.353205,-0.310671,-0.905758,0.686337,-0.324418,-0.001693,0.889530,
-0.714502,-0.266767,0.397265,-0.877698,-0.079110,-0.481552,0.855857,0.657662,
-0.160396,0.566527,-0.424001,0.517375,0.130124,0.115074,0.051963,0.649046,
.854047,-.881235,.126631,-.574343,-.489191,-.980439,-.470733,-.962436,
-0.333645,0.218596,-0.868193,-0.647308,0.894178,0.130114,-0.757778,-0.820324,
.863347,.639487,-.698022,-.215763,-.842064,-.842166,-.558100,-.002460,
0.724362,0.017898,-0.485085,-0.145514,-0.867028,0.566878,-0.496468,0.987019,
0.685643,0.630163,-0.587323,-0.803548,0.649724,-0.058057,-0.765984,-0.683921,
-.839461,-.634177,-.331229,-.945282,.495937,-.089007,-.765606,.359284,
-.449520,-.463628,-.856478,-.291584,-.305794,-.414579,.705956,-.581432,
0.603319,-0.779130,0.273053,0.736292,0.787748,0.776585,0.723311,0.473391,
0.406748,-0.864012,0.669843,0.056471,0.077931,0.903859,0.372550,0.238470,
-0.730318,-0.958679,0.293188,0.765619,-0.047685,0.527582,0.124903,0.502795,
-0.936046,0.268424,-0.788789,-0.241840,0.853845,0.917166,0.176727,0.457165,
-0.861964,-0.550219,0.193456,0.925785,-0.773634,-0.083233,0.399176,0.633114,
0.052755,0.069018,-0.310415,-0.869314,-0.027123,-0.937864,0.369156,0.242559,
-.896543,-.337656,.008178,.055772,-.810074,-.866920,-.441433,-.746120,
0.401504,-0.230223,0.012039,0.255350,-0.313056,-0.811233,-0.287486,-0.175020,
-.361452,.905971,-.249235,-.135086,-.177262,-.850060,-.501972,.875493,
0.218959,0.187613,-0.993821,-0.808164,0.249749,0.375336,0.434395,0.353206,
-.962320,-.557427,-.591022,-.772394,-.424347,-.032456,-.518514,.977157,
0.737322,0.493525,0.232507,-0.575735,0.682292,0.945021,0.249245,-0.679160,
0.850992,-0.999990,0.185754,-0.326270,-0.850050,0.683782,-0.450777,0.368909,
-0.128605,-0.444598,0.560745,-0.878856,0.930738,-0.004860,0.474350,0.968418,
0.437713,0.883328,-0.803976,-0.986635,-0.149128,-0.322490,0.990523,0.623662,
-0.169139,0.304542};

float snoise(vec Pt)
{
   // get ix,iy,iz, then look up noise at corners
   float res=256;
```

```
float x = Pt.x;
float y = Pt.y;
float z = Pt.z;

float ax = abs(x);
float ay = abs(y);
float az = abs(z);

ax=x;ay=y;az=z;
ax += 100000;
ay += 100000;
az += 100000;

float dx = fmod(ax,1.0f);
int ix = fmod(ax,res-1);

float dy = fmod(ay,1.0f);
int iy = fmod(ay,res-1);

float dz = fmod(az,1.0f);
int iz = fmod(az,res-1);

int q00 = perm[(int)fmod((iy+perm[ix]),res)];
int q01 = perm[(int)fmod((iy+perm[ix+1]),res)];
int q10 = perm[(int)fmod((iy+1+perm[ix]),res)];
int q11 = perm[(int)fmod((iy+1+perm[ix+1]),res)];

float dx1 = dx-1;
float dy1 = dy-1;

float v00 = rndx[q00]*dx + rndy[q00]*dy;
float v01 = rndx[q01]*dx1 + rndy[q01]*dy;
float v10 = rndx[q10]*dx + rndy[q10]*dy1;
float v11 = rndx[q11]*dx1 + rndy[q11]*dy1;

// simpler:
// dx = (3 - 2*dx)*dx*dx;
// dy = (3 - 2*dy)*dy*dy;
// better:
dx = (10-15*dx+6*dx*dx)*dx*dx*dx;
dy = (10-15*dy+6*dy*dy)*dy*dy*dy;

float r0001 = v00 + dx*(v01-v00);
float r1011 = v10 + dx*(v11-v10);
```

```
  float r00011011 = r0001 + dy*(r1011-r0001);

  return (0.5*(1+r00011011));
}// snoise()

RSLEXPORT int cnoise_eval(RslContext* rslContext,
                          int argc, const RslArg* argv[])
{
  RslVectorIter result(argv[0]);

  RslPointIter P0(argv[1]);
  RslPointIter P1(argv[2]);
  RslPointIter P2(argv[3]);
  RslVectorIter dx(argv[4]);
  RslVectorIter dy(argv[5]);
  RslVectorIter dz(argv[6]);

  int numVals = argv[0]->NumValues();
  float midgray = 0.50196f;
  for(int i=0;i<numVals;i++)
  {
    // float df1dx =
    // noise(vec((*P0)[0]+(*dx)[0],(*P0)[1]+(*dx)[1],(*P0)[2]+(*dx)[2]))-
    // snoise(vec((*P0)[0]-(*dx)[0],(*P0)[1]-(*dx)[1],(*P0)[2]-(*dx)[2]));
    float df1dy =
    snoise(vec((*P0)[0]+(*dy)[0],(*P0)[1]+(*dy)[1],(*P0)[2]+(*dy)[2]))-
    snoise(vec((*P0)[0]-(*dy)[0],(*P0)[1]-(*dy)[1],(*P0)[2]-(*dy)[2]));
    float df1dz =
    snoise(vec((*P0)[0]+(*dz)[0],(*P0)[1]+(*dz)[1],(*P0)[2]+(*dz)[2]))-
    snoise(vec((*P0)[0]-(*dz)[0],(*P0)[1]-(*dz)[1],(*P0)[2]-(*dz)[2]));

    float df2dx =
    snoise(vec((*P1)[0]+(*dx)[0],(*P1)[1]+(*dx)[1],(*P1)[2]+(*dx)[2]))-
    snoise(vec((*P1)[0]-(*dx)[0],(*P1)[1]-(*dx)[1],(*P1)[2]-(*dx)[2]));
    // float df2dy =
    // snoise(vec((*P1)[0]+(*dy)[0],(*P1)[1]+(*dy)[1],(*P1)[2]+(*dy)[2]))-
    // snoise(vec((*P1)[0]-(*dy)[0],(*P1)[1]-(*dy)[1],(*P1)[2]-(*dy)[2]));
    float df2dz =
    snoise(vec((*P1)[0]+(*dz)[0],(*P1)[1]+(*dz)[1],(*P1)[2]+(*dz)[2]))-
    snoise(vec((*P1)[0]-(*dz)[0],(*P1)[1]-(*dz)[1],(*P1)[2]-(*dz)[2]));

    float df3dx =
    snoise(vec((*P2)[0]+(*dx)[0],(*P2)[1]+(*dx)[1],(*P2)[2]+(*dx)[2]))-
    snoise(vec((*P2)[0]-(*dx)[0],(*P2)[1]-(*dx)[1],(*P2)[2]-(*dx)[2]));
```

```
      float df3dy =
      snoise(vec((*P2)[0]+(*dy)[0],(*P2)[1]+(*dy)[1],(*P2)[2]+(*dy)[2]))-
      snoise(vec((*P2)[0]-(*dy)[0],(*P2)[1]-(*dy)[1],(*P2)[2]-(*dy)[2]));
      // float df3dz =
      // snoise(vec((*P2)[0]+(*dz)[0],(*P2)[1]+(*dz)[1],(*P2)[2]+(*dz)[2]))-
      // snoise(vec((*P2)[0]-(*dz)[0],(*P2)[1]-(*dz)[1],(*P2)[2]-(*dz)[2]));

      (*result)[0] = df3dy-df2dz;
      (*result)[1] = df1dz-df3dx;
      (*result)[2] = df2dx-df1dy;

      ++P0;++P1;++P2;++dx;++dy;++dz;
      ++result;
    }
    return 0;
  }// cnoise_eval()

  static RslFunction myFunctions[] =
  {
    {"vector curlnoise(varying point, varying point, varying point,
       varying vector, varying vector, varying vector)",
       cnoise_eval, NULL, NULL },NULL
  };
  RSLEXPORT RslFunctionTable RslPublicFunctions(myFunctions);
}; /* extern "C" */
```

We can use the curl noise result in at least a couple of ways—in a surface shader and for doing displacements. The surface shader version is shown first, followed by the displacement one. Figure 16.12 shows the results.

In the curlnoise surface shader, we evaluate curl noise at P (by passing to the plug-in call three separate points to lookup scalar noise and three offset vectors to carry out finite differencing). The resulting curl noise (which is vector valued) is scaled by an ampl factor after which its x and y components are used to offset texture coordinates (s,t) before lookup:

```
Ci = texture(texnm,s+vel[0],t+vel[1]);
```

The result is shown in the top two images of Figure 16.12. The curl field causes the texture lookup to be warped. By animating a variety of parameters (shift of point P, amplitude, frequency, noise lookup offset, finite difference vectors), we would be able to animate the ripples in the lookups. Having a 4D noise function would help too, since we can simply vary the fourth (time) value to cause all the noise values to change.

```
plugin "curlnoise";

surface curlnoise(float freq=1, ampl=.1; string texnm="warpme.tex")
{
  if(texnm!="")
    {
      float d=.1;
      float pshift=132.55; // arbitrary shift

      vector dx=vector(d,0,0), dy=vector(0,d,0), dz=vector(0,0,d);
      // snoise() at PP, PP2 and PP3 are used in place of
      // a true vector-valued noise at PP
      point PP = P*freq;
      point PP2 = PP+vector(-pshift,-pshift,-pshift);
      point PP3 = PP+vector(pshift,pshift,pshift);

      vector vel = ampl*curlnoise(PP,PP2,PP3,dx,dy,dz);
      Ci = texture(texnm,s+vel[0],t+vel[1]);
    }
}//curlnoise()
```

The curl noise plug-in functionality can also be used for displacements. Below is a curlnoisedisp shader that does this. After obtaining a curl output from the DSO and scaling it, we simply displace our point with it:

```
P += vel;
```

This produces the effect seen in the bottom row of Figure 16.12. At the left, you can see the Gumbo surface being altered (note that the displacements are not along surface normals since we did not do P += vel×N). At the right are shown two curve primitives that are warped by the curl noise. The white curve (polyline) contains control vertices for the b-spline curve shown in dark red. The high frequency used in this examples creates a lot of wiggles in the curves.

```
plugin "curlnoise";

displacement curlnoisedisp(float freq=1, ampl=.1; output varying vector
vel=0)
{
  float d=.1;
  float pshift=132.55;

  vector dx=vector(d,0,0), dy=vector(0,d,0), dz=vector(0,0,d);
  point PP = P*freq;
```

```
point PP2 = PP+vector(-pshift,-pshift,-pshift);
point PP3 = PP+vector(pshift,pshift,pshift);

vector vel = ampl*curlnoise(PP,PP2,PP3,dx,dy,dz);

P += vel;
N = calculatenormal(P);
}//curlnoisedisp()
```

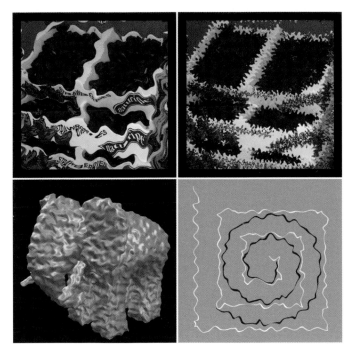

Figure 16.12 curlnoise surface and displacement shaders.

API Support

As you saw from the previous examples, there are some classes and methods that form the plug-in API whose functionality we rely on when we develop the plug-ins. This section very briefly lists the classes and mentions their use. Please consult the PRMan "RSL Plug-in API Reference" documentation page for a full list of methods and descriptions.

RslContext is a class which contains grid data that are needed by shadeops. Our DSO function receives a pointer to RslContext like so:

```
RSLEXPORT int add(RslContext* rslContext, int argc, const RslArg** argv)
```

The class helps with ensuring thread safety, for example, in situations where some common piece of data needs to be initialized. RslContext is derived from a class called RixContext.

As you can see from the above line of code, an array of RslArg pointers is passed to a DSO function call. We use the NumValues() method from RslArg to determine how many times to iterate over incoming grid points:

```
// ...
int numVals = argv[0]->NumValues();
for(int i=0;i<numVals;i++)
{
  // ..
```

IsVarying() and IsArray() query whether an argument is varying (across the grid) or is an array respectively. For array inputs, GetArrayLength() provides the number of elements in the array. Likewise, argument types can be inferred using IsFloat(), IsPoint(), IsVector(), IsColor(), IsMatrix(), and IsString().

Specific types of RslIter and RslArrayIter classes are used to access element and array grid data respectively. RslFloatIter is used to access a float argument (likewise for String/Color/Point/Normal/Vector/Matrix). Similarly, RslFloatArrayIter is used with a float array argument (likewise for String/Color/Point/Normal/Vector/Matrix).

In addition to the above, the API also contains RslFunction, which is a struct used to declare a single DSO function call, and an RslFunctionTable struct, which is required to declare the collection (array) of RslFunctions as a table of RslPublicFunctions:

Here is a sample array of RslFunctions:

```
static RslFunction myfunctions[] = {
        {"float sqr(float)", sqr_f, NULL, NULL},
        {"color sqr(color)", sqr_c, NULL, NULL},
        {"point mynoise(point)", mynoise, noiseinit, noisedelete},
        NULL
};
```

Each RslFunction has four members:

- RSL function prototype—This is how the DSO call will be invoked on the RSL side.

- pointer to entry function—This is the call that will be run on the C/C++ side, corresponding to the RSL call.

- per-frame initialization function for this DSO call (can be NULL).

- per-frame cleanup function for this DSO call (can be NULL).

Here is how the above array of RslFunctions is declared as an RslFunctionTable:

```
RSLEXPORT RslFunctionTable RslPublicFunctions(myfunctions, myinit, mycleanup);
```

Note that the RslFunctionTable should always be called RslPublicFunctions. It has three members:

- An array of RslFunctions declared prior to this call

- A per-frame initialization function for the whole group of RslFunctions (possibly NULL)

- A per-frame cleanup function for the whole group of RslFunctions (possibly NULL)

A DSO needs to have just a single RslPublicFunctions RslFunctionTable, which contains the name of a single RslFunctions array. That array needs to contain the declarations for all function calls in the DSO, even if they are defined in multiple source files.

In summary, the classes (RslContext, RslArg and typedefs for RslIter and RslArrayIter) provide thread support, inspector, and iterator calls, while the two structs (RslFunction and RslFunctionTable) provide means for declaring our DSO calls. As mentioned earlier in the PRMan documentation pages provide an exhaustive list of member variables, methods, and descriptions for each.

Multithreading

Most developers are not used to thinking of their code in terms of thread safety, for example, the possibility of a piece of code running simultaneously under multiple threads of execution. To keep the discussion simple our curlnoise example discussed earlier ignores the possibility that its initNoise() per-frame call can potentially be carried out by multiple threads. In this case, it merely leads to wasteful computation since the initialization is always the same. In general, global variables and functions need to be avoided, except when they involve just a one-time initialization with no subsequent changes to data involved. But in cases where the initialization relies on a specific user-defined argument or the current frame number or current time at the moment of initialization, you can see how with multiple threads, later threads might corrupt the initial state for earlier ones if those earlier ones have not yet finished executing while the later threads begin running. Likewise, memory allocation and freeing also needs to be carefully carried out in a multi-threading environment. Neglecting to do so might lead to invalid results due to memory corruption or result in outright program crashes.

From the earlier shadeop model where a separate call was made to a DSO for each shading sample, we have progressed to having to think about our DSO calls running in multiple threads of execution, each processing a grid of points. To help with proper implementation of our calls that accounts for such situations, the `RslContext` class mentioned earlier offers the following methods: `GetRixInterface()`, `GetGlobalStorage()`, `GetThreadStorage()`, `GetLocalStorage()`, `SetThreadData()`, `GetThreadData()`, `SetLocalData()`, `GetLocalData()`. In addition, the `Rix` API classes `RixMutex`, `RixThreadUtils`, and `RixStorage` contain additional calls that are helpful. Discussing the use of these classes and calls is unfortunately beyond the scope of this book, but we hope to provide detailed online notes on the topic of multi-threading in RSL plug-ins.

17

Anti-aliasing

In this chapter we will look at ways to avoid aliasing ("jaggies" or "crawlies") during shading. Such techniques are an important part of a professional shader writer's repertoire.

The Problem of Aliasing

Aliasing stems from inadequate sampling. Specifically, when a regular (not stochastic) sampling technique is used to discretize a high frequency signal and reconstruct the signal from the discrete samples, "high" frequencies will slip through the sampling, only to reappear as artifacts in the form of lower frequency "aliases." What constitutes high frequency? Any frequency higher than half the sampling rate (sampling frequency) is prone to aliasing. The theorem that states this is known as the *Nyquist Sampling Theorem*, and *Nyquist Limit* is the term for the cut-off frequency above which aliasing occurs. Aliases are objectionable artifacts and need to be addressed using a body of techniques known as *anti-aliasing*.

Figure 17.1 shows two occurrences of aliasing. On the left, there is a checkerboard pattern with a very high frequency (of alternating black and white squares). All that detail does not fit into the relatively limited set of pixels that comprise the object, and that is the source of the aliasing. As bad as this image looks, it is worse if there is an object or camera move, when these artifacts will appear to sparkle and crawl over the surface. The noise image on the right looks relatively benign, but it is hiding some aliases (the alias of high frequency noise is simply low frequency noise) that are not apparent in a static frame. During motion, these aliases become noticeable as they cause their own distracting motion over the surface.

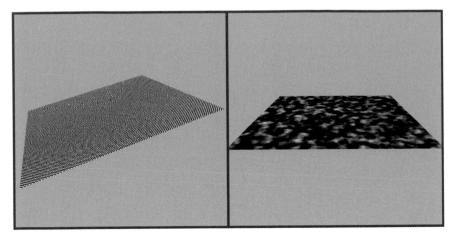

Figure 17.1 Two forms of aliasing.

During rendering with RenderMan, there are at least two forms of sampling going on. Scene geometry is stochastically sampled via micropolygons, and these samples are filtered to obtain pixel values. When micropolygon corners are shaded, the shading function is sampled at these locations, which form a regular grid in parametric UV space. Herein lies the problem. While RenderMan excels at micropolygon-based sampling and filtering, it offers almost no help with the shading sampling. This is because our shading functions can be arbitrarily complex and can contain arbitrarily high frequencies, and RenderMan has no way of estimating these. All it does is reconstruct the shading function over the micropolygon grids, making the results available for pixel-related sampling and filtering.

If regular sampling of shader functions over micropolygon grids is the source of shader aliases, maybe a raytracer can avoid this by sampling the shading function at stochastically derived surface locations (this amounts to stochastically sampling shading functions). While this is true, the aliasing problem has been traded for another (less objectionable for the visual system) problem, which is that of noise derived from the same stochastic sampling that eliminates aliases in the first place. The bottom line is that the only way to prevent aliasing artifacts is to keep the high frequencies at bay.

Anti-aliasing via Increased Sampling

To a limited extent, increasing the shading rate (or subpixel sampling grid size) can cause some reduction in aliasing. This is shown in Figure 17.2. The top two images were rendered at a coarser shading rate compared to the bottom ones. As a result, artifacts visible in the top-right image (look for discontinuities in color changes at boundaries) aren't apparent in the bottom-right image. The left images contain a lower frequency pattern, so the coarser sampling rate for the top image did not cause aliasing (the top and bottom images look identical).

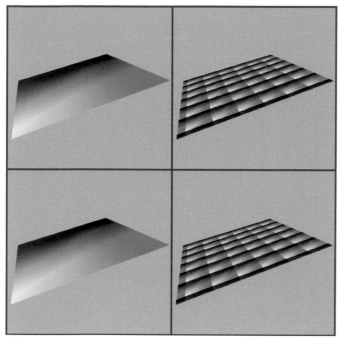

Figure 17.2 Anti-aliasing by increasing sampling rate.

Anti-aliasing Using Texture Lookup

RenderMan has stellar texture lookup (filtering) capabilities, precisely because it matches the area of the texture lookup to the area on the surface where the texture result will be utilized. We can use this to our advantage to avoid aliasing by creating texture maps out of our aliasing-prone functions and letting RenderMan filter out the high frequencies.

Figure 17.3 shows two views of a checkerboard. The closeup looks fine since the black/white squares are at a lower frequency. The smaller version on the right exhibits aliasing (run your eyes along the checker squares to see that they appear to lie on rather irregular lines).

For comparison, the same views are shown in Figure 17.4, this time with a texture map. You can see that the mapping holds up pretty well even in the smaller version.

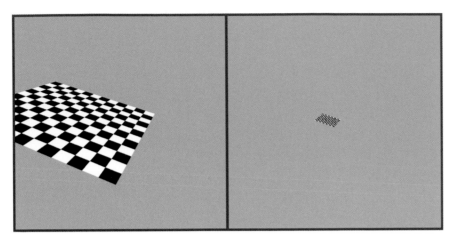

Figure 17.3 A checkerboard showing aliasing on the right.

Figure 17.4 Alias-free texture mapping, a hallmark of RenderMan.

We can try creating a texture map out of our checkerboard procedural shader by using it to render the pattern over a camera-facing square that fills the view (Figure 17.5).

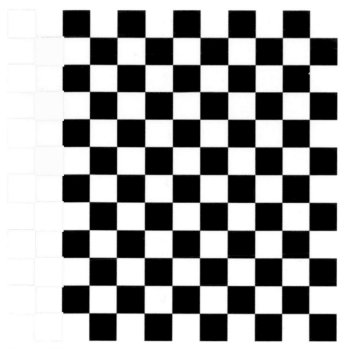

Figure 17.5 A checkerboard texture map created by "baking out" procedural texture.

Figure 17.6 shows that we can use the texture map to re-create the two views in Figure 17.3, finding to our satisfaction that the aliasing is absent. (You can make out clean diagonal lines on the smaller view.)

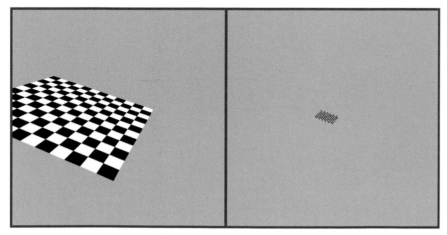

Figure 17.6 Checkerboard patterns re-created using texture mapping.

The advantage is obvious—we get clean, artifact-free rendering. But all the usual arguments against using maps for procedural patterns apply: The resolution is fixed, it is inconvenient to keep altering the maps to vary the looks, and so on. Nevertheless, it is a useful technique to keep in mind. For *y=f(x)* type of functions, note that just one scanline of pixels will do for use as a map.

Anti-aliasing by Clamping High Frequencies

As mentioned earlier, the surest way to prevent aliasing is to avoid the occurrence of high frequencies in our signals. This is particularly easy to do with "spectral synthesis" approaches of pattern generation, where complex patterns are generated by repeatedly summing simpler components at various frequency and amplitude scales. "Turbulence" patterns derived from Perlin noise are classic examples of this approach. We will now look at two examples of spectral synthesis.

Figure 17.7 shows three variations of a turbulence pattern. The image on the left is created using a shading loop of this form:

```
value = 0;
float ampl=0.5;
for (f = MINFREQ; f < MAXFREQ; f *= 2)
{
 value += ampl*snoise(f*P2);
 ampl *= 0.5;
}
```

The problem is that MAXFREQ can be quite large and hence mismatched with the surface area over which the pattern generation occurs. We would like ways to somehow estimate a bound on the higher frequency and use it as a cutoff to stop the loop from introducing aliases. Further, such estimates need to take the scene rendering parameters into account, specifically, how an RSL feature (such as the s texture coordinate) varies across the shading grid's u and v axes in the neighborhood of our shading location.

Figure 17.7 Antialiasing by clamping and fading out high frequencies.

RSL offers the following calls and variables to help with our estimation (please read the RiSpec or look online for more information on these): Du(), Dv(), Deriv(), area(), du, and dv. Du(x) returns the derivative of any x along u, likewise for Dv(x). du is the change in u across adjacent shading samples, likewise for dv. area(p) returns the area at location p and is derived from length(Du(p)×du ^ Dv(p)×dv).

Given the above, we can obtain two very useful filter estimates for anti-aliasing:

```
// from rmannotes.sl
/* sample rate metrics (from Apodaca92)
 *
 */
#define MINFILTERWIDTH  1e-7
#define MINDERIV        0.0003    /* sqrt(MINFILTERWIDTH) */

#define filterwidth(x) (max(abs(Du(x) * (du)) + (Dv(x) * (dv)),MINFILTER-
WIDTH))
#define filterwidth_point(p) (max(sqrt(area(p)), MINFILTERWIDTH))
```

filterwidth() is for use with a scalar quantity such as s, and filterwidth_point() is for use with a point, such as P.

In addition, we can also estimate a scalar filterwidth value at a point's neighborhood:

```
// x,y,z are components of a point
fwidth =   abs(Du(x)*du + abs(Dv(x)*dv) +
           abs(Du(y)*du + abs(Dv(y)*dv) +
           abs(Du(z)*du + abs(Dv(z)*dv) +
```

We can use the fwidth value above to estimate a cutoff frequency for our turbulence pattern and use it in the loop:

```
value= 0;
cutoff  = clamp(0.5/fwidth, 0, MAXFREQ);
float ampl=0.5;
for (f = MINFREQ; f < 0.5*cutoff; f *= 2)
{
  value += ampl*snoise(f*P2);
  ampl *= 0.5;
}
```

Rendering our turbulence pattern using the above code yields the image shown in the middle of Figure 17.7. As the surface recedes from us, the cutoff becomes more severe, and the loop stops executing earlier. The result is an incongruous "bald" spot over the surface. This boundary results from a hard cutoff value and can alias during motion. So we need to gradually fade out the high frequencies instead for a more natural look (right image, Figure 17.7):

```
for (f = MINFREQ; f < 0.5*cutoff; f *= 2)
{
  value += ampl*snoise(f*P2); // /f;
  ampl *= 0.5;
}
fade = clamp(2*(cutoff-f)/cutoff, 0, 1);
value  += fade * snoise(f*P2)/f;
```

Another example of frequency cutoff is shown in Figure 17.8, where we synthesize square waves using sin() curves, as per Fourier Synthesis (top row of the figure). The resulting shader produces stripes shown in the bottom row. The two
images in the top row demonstrate that the more we add higher frequency waves,
the better our approximation to the square wave (obtaining an exact square wave
require an infinite number of terms). But practically speaking, our shader will alias
horribly (bottom-left image) unless we take steps to establish a cutoff, whereby we
are able to get clean stripes (bottom right).

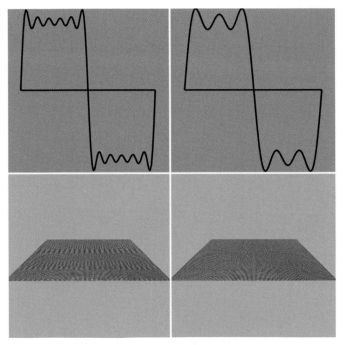

Figure 17.8 Square wave synthesis using sin() curves.

The shader used to obtain the two images in Figure 17.8 is this:

```
// 'k' is the number of consecutive sin() waves to add
// code adapted from Rick Sayre's SIGGRAPH '92 course notes
surface sqwave(float k=3, freq=1)
{
```

```
float ss = s*freq;
float n = k;


/////////////////////////////////////////////////////////////
// to antialias via freq. clamping, simply ignore incoming 'k',
// calc. our own
float dss = filterwidth(ss);
n = floor(1/(2*dss)-0.5);
/////////////////////////////////////////////////////////////


// Fourier sq. wave
float sum=0, i;
for(i=0;i<n;i+=1)
  {
    // please consult a calculus text or look online
    // for more explanation of the Fourier principle. It
    // be used to derive a variety of other waves such as
    // sawtooth, triangular, etc.
    sum += sin(ss*2*PI*(2*i+1))/(2*i+1);
  }
sum = sum*4/PI;

// normalize -1..1 sum to 0..1
sum = 0.5*(1+sum);
Ci = color(sum,sum,sum);
}
```

In the aliasing version, we are letting the user set the number of frequencies to sum. To get the pattern to antialias, we derive a filter width value using the macro shown earlier and use than in turn to set the iteration count n.

Analytical Anti-aliasing

We can generate many patterns using formulae or algorithms. Figure 17.9 shows an example of such a pattern. The clean bright look on the left might seem appealing, but the crisp boundaries are prone to aliasing while in motion. The softer boundaries in the image on the right, with their gradual transition between black and white, fare much better in comparison. *Analytical anti-aliasing* refers to ways of modifying shaders in order to provide soft transitions in hard-edged regions.

Figure 17.9 Hard (aliasing) and soft (antialiased) transitions in a pattern.

Below we offer a series of progressive examples to illustrate the idea. The math is lightweight and is kept that way on purpose—the visuals in the examples should be adequate to explain the basics.

Figure 17.10 is our "control" (nonantialiased) case. At the top-left, a step() function is shown (in blue), along with a pulse (yellow spike). The step() represents a hard transition (between colors or any other shader-related quantities, even nonvisual ones). The pulse is a filter function, which when "convolved" with the step() will produce a lookup curve (top-right image) that we would use in place of the step().

Because of the extremely local nature of the spike (it has no spatial extent), the resulting convolution or lookup curve is still the same step() function. Using such a lookup, which is essentially just the step(), produces well-defined black/white borders in the pattern on the bottom left and a well-defined vertical step in the displacement-mapped plane on the bottom right.

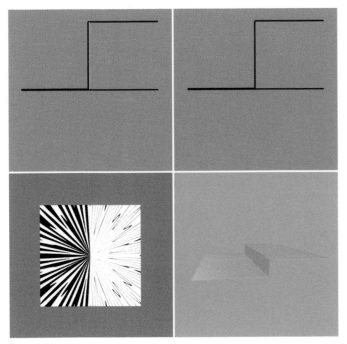

Figure 17.10 Use of a step() function.

The RSL step() function is used to create such step() functions: step(edge,value) returns 0 if value is smaller than edge, or a 1 otherwise. It is simply equivalent to this if() statement:

```
if(value<edge)
   return 0;
else
   return 1;
```

Using such conditionals makes it easy to program our shaders, but we always need to be wary of aliasing problems if we use them.

In Figure 17.11 we show that convolving our step with a "box" filter function (which does have a spatial extent, unlike a spike) produces a linear ramp lookup curve as shown at the top right. Visually speaking, the ramp makes the formerly steep wall more tractable by making it less severe. In terms of shading, the ramp region creates a blend (between colors or other quantities). The built-in RSL functions filterstep(), clamp(), lerp(), and mix() are all related to this ramp idea, as are boxstep() from Steve May's rmannotes.sl and *Advanced RenderMan* book's filteredstep().

The ramp lookup applied to the patterns (bottom left) and displacement (bottom right) makes their transitions softer. In the pattern, you can spot gray areas that signify blending.

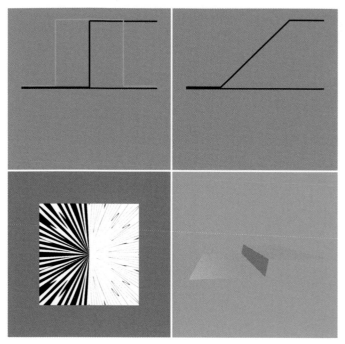

Figure 17.11 Antialiasing using a ramp function.

Also, in the pattern that you see in all these examples, there are two distinct regions—the filled areas on the left and outlines on the right. The filled areas are created using the various convolved step functions, while the outline areas use the subtraction of two functions to create a thin "pulse" region:

```
if(s>0.5)
  // solid regions
  Ci = filterstep(d,.49,.51);
else
  // outlines obtained from differences of steps
  Ci = 1-abs(boxstep(.49,.5,d) - boxstep(.5,.51,d));
```

As an aside, note that the filterstep() and boxstep() functions have different parameter orderings. Also, they can both be expressed in terms of clamp().

In Figure 17.12, we show that a triangle filter convolved with the step() function produces a quadratic lookup curve on the top-right.

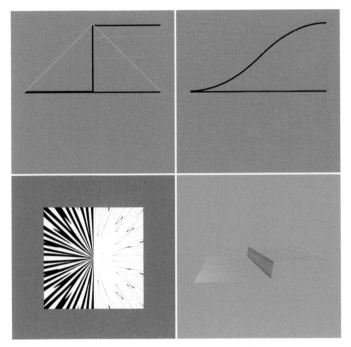

Figure 17.12 Antialiasing using a quadratic lookup curve.

As usual, we use the curve to antialias the pattern and displacement (bottom row). You can detect the lookup's curvy profile along the edge of the displacement—the vertical scaling up makes this a bit harder to see.

Next we use a parabola (whose equation is $y = -6x^2 + 6x$) as our filter function, ending up with a convolved lookup. This curve is exactly equivalent to the built-in smoothstep() call and is expressed by this cubic equation: $y = 3x^2 - 2x^3$. Figure 17.13 shows the curves and shader results.

Figure 17.13 Antialiasing using smoothstep().

smoothstep() is a workhorse function that produces good results at a reasonable execution speed.

In Figure 17.14, we show a sinc filter (which has two negative "lobes" that flank a central positive one) and its convolution with the step() function. The convolved lookup also contains negative lobes as expected. As an aside, the sinc filter looks a lot like the Catmull-Rom filter, and the convolution correspondingly looks like that resulting from convolving a Catmull-Rom filter. In his 1992 SIGGRAPH course notes, Rick Sayres includes code for catstep, which is the convolution resulting from convolving the Catmull-Rom filter with a step() function. Our image at the top right of Figure 17.14 looks a lot like catstep.

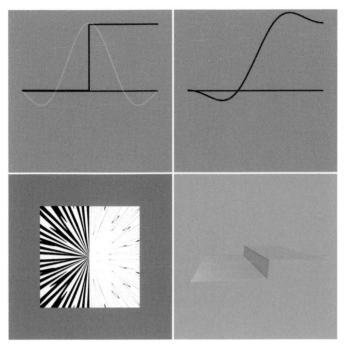

Figure 17.14 Use of a convolved sinc filter for antialiasing.

Note that the pattern at the bottom left of Figure 17.14 appears to contain some sharpened regions even in the middle of regular softening. This is because of the negative lobes in the convolution, which accentuate edges (instead of softening them) without leading to aliasing.

Finally, in Figure 17.15, we see two variations of lookup curves based on the gain() function, which we have encountered before:

```
float bias(float t;float a;)
{
    return pow(t,-(log(a)/log(2)));
}

float gain(float t; float a;)
{
  float g;
  if (t <=0.5)
  {
    g = 0.5*bias(2*t, a);
  }
  else
  {
    g = 1.0 - 0.5*bias(2.0-2*t,a);
```

```
  }
  return g;
}
```

The gainstep() call that uses gain() looks like this:

```
float gainstep(float a, b, e, g)
{
  if(e<a)return 0;
  if(e>b)return 1;
  float ee = (e-a)/(b-a);
  return gain(ee,g);
}
```

As you can see, gainstep() takes a range a..b, an edge value e, and a gain-control parameter g. If the to-be-filtered value e lies inside a..b, gainstep() creates a 0..1 value out of it and calls gain() together with the tuning value g. Depending on this additional tuning value, gainstep() behaves like step() for small values of g, and it behaves like filterstep() for g values close to 0.5. The top-left curve results from a g value of 0.00000004, and the top-right curve is a result of g being 0.4. The corresponding shader results are seen in the bottom row of Figure 17.15.

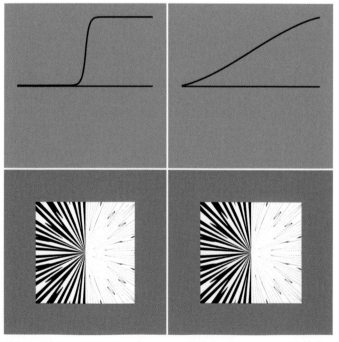

Figure 17.15 Antialiasing based on a gain() function.

In the above, we mentioned several filters: pulse, box, triangle, quadratic, sinc, and Catmull-Rom. If you want to explore alternate ones, here are some more names to look up in image processing and signal processing literature: Beckmann-Harris, Mitchell-Netravalli, Lanczos, Hann, Hamming, and Gauss.

These examples all deal with filters convolving a `step()` function, which is one of the simplest functions. In production work you might encounter more complex ones that need to be filtered so that they don't alias. As mentioned earlier, if the analytical approach proves intractable when you try on your own, consider creating a texture map out of the function and letting the renderer do the excellent filtering that it does. Alternately, using a symbolic math program such as Mathematica or Maple might help. Finally, you can carry out the convolution (which is based on integration) numerically and create a table that approximates the lookup curve. Whether you obtain a closed form solution or end up with a lookup table of values, you can consider creating a DSO shadeop to do the filtering efficiently and quickly.

Index

Numbers and Symbols

A